1 MONTH OF
FREE
READING

at
www.ForgottenBooks.com

By purchasing this book you are eligible for one month membership to ForgottenBooks.com, giving you unlimited access to our entire collection of over 1,000,000 titles via our web site and mobile apps.

To claim your free month visit:

www.forgottenbooks.com/free822494

ISBN 978-0-365-29950-9
PIBN 10822494

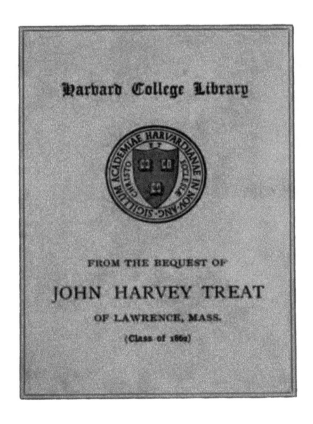

✝

A little Recreation for our
true old Friend Sir Patrick Kem
from his own grateful friends.

F.M. Clare Mullany

F.M. Vincent Whitty

RIGHT REV. DR. POLDING.

A HISTORY

OF THE

COMMENCEMENT AND PROGRESS

OF

CATHOLICITY IN AUSTRALIA,

UP TO THE YEAR 1840.

BY

VERY REV^{D.} DEAN KENNY.

———————

SYDNEY:

F. CUNNINGHAME & CO., STEAM MACHINE PRINTERS,

146 PITT STREET.

———

1886.

To

THE. BISHOP OF BIRMINGHAM,

RIGHT REVEREND

WILLIAM B. ULLATHORNE, O.S.B.

To you, my dear Lord, I dedicate these pages, in which I have endeavoured to narrate the commencement and progress of Catholicity in Australia. I know no one to whom in preference I could commend this small production. Several of those great and distinguished missionaries who laboured with you so successfully in cultivating this new portion of the Lord's vineyard in Australia, have gone to their rest; and amongst them, Archbishop Polding; he with whom you were united in heart and mind, whilst you were his Vicar-General in Australia. Your zeal and labours under his auspices changed the condition of the Catholic Church in Australia. By your writings you informed Europe of the restraints of the catholics in this far distant land, and their spiritual destitution; and you travelled in all parts to obtain an abundant supply of priests. You brought from the Colleges and Universities of Ireland and the Continent bands of zealous and enlightened missionaries, who spread the faith everywhere, and covered the land with churches. You exposed the inhuman treatment of your fellow man, by those who were in power, and greatly contributed to the amelioration of his unfortunate condition. By your pen and words you silenced the enemies of our holy faith, and reduced them to reason.

I lie under the deepest obligation to you. The young men whom you were preparing for the priesthood, were singularly favoured, of whom I was one. You spared no pains to develop our minds, by imparting to us the rich stores of philosophical and historical knowledge with which your luminous and acute mind was supplied. Many years have passed since you bade farewell to the Australian shores; but never ought the Catholic Church of Australia forget those days when, in all the vigour of your great intellect, you laboured so earnestly and incessantly for her welfare.

PREFACE.

THE object I had in view in writing the history of Catholic events in Australia, was to correct the mistaken notions in the minds of many, in regard to our history, and to reduce them to something like chronological order; and to show the wonderful progress of Catholicity in Australia in such a short time. I have been witness of many events recorded in the history. I came to the colony in the year 1835, with Bishop Polding, as an ecclesiastical student: it will soon be fifty years ago; and I was not unobservant of what was passing. I was ordained a priest with four others, by Archbishop Polding, in the year 1843, and have laboured ever since on the Australian Mission.

I am mainly indebted for the principal facts and events of the early history, to a small pamphlet of Dr. Ullathorne's, entitled, "Catholic Mission in Australasia"; and I have inserted an abridgement of his able reply to Judge Burton, one of the judges of the colony. I have carefully looked over the copies which remain of the old *Government Gazette*, and have perused many other papers, books, and periodicals, for catholic information. I must express my thankfulness to Mr. Halley and his assistants, of the Public Library, for their readiness in getting for me the books which I required. I have given some Colonial History connected with the events, which will enable the reader to remember better what occurred. I do not pretend to brilliancy of style, but I have adhered strictly to the truth in the narration of facts.

The extraordinary efforts and zeal of Father Therry, afterwards Archpriest, for the preservation of the faith, are not passed over, but portrayed with all fidelity: and the trials of Archpriest Flynn, and his expulsion from the colony by the Government, are detailed with all the particulars. Nor are the great labours of Archdeacon McEnroe unnoticed.

I intend the History to consist of two volumes, octavo, and I would have had the second volume ready now for publication, only a very severe attack of acute rheumatism, extending over three years, has prevented me from arranging the materials which I have collected.

The present book contains a complete narration of Catholic facts and events up to the year 1840, when Bishop Polding left Australia the first time for Europe. If this History gives satisfaction to the catholic public, I shall lose no time in getting the second volume published.

The year of our Lord, eighteen hundred and thirty-five, was a year memorable in the annals of the Catholic Church of Australia, for on the 13th of September of that year, arrived in Sydney the first catholic bishop of those colonies, the Right Rev. John Bede Polding. He came appointed by the successor of St. Peter, Gregory XVI., and intrusted with extraordinary powers to superintend the spiritual interests of Christ's church in these parts; to direct her energies for the glory of God and the salvation of souls. His labours extended over a period of about forty-two years, during which time his strenuous exertions in the cause of our holy faith abundantly testify to the wisdom, zeal and prudence with which he superintended the holy work committed to his care. The purpose of this History is not only to show the wonderful progress of Catholicity during the Pontificate of the Right Rev. Dr. Polding, but its commencement with the first catholics and the first priests who arrived in the colony.

I commence the History by giving an account of the discovery of this great South Land. It is interesting to know when Providence directed the helm of the mariner to the shores of this Great Island Continent, destined by our Lord to be a field where souls were to be saved and his praise and glory promoted.

St. Leonards, North Shore,
29th January, 1886.

CONTENTS.

PART I.

CHAPTER I.

CHAPTER II.

CHAPTER III.

CHAPTER IV.

CHAPTER V.

CHAPTER VI.

CHAPTER VII.

PART II.
—

CHAPTER I.

CHAPTER II.

CHAPTER III.

CHAPTER IV.

CHAPTER V.

CHAPTER VI.

CHAPTER VII.

CHAPTER VIII.

CHAPTER IX.

APPENDIX.

THE VERY REV. DR. ULLATHORNE.

S<small>T</small>. M<small>ARY'S</small> C<small>ATHEDRAL</small>, S<small>YDNEY</small>,

10th May, 1886.

I<small>MPRI</small>M<small>ATUR</small>.

✝ PATRICK F. CARD. MORAN,

A<small>RCHBISHOP OF</small> S<small>YDNEY</small>.

A HISTORY

OF THE

COMMENCEMENT & PROGRESS OF CATHOLICITY

IN AUSTRALIA,

UP TO THE YEAR 1840.

CHAPTER I.

*The Opinions of the Ancients in regard to the Great Austral
Land.—The Spanish Navigators.—Fernandez de Quiros.
Spanish Navigator, supposed by many the discoverer of
Australia, in 1606.—The Dutch landed early in Australia.
The famous Buccaneer, Dampier, visited Australia, 1688.
Captain Cook sighted Australia 18th April, 1770.*

AUSTRALIA is the largest island in the world; it is situated to the
south of the Malay Archipelago, and lies between the Indian and
Pacific Oceans. It extends from latitude 10° 40″ South to 39° 15″
South, and from longitude 113° 20″ to 153° 20″ East. In length
from East to West it is 2,400 miles, and breadth from North to
South, it varies from 1,600 to 1,900 miles. The area of Australia
is computed at three millions of square miles. It may not
improperly be termed a continent.

This great Austral Land, it is believed by many, was known
to exist by the ancients before the Christian era. Strabo, an
eminent geographer, who flourished fifty years before Christ,
mentions in his writings a large island which lay to the South-
east of India, and stretched far towards the West. Pliny (A.D. 77)
refers to a great island lying to the South of the Equator.

B

Ptolemy Claudius, celebrated as a geographer, who lived in the year of our Lord 150, states that from a great bay, 8° South, the land turned to the West and stretched to an unknown distance. The celebrated Venetian traveller, Marco Polo, visited the Indian Archipelago in the year 1293, and remained on the island of Lesser Java for five months, with the expedition fitted out by the Great Mogul, Emperor, Kublai Khan. He states that 700 miles from that island there was a country called Lochæ, which formed part of a great mainland. In the 14th century a Catholic missionary appears to have visited Java, and whilst there he heard of a great country which stretched so far to the South that its extreme regions, for several months in the year, were enveloped in darkness. For upwards of 200 years after Marco Polo's time no mention is made of the supposed island or continent lying to the South, except by this Christian missionary. From these testimonies, there can be little doubt but that some maritime adventurers in those early times had seen and coasted the shores of Australia; but their notions must have been very vague as to whether it was a continent or an island.

An attempt was made by the Spanish Navigator, Alvaro Mendana de Neyra, in 1568, to discover the great South Land which had been so much spoken about. He sailed from Callao in Peru, and held a course due West for nearly 4,500 miles, when he discovered the Soloman Isles. This group is in the latitude of Torres' Straits. Afterwards, during another voyage, in the year 1595, he was the discoverer of the Marquisas Islands; but he failed in finding the great Austral Land he was in search of. Mendana died on the voyage, and was succeeded in the command by his pilot, Fernandez de Quiros, who soon returned to Lima, in South America. Quiros became quite enthusiastic about the discovery of the great South Land; he maintained there must be a great country undiscovered lying to the South. He prevailed by his arguments with Phillip III. of Spain, who supplied him with three vessels for another expedition. Quiros was appointed Chief in command, and the second commander was Luis Vaez de Torres, a Spanish Navigator of great ability. The discovery fleet sailed from Lima, in South America, on the 20th of December, 1605, in the direction of West by South. The island of Tahiti was discovered by Quiros on 10th February, 1606, and on the 26th April he saw land which he believed to be the great South Land, and he named it Terra Austral del Espiritu Santo—the South Land of the Holy Spirit. Notwithstanding the perseverance and courage of Quiros, he is denied the honor of having discovered the great Austral Land; for many say that he mistook for it the group of islands known now by the name of the New Hebrides. Quiros, on account of disputes with his officers, loss of men, and sickness, was compelled to return to South America, before he had ascertained the extent and character of the islands which he had discovered. He reached Acapulco nine months after his departure. His companion, Torres, continuing to sail westward, in the latitude of the Straits, passed safely through those waters, which divide Australia from New Guinea. The straits have been called after him, Torres' Straits. He, Torres, sighted the mainland at the most northern point, viz., Cape York, but took it for a group of islands. When Quiros returned, he laid a memorial of his discoveries before the King of Spain, and mentioned twenty-three islands which he had discovered, together with "certain parts of a country which he believed was a portion of the Australian mainland."

About this time—the beginning of the 17th century—the Dutch were very persevering in their endeavours to discover the great South Land, which was so much spoken about throughout Europe. They maintain having landed on the Australian shores a few days before Quiros, if he did not mistake the New Hebrides for a part of the mainland of Australia.

It is difficult to suppose that a skilled navigator, such as Quiros was, would take three comparatively small islands for the mainland; he had been in those seas before in search of the great Austral Land, and had only recently discovered the island of Tahiti. My conviction is, with many, that he sighted the Australian Land; but the difficulties he had with his officers and crew prevented him from landing and surveying the coast.

The Dutch had wrested from the Portuguese the richest of the islands in the Indian Archipelago, and they lost no time in trying to ascertain the extent and riches of this great South Land. By the year 1622 they had surveyed nearly the whole of the Western Coast, and, in the year 1664, they gave the name of *New Holland* to the great discovery. It was in the year 1642* that Van Dieman's Land was discovered by Abel Jansen Tasman; but he thought it was a part of Australia, connected with the mainland.

There is no account of any one having visited the shores of New Holland or Van Dieman's Land for fifty years after the discovery of Abel Jansen Tasman. When the famous English buccaneer Dampier, visited the Island Continent, no doubt in quest of plunder, he landed on the western coast the 5th January

---

* Abel Jansen Tasman during the same voyage discovered New December, 1642.

1688, in latitude 16° 50" South. The ship commanded by him was named the Cygnet. He remained in this place whilst the vessel was re-fitted. He had some intercourse with the natives, whom he considered a very inferior race; nor did he form a very high opinion of the country which they inhabited. The locality where he landed was extremely barren and uninviting: Dampier, notwithstanding the unfavorable appearance of the country, must have taken a deep interest in the Great South Land, and he was not content with the partial view which he had obtained. He hoped, we may surmise, like others, to make a rich discovery on her shores, which would reward him for his pains, and give glory to England. He changed his colours, and through the patronage of his friend Lord Oxford, was appointed by King William III. to the command of an old ship of war, the Roebuck: in this vessel he left England in the year 1699, for Australia, and reached the western coast at Shark's Bay, latitude 25° South, on the 6th August of the same year. He does not appear to have surveyed any part of the coast: he remained only a few days at Shark's Bay and then put out to sea again: he went no further south, but steered north, touching at several places between Shark's Bay and Cape Bougainville; then he bore up to the island of Timor, and after that visited New Guinea. He visited many parts of this interesting island, and surveyed the coast. Dampier discovered many bays, capes, and channels on the coasts of New Holland and New Guinea, and they bear the names which he gave them. One hundred years transpired after the visit of Dampier to Australia before any settlement was formed on her shores, and this probably happened in consequence of the unfavourable account given by Dampier of the Great South Land.*

Captain Cook was the next after Dampier who conducted an exploratory expedition to the South Seas. He was selected by the English Government as the best qualified to make it certain as to whether there was a Great Southern Continent; although it is strange how Cook, or the English Government, could have any doubt about what had been made so certain by the discovery of the Spanish navigator Quiros, and by the Dutch. Captain Cook placed no reliance on the statements made by Quiros and the other navigators, that there was a Great South Land or Continent which they had seen, but attempted to prove they were mistaken in supposing that a Continent existed to the north of 40° of South latitude. Nor does it redound to his credit, when

* Vide : Dampier's Voyages.

he was convinced of the correctness of the reports and accounts of those grand old navigators, not to acknowledge his indebtedness to their skill and daring. But we do not wish to detract from the everlasting merit of Captain Cook, since to him we are indebted for the knowledge of the extent of Australia, the nature of the soil on the coast, and its adaptability for settlement. Captain Cook had only one vessel under his command, named the Endeavour, and only of 350 tons burden. His companions were Mr. Banks (afterward Sir Joseph), Mr. Solander, a Swede and a pupil of the celebrated Linnæus; they accompanied the expedition as naturalists; Mr. Green as astronomer, Mr. Buchan as draughts-man, and Mr. Parkenson as painter. The Endeavour left Plymouth on 26th August, 1768. Several islands in the Pacific Ocean were discovered by Captain Cook during his first voyage, and he staid for some time at New Zealand and then sailed for Australia: he sighted land at the southern extremity of Australia on the 18th April, 1770. He called the point of land which was first seen Point Hicks: it received this name from his lieutenant, Hicks, who was the first to obtain the sight of it. The Endeavour put in to Botany Bay, and there Captain Cook saw the natives for the first time, some of whom resisted his landing. At the spot to the south of the bay, where it is supposed the Great Navigator landed, a tablet has been erected on a projecting rock. In 1821 the Philosophical Society of Australia was established, and the President, the then Governor, Sir Thomas Brisbane, instituted enquiries among the Botany Bay natives to ascertain the exact spot where Captain Cook landed. After great difficulty a hoary-headed old Botany native stated that he saw the big ships arrive, the boats land the Chief of the party—a man with a big hat,—Captain Cook jump ashore, and that he could point out the exact spot. His account tallied with Captain Cook's historical records. The Governor and the Society firmly believed he was a reliable witness, and they organized an excursion to the landing place on Wednesday, March 20th, 1822. The excursionists proceeded from the north to the south side of Botany Bay, and the old white-headed native pointed out the rock on which Captain Cook landed. On a bold rock was fixed a brazen plate whereon was engraved the following inscription:—" A.D. MDCCLXX., under the auspices of British Science, these shores were discovered by James Cook and Joseph Banks—the Columbus and Mecænas of their time. This spot once saw them ardent in the pursuit of knowledge; now to their memory, this tablet is inscribed, in the first year of the Philosophical Society of Australia, Sir Thomas Brisbane, K.C.B., F.R.S.S. and E , (Corresponding Member of the Institute of France,) President. A.D. MDCCCXXI." This tablet was soldered about 25 feet from the level of the sea, on the face of the most remarkable rock in the vicinity. The Society then, in a natural arbour close by, drank to the immortal fame of the illustrious men whose discoveries they were there met to commemorate. The inscription on the tablet has not been obliterated by time; but it is somewhat overcast with branches of plants growing out of the fissures of the rocks. It is believed that Captain Cook landed on a beach near the rock, which corresponds with the account given in his journals, and that the rock was the most convenient place for affixing the tablet. Close by is a remarkable opening in the rocks by which the natives gained access to the elevated ground. The Hon. Thomas Holt has erected a monument on what he regards as the exact spot where Cook stepped on shore, and a flight of steps to very high land, for extensive views, has been cut near the spot.

When Captain Cook left Botany Bay he continued to survey the coast to the north for 2000 miles, that is to Cape York, the extreme point of the Australian Continent; and the time spent in coasting to the north was four months, during which time he discovered all the principal bays and harbours.

Captain Cook in his journal thus ends his account of New South Wales.—"As I was now about to quit the eastern coast of New Holland, which I had coasted from latitude 38 degrees south to this place (Cape York), latitude 10¼° South, and which I am confident no European had ever seen before, I once more hoisted English colours; and although I had already taken possession of several particular parts, I now took possession of the whole eastern coast, in right of his Majesty King George the Third, by the name of New South Wales, with all the bays, harbours, and islands situated upon it. We then fired three volleys of small arms, which were answered by the same number from the ship."—*Captain Cook's Journal.*

Had it been given to this great English navigator to see into the future, when the waters over which the keel of the Endeavour was the first to pass, carrying on their bosom ships laden with gold and rich merchandise of every kind, going to and from her shores; to see the coast, where he only saw the wild Aborigine, taken up by civilized man; the land richly cultivated in many parts, yielding abundantly, and covered with cities and towns. What more could he have desired!

CHAPTER II.

The causes which led to the foundation of the Colony.—Captain Arthur Phillip of the Royal Navy, selected by the Home Government to be the first Governor of the New Colony.— The landing of the Colonists.—The Inauguration of the Government, 7th February, 1788.—The Governor's Speech. —Two French Discovery ships anchor in Botany Bay.— The death of the Priest, Pere Receveur.—The resignation of Governor Phillip.

THE discovery of the eastern coast of Australia was made by Captain Cook in the year 1770 ; but it was seventeen years afterwards when the Colony of New south Wales was established by the British Government, in the year 1788. It happened in this wise :—The attention of the Home Government was drawn to select the shores of Australia for the foundation of a colony from the favourable account given by Captain Cook in the published narrative of his voyage. In all probability no settlement would have been made at this time, had it not been that the Government wanted a distant place to send her criminals. The jails throughout Great Britain were crowded with prisoners, because they could no longer be sent to the plantations in America. The Americans were victorious in the war of Independence, and would not allow any more traffic in white slaves. The convicts had been sold to the Planters of Virginia, and been sent to toil in the burning heat of the Barbadoes and other places. An account is given in Dr. Lingard's History of England, vol, xi, p. 145, that, during the Protectorate, 70 persons were sold at the Barbadoes for 1550lbs. of sugar each. Among them were divines, officers and gentlemen, who were represented as grinding at the mills, attending the furnaces, and digging in that scorching island, whipped at whipping-posts, and sleeping in sties, worse off than the hogs in England. These were persons obnoxious to the Government, being bought and sold from one Planter to another. In the time of Charles II. there were sold, of those who had taken part in the rebellion of Monmouth, 849 persons, to the Planters of Jamaica. "The Mayor, Aldermen and Justices of Bristol were accustomed to transport convicted criminals to the American plantations and sell them by way of trade. Now, the English nation abhors such inhuman conduct as that of one man selling his fellow-man for gain ; but it is most humiliating to think that the great in the land at one time sold their christian brother as they would a piece of merchandise."—*Samuel Sydney—Three Colonies, p. 22.*

8

The English Government came to the resolution, some time after the voyage of Captain Cook, to send her criminals to that island continent, lately re-discovered, and the coasts of which had been so favourably described by that illustrious navigator. The place selected for location was Botany Bay, situated on the eastern coast. In coming to this determination the first object was to clear out the jails and houses of correction, and send the prisoners beyond the seas, to where they would be as little trouble as possible to the parent country. The second object was, which is evident from the great preparations made, to secure this great South Land by founding a colony, which might in course of time compensate for the loss of her American possessions.

The Order for the establishment of a Settlement in New South Wales was issued by the Executive Council on 6th Dec., 1786. The Government selected Captain Arthur Phillip, of the Royal Navy, to conduct the expedition, and to be the Governor and Commander-in-Chief of New South Wales; and officers were appointed under him for the different departments, both military and civil. When the expedition for the new colony embarked, they numbered 1044 persons; but 14 died during the voyage; thus 1030 landed in New South Wales. The persons belonging to the expedition were distinguished:—Civil Officers 10; the Military, including Officers, 212; wives and families of the Officers, 28 women and 17 children; other free persons 81; the prisoners amounted to 696: in all there were 348 free persons and 696 convicts.

When making preparations for this exodus the spiritual wants of the bond or free were not taken into consideration of the unfortunate men destined to people this desert land. What ought to have been thought of in the first instance was left to the last. No minister of religion or schoolmaster was appointed to instruct the ignorant. Before the fleet sailed a Protestant Bishop charitably reminded them of the omission, and then the Rev. Richard Johnson was appointed chaplain. Such conduct of the then Government merits great reproach — not to think of supplying those unhappy beings with the means of religious instruction and consolation. Is it not the duty of a Christian Government to endeavour, by providing ministers of religion, to raise the fallen? otherwise what is it better than the heathen rulers of Greece and Rome?

The fleet, consisting of one frigate, the "Sirius," with a tender, three store ships, and six transports, set sail on 13th May, 1787. It had a prosperous voyage and touched at several ports on the way—at Cape de Verd Islands, Rio Janerio, and Cape of

Good Hope, where they were kindly received and their wants supplied. They arrived at Botany Bay 20th January, 1788. When Governor Phillip examined the land near the bay he came to the conclusion that it was unsuitable for a Settlement. Some of the peeple were allowed to go ashore and they began to clear the land, but found the surrounding parts not adapted for occupation. The bay, although spacious, was found to be shallow, and not safe from the easterly gales, and the shores were low and swampy. No debarcation of the people in general took place, and no Settlement was formed.

Governor Phillip, having manned three boats, proceeded to explore the coast to the north, and when examining Jackson's Bay, as laid down in Cap ain Cook's chart, he entered the Heads, and discovered a magnificent harbour, deep, wide, and land-locked on all sides, the shores high and richly wooded. He sailed round the bays in the spacious harbour and selected a cove where flowed a clear spring from the rocks, which was afterward called Sydney Cove. The fleet, which consisted of eleven sail, was ordered to sail for Port Jackson on 26th January, 1788: it entered the Heads and sailed down the harbour to the cove selected by Governor Phillip and there cast anchor. On the second day the debarkation took place, which was made with some formality. The first who landed was a detachment of Marines and some Blue Jackets. There were a great many of the Aborigines on the shore when they landed, and they seemed disposed to defend their country against the intruders. The natives were armed with spears and shields and bomerangs: they were quite naked; but through the conciliatory conduct of the Governor and officers, and seeing no doubt that a far superior force was opposed to them, they submitted and laid down their arms. The natives on this occasion showed more bravery and natural intelligence than at first they got credit for. The number of Settlers who then landed were one thousand and thirty souls: during the voyage the expedition had lost fourteen persons.

The first colonists of New South Wales being safely landed, after having been delivered from the perils of the sea, and having traversed 16,000 miles of water, we do not find them manifesting gratitude to the Almighty for His protection; they did not assemble around the cross—the symbol of our redemption—and chant the Te Deum in thanksgiving; no: but that same evening, when the Royal Standard was erected, the Governor with his officers assembled round and drank the King's health and success to the Settlement.

It was in the vicinity of the Sydney Cove, 7th February, 1788, that a portion of the ground was cleared for habitation: it was laborious work, for the land was thickly timbered to the water's edge, and there were gigantic trees: the sound of the axe reverberated for the first time in that primeval forest and soon fell by the sturdy arm of the exile, with a loud crash those aged denizens. The Governor then lived in a tent and every one erected a covering of the best kind available; some lived in hollow trees, and huts were made out of the cabbage tree which grew there in great abundance, others made of branches and twigs plastered with clay. There was a clear running stream of fresh water close by where they were encamped. The locality where Sydney took its rise was on the level ground, from Hunter-street towards the Circular Quay. No house, then, nor for a long time after was put up for divine worship. There was a clear piece of ground on the west of the Cove, now called *Dawes' Point*, where a battery is placed, and it was there on the 12th day after landing, 7th February, 1788, that the government of the Colony was inaugurated with all the formalities. The Royal Standard was raised, all the colonists were there, the Military were drawn up under arms, and the Governor was surrounded by his officers. The prisoners were placed on one side. The Royal Commission was read in the first place by the Judge Advocate, David Collins, then the Act of Parliament was made known, which authorized the establishment of Courts of civil and criminal judicature in the Colony, and finally the letters patent under the great seal which give power to the proper officers to summon and hold those Courts. The Governor was entrusted with extraordinary power, by the letters patent of the Seal of England, which had never been exercised by any other official in the British Dominion. He could sentence to five hundred lashes, fine five hundred pounds, regulate customs and trades, fix prices and wages, remit capital punishment, bestow grants of land, and create a monopoly of any article of necessity. All the labour of the Colony was at his disposal; all the land, all the stores, all the places of honor and profit."*

The Governor on that occasion delivered a very well prepared and appropriate address, although rather boastful. "He considered that a Special Providence had watched over them and directed their course, made the winds and seas propitious and brought them in safety to their destination. England the especial favorite of Heaven. No power on earth equal to that of England, her

* The Three Colonies of Australia, by Samuel Sidney, page 29

sway reaches from pole to pole, and this is an earnest of the protection which will be afforded the offshoot of the parent stem, which that day sprang into existence. She has surpassed all nations in colonization. Other nations have conquered by force of arms, destroyed communities and made homes desolate; but England created new communities and established happy homes. He acknowledged that young America had obtained the victory in the late contest with Britain, and Britain resigned the dominion of the Continent into her hands. She sought now to lay the foundation of another empire in this region of the earth, which will rival in strength the one recently lost. This project had the authority, sanction, and encouragement of the Sovereign, the parliament and the people, he said that the enterprise was wisely conceived, deliberately devised, and efficiently organized. That they took absolute possession of this fifth division of the globe on behalf of the British people and hope to occupy and rule this great country and to be the patron of the whole Southern Hemisphere. They will have the surpassing honor of having introduced the christian religion, and European civilization into the Southern Hemisphere. It will be their honor to plant the Standard of the Cross, and the ensign of their country, at no distant time amongst populous nations to whom both of these have been little known. Such are the objects which will arouse the enterprise and stimulate the energies of the people of this young country. Enterprise and energy directed towards the extension of commerce, spread of the English language, the promotion of the arts and sciences, and the *extension of the true faith*. Next after the protection of Providence they will have to rely upon their own fortitude, energy, and discipline."

This is the substance of the address which was delivered by Governor Phillip, when he initiated the Government of the Colony. It is difficult to know what induced him to speak in such flattering terms of the territory, to the young colony; there was no appearance of fertile land; he had abandoned the shores of Botany Bay because they looked so barren, and the land they had encamped upon seemed to be of the same character; and as for the mineral wealth, which was known, he said, to be so great, as to promise "that it may yet rival the treasures which fiction loves to describe." How was it known? We have no accounts previous to that time of the discovery of gold, or any other mineral: except the reports of the ancients about the golden treasures of the Great Austral Land. Probably the Governor indulged in this fabulous description, (which is becoming a reality), to reconcile the unfortunates to their unhappy lot by filling them with hope, and that they might be the more subordinate. Sad must have been their disappointment, on the third year of their settlement, when they remembered the encouraging words, and found themselves nearly starved to death from want of provisions; partly occasioned by the ungenerous soil and the drought! A land without native fruit of any kind, no vegetables, no wild fowl, no beast except the kangaroos, and few of them to be seen—to satisfy the cravings of hunger. The timely arrival of the store ship Justinian saved the entire colony from perishing by famine. A few days after the arrival of this ship four transports arrived filled with convicts, and the population of the colony was increased by 1250; and had they come before the store ship nothing could have saved the colony from destruction.*

There appears to have been no zeal for the advancement of religion, in the beginning of the colony. The Governor, and probably his officers, did not attend the service of the Church of England until afterwards. There was no church erected during the stay of Phillip; but *all the convicts*, composed of different religious denominations, were compelled to hear the liturgy of the English Church on every Sunday, and that under the penalty of having so much deducted from their rations—overseers 3 lbs. flour, labouring convicts 2 lbs. Divine service was generally performed in the open air, and then the poor convict was exposed to the inclemency of the weather in this ever changeable climate; the burning sun, the scorching wind, and the cold, biting, westerly blasts of winter. The Governor, who was a man of great ability, shrewdness, and intelligence, and of some religious sentiment, must have seen the utter impossibility of reconciling the Catholic convict to the liturgy of the Church of England : he must have been convinced that the Roman Catholic priest was necessary to effect a reformation in the Catholic prisoners. We can well imagine, in those times, the piously disposed of the Catholics assembling in a shady place, saying the Rosary, reading the Litanies, and prayers of Mass : making fervent Acts of Contrition, and asking a merciful God to send them His teacher to instruct and console them, and to offer up the Holy Sacrifice. When they met for this holy purpose they would be accused of plotting rebellion, and forbidden, under the severest penalty, to be seen together.

A week after the Government was established, Lieutenant Philip Gidley King went with a small party to form a settlement on Norfolk Island. Captain Cook had recommended this to be done.

* Flanagan's History of New South Wales, page 56.

When Governor Phillip and the fleet arrived at Botany Bay there were lying two French Discovery ships which had put in to get re-fitted. During the time they remained in the harbour a French priest died, from wounds which he had received at the Navigator's Islands. His name was Pere Receveur. He was the Naturalist of the expedition. Those Discovery ships had been sent out during the reign of the unfortunate Louis XVI. The remains of Pere Receveur were interred on a slope of rising ground on the north side of the bay, not far from the entrance. A monument was erected over his remains with the following inscription : —"Hic jacet Le Receveur E. F. F. Minimis Galliæ Sacerdos, Physicus in circum navigatione Mundi. Duce M. de la Peyrouse. Obut 17 Febi. 1788." This monument was destroyed by the aborigines; but Governor Phillip, by a christian and friendly act, ordered another to be erected, and had the inscription engraved on a copper plate and attached to the nearest tree. The names of the two ships under the command of Monsieur de la Peyrouse were the Boussole and Astrolabe : they remained at Botany Bay until the 10th March, same year, when they sailed, and were never more heard of. Forty years after remains of the vessels were found at the island of Malicolo. There is now a large slab over the grave of Pere Receveur, with the inscription engraven on it, and surrounded by a substantial iron railing. This improvement was effected by the late Father Nesbert Woolfrey, the priest of Waverley.

Governor Phillip resigned the Government of the colony in December, 1792, and returned to England. He was the best of the four first Governors. Had he not removed the colony from Botany Bay to Jackson's Bay, Sydney harbour, in all probability the Settlement would have been abandoned. The low swampy land at Botany was found to be quite unsuitable for habitation and cultivation. He guided the young colony with great ability during the short time he had authority. He was well adapted for governing those over whom he had power. Brought up himself under the severe discipline of the Navy, he knew well how to command others. He repressed vice by the maintenance of good order, and he made himself feared by terrible examples of punishment. He restrained those in the Military and Civil service by keeping them to their duty and making them respect the laws; and had they been under similar control, they would not have been guilty of those escapades which afterwards demoralized, and retarded the progress of the infant colony. There is one thing of which this Governor was greatly deficient; he does not appear to have understood the benign influence of religion upon the soul of man : he would have left England without a minister of religion had he not been reminded of the expediency of providing a clergyman : and during his time no place of worship was erected. But the Home Government was more to blame in this matter than Governor Phillip. It was hard enough to transport the unfortunate convicts to an unexplored island 16,000 miles away, and deprive them almost of hope to return to their native land ; but persecuting in the highest degree, to deprive them of the consolations of religion and the means of arriving at their everlasting kingdom, drowning all hopes in them for time and eternity. He looked well after the material interests of the colony : he lost no time·in getting the land cleared of the heavy timber, and how could that have been done without the prison labour ? At the time of the departure of Governor Phillip the statistics show that 1703 acres of land were in cultivation, which belonged to sixty-seven settlers ; and the Government had in cultivation 1012 acres ; the whole under cultivation amounted to 2715 acres : Governor Phillip had only granted, in his time, 3470 acres. He encouraged industry, and caused the country to be explored : he discovered the river Hawkesbury in the second year after his arrival, 6th July, 1789, and sailed up the river for 100 miles, till he came to shallow water at the foot of a hill, which he called Richmond Hill. In the same year an attempt was made to penetrate to the Blue Mountains, which are distinctly seen from Sydney. It is much to the credit of Governor Phillip that he was most kind and humane to the Aborigines, and did all he could to conciliate and establish a good understanding between them and the colonists ; and tried to ameliorate their forlorn condition. An accident occurred to him on one occasion when he ventured too far among a tribe of blacks, on the coast at Manly beach : Several hundreds were congregated ; one of them mistaking his kindness for an act of aggression, hurled a spear at him, which lodged in his shoulder, above the collar bone, and remained there, and was extracted with difficulty. No vengeance was taken ; one of them boldly came to the Governor, and represented that the black fellow who threw the spear did not understand what the Governor meant. A better understanding would have existed between the two races, and more could have been done for the civilization of the Aborigines, had the conduct of Governor Phillip been imitated, by not retaliating on the poor savage when it could have been helped. Governor Phillip resigned and returned home through ill health. He sailed 11th December, 1792, after ruling the colony for five years : and although he had been compelled to preserve order,—frequently to punish by the last penalty of the law, he took with him the good wishes of all the colonists, and an expression of their hope that he would soon be restored to health. When he returned to England he lived in retirement on the small salary of £400 a year. He died there a few years after.

In the year 1790, during Governor Phillip's rule, three transports arrived with 1250 additional convicts,—1000 males and 250 females; and detachments of some companies of soldiers belonging to the N. S. W. corps. Amongst the officers was Mr. John McArthur, who afterwards became a leading man in the colony, and acquired great wealth. He was at first Captain and Paymaster of the force—the New South Wales corps. On account of bad treatment nearly 300 of the prisoners died on the voyage. In their desperation they tried to take the vessel, but were overpowered and chained down in the hold. The contractor with the Government got £17 7s. 6d. per head for bringing them out, and no deduction in the event of any one dying, so that for them the more deaths the more gain. The dead were permitted to remain festering with the living.

It was not until September and October of 1791, that the remainder of the second fleet, consisting of five vessels, arrived, and anchored in Port Jackson, with a large number of convicts. These were five of nine vessels, which left Plymouth the previous year, with 2050 male and female convicts.

When the Governor left, in 1792, there were *2715 acres* of land under cultivation, as stated above, and the population, not including Norfolk Island, numbered 3,500, and one-third of these, our historian states, were Roman Catholics : including Norfolk Island the population amounted to 4,414. The ship " Bellona," in the year 1793, brought out a number of emigrant settlers. They were to have grants of land. Land was assigned to them eight or ten miles to the west of Sydney, called Liberty Plains : so named because they came free to the colony.

CHAPTER III.

*The Religious and Social Condition of the Colony after the
departure of Governor Phillip.—The arrival of three
Priests in 1799.—Governor King, by directions of the
Home Government, gives permission to Father Dixon to
exercise his clerical functions.—The insurrection at Castle
Hill.—Extreme liberality of the Home Government to the
Church of England.—Father Dixon falsely accused of
complicity in the rebellion at Castle Hill.*

WHEN Governor Phillip left, the government of the Colony
was entrusted by him to Major Francis Grose, the senior officer
of the 102nd Regiment, or N.S.W. Corps, and he had as
assistants David Collins, Esq., Judge Advocate, the Rev. Richard
Johnson and two magistrates.   Major Grose after a time
resigned and went home. He was succeeded by Captain Paterson
as Lieutenant Governor.   These two officers governed the Colony
for nearly three years, and "secured for themselves a monopoly
of land, labour and traffic."   Nothing was allowed to
be bought, either from the public store or from the private
ships which visited the por , without passing through the hands
of a set of greedy and grasping officials.*
   They were accused of having abused the power which
was in their hands ; that they withdrew all authority from the
civil magistrates, prevented them from making inquiry into cases
and giving judgment; that they were guilty of self-aggrandise-
ment by obtaining for themselves large grants of land. Governor
Philip was very judicious in portioning out the land. He had
not given away more than 3,470 acres, but the officers of the
new Government and their immediate friends were soon in the
possession of 15,000 acres.   They aimed seemingly at becoming
the principal proprietors of the land and stock, the founders of
wealthy families and of a Colonial Aristocracy.
   They interfered with the commercial interests, small as the
Colony was, for they restricted the sale of merchandise.   When
a ship arrived with a cargo of merchandise, instead of allowing
the owners to sell it out to the best advantage, they monopolized
the cargo, fixed the price, and then retailed the articles at an
enormous rate of interest—as high as 1200 per cent. and more.
This was crushing to the infant Colony, which had the greatest
difficulty to produce at the time, and such an unlawful restriction
weighed heavily upon the new settler, who had to sell cheap to
the Government and purchase at a famine price.   However, this
insignificant oligarchy made a sure footing on the lands of the

------

* P. 195. Hist. A. D., Part II.

colony, and were able to control future Governors and dictate their own terms; but some of these officers, to do them credit, in course of time improved their estates; the land was cleared by them and cultivated, the stock improved, and they redeemed themselves to a certain extent by their energy and enterprise. Exploring the country, they opened up its resources, and whilst they enriched themselves they added to the prosperity of the colonists. The worst of it was, that during those three years and afterwards a traffic was created in spirituous drinks, especially rum.*

Rum became the common currency amongst all classes. Land and goods of all kinds were bought and sold with it. There is an instance on record of an officer who, with a hogshead of rum, purchased 100 acres of land, which had been granted to some soldiers in half-acre allotments. Wives have been bought from their husbands for rum, as there was little respect for the marriage bond. The vice of drunkenness was rampant in the community, and the highest class was not free from it. It is recorded that a Judge, in those early days, " pronounced sentence of death when in a state of intoxication."†

The greatest licentiousness prevailed during these three years, and continued during the times of succeeding Governors. The most baneful of the human passions—avarice, drunkenness and lust—were in the ascendancy. Had these demons not been arrested in their course, it must have eventuated in the ruin of the colony. Then, in a small community consisting of only 4,000 persons, were found all the elements of evil which have caused the destruction of mighty empires. Such was the social condition of the colony, during three years of military despotism; the civil authority was dispensed with, and the military alone governed. On the first Sunday after the arrival of Governor Hunter, September, 1795, the Rev. Mr. Johnson, the colonial chaplain, and the only clergyman in the colony, had the boldness, after his sermon, (although generous, it would have been more magnanimous had he confronted the evil in the beginning), " to expose the last government, their extortion, their despotism, their debauchery, the ruin of the colony, reducing it almost to famine by the sale of goods at 1200 per cent. profit." He congratulated the colony on the abolition of the military government, on the restoration of a civil one, and on the laws; and orders this day given out " *that no*

* Reminiscences of N.S.W. by Judge Therry.
† Reminiscences. page 74.
C

officer shall sell any more liquor."—* It is not my intention
to write a general history of the colony; but only to advert
to the state of the politics, as an elucidation of the condition
of the colony. Religion and politics are the two points upon
which all human affairs turn. When religion is wanting in
a state, the superstructure will be frail and tottering:—Such was
the condition of the colony during the interregnum from departure of Governor Philip to arrival of Governor Hunter. It seemed
to have been the intention of the Government in the beginning
to plant the true religion, and extend the true faith, when the
colony was founded.† The colony was woefully in want of
religious instruction; there was only one clergyman sent out by
the Christian Government to administer to the religious wants of
the young community, and no place of worship was erected until
after the departure of Governor Phillip: and then, in July (1793)
after a period of five years, the first place of worship was erected.
This Church was opened for service of the Church of England,
25th August, 1793; but this House of Prayer was not erected at
the expense of the Government but by voluntary contributions of
the colonists and by the exertions of the Rev. Mr. Johnson, the
protestant colonial chaplain. Everything else had been diligently
attended to, except the interests of religion, which was the last
consideration. Commodious dwelling houses were erected by
the Government. Stores, barracks, workshops, &c.‡

A priest who was the chaplain of one of two Spanish vessels
which arrived in the port, in March, 1793, expressed his astonishment when he ascertained that no place of worship had been
built: he said "that had a settlement been made by his nation, a
house for the service of God would have been erected before
any habitation for man."

It does not appear that much interest was taken by the community in erecting a place of worship for their protection from
sun and rain; for the building only cost £40, and the materials
of which it was constructed were very unsubstantial; the walls
were made of posts, wattles and plaster, and the roof was thatch.
Nor is the want of ardour on the part of the inhabitants to be
wondered at; the third of the population were Roman catholics,
and they were required by the regulation of the Government to
be present during the service of the Church of England; and the

* History of Australia. Discovery and Colonization, in 4 parts.
† Address of Governor Philip.
‡ Flanagan's History of N. S. Wales. Pages 78—93.

other two-thirds were members, we presume, of the Church of England and Dissenters. It was great oppression to compel the catholics to attend a worship they disliked and believed to be erroneous, and which brought to their mind all that their forefathers had suffered for conscience sake. They were there in punishment for their violation of the laws, but they should have been at liberty to worship God according to their belief. Such an attempt to fetter the soul whilst the body was in chains could only nourish discontent, and breed revolt. The authorities should have seen the impossibility of making at least the catholic prisoners conform to the worship of the Church of England; and therefore the necessity of providing clergymen to supply the religious wants of the catholics and others. The Rev. Mr. Johnson must have been very distasteful to the members of the Church of England when he turned a Moravian Methodist; and notwithstanding all that is said of his zeal and piety, he spent a great deal of his time, away from his charge, on his farm at Kissing Point. He was very successful in horticultural pursuits, and his oranges sold sometimes at a shilling each. He returned to England with a good fortune, after having spent twelve or thirteen years in the colony.

There was no school for the children until the year 1797, when a school-house was built for the accommodation of 300 children; and it is astonishing that some provision was not made for the secular education of the children during these nine years of the existence of the colony. It was not before, but when the school was built, that the Rev. Mr. Johnson began to catechise the children after the service on each Sunday. A great many of these would be catholic children, who were compelled to be present, as the catholic adults were compelled to be present to hear the service of the Church of England.

The tenets of the Moravian Methodists are very objectionable. It is said the doctrines preached by their founder, Zinzendorf, were of the most revolting and horrible nature.* An author remarks, referring to his doctrines, "It is truly melancholy to behold the sacred name of religion prostituted to such vile abomination." Such were the dangerous occasions in regard to Faith, to which the catholics were exposed in the beginning of the colony. An historian of the colony writes, "One chaplain of the Church of England enjoyed a salary for preaching occasionally to an ignorant uninstructed multitude, of whom one third were *Irish Roman*

---

* History of Heresies, by St. Liguori. Vol. II., p 73.

Catholics, transported for political or agrarian offences. Religious teaching, the bedside prayer, the solemn call for repentance, were seldom heard in that miserable Gomorrah.*

The church which had been erected at the cost of £40, was on the evening of the 1st October, 1798, consumed by fire. It was thought to be the work of an incendiary and a reward of £30 was offered by the Government to find out the transgressor ; but no one was found charged with the offence. A very strict order had been made compelling all the prisoners, under certain penalties, to attend, without distinction of creed, Divine Service on Sunday. And because it was suspected to be the work of an incendiary, all the men were compelled to work on Sunday for the erection of another place of worship. But can anyone be surprised if it was set on fire by someone ; since could anything be more intolerant than to compel the unfortunate prisoners to hear what which was contrary to their faith and conscience, and calculated, at least in respect to the Roman catholics, to awaken all their animosities to a Liturgy, an account of which their forefathers had suffered so much by the penal laws.

A singular notion took possession of the minds of the people, in the beginning of the colony, and for many years after, that Australia was united to China ; and that if they could cross the country to the north they would reach China : deluded by this notion, a considerable number made the attempt. The colony was only three years (1791) in existence, when the first attempt was made. Twenty convicts ran away, seven of them perished in the bush, the remainder, when discovered, were almost naked and dying with hunger : still this did not deter others from making a similar attempt. In the beginning of the following year, 44 men and 9 women were missing from the establishment, and it was believed they had lost themselves on the way to China, and had died of starvation; nor did the fate of these deter others, a few years afterwards, from trying the experiment. It is related by Collins, writing in January, 1798, "that numerous bodies of the Irish convicts left the settlement to regain their liberty, by making their way through the bush to China, but no doubt they perished in the attempt." A man by the name of Wilson, who had lived with the aborigines, returning to the settlement gave information that he had seen more than fifty skeletons of those, which the blacks said were skeletons of white men who had lost their way in the woods. It was the greatest infatuation for men to attempt what they knew had been fatal to so many, but the

---

* **Three Colonies of Australia, Sidney, p. 31.**

innate love of liberty prompted them to try or perish in the attempt; and death was preferable to the cruel treatment they were undergoing, working in chains, under the scorching Australian sun; subjected to the lash for the least infringement of regulation; and the despotic conduct of overseers and no abridgement of punishment for good behaviour; associated with the vilest of men, and the voice of religion never heard in that Pandemonium. These are extenuating circumstances. Who would not excuse them for trying to get to China? It is very illiberal to reproach, as some have done, these men with their ignorance of the Geography of Australia, a land 16,000 miles distant from the Green Isle; and the more, because in their youth they were deprived of the opportunity of acquiring any knowledge. It should be remembered that those Irishmen were brought up under the penal laws, and it was not until the year 1791, that the following enactment was expunged from the Statutes:—" If a catholic kept a school or taught any person, protestant or catholic, any species of literature or science, such teacher was for the crime of teaching punishable by law, by banishment—and if he returned from banishment, he was subject to be hanged as a felon."

It is not to be doubted but that it was the intention of the Home Government in the beginning of the colony to establish the Church of England upon such a basis that she could not be shaken, and to make her the dominant church, to the exclusion of all dissenters. The colony was only two years in existence whan provision on an extensive scale was made by the Home Government for the "church and schools." Instructions were sent to Governor Phillip to set apart in each township, in the name of His Majesty George III., 400 acres for the minister, and 200 acres for the maintenance of a schoolmaster. The same provision was repeated to Governor Macquarie in the year 1809.

There was a new measure—a most bountiful measure—put in force in the year 1826, thirty-nine years after the establishment of the colony, giving to the Church of England the most extensive support. This measure was planned by George IV. and His Majesty's advisers, and issued under the Royal Sign Manual. By this Royal enactment (purporting to provide for the maintenance of religion—that is the Church of England—and the education of youth in the discipline and according to the principles of the united Church of England and Ireland) a Body Politic and Corporate was formed to carry out the Royal provisions, consisting of the Governor and the Government officers, together with the Archdeacon of the Church of England, and the nine senior chaplains. The Governor is commanded by his instructions under the Royal Sign Manual, dated 17th July, 1825, to see that there be set apart in every county for the above purpose " the seventh part in extent and value of all the lands in each and every such county, and to be known by the name of the Clergy and School Estate of such county."

How exclusive and unjust to the Roman catholics—one-third of the population, numbering 17,000 at that time—and all dissenters from the Church of England !—a most determined attempt to establish a State Church in the colony, and force the colonists in a manner to conform to the Church of England. Nor was there a shadow of excuse for such an exclusive measure. Had the colony been composed only of members of the Church of England. with not much likelihood of divergence from her views, then there would not be so much cause for complaint. But when the most of the people of the colony, both bond and free, were adverse to the principles of the Church of England, and not likely to be reconciled to her, such a Royal piece of legislation was, to say the least of it, very short-sighted and one-sided, and calculated to breed the greatest discontent in the State. In all probability the measure was concocted in the colony by the would-be aristocrats and sent home for the approval of His Majesty's advisers. This would be making the *amende honorable* for their insubordination at the time of the *coup d'etat*—a manifestation of their loyalty and fidelity to the Church and State. It was intimated to the corporation by the Governor, at the close of the year 1829, that it was His Majesty's (George IV.) intention to revoke the charter. The charter was actually revoked on 4th February, 1833. The revocation was notified in the *Gazette*, 28th August, 1833.*

Very little is on record about the catholics in the early days of the colony; only that about one-third of the prisoners were Roman catholics; some statistics were kept, but not one giving the number of each religious denomination; the entire population seemed to be considered as members of the would-be State Church. In my opinion there were very few catholics amongst the convicts of the *first fleet*, who came out under Governor Phillip. They, in all probability, were the deliverances of the jails and houses of correction, throughout England. Collins states in his History of New South Wales, that the first Irish convicts arrived in the year 1791 : No doubt, a great many of these were catholics. The unfortunate Irish Catholic prisoner, when he landed, found no priest to whom he could pour out his

* State of Religion and Education in N. S. Wales (Burton's), page 30.

afflicted soul, and receive the strengthening graces of the sacraments. The Home Government were too apathetic to care about his spiritual wants ; and the colonial authorities too bigoted and averse to the catholic church to trouble themselves in procuring spiritual aid for the catholic convicts. We are sure the prayers of the poor prisoners were unceasing to the God of all consolation to send them a priest. Their petition was heard, and He sent them three priests under the garb of political prisoners, but they were innocent of the charges made against them. In 1799, the year following the Irish Rebellion, a great many persons were banished, on the charge of being implicated in the outbreak of '98, and amongst these were three priests, viz., Fathers Dixon, Harold, and O'Neil, and a protestant clergyman, the Rev. Mr. Fulton. Father Harold was placed at Norfolk Island, where he officiated for some time. Father O'Neil obtained his liberty, the Home Government having discovered that he was innocent. He returned to Ireland in 1802. Father Dixon was appointed by the colonial Government to administer to the religious wants of the catholics of the colony in 1803. And at the same time that Father Dixon received permission from the Government to exercise his clerical functions, he received faculties from his ecclesiastical superiors. Father Dixon was appointed by the Proclamation of Governor King, on 19th April, 1803. The Proclamation ran as follows :

"Whereas I have judged it expedient and admissible, in consequence of a communication from His Majesty's Principal Secretary of State for the Colonies and War Department, to grant unto the reverend Mr. Dixon, a conditional emancipation to enable him to exercise his clerical functions as a Roman Catholic priest : which he has qualified himself for by the regular and exemplary conduct he has manifested since his residence in the colony ; and his having taken the oath of allegiance, abjuration, and declaration prescribed by law."

" Which permission shall remain in full force and effect, so long as he, the said Reverend Mr. Dixon, and (no other priest) shall strictly adhere to the rules and regulations which he has this day bound himself by oath to observe, as well as all the other regulations which may hereafter be made thereon by His Majesty's Governor of this territory for the time being ; and in case of any deviation therefrom by the said Mr. Dixon, or any of his congregation, it will remain with the Governor of this territory to suspend such religious assemblies, and to deal with the offenders according to law."

To His Majesty's Justices assigned to keep the peace, &c., &c
Given under my hand and seal, this 19th day of April, 1803.

(Signed)   P. G. KING.

To which proclamation are appended the following regulations :—

General Orders, April 21, 1803.

Regulations to be observed by the Rev. Mr. Dixon and the catholic congregation in this colony :—

First—They will observe with all becoming gratitude that this extension of liberal toleration proceeds from the piety and benevolence of our Most Gracious Sovereign, to whom, as well as our present country at large, we are (under Providence) indebted for the blessings we enjoy.

Second—That the religious exercise of their worship may suffer no hindrance, it is expected that no seditious conversations that can in any way injure His Majesty's Government or affect the tranquillity of the colony will ever happen, either at the places prescribed for their worship or elsewhere ; but that they will individually manifest their gratitude and allegiance by exerting themselves in detecting and reporting any impropriety of that or any other nature that may fall under their observation.

Third—As Mr. Dixon will be allowed to perform his clerical duties once in three weeks at the settlements at Sydney, Parramatta and Hawkesbury, in rotation, the magistrates are strictly forbid suffering those catholics who reside at the places where service is not performed from resorting to the settlement and district at which the priest officiates for the day.

Fourth—The catholic service will be performed on the appointed Sundays at 9 o'clock in the morning.

Fifth—No improper behaviour during the time of service is to be allowed by the priest, who will be responsible to the magistrates for his congregation going regularly and orderly to their respective homes, after the offices are ended.

Sixth—And to the end that strict decorum may be observed, a certain number of the police will be stationed at and about the places appointed during the service.

Seventh—Every person throughout the colony will observe that the law has sufficiently provided for the punishment of those who may disquiet or disturb any assembly of religious worship, or misuse any priest or teacher of any tolerated sect.

(Signed)   JAMES DIXON.

Subscribed before us this 19th day of April, 1803.

(Signed) RICHARD ATKINS.
THOMAS JAMIESON.

Where was the need of all this formality in appointing Father Dixon, and why expect such immense gratitude for an act of simple justice?—for had two or three priests been appointed by the Government before that time it would have prevented an accumulation of crime. And why were the Governor and others so full of fear and apprehension of the unfortunate priest and Irish rebels ; did they think that if they were treated humanely, they would rise up and murder their keepers in cold blood ? And for what end would they rebel ? to seize upon the miserable uncleared land about Sydney, and a few shabby weatherboarded cottages, including the Government House ? No, the only motive by which they could be actuated, would be to rid themselves of the cruel tyranny by which they were oppressed.

Father Dixon immediately availed himself of the permission granted by the Governor, to discharge his clerical duties : I find a notice in the *Sydney Gazette* of May, 1803, that the Roman catholic congregation in that year, assembled for the *first time* at Sydney. It is there stated, " That on Sunday Morning, 22nd May, 1803, the Reverend Mr. Dixon will perform the duties of his functions at Parramatta, and on Sunday next, at the Hawkesbury ; in which succession the meetings are to be held at these three principal settlements." The first meeting of catholics was held in Sydney by the Rev. Mr. Dixon, on 15th May, 1803. He was, according to all accounts, a good, zealous and charitable priest, and was ever ready to give consolation to the afflicted, and he spent his time in administering the Sacraments of Baptism, Marriage, offering the Holy Sacrifice, absolving the penitent from his sins, and feeding him with the Bread of Life. A marriage which he solemnized is notified in the *Government Gazette* in the following terms : " May 15th, 1803, married by the Rev. Mr. Dixon, of the Church of Rome, Henry Simpson, shipwright, to Catherine Rourke, of the Rocks, widow.

But the good priest was not allowed to remain long in the quiet enjoyment, like his Heavenly Master, of going about and doing good ; the hatred, bigotry and jealousy with which he was surrounded, soon found a pretext to deprive him of the power of doing good. "He was interrupted," says a respectable writer, " by the report that meetings for worship were gatherings of traitors, and the medium of communication for another attempted rebellion. An order closed the services." And yet when the insurrection did burst forth, and a second "Vinegar Hill " battle took place on the other side of the world, the Rev. Mr. Dixon accompanied the Commanding Officer and exerted himself nobly on the side of order and humanity.

The same vessel which brought out the three priests to the colony, brought Joseph Holt, called General Holt, because he was one of the leaders in the rebellion of 1798. He was fourteen years in the colony, at the end of which time he returned to Ireland. He wrote a very interesting biography in which he makes known his experiences of colonial life and gives a very truthful and correct account of the "oppressions, woes and pains" inflicted by those in authority. I will give an illustration drawn by him, which shows the barbarous and cruel treatment to which the unfortunate prisoners were subjected by the myrmidons of power. He was taken shortly after his arrival by the Rev. Mr. Marsden, one of the colonial chaplains, who wished to secure his services, to see a Government gang at work. He writes: "At a distance, I saw about 50 men at work, as I thought dressed in nankeen jackets, but on nearer approach I found them naked, except a pair of loose trousers. Their skin was tanned by the sun and climate to that colour. I felt much pity for the poor wretches : they had each a kind of large hoe about nine inches deep, and eight inches wide and the handle as thick as that of a shovel, with which they turned up as with a spade, the ground which was left to rot in the winter. They cannot bear any clothes when at work in the heat of the day. Captain Johnstone addressed me saying, 'Mr. Holt, you are a good farmer, I suppose?' 'I do well enough with horses and oxen, but not with men,' said I. Dr. Thompson then said, 'Do you think those men would understand you better than horses or oxen ?' 'Yes sir,' I replied, 'but it appears great brutality to work men in this manner.' 'Well,' said he, 'it matters not what you think about it, you will soon come into it.'" On another occasion not long after, Holt says : "I marched to Toongabbee, where all the Government transports were kept, who were called out to witness the punishment of the prisoners. One man, Maurice Fitzgerald, was sentenced to receive 300 lashes, and the method of punishment was such as to make it most effectual. The unfortunate man had his hands extended round a tree, his two wrists tied with cord, and his breast pressed closely to the tree, so that flinching from the blows was out of the question, for it was impossible for him to stir. Here is a picture of the working of the convict system in those days. Father Harold was ordered to put his hands against the tree, by the hands of the prisoner, and two men were appointed to flog, namely Richard Rice a left handed man, and John Johnson the hangman from Sydney, who was right handed. They stood on each side of Fitzgerald, and I never saw two thrashers in a barn move their flails with more regularity than those two man-killers did, unmoved by pity, and rather enjoying their horrid employment than otherwise. The very first blows made the blood spout from Fitzgerald's shoulders, and I felt so disgusted and horrified, that I turned my face away from the cruel sight."

What a revolting scene, what inhuman treatment to a fellow man, made to the image and likeness of God. It puts one in mind of pagan times when the master would order his slave to be scourged or slain for the slightest offence, merely through capriciousness. In all probability Fitzgerald had to suffer those 300 lashes on account of a little insubordination or impertinent reply to his hard task-masters; but what prompted those petty tyrants to order the priest, Father Harold, "to put his hand against the tree by the hands of the prisoner?" Was it to nerve Fitzgerald to bear his punishment with more firmness? But such tigers could have no sympathy. No, it must have been to degrade Father Harold, to lower him in the eyes of all present, to remind him he was a political prisoner, a rebel, and that he might expect similar treatment if he dared to evince a spirit of discontent. Whatever was their reason for such an order, it was treating Father Harold with the greatest indignity. I cannot find for what Fitzgerald was flogged, but the punishment surely was excessive.

An outbreak of the prisoners and others happened in March, 1804, said to have originated with the Irish State prisoners; but Mr. Holt, and others, assert that they were not the only prisoners who broke out. The gangs of prisoners employed at Toongabbee, Castle Hill, near Parramatta, took part in the insurrectionary movement; and amongst them there were Englismen and free men, and assigned servants belonging to the settlers in the surrounding parts. They numbered from 200 to 300, and were well armed. They were met by Major Johnstone, at the head of 25 soldiers and some settlers, at the Ponds, a place between

Parramatta and Windsor. The insurgents, seeing such a small force against them, halted at the side of a hill, not to offer battle, but they sent two men, Cunningham and Johnson, to represent their grievances, and Major Johnstone, if he had had any humanity, might have listened to their tale of woe ; but instead he laid hold of Johnson and placed a pistol at his ear, whilst his quartermaster, Laycock, killed Cunningham with one blow. They then fired at the insurgents, killing some, and the rest fled. It is evident the rebels had no intention to take life. If they had, it would have been easy for 300 well-armed men, in their desperation, to have slain or put to the rout twenty-five soldiers. It cannot be concealed, although the '98 business was made a " cloak for malice," that it was the tyranny and cruelty of those in authority, and of the settlers to whom the prisoners were assigned, which instigated them to rise up against their hard taskmasters.

In order to hide their cruelty and mismanagement, the Government of the day was easily persuaded that the Irish political prisoners were the instigators of the late disturbances and cause of all the discontent, and they pretended that Father Dixon was implicated, for he was obstructed in the discharge of his clerical duties, and the allowance which he received from the Government was withdrawn, and his rations were stopped. This was no doubt tantamount to a dismissal from the Government. It is very natural to suppose when Father Dixon saw the way he was treated, and could do no good, that he made up his mind to leave the colony, which he did in the year 1808. Father O'Neil had also been sent to the colony for being implicated in the Rebellion of 1798, together with Father Harold. The Home Government became convinced in due time that the Rev. Mr. Dixon and Rev. Mr. Harold had no participation in the acts of the Irish Rebellion. Father O'Neil received his pardon and returned to Ireland in the year 1802. Father Harold officiated at Norfolk Island for a time ; and when the Rev. Mr. Dixon left, he came to Sydney and officiated in his place.

The Colonial Government now became thoroughly religious, and persuaded of the necessity of the ordinances of religion being attended to ; accordingly they determined to enforce the observances of the Church of England, and compel all without distinction to give their attendance. A regulation was made and enforced, that the whole of the prison population should attend Divine Service in the Church of England ; and, if anyone kept away, for the first offence he should receive twenty-five lashes, for the second fifty lashes, and if he refused the third time be sent to a penal settlement. The regulation was vigorously enforced. Here was persecution for conscience's sake with a vengeance.

The priest was now separated from his flock, he could neither preach, baptize, nor attend the sick, in all probability he had no means of subsistence. He asked permission from the Government to return home, and immediately it was granted. This priest was the Rev. Mr. Harold. Now was the time, when the three priests had left the colony, to compel all to conform to the Church of England; but the means resorted to were not the mild and persuasive words of the gospel, but the painful and bloody strokes of the lash. They borrowed from the penal code to carry out their ends. The inhabitants of the colony, bond and free, amounted to 10,500 souls at this time, 1809, and a great number were Roman catholics. In the year 1807, Rev. S. Marsden, one of the protestant chaplains, the senior, went to England to procure more clergymen for the Church of England. In 1808 the Rev. Wm. Cowper and Rev. Mr. Cartwright arrived in the colony, and between 1810 and 1817 the church establishment was increased by an assistant chaplain. Observe with what care the protestant church was fostered.

A literary person, by name James Benwick, F.R.G.S., writes: " New South Wales in the beginning was regarded as England over the way, and absolutely attached to the State Church of England, and Roman catholics could expect no favour. All had to go to church, they were driven as sheep to the fold, and whatever their scruples the had to go: Fallen as many were, they were not to be supposed aliens altogether in principles, and indifferent to Faith. In some, the very consciousness of crime had developed an eagerness after Faith, and that the Faith they had known, the Faith of a mother. But expostulations were unheeded. If a man humbly entreated to stay behind, because he was a presbyterian, he incurred the danger of a flogging. It is said that upon a similar appeal from another, who exclaimed ' I am a catholic,' he was silenced by the cry of a clerical magistrate, ' Go to church or be flogged.' "

Contrast the prosperous condition of the Church of England with the deplorable and neglected state of the catholics. They are denied all help: not an acre of land for them to build a church or school upon: no priest to administer the rites of their holy faith: no catechist to instruct them in the elements of religion: no schoolmaster: which meant, as clearly as possible, that their only help was in the Church of England, by law established in the colony. Was this not religious oppression?

Father Harold must have left the colony about the year 1809. Father Dixon left in 1808. From this time until 1817, when the Very Rev. Father O'Flynn arrived in the colony, that is eight years and more, there was no priest in the colony to administer to the religious wants of the catholics, amounting to nearly a third of the population, and they were compelled to attend the protestant service of the Church of England. What a state of spiritual destitution during those eight years! No priest to offer up the adorable Sacrifice: no church for the catholics: the catholic child left without the saving waters of baptism, or doubtfully baptised by the Protestant minister: the sick and oppressed without the spiritual consolation of their pastor; and they go into their grave unconfessed and unanointed: no catechist to instruct the children in the only true and saving faith. And this continues for the long time of eight years. The poor catholics had one resource—they could pray that the Almighty would soon relieve them and send them priests. They did pray, and in due time their prayer was heard.

CHAPTER IV.

1808—The Coup d'Etat, when Governor Bligh was deposed, and Mr. John McArthur appointed himself Colonial Secretary. —Arrival of Governor Macquarie, in 1809.—The Very Rev. Jeremiah O'Flynn arrived, 9th November, 1817.—Archpriest O'Flynn compelled by the Governor to leave the Colony.

THE very year in which Father Dixon left the colony was the year when Governor Bligh was arrested, and his administration put an end to by Major Johnstone, at the head of a number of soldiers. This little coup d'etat took place 25th January, 1808. The Governor was imprisoned until 20th February of 1809. Those who had seized upon the Government dismissed all the civil officers and appointed others in their place. Mr. John McArthur, who had chiefly been instrumental in deposing Governor Bligh, was placed at the head of the Government, or rather, it is recorded, appointed himself Colonial Secretary.

The way these things came about was this:—Mr. John McArthur had been imprisoned by the Governor because he refused to pay the forfeit, which he had incurred, by a prisoner being found in his craft, which was cleared for New Zealand. The Governor had taken a piece of land from Captain John McArthur, which he had selected for a residence, on Church Hill, —an elevated healthy situation—and given him in lieu an allotment at the end of lower Pitt-street, then called Pitt's Lease, which allotment was very objectionable, because it was the place where the gallows stood, and surrounded by all the vile and infamous characters of the town of Sydney. These were the immediate causes which brought things to a crisis; but there had been a very bad feeling and misunderstanding between the Governor and McArthur from the beginning. Governor Bligh entered upon his rule of the colony with the firm determination of crushing monopoly in all its branches, and all its adherents; and he seems to have looked upon McArthur as the ruling spirit of the movement. The sentiments of the Governor in regard to the condition of the colony when he arrived, may be gathered from his own words. He wrote:—"To ascertain the state of the colony I visited many of the inhabitants individually, and witnessed many melancholy proofs of their wretched condition. A want even of the common necessaries of life *was too prevalent*, particularly at the extensive settlement on the Hawkesbury; and although Sydney formed some exception to the general aspect, yet even there the habitations and public store-houses were falling into decay; industry was declining; while a pernicious fondness for spirituous liquors was gaining ground, to the destruction of public morals and private happiness. Knowing the sentiments of the British Government on the subject of the existing abuses, and the solicitude entertained for their correction, I used every exertion to accomplish this, and particularly in relation to the barter of spirits." It would appear from this statement that the Home Government was perfectly cognisant of the abuses which existed in the colony, and that the Governor had particular instructions to use all his endeavours to remove them. Captain John McArthur called to see the Governor shortly after his arrival, and fully alive to his own interest, and no doubt in the second place, to the interest of the colony in general, began to impress upon his mind the great advantages which he thought must accrue to the colony and the mother country from the production of fine wool. The Governor answered in his gruff seaman style; and seeing Mr. McArthur had an eye to business, said— " What have I to do with your sheep, sir? What have I to do with your cattle? Are you to have such flocks of sheep and herds of cattle as no man ever heard of before? No, sir." The captain replied that he understood the Home Government had particularly recommended him to his notice. " I am well aware of your concern, sir; you have got 5000 acres of the best land in the colony, and in the finest situation, but by God, you shan't keep it."—*Judge Therry's Reminiscences of N.S. Wales.*

This was rather hasty language on the part of the Governor, a comportment perhaps suited for the quarter-deck, but not for the floor of the Government House, with a wealthy and ambitious man like Captain McArthur, who was supported by a powerful oligarchy. The Governor had no intention of taking the life of McArthur, but was not reluctant to put him in prison from a desire to break up the combination by securing the ringleader. When the Governor was put under arrest by Major Johnstone, at the instance, it is said, of McArthur and others, he ignominiously, his enemies declared, concealed himself under a bed in the Government House. Now it should be known that the residence was suddenly surrounded by the soldiers, and a number of them with their muskets and fixed bayonets rushed up stairs, at the top of which Governor Bligh was standing, sword in hand; he thought they were about to seize his person, and he retired to prevent them laying hold of him. Now I do not think the Governor was so much to blame for trying, as he supposed, to save his life: he knew well, a hero of many fights, what infuriated soldiers might do; and his conduct under such dangerous circumstances was not worse than that of Charles II., who concealed himself in the oak tree from his enemies.

No doubt John McArthur and his party had no intention of taking the life of the Governor, but it seems as if they were fully bent on sending him out of the colony, and thus getting rid of one who was most inimical to their scheme of aggrandisement. Governor Bligh, at the court-martial in England (for he brought Major Johnstone before the court on a charge of mutiny, and John McArthur was also arraigned before the same tribunal) declared it was a slander on the part of Major Johnstone to make such a statement. It is difficult to believe that an old naval hero would have been guilty of such an undignified retreat. He commanded the man-of-war ship, Director, at the battle of Camperdown, and he first silenced and then boarded the ship of Admiral De Winter. At the battle of Copenhagen Bligh commanded the Glutton, and was publicly thanked by Lord Nelson on the quarter-deck.

The result of the trial was that Major Johnstone lost his sword, and was cashiered. Mr. McArthur had left the army for some years before, and on this account could not be brought before a court-martial for the par he had taken, but he was interdicted from returning to the colony for a period of eight years.

This little coup d'etat had rather a beneficial effect upon the affairs of the colony; it broke up the oligarchy of would-be rulers and caused a Governor of superior character to be sent to the colony, the very able and sagacious Governor Macquarie. With

VERY REV. J. O'FLINN, ARCHPRIEST.

all the noise and agitation caused by this stroke of policy there were no lives lost: it ended happily, like a comedy, by marriage. Young Lieutenant O'Connell, one of the officers of the 73rd Regiment, who came to the colony with Governor Macquarie, married Mrs. Putland, widow, and daughter of Governor Bligh. The festivities consequent upon the nuptials allayed much of the ill-feeling which had existed amongst some of the principal colonists.

The colonists presented an address to Governor Bligh before he left the colony, testifying in the strongest terms their respect and veneration towards him. The address was signed by 833 country settlers and landholders; date, 1st January, 1808.— *Discovery and Colonization of Australia, p. 382 & 386.*

This should be said in favour of Captain John McArthur, that although he was bent on the acquisition of wealth and influence, he never forgot the general interests of the colony. On the trial, at the court-martial, he stated, and there is no reason to disbelieve his statement, that he had disposed of breeding cattle, amongst the settlers, to the amount of £20,000; that he had raised about 12,000 head of horned cattle and 12,000 sheep; that at that time he was in possession of 4,600 sheep and 300 head of cattle; and that the consequence of his management was to lower the price of beef and mutton from 2s. 6d. per lb. to 9d.

The descendants of John McArthur are still wealthy and influential, and hold part if not all of the 5000 acres originally granted to the founder of their family, They have cultivated their land to the highest degree, and planted vineyards; and they are ever foremost in whatever movement is set on foot for the advancement of the colony.

The reader will pardon this digression from the ecclesiastical history; but it will be well for him to know what were the current events, the disorderly state of the Government, and the wretched condition of the people. A new state of things was inaugurated with Governor Macquarie, who arrived in the colony 28th December, 1809.

After the departure of Father Dixon the catholics were for ten years, as I have stated, without a priest to administer the sacraments and rites of the church: there were no influential catholics to represent their spiritual grievances: many of the Irish catholics had been sent to the colony on account of the '98 rebellion and for agrarian outrages, and a good number for offences of quite a different character, which ranked them with a degraded class. Very Rev. J. O'Flynn arrived in the colony in the year 1817. He was appointed by Rome to administer to the

D

spiritual wants of the catholics of the colony, and had authority to confer the sacrament of Confirmation. He was a man of meek demeanor, and very zealous for the salvation of souls. I have seen several who were baptized by him, and there was pointed out to me by an olde resident of Sydney, a place in George-street, where he administered the Sacrament of Confirmation. He went from one part of the colony to another, seeking out his people, celebrating the Divine Mysteries, and giving instructions. From the time he landed the most determined opposition was raised against him. His zeal and piety attracted the notice of the anti-catholic party, and they cried out for his expulsion from the colony. As a pretext for sending him away it was alleged that he had come to the colony without the approval of the Home Government. Judge Therry, in his "Reminiscences of New South Wales and Victoria," states, that there was no law which required the sanction of the British civil authorities. Father O'Flynn was cast into prison and sent away by the first ship sailing for England. It is said that he left the Blessed Sacrament for the adoration of the faithful in the house of Mr. William Davis, near where now stands the Church of St. Patrick. We can well imagine the fervent prayers which the afflicted souls would offer to their Saviour in the sacrament, to send labourers into the vineyard, which was arid for want of cultivation. Nor was it long before their prayer was heard. The Arch-priest, Father O'Flynn, arrived safely in England, and the hardship of the poor catholic prisoners being deprived in this summary manner of his ministry was brought before Parliament, by Lord Bathurst,, who made provision for two catholic clergymen. Lord Donoghmore represented the arbitrary conduct of Governor Macquarie, in compelling Father O'Flynn to leave the colony, in the House of Conmons. The representation caused considerable excitement, and the British public acknowledged that a great injustice had been done to the poor catholics of New South Wales. It was ordered by the Executive that two priests be selected, and salaries given them, to proceed to New South Wales to attend to the religious wants of the Roman catholics.

To show how deeply the catholics felt the deprivation of their spiritual adviser, it is related by Dr. Ullathorne in his account of the Catholic Mission in Australasia, that shortly after his arrival a venerable old man came to him from a distance to go to his religious duties, and expressed his regret for the departure of Father O'Flynn by saying, "Oh had Father O'Flynn remained what would he have done! He had the sweetest and the swiftest tongue of Irish that ever my ear heard." The old man excused his bad English and said that he "had never spoken one word of English until it was made fifty lashes to speak a word of Irish." The anti-catholic clique of bigots who surrounded the Governor of the day must have been sensible of their injustice towards the catholics.

A petition was got up by the catholics and liberal-minded protestants requesting the Governor not to send the *Very Rev. J. O'Flynn* out of the colony. They were told very coolly that it was a piece of presumption on their part to make any such request. Some over zealous protestant officials were accused of influencing the Governor to do this despotic act: and it is said that the Governor was incessantly entreated by settlers to send Father O'Flynn out of the colony, because he was constantly inducing, by Divine Service, the prisoners to leave their work. In a letter which appeared in the "Freeman's Journal," a few years back, the writer states, "That the name of the Arch-priest was not Rev. William Flinn, as given by a correspondent, but the Very Rev. Jeremiah O'Flynn, and a very fine looking man he was. He confirmed me, and I quite well remember him." Again, the writer states, that "Father O'Flynn left the Blessed Sacrament in the house of a devoted catholic (in a Pix), the late Mr. James Dempsey, of Kent-street, near to Erskine-street, and next door to the then residence of Mr. Thomas Day the boat builder, which is not near St. Patrick's Church, as has been asserted." He also states that before the arrival of Father Therry the catholics met in Sydney, for their devotions, at the house of this good old man, James Dempsey, on all Sundays and holidays; and that the priest of a French Frigate frequently said mass there. I find it attested by Bishop Polding, in his report of the Mission, for the Propagation of the Faith, that the Blessed Sacrament was consumed, and the species found uncorrupt, when the two priests, F. Connelly and Father Therry arrived, in the year 1820.

There is no record in the *Government Gazette* of the imprisonment of Father O'Flynn, or of his compulsory departure from the colony, that I can find. There were said to be at the time, in New South Wales and Van Dieman's Land, not less than 10,000 catholics, which is a most aggravating circumstance in connection with the treatment of the Arch-priest—to deprive that number of people, firmly attached to their religion, of the ministrations of a priest, and who had been already without a clergyman for ten years. But I suppose penal laws were to be expected in a penal settlement. Father O'Flynn concealed himself for a time, whilst a petition was being prepared. The petition was signed by 400 respectable colonists, who prayed the

Governor to allow Father O'Flynn to remain, otherwise a great number of the community would be deprived of religious instruction. It was to no purpose; he had to depart from the shores of Australia.

In course of time Archpriest O'Flynn arrived in his native land; he represented the treatment he had received from the Colonial Government to the Right Rev. Dr. England, Bishop of Charleston, who was in Ireland at the time. Bishop England put the case into the hands of Lord Donoughmore, who was then member for Cork, and he brought it before the House of Commons.

When Father O'Flynn returned to Ireland, there was a young priest, lately ordained in Carlow College. This priest was the Rev. John Joseph Therry. He had greatly distinguished himself during his college career for learning and piety. He was most anxious to devote himself to the service of God and of His church in a foreign land: he had formed a small band of students into a society to offer up prayers for the success of foreign missions. This zealous young priest saw Archpriest O'Flynn, and heard from his lips the tale of the sorrows and spiritual wants of his fellow countrymen: he did not hesitate, but offered himself at once for the arduous duty. He applied and obtained the consent of his bishop to go out to Australia. Another priest, somewhat older, the Rev. P. Connelly, joined him in the noble object. They were furnished with the requisite papers by the Government: Lord Bathurst having made provision for two catholic clergymen to be sent to New South Wales.

CHAPTER V.

*2nd May, 1820.—The arrival of Fathers Therry and Connelly.—
Extraordinary instructions of Governor Macquarie to these
two clergymen.—Foundation-Stone of St. Mary's laid by
Governor Macquarie, 29th October, 1821.—The reason why
Father Therry was deprived of his salary, and forbidden to
officiate.—In the year 1829 Mr. Roger Therry arrives as
Commissioner of the Court of Requests.*

THEY sailed from the Cove of Cork, in the ship "James," on the
5th December, 1819, and arrived in Sydney Harbour on Tuesday,
2nd May, 1820. They lost no time after their arrival in obtaining
an interview with the Governor, then General Macquarie, when
their credentials were acknowledged. There being now no
hindrance on the part of the Government, they immediately
began to discharge the functions of their sacred ministry. Fathers
Connelly and Therry received their spiritual powers from the
Right Rev Dr. Slater, who was Bishop of the Mauritius, and held
from the Holy See Ecclesiastical Jurisdiction over New South
Wales, and all the islands in the Oceanique-Southern Seas. They
had from the Home Government £100 each as an annual salary.

The catholics, although numerous, were without a church
wherein to offer the Holy Sacrifice, and hear the word of God ;
and had been so since the foundation of the colony, and these two
devoted men resolved without delay to exert themselves to have
this great want supplied.

Soon after the arrival of the Missionaries, 6th June, 1820,
the Governor sent them written instructions, to direct them in the
discharge of their clerical duties. "He advised them not to try to
make converts from the members of the church of England, nor
protestants in general, to confine their labours to those of their
own flock, and warned them on their peril." This was certainly an
uncalled-for admonition on the part of the Governor to the
catholic clergymen He should have left them to their own
judgment and discretion as were the protestant clergy ; but it may
be supposed that as he and his advisers could not send them out
of the colony, like Father O'Flynn, they were determined to
restrict their action in every way they thought that action would
be detrimental to the would-be state church, by changing the
minds of her subjects, and drawing them over to the catholic
church. He also enjoined that the mass should not be celebrated
publicly, except on Sundays and holidays of the church of
England. He seemed to regret he could not enforce the "Act of

Conformity," passed in the reign of Queen Elizabeth, which prohibited any one from attending the ministration of any clergyman except those of the church of England, and inflicted a fine for not attending service on Sundays, and the prescribed holidays. Governor Macquarie further regulated, that Fathers Connelly and Therry were not to interfere with the religious instruction of the catholic children belonging to the orphan schools; all the inmates of which were to be instructed in the faith and doctrines of the church of England. The Governor ended his instructions by saying, " he was ready to advocate and support the religious liberty of his flock and maintain their just rights and privileges."

This last regulation was a block thrown in the way of the two zealous priests, who had just arrived in the colony, of no small magnitude; to prevent them from instructing the children of their flock, who were being brought up in the Government charitable institutions. The Government had no power to interfere in this way with the parents, who have a natural right to get their children educated in their own religion. To deprive them of this right is unjust, it is to sever the most tender ties which bind the parent to the child—the tie of faith, the tie of hope, the tie of charity in God. If the Governor had received a warrant from Heaven that the church of England was the church of Christ, then he might have exercised control over the souls of those children; but the church of England can lay no substantial claim to this high prerogative, there is no argument in her favor. It is the more to be regretted that he acted in this manner, as Governor Macquarie had many good qualities, but the arbitrary treatment of Father O'Flynn and these stringent regulations are blots upon his administration. They soon commenced their labours. In the Court House a meeting of the catholics was held in the month of July, about two months after the arrival of the catholic clergymen. It was resolved at this meeting, without delay to use their best endeavours, to commence a church, suitable for the catholics of Sydney. The Rev. Philip Connelly presided at this meeting. It was arranged, soon after, that in order to do more good, one of them should go to Tasmania, and labour amongst the catholics, of whom there was a considerable number. The lot fell to Father Therry, who was the junior. He proceeded for his destination and was at sea about a fortnight, when adverse winds drove the vessel back to Sydney; the catholics of Sydney were wont to say from their appreciation of Father Therry that " it is an ill wind which blows nobody good." Father Therry then remained in Sydney, and Father Connelly went to Hobart Town.

When a suitable site had been secured from the Government and all the necessary preliminaries settled upon, the day was appointed for the laying of the foundation stone, and Governor Macquarie was invited to perform the ceremony : he accepted the invitation. It was on the 29th October, 1821, the event took place ; when the Governor received from the hand of Father Therry a silver trowel, and laid the foundation stone of the first catholic church commenced in the colony. On this occasion the reverend chaplain was robed in his priestly vestments.

Government Gazette and New South Wales Advertiser, 3rd Nov., 1821.

FOUNDATION STONE LAID 29TH OCTOBER, 1821.

On Monday last the first stone of the first Roman catholic chapel was laid in this part of the world, in the presence of a vast assemblage of respectable persons, who were anxious to witness so important and interesting a ceremony. The site chosen for the erection of this edifice, which is intended to be spacious as well as handsome, is to the east of Hyde Park, the front of the chapel facing the town. The spot in every way seems extremely eligible, and there can hardly be a doubt entertained but that the structure, when completed, will join with the other superb buildings in that attractive end of the town in affording additional and consistent beauty to the rapidly improving Australian capital. His Excellency the Governor performed the grateful ceremony, for which purpose a very handsome silver trowel had been prepared by Mr. Clayton, which was adorned with an appropriate inscription. " St. Mary's Chapel " was the designation which this intended place of worship received from His Excellency. The Rev. Mr. Therry's address on this occasion and His Excellency's answer have been transmitted to us for insertion, and are subjoined for the information of the public.

" In presenting to your Excellency this humble instrument (which, undervalued as it may be by the supercillious and the unscientific, will not be contemned by any who have studied and patronized, as your Excellency has done, the sciences and useful arts), we, the catholics of this colony, cannot refrain on such an auspicious occasion from expressing our most sincere and heartfelt gratitude to your Excellency for having deigned to honor us by personally laying the first stone of the first Roman catholic chapel attempted to be erected in this territory.

"As a worthy representative of a benevolent king, you, by this act of condescension, give an illustrious example, which will prove to be not less beneficial to society than meritorious to your Excellency. You will have the merit of laying the firm foundation of a moral edifice of unanimity, mutual confidence and fraternal love, and of more strongly cementing the respect and affection of all persuasions and parties in this country to our sovereign, to yourself and to each other.

"In the temple whith you now commence, prayers shall be frequently offered to the Throne of God to invoke upon yourself and your amiable family the richest blessings of heaven, and we venture to predict that whilst it shall continue to be appropriated to the sacred use for which it is intended, neither the name nor the virtues of your Excellency shall at any time be forgotten.

"(Signed) JOHN JOSEPH THERRY,
"Roman Catholic Chaplain.

" For himself and his Roman catholic brethren of New South Wales.

" His Excellency LACHLAN MACQUARIE, Esq., Governor-in-Chief, &c., &c."

" 29th October, 1821.

" Reverend Sir,—I receive from your hands with much pleasure, in your own name and that of your Roman catholic brethren of New South Wales, the very handsome silver trowel now presented to me, and I feel myself very much honored in having been thus selected to make use of this instrument in laying the first stone of the first Roman catholic chapel attempted to be erected in Australia The sentiments you have addressed to me are congenial with my own—in the beneficial result to be derived from the erection of the proposed edifice.

" It has been a great gratification to me to witness and assist at the ceremony now performed, and I have every hope that the consideration of the British Government in supplying the Roman catholics of this colony with established clergymen will be the means of strengthening and augmenting (if that be possible) the attachment of the catholics of New South Wales to the British Government, and will prove an inducement for them to continue—as I have ever found them—to be loyal and faithful subjects to the Crown.

" I beg you will accept of my best acknowledgments for the sentiments of friendly regard and kind good wishes you have been pleased to express for myself and my family.

                    " LACHLAN MACQUARIE,
          " Governor-in-Chief of New South Wales.

"To the Rev. JOHN JOSEPH THERRY and the Roman catholics of N. S. Wales.

" Sydney, 29th October, 1821.

It is related, there were dissensions amongst the catholics about the size of St. Mary's, and no doubt had the plan not been so large the Government would have contributed more readily and liberally. The Colonial Architect objected to the plan being so large, and said that the catholics would not require such a building for a hundred years. Mr. C. Fitzpatrick, in a letter, states, that there were catholics from all parts of the colony at the laying of the foundation stone ; and that he was a boy serving mass on the occasion ; he held the trowel until the time came for Father Therry to present it to the Governor; the following inscription was on the trowel :—" This trowel was presented by the catholics of New South Wales to Major-General Lachlan Macquarie, Governor in Chief, &c., &c., on the auspicious occasion of his laying the foundation stone of St. Mary's Catholic Church." The Governor wiped the trowel with his own handkerchief, and put the trowel in his bosom saying, " You must know Mr. Therry that, although I never laid the first stone of a catholic church before, I am a very old mason," meaning he was a Freemason, " and I shall keep this trowel as long as I live, in remembrance of this day, and I wish you and your flock every success in your pious undertaking." Mr. Fitzpatrick also states that Father Therry won the esteem of Mr. Commissioner Bigge, who made a present of two silver branch candlesticks of great value for the especial use of St. Mary's church.

Governor Macquarie did not long enjoy the vice-regal power after the laying of the foundation stone of St. Mary's church ; he was recalled by the King's Commission, on the 1st of December following, when Major-General Sir Thomas Brisbane was appointed in his stead, as Captain General and Governor in Chief of these colonies.

I cannot allow the time of the administration of Macquarie to pass by without recording my small meed of praise; he is considered by the majority, who have written on the affairs of the colony of New South Wales, to have been the best Governor the colony had, up to the time of his removal. He held the Government for eleven years. One of his first acts was to declare all trials since the arrest of Bligh illegal, and all the acts of the provisional management null and void. He arrived in the colony, as Governor, when it was in a very distracted state with much dissension and discord, monopoly of trade and commerce, depression, great dissipation and lax morals; he destroyed the monopoly, and broke the power of the would-be oligarchy; he restored credit and confidence which were at a minimum, and by wise regulations, he established order and due subordination. Besides looking to the general interests of the colony, he considered it a special duty to attend to the welfare of the prison population, and encouraged them in every way; he ameliorated their unhappy condition, and strove to bring about their reformation; he held, as a principle, that when a man had gained his freedom by good conduct, his days of punishment should not be remembered against him; and he expressed a hope that the British public would never be so resentful as not to pardon the injuries which lawless men had committed against her. This was the best of ethics, and it must be said that the Governor endeavoured to carry out these principles in his conduct. He caused to be erected by prison labour, and the prisoners could not be better employed, many large, commodious, and not inelegant, substantial public buildings; and that not only in Sydney, but in all the adjacent towns. Hyde Park Barracks were erected for the accommodation of the prisoners, and Sydney Infirmary, now being pulled down, which has done the greatest service, during the time of the penal settlement and till the present. It was also during his administration that two orphan schools were erected at Parramatta, one for boys and another for girls.

It was in his time that Bathurst and the adjoining country was discovered by the enterprising explorers, Messrs. Blaxland, Lawson and Wentworth. He connected Bathurst with Sydney, by prison labour.

He opened up the resources of the colony by the construction of roads and bridges, but the crowning achievement of his administration was, the finding of a passage across the Blue Mountains, and the making of a road to Bathurst Plains. It is by such men, endowed with the faculty of organisation, as Governor Macquarie, men of capacious minds, and far seeing, that empires are founded. Judge Therry, in his "Reminiscences of New South

Wales and Victoria," remarks :—"His merits are summed up in a sentence—He found a garrison and a gaol, and left the broad and deep foundations of an empire." (The retiring Governor, in recognition of his worth for the good he had done, was presented with a golden cup, valued at 500 guineas. This was done at the instigation of Messrs. D'Arcy Wentworth and John Piper.—*Flanagan's History.* Vol. 1, page 230.)

He was not so happy in his views about religion ; he was warmly attached to the church of England, because she was the church of the state, and he considered that she ought to be the only church in the colony, to the exclusion of all dissenters : he would give no encouragement to the catholic religion: he left during the most of his time, the catholics without a religious instructor, and compelled Father O'Flynn, at the instigation of the bigots who surrounded him, to leave the colony, because he had no credentials from the Home Government. He found out his mistake in the end, when Fathers Connelly and Therry arrived in the colony, appointed by, and with salaries from the Home Government. He very graciously consented and laid the foundation stone of St. Mary's cathedral. He did more, knowing that the catholics were not the most wealthy in the colony, and the funds nearly exhausted, he promised on the eve of his departure from the colony, to use his influence with Earl Bathurst, to obtain further help for the completion of St. Mary's—I find the words of the note, in Dr. Ullathorne's reply to Judge Burton.

Ship Surrey, Port Jackson,
15th February, 1822.

Dear Sir,—I shall not fail to move Earl Bathurst, on my arrival in England, to instruct Sir Thomas Brisbane to extend further assistance towards completing the Roman catholic chapel at Sydney.

I remain, in haste, dear Sir,
Yours very truly,
L. MACQUARIE.

To the Rev. J. J. Therry, &c., &c.

Nor was he unmindful of his promise, it would appear ; for when a memorial was presented to His Excellency, Sir Thomas Brisbane, supported by one of the ju ges and twenty-six magistrates of the territory, praying for pecuniary assistance towards the completion of St. Mary's, the following reply was received from his Excellency, through his secretary.

" After the anxiety so generally felt, the propriety of opening a fresh subscription for the consummation of that religious, political, and elegant undertaking, naturally suggests itself ; and in any list that may be opened, I am directed by the Governor, to enter the name of the Government for a sum equal to the sum total of all such additional donations.

I have the honor to be, rev. sir,

Your most obedient servant,

F. GOULBURN,

Colonial Secretary.

It would have redounded to the everlasting honor of Macquarie had he before his departure, expunged from the regulations of the orphan schools, which were made by him and his confidential advisers, that one which required that all the inmates, whether of catholic parents or dissenters, should be instructed in the doctrines of the church of England ; but the honor of erasing it was left to others.

Most strenuous efforts were made by the catholics to supply the requisite funds for the building of St. Mary's church ; collections were made in every place, and even collectors were sent to the Dutch settlements in the Islands to the North of Australasia, but the results were inadequate, and no aid was received from the Government. The leading protestant gentlemen of the colony had contributed handsomely to the erection of the building ; I have given a list of their names in Appendix A. at the end of the volume. We find there the honored names of Wentworth, Campbell, Goulburn, the Governor's Secretary, Wm. Bland, McHenery, Capt. King, Royal Navy, Sir John Jamieson, Lord, and many others. It may be said of them in regard to the catholic community that they were friends in need and therefore friends indeed. Be their names ever remembered—From papers left by Father Therry, I find that from the commencement of the building, that is from 29th October, 1821, to 14th August, 1824, the subscriptions amounted to £2,602 4s 2d. and work worth that and more had been done. No assistance had as yet been given by the Government. It is true that to undertake such a large building at that time, when the catholics did not number more than 10,000, one-third of the population, and these comparatively poor, required no ordinary foresight and fortitude. It was a question, when the structure was nearly at a stand still, whether it would not have been better to have built a church not so large, that the Government might help more willingly, and the catholics assemble in it, for divine worship, within a time not far distant. However, the work was proceeded with by separate contracts, and Father Therry lived to see St. Mary's cathedral nearly completed and filled with faithful and devout worshippers.

When Father Connelly went to Tasmania—in 1820, shortly after his arrival in the colony—Father Therry had no assistance until the year 1826, when Father Power arrived. During those five years he had to discharge all the duties of a priest, which was no light obligation, as the catholics were scattered in the surrounding country. He had to celebrate the divine mysteries at Parramatta, Wollongong, Hawkesbury, Penrith, Liverpool and other places, and to be ready to attend to sick calls at any time. And all the salary he had as colonial chaplain was £100—not sufficient to keep a horse in those days, when feed was so dear. In a very arbitrary manner (as I will show a few pages further on) he was deprived by the Government of his salary. Father Therry was actuated by the true missionary spirit, and many instances are on record of the promptitude with which he attended to the salvation of souls. A catholic who lived in those times, now far advanced in years, informs me that he remembers one occasion when Father Therry had returned to Sydney from Wollongong, where he was attending a sick person. Without any time to rest he was sent for to see another person said to be dying. It was a Sunday, and a very wet day. He immediately prepared and proceeded to Wollongong, distant seventy miles, on horseback, and then by an exceedingly bad road. I have heard that every day his gig was ready at the door to start for wheresoever he was required.

I have before related that Commissioner Bigge was sent out by the Home Government to investigate the affairs of the colony. He had for secretary Mr. Thomas Hobbes Scott, who had been in early life a wine merchant. The commissioner with his secretary had not long returned, when Mr. Scott was appointed archdeacon of the colonial protestant church. He arrived in May, 1825, and soon after made his charge to the clergy of the church of England, when he said "he communicated the gracious intention of His Majesty to divide the colony into compact parishes and to prosecute the work of education on a more liberal and comprehensive system than that which had hitherto been pursued." Accordingly in the following year a royal charter was issued, with instructions under the royal sign manual to Governor Darling, dated 17th July, 1825. The preamble of the charter shows the end for which it was designed —" Whereas we have taken into our royal consideration the necessity of making provision for the maintenance of religion and the education of youth in our colony of New South Wales, and for that purpose have thought proper to erect into one body politic and corporate such persons as are hereinafter mentioned, and to vest in them and their successors such lands and tenements as will be sufficient to make a provision for that purpose, as aforesaid." And in the instructions under the sign manual to the Governor are the following: "Whereas it is necessary that sufficient provision should be made for the establishment and support within our said territory of the pr t s an reformed religion, as by law established in England amdt Ireland, and for the education of youth in the discipline and according to the principles of the united church of England and Ireland. And we have for that purpose thought fit that such part as hereinafter mentioned of the waste and unoccupied lands within our said territory and its dependencies, should be appropriated and set apart, and should be placed under the control and superintendence of one body politic and corporate, to be established within the said territory by letters patent, to be for that purpose issued under the public seal of New South Wales, &c., &c."

When Father Therry saw what was the intention of the Home Government, viz., to give *no* assistance for the education of children of catholic parents, in the catholic faith and to provide only for the education of children in the protestant belief, he resolved to form a Catholic Education Society to prevent the children of catholic parents from being taught the doctrines of the church of England. There appeared in the *Sydney Gazette* of 16th June, 1825, a letter written by Father Therry, in which he makes known the measure intended, and how prejudicial it would be to catholic education, and in the same letter he exposes the grievance which compelled the catholics to bury their dead in the protestant burial ground; and it is in this letter that appeared the expression "qualified respect" in regard to the protestant clergy. Here are the words of the letter—

Sydney Gazette.—Thursday, June 16, 1825.

The Roman catholic chaplain has publicly to express his grateful acknowledgements to Mr. James Burke, of Airds, a native of this colony, for his offer of five acres of cleared and valuable land, contiguous to Campbelltown, as a burial ground, and site for chapel and school-house; and for his still more liberal promise of giving double that number of acres, if so many should be required, for these purposes.

"It may be necessary here to state that the Roman catholics, who form the greater number of, at least, the free inhabitants of that and some of the adjoining districts, having no place to assemble in on the Lord's day, for the purpose of divine worship, but the open air (in which the prisoners of that persuasion are obliged to continue for hours together on every Sunday, exposed to all the vicissitudes of the weather, in order to be exempted from a necessity of attending at ceremonies of which they cannot conscientiously approve), and having already liberally subscribed to the erection of the Sydney chapel, the funds of which are indeed nearly if not completely exhausted, decline to contribute any further to that edifice until they shall have first erected a temporary chapel in their immediate neighbourhood."

"And as from a document which has been recently published, it may be inferred that public provision is to be made for protestant parochial schools exclusively, and that the children of the catholic poor are to be either excluded from the salutary benefit of education, or compelled, or enticed to abandon the truly venerable religion of their ancestors, according to the past and present system of the orphan school institutions of the colony; and as the lesser of these evils must be deprecated as a most serious one, the Roman catholic chaplain, with the fond hope of obviating both, is determined, Deo adjuvante, immediately to form a Roman Catholic Education Society, into which, however, persons of any denomination may be admitted on subscribing to its fund fifteen shillings a-year, or one shilling and three pence per month. But he has seriously to regret that this design has not been anticipated, or that its execution has not been reserved for less humble and more efficient instrumentality than his."

"The intention of the Roman catholic chaplain to procure burial places separate from those of the establishment, will not be ascribed, by any person who happens to know him, to a spirit of illiberality: so far from it that the idea was first suggested to him by a personage of high and distinguished liberality and benevolence, of another persuasion, who had known by experience that it was in strict accordance with the discipline of the Roman catholic church, and calculated to prevent the clashing or inconvenient interference of the respective duties of clergymen of different societies, and the recurrence of an instance which had more than once taken place, in which burial or surplice dues were required from surviving friends of deceased catholics by a minister who had not officiated at the interment, and on payment of them being refused, were enforced by him in his capacity of magistrate."

" This precedent, however, he feels it his duty also to state, has neither been, nor is likely to be adopted by the other reverend gentlemen of the establishment, who, with the exception of the reverend gentleman alluded to (who, I sincerely believe, on these occasions, merely vindicated what he considered to be his just rights), are in every way entitled to, and possess his qualified respect."

Sydney, 14th June, 1825.

Written communications intended for the Roman catholic chaplain may be left at the residence of Mr. William Davis, Charlotte-place; Mr. Thomas Byrne, master of the chapel school. Hyde Park; or at his lodgings, Campbell-street, Brickfields.

It is evident from the context that Father Therry meant the expression *unqualified* respect " the protestant clergy are in every way entitled to his *unqualified* respect." When brought to an account for the expression he declared it was the word unqualified he wrote, and the printer admitted that it was his mistake. It was only a pretext to find fault with Father Therry; the head and front of his offending was because he had in this article exposed the exclusiveness of the intended measure to provide only for protestant parochial schools, and because he reminded the Government of its promise to assist in the erection of St. Mary's, and informed them that the catholics were entitled to burial grounds separate from the establishment. However it was through this letter that Father Therry was deprived of his salary, and prevented by order from officiating in any of the public institutions; nay more, he was offered £300 to leave the colony: but Father Therry was made of sterner stuff, he worked on and would not desert the flock entrusted to his care by the Supreme Pastor. Had he left the little flock forlorn, he would have been like the hireling described by our Lord, who abandons the sheep when he sees the wolf coming. More anon about Father Therry.

Sir Thomas Brisbane was recalled through misrepresentations made against his administration to the Home Government, before the expiration of the time alloted for the stay of a Governor. Sir Thomas was a man of well cultured mind, and possessed of scientific attainments. He was distinguished as an astronomer. It was he who established the first observatory in the colony and appointed a well-qualified astronomer to superintend it. In his reply to the address which was presented to him by the

VERY REV. JOHN JOSEPH THERRY.

colonists, when about to leave, he said: "he had been bred in the profession of a soldier and spent the last years of his life in the campaigns of his country." He had very much distinguished himself during the Peninsular War. In the address (*vide* Wentworth's and Lang's History) he was complimented by being told, that "during the four years he held the reins of Government, the colonists enjoyed three of the greatest political blessings, to wit, a *mild*, an *impartial*, and *firm administration*," It is not recorded that Governor Brisbane during his time performed any great work; but he is thanked for having established trial by jury, and given freedom to the Press. Many distressful events occurred, in the time of his administration, and several beneficial happened. Through some mis-management, by selling too cheap, the wheat became scarce; the wheat fell from 10s and 7s 6d to 3s 9d and then rose to £1 4s per bushel. There was a disastrous flood in the Hawkesbury River, and the finest crops were destroyed. Many of the small settlers had to dispose of their farms which fell into the hands of the public-house keepers and money lenders. The colony was gradually extending its limits, a Captain Currie of the Royal Navy explored the plains of Maneroo, which are from two to three thousand feet above the level of the sea, divided from Twofold Bay by a lofty range of mountains.

In the year 1824 Messrs. Hovel and Hume, after great hardships, crossed the country to Port Philip. In the north Mr. Oxley, Surveyor-General, was ordered by Sir Thomas Brisbane to make an exploration, and he discovered the l River Brisbane, which is navigable and leads to rich agricultural and and pastoral districts. And in 1825 Mr. Allen Cunningham discovered the Pandora Pass, by which you enter from the Upper Hunter to the Liverpool Plains, and to extensive and rich districts beyond.

Sir Thomas Brisbane is praised for having ameliorated the condition of the prison population and improved the financial affairs of the colony. He seems to have left Australia with the goodwill and esteem of all the colonists, and he was no ordinary person to have won this honor in the midst of parties who were so discordant.

There was not much immigration before the time of Governor Macquarie. Towards the end of his vice-royalty immigrants were encouraged to come to the colony by grants of land being given, and a good many possessed of small capital took advantage of the premium held out by the Government. The prospects of success in commercial pursuits were full of hope, and the soil was reported in many parts to be of the best description, and

E

well adapted for agricultural purposes. When immigration fairly set in, the giving of grants was discontinued. During the administration of Governor Brisbane many retired officers of the naval, military and civil service, induced by the salubrity of the climate and other decided advantages, settled down in the colony. Their morals generally gave edification, and their upright conduct inspired confidence. Then also were added to the population men of superior education and intelligence, most of whom speculated in taking up sheep and cattle stations, and in the end became immensely rich, through the profits on their wool and cattle.

Governor Darling succeeded Sir Thomas Brisbane, and arrived in the colony 19th December, 1825. On his way out to the colony he called at Hobart Town, capital of Van Dieman's Land, and by virtue of the power entrusted to him by the Home Government he declared the island colony independent of New South Wales and a separate Government, except that the Lieutenant-Governor of Tasmania was subject to the Governor-in-Chief of New South Wales. When he arrived in Sydney he appointed the first Legislative Council, composed of the following members, viz.: Lieutenant-Governor Stewart, who had administered the affairs of the colony before his arrival; Chief Justice Forbes, Archdeacon Scott, Macleay, Colonial Secretary; John Macarthur, Robert Campbell, sen., and Charles Throsby. At the same time the Executive Council was formed, consisting of the Lieutenant-Governor, the Chief Justice, the Archdeacon and the Colonial Secretary. Whilst Darling was Governor that inestimable privilege of the British Constitution was conferred by the Home Government, viz.—trial by jury in a full and complete form. The colony had enjoyed trial by jury since 2nd November, 1824; but not complete, because it was only in criminal cases that a ju was impanelled. The civil cases were decided by a judge a ry two magistrates, as assessors; unless both parties agreed to have a jury, and then the Court was empowered to supply jurors.

It was during the governorship of Darling that Father Therry was deprived of his salary, and offered £300 to quit the colony. A very old and respectable man, still alive in the colony, told the writer that Father Therry, being very disconsolate at thinking he might be compelled to leave his flock, as Father Flynn had been to leave the colony, called upon Mr. C. Wentworth, the leading barrister then in the colony, and a most determined foe to any thing like oppression, who, having heard his case, told him not to fear, that "he defied the Governor to send him out of the colony." The condition of the catholics in the colony at this time was very disheartening. Subscriptions were coming in very slowly for the completion of St. Mary's church; and the Government was not redeeming its promise, to be at half the expense; to add to their troubles, the chaplaincy was taken from Father Therry, and he had to be supported by the people. The catholics were becoming numerous, but the majority of them were poor: they had subscribed liberally towards the erection of St. Mary's, but it was a great undertaking, and a heavy tax upon their resources. I have given in the Appendix a list of those who subscribed their Christmas dues at St. Mary's in 1824, amounting only to £28. No doubt he received more than this: at the different stations he would receive support according to the means of the congregation. This would be considered now a small Christmas dues at the stations. And what must have been the greatest affliction to the Rev. Father was to be prohibited from visiting the sick in the hospitals and infirmaries—when, he could not administer to them the consolations of our holy religion. To show the fortitude and address of this apostolic man, whilst under ban, he went to visit a dying man at one of the hospitals; he was stopped by the guard when about to enter: Father Therry said to him, "the salvation of this man depends on my ministration; which is your first duty? The guard, recognizing the right of the man of God, lowered his arms and permitted him to pass. Another time he was going into the Infirmary to attend a sick person, when the door-keeper told him to stop until he ascertained from the attendant surgeon whether he could be admitted. Whilst he was away, Father Therry, who knew all the passages of the place, entered, gave the sick person consolation, and when returning he met the official, who told him he could *not* be admitted. Many of the petty officials were very insolent to Father Therry and his flock, taking advantage of the circumstances. It was permitted the catholics to have divine service in the old Court-house, a large building, now a Public School in Castlereagh-street; but because their pastor was not recognised by the Government the door was locked against them! but in defiance of such insolence the door was forced open. It is said Mr. Wentworth was consulted as to what steps the catholics ought to take to secure the court-house for divine service, as they had as good a right as others to use it for that purpose. "What will you do?" said Wentworth, "why take a crowbar and break the door open; and if they take you to court, send for me, and I'll defend y u." In the m dst of all this trouble Father Therry was ever cheerful, and his sorrows only tended to make him more zealous and laborious for the cause of God and good of his fellow men; which reminds one of the words of St. Paul, when he says "There is a sorrow of the world, and a sorrow that is according to God." Father Therry was widely respected by all classes, and highly esteemed. When travelling in the discharge of his sacred duties every door was open to him and every assistance given to further the sacred ends he had in view. In disputes the decision of Father Therry was accepted, and oftentimes the matter was referred to him for arbitration. He had a kind word and shake of the hand for every one.

The administration of Governor Darling extended over six years; he retired on 21st October, 1831. His Vice-royalty was certainly not popular. He came seemingly to govern with a high hand, it being then a penal colony. His acts would lead one to suppose that severe measures were necessary to keep the colonists in subjection. He was a soldier, accustomed to the routine and exactness of military life, which brooks no delay or reply, and he expected every one should bend to his will. He introduced again the lash and short rations in regard to the unfortunate prisoners, which had been partly done away with in the time of Governor Macquarie. He, writers say, meddled and interfered too much in the details of the Government departments instead of casting the responsibility on the heads of offices. He is said to have ignored the control of the Executive and Legislative Councils, which could have shielded him from much of the opprobrium which he suffered from the public. Governor Darling estimated himself rather highly: confiding too much in his own ability, he fancied he could manage efficiently all things civil, judicial, and financial. He wanted more experience in governing a community, and better knowledge of men and things. He quarrelled with the Press because it criticised severely and condemned some of his public measures: and he enlisted the antagonism of several of the leading and most popular men of the day, such as Mr. C. Wentworth, Mr. Wardell of the *Monitor* newspaper, and Mr. Hall of the *Australian*. Two of the editors were prosecuted for libel against the Government, and lodged in jail. They were sued for penalties and forfeitures incurred by infringement of the Act for regulating the Press. Governor Darling was severely condemned by the public for cruelty towards two soldiers who had committed a petty larceny, to get out of the army. Their names were Sudds and Thompson. No doubt it was a very critical time for the King's representative to administer the affairs of the colony. The colonists were very much agitated in demanding the rights and privileges to which they considered they were entitled by the

53

British Constitution. They wanted complete trial by jury, and a Legislative Assembly, to have the power of taxing themselves. The Home Government was not disposed, as yet, to grant all they demanded, and the Governor stood between, to carry out the behests of Downing-street. But he would have succeeded better had he been more conciliatory. Yet Darling was most exact and attentive to business, and he cannot be accused of want of zeal for the common good and advancement of the colony. He encouraged explorations of the interior which were made by Major, afterwards Sir Thomas Mitchell, Captain Sturt and others. Captain Sturt and party were the most fortunate, they went in a boat on the Murrumbidgee until they came to its junction with the Murray; which noble river brought them to South Australia, near Lake Alexandria. Thus Captain Sturt was the discoverer of that beautiful country of South Australia and of the Murray River, which now is the boundary between New South Wales and Port Philip. These rivers are sometimes navigable, for vessels of small tonnage, a distance of 600 and even 1000 miles. By them the produce of the settlers on their banks is conveyed to market and they receive their supplies by those rivers. In the time of Governor Darling Sydney was supplied with water, from the Botany swamps and lagoons, by means of an aqueduct, constructed by Mr. James Busby, Mineral Surveyor and Engineer to the Government.

The catholics during the time of Governor Darling were becoming numerous and almost equal in number to the members of the more favoured community of the protestant church. It is a fact that all the prisoners from Ireland were sent to New South Wales, for the last 40 years; and the majority of these being Roman Catholics, accounts for the catholics being so numerous in New South Wales: It is said they were not sent to Tasmania, alias Van Dieman's Land, because it was intended to make that a protestant colony: The most of those who were sent from Ireland were transported for political and agrarian offences. The political prisoners were exiled for loving their country too well and desiring to see her free and independent, and their religion delivered from the oppression of the penal laws. Many of them were excellent men, and left their native land without a taint on their moral character, and their children's children at this day do honour to their sires.

Many of the catholic emancipists were scattered over the colony following agricultural pursuits; and by their skill and industry in farming, had become wealthy. Very few were employed by the Government; their religion, country, and name rebel operated powerfully against them in the social scale. The catholics were very much depressed in the time of Governor Darling's administration : there was no one amongst them of social standing and influence to advocate their wants and represent their grievances. The voice of Father Therry would not be heard : he had quarrelled with the Government and was deprived of his salary, and there were only six families of catholic gentry in the colony. The sad condition of the catholics then, and their subsequent deliverance and liberation would remind one of the words of our Saviour to his disciples before his passion and resurrection, where he said, "Amen, amen I say to you, that you shall lament and weep, but the world shall rejoice ; and you shall be sorrowful, but your sorrow shall be turned into joy." The time of sorrow for the catholics of New South Wales was about to be changed for a time of joy : real joy was about to succeed to the sorrow of those days.

Towards the end of the year 1829 there arrived in the colony Mr. Therry, with the appointment, from the Home Government, of Commissioner of the Court of Requests. He was a catholic gentleman, who had taken part in the struggles for catholic emancipation, and had been secretary of the "National Society for the Education of the Poor in Ireland," which was formed in Dublin in the year 1822. Mr. Roger Therry was a firm and true catholic : he deplored the humiliating condition of his co-religionists in New South Wales, and he determined to do all which lay in his power to raise them in the social scale. During his stay in England he had made the acquaintance of Mr. Blount, the member of parliament for Steyning. Mr. Blount had been, previous to the passing of the Emancipation Act, secretary to the Catholic Association in England, and he enjoyed the confidence of the liberal administration of the day. To this amiable and energetic man he represented, by writing, the great grievances under which the catholics suffered, and entreated him to use his influence for them and obtain redress. Mr. Therry has quoted in his book of Reminiscences of New South Wales and Victoria, a letter which he received from Mr. Blount in reply, which shows how strongly he sympathised with the catholic population in the wrongs which they were enduring, and how anxious he was to assist in obtaining justice for them. The letter was dated, London, Dec. 1833.

These are the words of Mr. Blount :—" Nothing can be more palpably absurd, or more abhorrent to every feeling of christian charity than to transport many thousand abandoned wretches to a distant land, that they may be reformed and become good members of society, and debar them from the means of learning the morality or practicing the precepts of religion. Such conduct would have been too bad in any times; but it is intolerable that an administration boasting peculiar liberality, and teaching the people their physical strength, and confiding in the schoolmasters to enforce obedience to the laws, should condemn so many poor creatures to the sad necessity of remaining in ignorance of their social duties. Such however is the state of the catholic convicts in Australia. It is well worthy of your philanthropic exertions to remove an error in legislation from our liberal government, such a danger from the colony, and such a curse from those wretched beings: and you ought to be zealously seconded by every friend of humanity at home and abroad, be his creed in religion or politics what it may. But how is this desirable object to be obtained? By giving to catholics, who, though they may have deviated from the precepts of their religion, yet are convinced of the truth of its doctrines, adequate protection, places of religious worship, and spiritual instructors. Whence must funds be provided for such objects? Not from charity, but the policy of the Government; from their intimate conviction that not only justice and humanity, but the well-being of the colony essentially depend on the maintenance of public morality."

Mr. Blount was faithful to his promise, and lost no time to impress upon the leaders of the Government the policy of sending religious instructors to the poor outcasts in New South Wales. The question which he kept constantly before them was —" Are the catholics of our foreign dependencies to be good or bad subjects?—loyal, orderly, and educated, or factious, ignorant, and degraded?" He exerted himself very much in obtaining a catholic bishop and clergy to be sent to the colony.

CHAPTER VI.

*The Arrival of Governor Bourke, 3rd December, 1831.—Great
Meeting of the Catholics on March 30th, 1832.—The Speech
of Roger Therry, representing the grievances of the Catholics
—Memorial carried at the meeting in favour of Father
Therry.—The arrival of Rev. John McEncroe with the ap-
pointment of Roman Catholic Chaplain, and John Hubert
Plunkett, as Solicitor-General, in May, 1832.—The Very Rev.
Dr. Ullathorne arrives as Vicar-General, 1832.—The Origin
and Provisions of Sir Richard Bourke's Church Act.*

GOVERNOR Bourke succeeded Darling, and landed on 3rd Dec.,
1831. He was received by the colonists with great welcome and
rejoicings. His fame had gone before him as a man of enlightened and liberal views; a soldier who had greatly distinguished
himself in the wars of South America, and gained there an
experience well suited to enable him to govern the colony. With
his comprehensive mind it was not long before he became master
of all the details of the government, and the state of affairs both
ecclesiastical and civil. He determined to do justice to all, as far
as lay in his power. One of the first steps which he took was to
allay religious discontent, by proceeding to procure assistance to
the different christian denominations in proportion to their
numbers.

The arrival of Sir R. Bourke filled the Roman catholics with
great hope : they expected he would prove himself to be what
report made him, an able, just, and liberal Governor, and as the
sequel showed, they were not disappointed.

Not long after the arrival of the Governor the catholics determined to hold a meeting, and agree upon a memorial, representing
their wants and grievances, and present it to the Governor. One
particular object of the meeting was, to induce the Government
to redeem its promise of assistance towards the building of St.
Mary's church. At that time the work done, when valued by a
competent architect, amounted to £5,900, and when all deductions
were made, there remained due to the church by the Government,
£3,000—a just and legitimate claim.

This meeting was held in Sydney 30th March, 1832, at the
time a Roman catholic gentleman, by name Lieutenant Paett, an
officer of the Indian army, on leave of absence, was here, and he
presided at the meeting. The mover of the memorial was Mr.
Therry, then commissioner of the Court of Requests. He spoke

to the following effect:—" Though," he said, " they were bound to be thankful for the £500 that had been recently appropriated for the completion of the chapel, yet their thanks should partake somewhat of that gratitude which was described as 'a sense of favours to come.' Their thankfulness for what they have received should not be construed into an admission that what had been done was all that ought to be done. The Chief Justice, he was bound to state, had been their warm advocate on the occasion of this recent grant, but as the proceedings of the Council were not published, of course he could not ascertain who were their supporters, and who were not, but he believed the general disposition of the council, on the occasion, was kind and friendly towards the Roman catholics. Upon the part of the memorial which referred to education, he would only remark, that whilst the protestant church was unquestionably entitled to those facilities to which its importance and numbers gave it a claim, yet the Roman catholic community and the dissenting congregations had a claim to corresponding facilities according to their importance and numbers. Now it was admitted that the Roman catholics constituted more than one-third of the population of the colony; yet they were excluded from the school for teaching trades at Carter's Barracks, from the School of Industry, and from the Orphan Schools; nor was there any endowment which made a provision for the education of Roman catholic youth. It was but justice to say, however, that a recent resolution of the Legislative Council had recommended a provision to supply this desideratum. The Roman Catholics owed it to themselves and to their advocates at home, to invite the attention of the Council here, and of the parliament, to the pressing and urgent necessity of their condition. There were some persons who refused to sanction any appropriation of the public money for the uses of the Roman catholics, lest thereby, forsooth, they might assist in propagating a false religion. No man had a right to use this doctrine, however privileged or orthodox he might fancy himself to be. A man's religion was between God and his conscience, and he was bound to abide by that faith of the truth of which he was conscientiously convinced. The public money was supplied by the catholic as well as by the protestant tax, and should be applied to the uses of each according to the exigencies of each. While on this topic he could not forbear from presenting to their consideration one view of the Roman catholics of the colony which had always impressed itself forcibly upon his mind. To him the condition of the catholics of the colony appeared to be, in one respect, particularly hard. He adverted to

the circumstances of that portion of their body who resided out
of the district of Sydney: and how vast that portion was might
be easily estimated from the fact, that all the transports from
Ireland, freighted with prisoners, had been invariably sent to
New South Wales: none from Ireland, certainly within the last
eight or ten years, had been sent to the sister colony. The reason
of this arrangement it was immaterial to consider; but it was
material to consider that the fact was so; for it was the fact that
accounted for and explained why it was the Roman catholics
constituted so large a proportion of the population of the colony.
Now it was not an exaggerated estimate to say that *three-fourths*
of those sent to New South Wales from Ireland were Roman
catholics. In the ship in which he came out there were 200
prisoners. and of these 175 were Roman catholics. This average,
from accurate information which he had obtained, was applicable
to all the ships from Ireland. Let him now trace the progress of
these men, these 200 Irish prisoners, after their arrival in the
colony, sent thither, it should be borne in mind, for the purpose
of being reformed. Perhaps twenty or thirty of them were
assigned as servants in different employments in the district of
Sydney, whilst the remainder were drafted off to Bathurst, Illawarra, or Maitland, each place one hundred and fifty miles distant
from Sydney, and where, during the whole term of their sentence,
—and if their sentence were for life, during the whole term of
their existence—no opportunity for religious instruction was
afforded them; and should death overtake them in their calami-
tous position, their pillow was not soothed by the consolation of
the minister of religion; nor over their untimely grave could their
pastor pour his pious requiem. To the Irish Roman catholic
exile this deprivation added a deep and bitter—and the more
bitter, because an unavowed, and, he believed, an unattended—
aggravation of the punishment of evil to which his sad destiny
had doomed him. In regard to Father Therry, he had now been
for twelve years a Roman catholic clergyman in this colony:
during the greater part of that time he had been the Roman
catholic chaplain: during the whole of that time, in point of zeal,
activity, of useful and efficient discharge of the functions of the
ministry, he had been indefatigable as an officiating priest.
Neither time, nor distance, nor danger—and his duties were often
performed at the real peril of life—ever impeded or obstructed
him in the zealous performance of the sacred duties of his mission.
The duties of the office which he held brought him into frequent
contact with all classes of persons in every district of the colony,
and he never made an assertion of the truth of which he was

more convinced, than that the Rev. Mr. Therry possessed the unbounded esteem, confidence and affection of all classes of Roman catholics; and with corresponding confidence he would assert, that he knew of no act which the Government could perform towards that body that would be hailed by them with more delight and gratitude, than the re-appointment of that rev. gentleman to the Roman catholic chaplaincy of the colony. But it would be remembered, he added, that similar testimony had been borne on his behalf in a memorial presented to the Council, to which the signatures of forty magistrates, the principal civil and military officers in the colony, and several hundred other persons were affixed."

Mr. Therry then read the memorial, and proposed the adoption of it to the meeting. The memorial represented that the Government had been most liberal in providing for the education of the youth of the established church, and of the other denominations; but that for want of means the majority of the catholic poor were uneducated and without religious instruction. His Excellency was also requested to restore the Rev. John Joseph Therry to his position of Roman catholic chaplain.

The motion for the adoption of the memorial was seconded by John O'Sullivan, and unanimously adopted by the meeting.

This memorial was not presented to Governor Bourke until more than four months after, and in the mean time arrived in the colony the Rev. John McEncroe, with the appointment of Roman catholic chaplain, and John Hubert Plunket, Solicitor-General: they came in the same vessel. The memorial of the catholics was presented to the Governor on the 17th August, 1832. The deputation consisted of five gentlemen, two of whom were protestants; viz., Major Mitchell, Surveyor-General; J. H. Plunket, Solicitor-General; S. Moore, senior magistrate of the colony; the Rev. J. McEncroe, and R. Therry. The names of two thousand persons, free inhabitants of the colony, were appended to the memorial. His Excellency gave them a very gracious reception, and having listened attentively to the reading of the memorial, said: that he was most anxious to secure for his majesty's Roman catholic subjects in the colony a suitable provision for their education and religious instruction; and he had made known immediately the resolution of the Legislative Council on the subject. It was not within the scope of his commission to add to the Roman catholic chaplains of the colony; but he would lay before the Secretary of State, without delay, the application of the memorialists in favour of the Rev. John Joseph Therry. He said he had endeavoured to place upon a better footing the catholic schools

Emancipation Bill, which removed from the case

disabilities. There was now a liberal government, :
tories were disbanded : a new era was dawning over
Isles, and the long and dark night of persecution and
was disappearing. The British Government had now :
of fondling and pampering a dominant church in
dependencies. There was a good deal of work to be d
away the accumulated injustice of years. The Rom
especially, and dissenters from the church of Eng
colony, were most unfairly dealt with in the distribu
public funds, *to which all contribute*. The monies to
by the government, in the year 1833, were estimated
sum of £110,252, and more than £19,071 (one-sixth (
was devoted to the expenditure of the church of Engl
only £800 was allotted to the Roman catholics, wh
more than one-third of the population, for the suppo
and maintenance of schools ; and £600 appropriated :
of Scotland. Here was the greatest disproportion :
equalization in the distribution of the public revenue
Bourke took the first steps to promote religious equa
South Wales.

Contrast the means and appliances of the cathol:
the colony in the year 1833 with the state of the ch
land, and the greatest difference is evident. The :
establishment then consisted of an archdeacon and I
and they were possessed of eight churches and six cha:
mention that the church of St. James, at the head of
in Sydney, and which was first intended for a cour
nearly roofed in so far back as the year 1820, and

that time a fine stone church in Parramatta, capable of containing 400, and commodious churches in Windsor and Liverpool; and the poor catholics had "not where to lay their heads," except to attend the divine mysteries in the court-house of Sydney; and outside of Sydney, in the towns of Parramatta, Windsor, and Liverpool, in the houses of the catholics: there is no question, therefore, of the extreme partiality of the government of the day to the church of England.

Before I give an account of the Church Act, I may state, it was in the year 1832 that the Very Rev. Dr. Ullathorne arrived in the colony. The origin of his appointment as Vicar-General was related to me by the late venerable Arch-bishop Polding. On account of the disagreement of Father Therry with the colonial authorities, the Home government applied to Dr. Bramston, then the Roman catholic bishop of London, for the appointment of a Roman catholic Ecclesiastical Superior for New South Wales. Dr. Bramston applied to the Benedictine congregation of Downside, and the appointment fell upon Dr. Ullathorne, who came to the colony as Vicar-General of Bishop Slater of the Mauritius. Bishop Slater held jurisdiction from the Holy See over all the islands to the east of Mauritius; consequently over New Holland, Tasmania, New Zealand, &c. An amusing occurrence was told to me when I was in England, by the late estimable Dr. Heptonstal, illustrative of the disinterestedness and devotedness of Father Ullathorne, when he was leaving for Australia. Dr. Heptonstal met him in London just on the eve of his departure, and in bidding him adieu, the young ecclesiastic, about to embark on such a long voyage, and for what was then a comparatively unknown land, manifested not the slightest regret at breaking the dearest ties, no more than if he were going to see the brothers of his order at Downside or Ampleforth. Before Father Ullathorne came to the colony he had been assisting Father Sinnot in the management of Ampleforth College, a Benedictine establishment, for two years, because of a reconstruction which had been brought about by Dr. Bains, the bishop. Father Ullathorne, on his way out, touched at Hobart Town, in Van Dieman's Land. The state of that very small portion of the church very much displeased him. Father Connelly had been there alone twelve years and not much was done; not even a suitable church was built. It should be considered that the government there were just as remiss and disinclined to help the catholics as they were at Sydney. The catholics were few and very poor; the protestants had there a commodious and substantial stone building, capable of containing 1,000. It was opened for divine worship in the year 1819.

The famous despatch of Sir Richard Bourke to the Right Hon. E. G. Stanley, Secretary of State for the Colonies, was dated 30th September, 1833; in which his Excellency, in clear and unmistakable language, represents the religious wants and wishes of all sections of the community, and proposes measures calculated in his estimates to give general satisfaction.

He began by stating that he had received the order of the King in Council (W. IX.), dissolving the church and school corporation in New South Wales; but without any information of the views of his majesty's government as to the future maintenance and regulation of churches and schools within the colony. He observed that the inhabitants of the colony were of many different religious persuasions; that the members of the church of England were the most numerous; but there were large bodies of Roman catholics; and presbyterians of the church of Scotland, besides protestant dissenters of many different denominations,..........and that probably one-fifth of the whole population of the colony was catholic. He said that the clergy of the church of England were supported chiefly by payments from the Treasury, and to a small amount, by the rent and sale of lands, formerly granted to the church and school corporation. That the charge for the church of England in the following year would amount to £11,542 10s. The whole charge on the public treasury for the church of Scotland was £600, and for the Roman catholic chaplains and chapels £1,500...................."In regard to the catholics," he said, "they possess one large and handsome church, in Sydney, not yet completed. In aid of its construction, donations, amounting in all to about £1,200 have been at different times granted by this government. The sum of £400 (included in the £1,500 before mentioned), has been appropriated by the Council to be paid in the next year, in aid of a similar sum to be raised by private subscriptions, for erecting Roman catholic chapels at Maitland and Campbell Town." A chapel was begun at the latter place, as well as at Parramatta, some years ago; but neither have been completed for want of funds. "The chaplains" says Sir Richard Burke, " of the church of England are provided with glebes of 40 acres each, or with a money allowance in lieu, and with houses or lodging money. No advantage of this kind is possessed by the clergy of the church of Scotland, or by the Roman catholics......; Such an unequal distribution of support cannot be supposed to be acceptable to the colonists, who provide the funds from which this distribution is made. Accordingly, the magnitude of the sums annually granted for the support of the church of England in New South Wales, is very generally complained of, and a petition to the Governor and Legislative Council has been lately prepared at a public meeting, and very numerously signed, praying for a reduction of the expenditure."...............The Governor goes on to remark, that in a new country, to which persons of all religious persuasions are invited to resort, it will be impossible to establish a dominant and endowed church without much hostility, and great improbability of its becoming permanent. The inclination of these colonists, which keeps pace with the spirit of the age, is decidedly adverse to such an institution ; and I fear the interests of religion would be prejudiced by its establishment. If, on the contrary, support were given as required, to every one of the three great divisions of christians indifferently, and the management of the temporalities left to themselves, I conceive that the public treasury might in time be relieved of a considerable charge ; and what is of much greater importance, the people would become more attached to their respective churches, and be more willing to listen to, and obey the voice of their several pastors.

The following were the arrangements proposed by Sir Richard Bourke. The first was, that whenever the congregation subscribed £300 for the erection of a church and a clergyman's residence, that upon application, an equal sum should be issued from the colonial treasury in aid of the undertaking ;.........that the building be vested in trustees. A chaplain of the creed of the congregation shall then be appointed by the crown in the manner now practised, and his stipend shall be issued by the Governor at the following rate :—If, in the district where the church or chapel to which he shall be appointed, is situated, there be a resident population of one hundred adults, who shall subscribe a declaration setting forth their desire to attend such place of worship, the chaplain shall receive from the treasury *one hundred pounds a-year;* if there be two hundred adults, one hundred and fifty pounds ; and if five hundred adults, then two hundred pounds ; which is proposed as the maximum salary to be paid by the government to a chaplain of whatever persuasion. In regard to the appointment of Dr. Ullathorne as Vicar-General of the catholic church in the colony, he says :—"And the recent appointment of a Vicar-General, with whose discretion, character, and morals I have the greatest reason to be satisfied, will, I hope, effect what is required in the Roman catholic church. I am inclined however," he continues, " to think that the salary of £200 a-year is too low for the office, and that it might be advantageously raised to £400, to enable the Vicar-General to visit frequently the chapels in the interior."

His Excellency states, in the foregoing outline, "I have limited the support of the government to the three principal christian congregations in the colony." He states, that "in both the male and female orphan schools, the children are brought up exclusively in the doctrines of the church of England."

There is in Parramatta a considerable boarding school, called the King's School, at the head of which is a clergyman of the church of England, with a salary of £100 a-year only, but who has been promised the occupation of a house at the public expense, to contain from sixty to eighty boarders and day scholars. The three schools thus described, now are, and will in all probability continue to be, exclusively for the church of England. They may be supported, and the orphan schools extended, by means of the income which will, at no great distance of time, be derived from the lands granted under seal to the Church and School Corporation; and which, in its dissolution, became, by the terms of the charter, vested in the crown, to be disposed of by his majesty, his heirs and successors, "in such manner as shall appear most conducive to the maintenance and promotion of religion, and the education of youth in the said colony." "Under these terms," says Sir R. Bourke, "the income of the lands may be applied to the support of any of the churches or schools referred to in this despatch."

"The primary schools, or parish schools established by the corporation, which are thirty-five in number, situated in various parts of the colony, attended upon an average by 1,248 children of both sexes, are charged in the estimates for 1834, at £2,756: in all of them the catechism of the church of England is taught. Thus the charge for all the schools of this description for the year 1834 is taken at £5,736, to which should be added a vote of the Legislative Council of £2,300, for the site and buildings for the King's School at Parramatta............The sum of £800 has been voted for the Roman catholic schools for the year 1834."

"You may thus perceive, sir, the great disproportion which exists in the support given by the State to schools formed for the use of the different denominations of christians in the colony; a disproportion not based on the relative numbers of each, but guided, it would seem, by the same principles which have regulated the support afforded to the different churches."

I have given in the above extract the principal matter contained in the despatch of Sir Richard Bourke in regard to ecclesiastical matters. These suggestions of his Excellency must have been most acceptable to the Home government; since, having dissolved the Church and School Corporation, and the

REV. JOHN MCENCROE.

lands of same reverting to the crown, they were enabled to sanction those measures of the colonial government which seemed to be most conducive to the public good.

The Home government took time (two years) to consider the matter; but a most gracious reply was received from Lord Viscount Glenelg, then at the head of the colonial department, during the administration of Lord Melbourne. His communication to Sir Richard Bourke bears date 30th November, 1835; in which document he acknowledges with pleasure, both on his part and the part of the others of His Majesty's government, "for the full and clear statement which he transmitted to them, of the existing means of religious instruction and education, in connection with the wants and circumstances of the colony; and also for the suggestions with which you have followed up that statement.

Further on His Lordship states :—" I am disposed, therefore, to commit to the Governor and the Legislative Council the task of suggesting and enacting such laws and regulations for the distribution and appropriation of the funds applicable to the general purposes of religion and education, as they consider best adapted to the exigencies of the colony."

"In the general principle upon which that plan is founded as applicable to New South Wales, His Majesty's government entirely concur. In these communities," he goes on to state, "of the Australian colonies, formed and rapidly multiplying under most peculiar circumstances, and comprising great numbers of presbyterians and Roman catholics, as well as members of the church of England, it is evident that the attempt to select any one church as the exclusive object of public endowment, even if it were advisable in every other respect, would not long be tolerated. To none of the numerous christians of those persuasions should opportunities be refused for worship and education on principles which they approve."

"The plan which you have suggested appears to me fully in accordance with these views in both its branches ;—in that which relates to the places and ministers of worship, or, as it may be more briefly described to public religion; and in that which concerns public education."

Now nothing could be more just than the conclusion come to by the Home government, and communicated to His Excellency through Lord Glenelg; and it would have been inconsistent for them to have acted otherwise. It is strange how things happen, at times : this reply emanated from the whig liberal government, under Lord Melbourne. The administration of Sir Robert Peel

F

was adverse to making any alterations in the protestant church establishment, and were defeated in April, 1835, on a motion to appropriate a portion of the church revenues to education.

The Church Act, initiated by Sir Richard Bourke, became the law of the colony on the 29th July, in the year 1836. This memorable Act, which, to a certain extent, put down religious dissensions, established also equality amongst the different christian bodies, although chiefly framed by the Governor. Nevertheless, as he intimates in his despatch, he was indebted for several of its clauses to suggestions from experienced liberal and enlightened men, both protestants and catholics, of the colony.

I come now to the time when Dr. Polding was appointed bishop. I have heard from his own lips, that he was appointed, at first, by the Holy See, Vicar-Apostolic of Madras, in India, with the title of Hierocœsarea; but Dr. Polding declined the appointment, after full deliberation, although, in some respects, there were strong inducements. It was a very important charge and well able to support the dignity of a bishop: but it had also its drawbacks; a terribly hot climate; and there were differences with the Portuguese clergy—a kind of schism. It was about this time that Father Therry, being the senior priest in the colony, had disagreed with the government: and on account of this an application was made to Dr. Bramston, bishop of London, for the appointment of a Roman catholic Ecclesiastical-Superior for New South Wales. Dr. Bramston applied to the Benedictine congregation of Downside. I have related that the appointment fell upon Dr. Ullathorne. In course of time Governor Bourke wrote home that Father Ullathorne was giving them every satisfaction, and had secured the confidence of the catholic population. Dr. Polding received a letter from Father Ullathorne in the year 1833, describing the mission, and giving an account of his missionary labours.

CHAPTER VII.

The appointment of Dr. Polding as Bishop-Vicar-Apostolic of New Holland.—Consecrated Feast of S.S. Peter and Paul, 29th June, 1834.—Arrives at Hobart, 6th August, 1835.— Arrives in Sydney 13th September, 1835.—Installation of the Bishop in St. Mary's, 22nd September, 1835.—The plan of the Bishop for the reformation of the manners of the people.—The acknowledgements of Governor Bourke as to the change of conduct.—Laying, by the Bishop, of the foundation stone of St. Patrick's Church, at Parramatta.—Petition of Bishop Polding, to Government, for more Priests.

REPRESENTATIONS of the state of religion in Australia were sent to Rome, and in the year 1834 Dr. Polding was requested by the Holy See to accept of the appointment of Vicar-Apostolic of New Holland, Van Dieman's Land, &c., as bishop-in-partibus. He gave his consent, and on 2nd May, 1834, was appointed; in the following month, the Feast of Sts. Peter and Paul, he was consecrated.

Full of zeal and fervour, the new and first bishop of Australia immediately began to select subjects for his distant and extensive vicariate. Many were the applicants to help him in his arduous mission; nine persons were chosen to accompany him, viz., three priests, Revs. Fisher, J. Corcoran, and A. Cotham, O.S.B.; Rev. J. B. Sumner, O.S.B., sub-deacon; catechists and ecclesiastical students, Rev. John Spencer, O.S.B., professed; Rev. H. Gregory, O.S.B., professed; and Messrs. Harding and Kenny. The bishop applied to the Home government for pecuniary aid to assist in bringing out those missionaries to the colony. It was in February, 1835, that Lord Aberdeen appointed four additional Roman Catholic chaplains for New South Wales, with an annual stipend of £150 to each, and in this number was included Dr. Polding, the bishop; the catechists received £100 each. When all things were ready, the heroic party met in Liverpool at the Misses Slater, relatives of the bishop, and nieces of Bishop Slater of the Mauritius.

It was in the month of April, 1835, that the company, with the Right Reverend Dr. Polding, sailed from Liverpool in the good old ship "Oriental"; she was towed to Birkenhead by a steamer, on which were a great many of the bishop's friends and admirers, wishing him God speed and praying for the success of his glorious mission. When the "Oriental" was leaving Liverpool and moving down the Mersey, the poor Irish labourers at the docks gave three hearty cheers for a prosperous voyage.

Alas! Some of them had friends in that far distant land, to whom they hoped the bishop and clergy would give consolation. It was all well with us, (the writer was one of the party) till we reached the Bay of Biscay; then old ocean seemed to dispute our passage; we encountered a terrible sea, and were tossed to and fro by the winds and waves, and never shall I forget the last assault, when a towering wave, erect as a wall, fell over us, forced in the front of the cuddy and cabins; their contents and seats were floating in the saloon. But the old East Indiaman stood it bravely, and this was the first and last rude shock she received. After this we enjoyed fine weather and fair winds, with nothing to incommode us except *le mal de mer*. So soon as we were recovered from our sickness, and able to keep our equilibrium, by the directions of the bishop we were engaged in study—some studying theology; and there were frequent religious conferences, over which Dr. Polding always presided; and others employed in preparatory studies, under the direction of a priest—so that the ship became like a small ecclesiastical seminary. When the vessel was steady we had mass every morning, and the bishop gave us a discourse every Sunday. We were becalmed at the line, and had only crossed it about a fortnight when a great affliction befell us in the loss of one of the priests, the Rev.— Fisher. He was sickly when he came on board, but it was hoped that the sea voyage would restore to him his health. He died calmly and resigned to the will of God, having received the last rites of the church at the hands of the good bishop. Most serene was the afternoon, when wrapped in a canvas shroud his remains were lowered from the Archbishop's cabin into a watery grave; both sea and sky in their solemn silence seemed to condole with us. The sacred mysteries had been celebrated that morning by every priest for the repose of his soul, and matins and lauds were said around his remains before he was committed to the deep. "Requiescat in pace."

The "Oriental" had favorable winds and fine weather till we neared the Derwent River, in Tasmania, where we were prevented by contrary winds for some days from reaching Hobart Town. We cast anchor in the Derwent, some distance from the town, on the 6th August, 1835. There for the first time we enjoyed the delights of an Australian climate; smooth as glass were the waters of this majestic river, and not a leaf stirred on its thickly wooded banks, nor did a cloud float on the rich blue expanse of the heavens, not a breath of wind to stir the sails. The brave old ship after the travel of 16,000 miles lay motionless on the bosom of the waters, with her image perfectly reflected from the glassy surface. We were soon surrounded by many boats, full of people curious to see the new arrivals and gather some news from home. Lieutenant Small was the first visitor. Some of us were rather disappointed at the civilized appearance of our visitors; for wo expected to see canoes filled with sable strangers, the native blacks; we thought the former rather common place, not differing in face, clothing, or manners, from those we might have seen had we only reached as far as the Firth of Forth, in Scotland. Two of the bishop's party went to Hobart Town, the Reverends Corcoran and Sumner, and they brought us the news that the town was larger than they thought, and that an old priest, viz. Father Connelly, had been there alone for twelve years: that there were some respectable catholics, but his flock was not numerous; but it gave us a good opinion of the land and climate when we saw in their hands a few apples which they brought from Father Connelly's garden. His Excellency, Governor Arthur, sent his boat, well manned, to take the bishop ashore. The day we left the ship we were introduced to Father Connelly, at his residence, by the bishop, and dined there. His place was situated a little above where the catholic cathedral now stands and contiguous to his small church. This structure was certainly not creditable to the catholics of Hobart Town—a small oblong rough building for divine worship, and the flooring boards were not laid. Still it must be taken into consideration that the catholics were few and not wealthy, and the Government was by no means liberal in those days.

Father Connelly was a man of no small ability and attainments; but he had become rather antiquated in his manners, on account of being so long by himself. He was a native of the North of Ireland, very witty and full of dry humour and caustic remarks, and had often shown great adroitness in his correspondence with those in authority. A singular story is related of him in regard to a convert whom he had converted to the catholic church. The name of the man was Pierce. The narration is, that this man Pierce escaped from Macquarie Harbour in Van Dieman's Land, with six companions; they lost their way in the bush and were reduced to the last extremity by hunger. The demon provoked Pierce to that extent that he rose up against his companions, killed and eat them. He gave himself up and was sent back to Macquarie Harbour. He again escaped with a man named Cox, whom, in like manner, he killed. Pierce appeared in the settled districts with a bag containing an arm of his victim, Cox. Father Connelly wrote an account of Pierce's life, in Irish, when he Pierce was in prison awaiting the fulfilment of the last sentence of the law. Father Connelly read it on the scaffold, folding up the paper and putting it in his pocket Governor Philip, who thought Father Connelly rather a simple kind of man, sent his orderly with the request to favor him with the account of Pierce's life. The priest sent it, but the Governor nor any of the officials "could make it out." They thought it was Hebrew, and had to send for Father Connelly to translate it. This was a standing joke ever afterwards on the Governor, who had thought very little of the attainments of the humble priest.— *Taken from a letter of C. Fitzpatrick.*

The bishop was cordially received by the catholic laity; and those of them who were in good circumstances and influential showed him every respect. There were amongst these Messrs. Halket, Driscol, Doctors Hall and Rowe, Lieut. Small and others. Dr. Hall is still alive, having reached the ripe and mellow age of seventy-three. During the short stay of the Bishop a great deal was done for the spiritual well-being of the catholics of Van Dieman's Land, alias Tasmania. He appointed the Rev. A. Cotham to the spiritual charge of the Mission with Father Connelly, who had been there for so many years; he also established a catholic school in Hobart Town and obtained from the government £90 as a salary for the teacher. The first teacher was Mr. John Kenny, one of the ecclesiastical students, who came with the bishop to the colony. At the request of Dr. Polding he remained for six months to organize the school, and instruct the children in the christian doctrine. Whilst the bishop was in Tasmania, he laid the foundation stone of a church at Richmond, and visited various parts of the colony, forming congregations and imparting new life into the catholics, who rejoiced to see the day when they were visited by a bishop appointed by the successor of St. Peter.

Bishop Polding left Hobart Town on 5th September for Sydney, in the same ship the "Oriental," in which he came. accompanied by one priest, three religious who were professed monks of the order of St. Benedict and two ecclesiastical students viz:—Messrs. Harding and Gorman. He left in Hobart Town Reverend A. Cotham and Mr. John Kenny. The "Oriental" arrived in Sydney with the Bishop and his party on Sunday, 13th September, 1835. The installation of the bishop in the cathedral of St. Mary's took place on Sunday, 20th of the same month. It was an imposing ceremony. The bishop, clad in mitre and cope, and holding the crosier, proceeded with his chaplain to the principal entrance of St. Mary's church, where he was received by the vicar-general, the Very Reverend W. Ullathorne and the clergy.

they then walked in procession to the sanctuary, where they kneeled in prayer for a time; during the procession the Te Deum was sung by the choir accompanied by the organ; then the bishop ascended the steps of the altar, and took his seat in front of the congregation. The bulls of consecration from the Holy See were read by the vicar-general and then the clergy one by one kneeled before the bishop and made their submission. The vicar-general when introducing his lordship to his flock, delivered an appropriate discourse which deeply moved the bishop. His lordship then for the first time addressed his flock in a most feeling and impressive manner, when he dwelt with considerable force upon the merits of the reverend gentleman, who had filled for some time the office of vicar-general; and spoke of the excellent qualities of Father Therry, the pastor to whose zeal they were indebted for the noble structure in which they were then assembled and whose absence on this occasion seemed to be much felt by the congregation. He concluded by complimenting the gentlemen who had accompanied him, and hoped that the flock would abide by the instructions of those who had forsaken their country and friends to administer to their spiritual wants. High mass was then celebrated by the bishop; at the end of which he gave the solemn benediction, standing with mitre on head and crosier in hand. There was a very crowded congregation, and a great many protestants, both ladies and gentlemen, were present. The choir was very efficient, and Mrs. Russ, who will be well remembered by many of the old colonists, with her exquisite voice sang the most difficult passages of the mass, to the delight and admiration of all. It was remarked by a contemporary print, that from what had been heard of Dr. Polding, they were led to anticipate the best results, both in a religious and moral point of view, and hailed his arrival with the greatest satisfaction.

The Bishop, Dr. Polding, was only provided by the Home government with the same salary as the priests who accompanied him, viz.: £150 per annum; but that was certainly a very small allowance for a bishop, under the circumstances, to enable him to support his dignity and to answer the many demands sure to be made upon him. The committee of St. Mary's taking these things into consideration, memorialized the Governor, praying that an adequate salary be provided for the Right Reverend Dr. Polding. This memorial was laid upon the table of the Legislative Council by His Excellency Governor Bourke on 18th September, 1835. After the deliberation of the council, it was moved on the twenty-second of the same month, that His Excellency the Governor be requested to convey to the Right Honorable the

Secretary for the Colonies, the recommendation of the council, that an annual salary of £500 be allowed to the Roman Catholic clergyman exercising episcopal authority in this colony, with the sanction of His Majesty's Government. I would here remark from the wording of the motion, viz., "Roman Catholic Clergyman" that the gentlemen of the council had a difficulty in recognising Dr. Polding as a real bishop, although eighteen centuries of apostolic succession gave him an undoubted claim to the title; it was only pressure from without which forced them to acquiesce in the proposal.

In commencing to give an account of the labours of Bishop Polding as vicar apostolic, it will be well to inform the reader of the vast extent of his vicariate : He had to administer to a territory in New Holland, extending from Sydney to Queensland in the north, distant 500 miles ; to Cape Howe in the south, distant 300 miles ; and reaching from Sydney to Bathurst on the west, distant 144 miles ; beyond these places at the time, in the year 1835, the population was very sparse, and the towns which have risen to such great importance were only being formed, or not yet in existence. The bishop had also to attend to the spiritual wants of Tasmania, i.e. Van Dieman's Land. The catholic population of New South Wales, according to the census taken one year after the arrival of Dr. Polding, amounted to 21,898, and in Van Dieman's Land they numbered not less than 7,000 souls. The bishop did not delay in sending the few labourers at his disposal into this portion of the vineyard of God's church, which had been entrusted to his pastoral care. Father Cotham, as stated, he left in Tasmania with Father Connelly : he removed Father Therry from Sydney and placed him in Campbelltown ; Campbelltown contained 287 catholics, Appin, Menangle, Narellin and Cooke, 810; and he had charge of Appin, Illawarra and Argyle. There was great discontent, on the part of the catholics in Sydney, to the removal of Father Therry, who had done so much for the catholic cause there; but his new appointment was a larger honor, and he preferred to labour in those districts. The bishop arranged that Father Therry, who had been deprived of his salary, should receive in testimony of his merits, a stipend equal to that of the colonial chaplain. The Reverend J. Corcoran was appointed to Windsor, Richmond and Currajong ; the Reverend J.V. Dowling was placed at Maitland, on the Hunter River. Windsor at this time contained 228 catholics, Richmond 171, Hundred of Richmond 102, County Cook 534, West Maitland 365, East Maitland 200. The very reverend the vicar-general, Dr. Ullathorne, remained for some time with the bishop in Sydney and then took charge of

Parramatta, and resided there. The bishop retained in Sydney the Reverend John McEncroe, a priest most devoted to his duties in visiting the sick and comforting the poor afflicted prisoners, and withal a man of learning and great energy of character. Like a true missionary, the first object of the bishop was to reform the morals of his people, and enforce the discipline of the church. Vice was to be removed : Many were at variance with the laws of God and His church : Intemperance was very prevalent, with all its attendant evils; the marriage bond was not respected, and licentiousness of manners was general, and much fraudulency and overreaching in business; yet there were those, not a few in the catholic community, whose conduct was most exemplary, who flourished in faith and virtue, and had contributed much to preserve the faith and maintain virtue. The bishop and his clergy were indefatigable in their exertions to bring about a reformation of manners, and the greatest success, by the grace of God, resulted from their exertions. In the first relation of the mission of New Holland, which Bishop Polding presented to the congregation of the propagation of the faith in Rome, he details the plan adopted to obtain that good end. "We have," he says, "the inexpressible satisfaction of being eye witness to a decided change in the conduct and manners of our flock. The simplicity of the first ages seemed to be renewed, in the promptness with which they heard and obeyed the admonitions of their pastors. From week to week we have been employed in hearing the general confession of individuals, who, on account of their circumstances, or through negligence, have remained immersed in sin for forty or fifty years, and even a longer time. It being of the greatest importance to have order in our missionary life, we formed a plan which we follow to the present day. We commence at an early hour in the morning, and place ourselves in the church, or house used for that purpose, and remain there until some one comes to confession. At 10 o'clock a.m., the sacraments of baptism and matrimony are administered ; afterwards the hospitals are visited, the prisons, the jails, and finally the sick living in the city and suburbs. Thus is occupied the day until the evening, when the funerals are attended. Then only can we repose for awhile, and apply ourselves to our spiritual exercises, although they are frequently interrupted, and even our sleep during the night. In the evening we instruct our converts. It need not be added that the Sunday is a day of incessant occupation Each one celebrates mass twice, and it is necessary to give two or three instructions, besides continual attendance in the confessional. In the course of a few months there was a visible change in the entire population, it being impossible that a reform such as this should take place in one third of the population without producing a certain effect in the remainder. In consequence, the public authorities acknowledged that there was an amelioration, concluding from the general tranquillity throughout the colony, and from the diminution of public crime."

The writer well remembers the complete disinterestedness shown by the bishop in the discharge of those duties : he took his share, as a simple priest in the labours with his priests, without reserve, except when the general interests required his attention. Every day he attended in the confessional, and I have seen him delayed on the Saturdays till nearly midnight in the old chapel of St. Joseph : his confessional was always thronged, for he was a wise, prudent, and consoling confessor, and well knew how to pour oil and wine into the wounds of the soul. · He took his turn in preaching, and some will recollect the great power and unction of his words in those days. He visited the hospitals and prisons, inspiring patience and resignation, and encouraging the poor sufferers to be fervent and to lay aside all tepidity and repugnance in the service of God. I once accompanied him late at night to the old jail, then at the end of George-street, where lay a young man. in the prime and vigour of life, under the sentence of death for bushranging; he went to strengthen him for his terrible end, and remained a long time praying and instructing him; the man was executed the following morning, and to show the kindness of the good bishop, he brought him two large apples from his own garden, to cool his feverish mouth.

There was one cause which contributed very much to the moral improvement amongst the prisoners : Every month, and sometimes more frequently, there arrived in the colony vessels filled with prisoners, who were transported from England, Ireland, and Scotland ; a great many of these were catholics. (From the beginning of the year 1836, to the year 1841, there were sent to New South Wales upwards of 18,000 prisoners : each prison ship carried from 200 to 300). They remained, when the vessel arrived, according to the Government regulations, for fourteen days on board the ship, until the necessary preparations were made for their assignment to masters in different parts of the colony. As might be supposed, they did not spend these days of indolence profitably, but sometimes rather sinfully. Bishop Polding considered it his duty to represent to the Governor, that the time could be employed very usefully if they were permitted to land and receive instructions, and other means which religion offers. The Governor very willingly consented to the request, and the prisoners were allowed, for ten or twelve days, to attend the instructions of their respective pastors, catholic and protestant.

Dr. Ullathorne, in his evidence before the committee on transportation, gives the following account:—* "The catholic prisoners, who are about one-third of those who arrive, with the consent of the Government, remain ten days in Sydney before they are assigned, for the purpose of obtaining religious and other instruction. They are marched to our church at six in the morning, and remain till about 11 o'clock, they are then again marched to the church at three, and remain till about six. The bishop himself appears personally amongst them, and after giving them an exhortation they are then classed; those who have neglected the duties of religion altogether for the course of one year, those for three, those for seven, those for ten, and those for life. They are then subject to an examination as to their dispositions, and the amount of religious knowledge they may possess. After this they are again classed: the best of them are selected as monitors: our ecclesiastical students act as catechists; a clergyman is called to assist from the interior, and after they have gone through a series of religious exercises and through a series of individual converse with the clergy, they then after that course of their instruction, go through another series of instruction with regard to their condition as prisoners, and also in reference to their masters, and the law, and the Government, and the particular dangers that surround them. After this they proceed to their assignment." These exercises were introduced 1st January, 1837.

There can be no question as to the beneficial moral effects of this plan to the prisoners; and many of them attribute their future virtue and welfare to this spiritual retreat of ten days, under the eyes of the bishop and clergy. Nay, the sincerity and piety with which those unfortunate men comported themselves, made a deep impression on the minds of the faithful. It is related that on one of these occasions, when the bishop was administering the holy communion to about one hundred of them, he was interrupted by the sobs and cries of a person present in the church; she was at first taken to be a maniac; the bishop sent her word to remain quiet, and he would speak to her after the service. After mass, and whilst he was yet in the sanctuary, she came to him and said she had been a great sinner, and that for thirty years she had not been at confession, that Father Therry and the other priests had frequently admonished her; that she had

---

* Page 36, No. 324.

abandoned the church in order not to be disturbed by the sermons of the bishop and the other clergy : but what she had seen that morning had made a strong impression which she could not remove ; that she wished to turn to God, and begin by making her confession without delay. She made her confession, and continued to persevere in her good dispositions.

It was remarked by Bishop Polding, in his relation to the Holy See, that before this plan was adopted of preparing the prisoners, who had newly arrived, by giving them a spiritual retreat, instruction, and the sacraments, it was observed that many of the newly arrived were pu in prison, either through their folly or wickedness; but more frequently hy the persuasions of designing rogues who took advantage of their ignorance and induced them to steal and rob their masters, in the hope of having part of the plunder. "We put the unfortunate penitents on their guard against such artifices. We do not permit them to depart to their destination until they are fully instructed in their religious obligations, and well advised how they are to conduct themselves to obtain an amelioration of their unhappy condition, particularly insisting on industry, sobriety, fidelity, and obedience to their masters. After this the prisons were not filled with the new arrivals. It was universally remarked that a great change had taken place in the behaviour of the prisoners throughout the colony ; and it is worthy of observation, that of those who were condemned to death within three years after our arrival, scarcely one of the many was of those who had been instructed and prepared by us. The number of the public executions were considerably diminished. In the year of our arrival twenty-two were condemned, several of whom were converted in the prison ; the year following twelve; in the next seven; and since the number has gradually decreased."

Governor Bourke, in reply to certain questions proposed by the Secretary of State, wrote as follows: "They, the prisoners, on their arrival were granted a few hours in the day to receive instructions from the clergy of the different communions. To give a longer time for this instruction, Dr. Polding, the Roman Catholic Bishop, shortly after his arrival in New South Wales, requested that the time be prolonged between the arrival and consignment of the prisoners, which was granted. The attention paid to those of his communion has been given with great earnestness and regularity ; and there is reason to believe that the result has been beneficial, both to those who have received his admonitions and to the public in general."

The first year after the arrival of Bishop Polding was filled with many important events in connection with religion. The first time the bishop administered the sacrament of confirmation was on Sunday, 28th February, 1836; it was then given to 60 or 70 soldiers of the 17th Regiment. It was remarked at the time by a correspondent, that he often heard it said, " better the christian better the soldier," and he had no doubt of the truth of the saying; for a man who goes into the battle field in the peace of his Maker cannot have the dread of death staring him in the face, but advances boldly to meet the enemies of his country, feeling confident, if he falls, of doing his duty to both God and man. This holy rite had been administered in the colony before, by the Very Rev. J. O'Flynn, who had the power to give confirmation, but this was the first time a Bishop had administered the sacrament in the colony.

The next catholic work of importance done by the bishop was the blessing and laying of the foundation stone of St. Patrick's Church, at Paramatta. It was said, then, it is high time that in the thriving and flourishing district of Parramatta something in the shape of a decent place of worship should be erected for the catholics, who comprise so great a portion of the community. On Thursday, 17th March, 1836, St. Patrick's Day, the inhabitants of Parramatta witnessed a religious spectacle, the first of its kind in the colony.

All the catholic clergy of the colony were in attendance, and a very large assemblage of catholics from all parts, with many persons professing other creeds, were gathered round the foundation at the time appointed. The bishop, clergy, and assistants walked in procession to the site. The bishop was richly vested in rochet, stole and cope, with mitre and crosier, the clergy were vested with beautiful chausibles of silk, gold and embroidery work, and the cantors had on copes of costly material.

The bishop delivered an address on the occasion. He spoke as follows: "A foundation of religion had been commenced amongst them, and from these beginnings he prayed God to be propitious. A temple would arise, in which would be offered up the great sacrifice, a temple in which they would assemble to worship and glorify God and to learn lessons of love to all mankind. When the children of Israel passed the Jordan they collected, by command from on high, stones from the bed of the river, which had miraculously opened a way to their feet, and erected a monument of the event, to the end that their children's children might remember the protection which God had given their fathers. So the monument commenced

this day would be a sign to those who came after them in future
generations that God had visited and protected His people amidst
their difficulties; that in bringing them into a strange land He
had not forsaken them; He had redeemed them from captivity,
had blessed their flocks and herds; wherefore then, not unmindful
of His goodness, they had raised this temple to His holy name. The
bishop then exhorted all according to their means to contribute
cheerfully and generously towards its erection, following the
example of the people of Israel, who brought their gold, their
silver and brass, when David invited them to build a house unto
God, and rejoiced because they offered their gifts with all their
hearts. The church was dedicated unto God, under the name of
St. Patrick the Apostle of Ireland, whose festival was this day
celebrated. This day would be remembered memorable amongst
them by the erection of a material temple. There was also a
spiritual temple, in which God loves to dwell; let the spiritual
temple be this day commenced by a renunciation of all excess and
a change of life. In conclusion the bishop, with the authority of
a father, and in the name of the glorious St. Patrick, entreated
his people as they reverenced the land of their forefathers and
rejoiced in its power, to show forth the power and purity of their
faith, in the propriety of their conduct: to shun all excess
and drunkenness, as most offensive to the Almighty, derogatory
to the memory of a saint, distinguished for his abstemiousness,
and degrading to the descendants of those whose holy lives obtained
for Ireland the title of the Island of Saints. When the illustrious
Daniel O'Connell called on the men of Clare to abstain, during the
period of the election, from intoxicating drink, they obeyed, and
their obedience was rewarded; their moral triumph was followed
by another which spread rejoicing through the world. The men of
Clare will be remembered with feelings of gratitude and respect; so
also will the people of Parramatta if they set this day an example
of temperance to present and succeeding generations, which shall
contribute to emancipate them from the power of evil habits; by
many deemed invincible. In this hope the bishop entreated all to
retire early to their homes, blessing and praising God for that He
had vouchsafed to choose unto Himself a dwelling amongst them."

The priests, at the commencement of the year 1836, were few
in number, but the bishop did not delay in striving to have the
number augmented. On the 6th May, 1836, he forwarded to His
Excellency, Sir Richard Bourke, an application for an increase to
the number of priests; and I consider it would not be fair to the
reader if I did not quote this communication in extenso, as it gives
a particular account of the condition of the catholics at the time
in New South Wales.

The application was made in the following terms: " Sir,—In forwarding to the Colonial Office the estimate of the probable expenses of the department of the Roman Catholic Church and School Establishment for the year 1837, and also the supplementary to the estimate for the year 1836, I have the honor respectfully to submit to the consideration of your Excellency, and of the Honorable the Legislative Council, the justice and expediency of augmenting the present number of Roman catholic chaplains in this colony and penal settlement. Before I state the reasons on which I ground this application, your Excellency will permit me to trace the measures that have been adopted within the last three years to provide the catholic population of New South Wales with religious instruction. In the year 1833, on two chaplains, with the presiding clergymen Father Therry, Father McEncroe, and Dr. Ullathorne, devolved the duty of imparting religious instruction and of administering to the spiritual wants of one-third of the entire population of the colony, diffused throughout every part of this extensive territory. By so small a number of clergymen, not more than sufficient for Sydney alone, little could be done, except to keep from entire decay so much of the spirit and form of religion as had been preserved by the zealous labours of their predecessors, to run hastily from place to place, perhaps at great distances, to supply the most pressing wants of their flocks—to administer the rites of religion to the child, and to those in danger of death. In such a state of things even the individual efforts of a clergyman must of necessity have been limited in their application and weakened in their power, the greater portion of his time being consumed, and his energies exhausted, in the act of passing from locality to locality. The efficiency of clerical labour is intimately connected with the continued residence of the clergyman amongst his people ; thus only can the pastor know the habits of the individuals of his flock ; have frequent communication with them, become enabled to adapt his instructions, public and private, to their respective dispositions and circumstances. In the course of the same year the urgent petition of the catholic community for religious assistance was taken into consideration, and provision was kindly made by your Excellency and the Honourable Legislative Council, for four additional chaplains. Towards the latter part of last year, the bishop arrived with three chaplains, and the result of the combined labours of the catholic clergy thus augmented in numbers tends to show, in the effect, the absolute necessity of a resident, in order to secure an efficient, clergy.

"During the last seven months, two clergymen and the Bishop have devoted their labors permanently to the inhabitants of Sydney and its various establishments. The result has shown itself as well amongst the prison population as amongst the free, in the inmates of the gaol, prisoners' barracks, the hulks, and amongst the inhabitants of the town, by a marked and acknowledged improvement of morals, and in the case of a, by no means, inconsiderable number of persons hitherto regardless of religious duty, by a total reformation of conduct; and your Excellency will participate in the pleasure with which I state that this moral improvement amongst our people is, under the Divine blessing, still steadily progressing.

"Since the month of October last, each Sunday ecclesiastical Students have read prayers, and instructions selected by the Bishop, to the prisoners in Carter's barracks, at the treadmill, in the gaol, and recently to those employed at the new gaol.

"Sydney being thus provided, there remain only four chaplains for the whole of the interior of the colony and the remote penal settlements. Duty is performed at Parramatta by the Vicar-General, Dr. Ullathorne, but in consequence of our limited numbers, he is liable to be required to attend other and distant settlements. Clerical attendance is also provided for Liverpool, a position important on account of the hospital. A chaplain is also established at Windsor, but as the field of his labors extends from Penrith and its vicinity down to the mouth of the Hawkesbury, a distance of more than sixty miles, over a populous country, he cannot be considered as resident; each part of this extensive district can only be occasionally attended to; still a manifest improvement has taken place at Windsor, and in its vicinity. The same may be said of Maitland. The chaplain stationed at Maitland has to extend the sphere of his duties to Newcastle, across the Hunter, up the whole of the Williams River, and over Patterson's Plains on the one side and on the other to the distant districts of the Upper Hunter, the Patrick's, and the Liverpool Plains. The population of the township of Maitland alone, of which a great portion is catholic, according to a census taken by a police magistrate in the commencement of the last year, amounted at that time to 2,000 souls; since it has been considerably increased. And there still remains Campbelltown and Appin, the Cowpastures, and the district of Illawarra, divided from the rest of the colony by its precipitous range of mountains, chiefly catholic, the vast district of Argyle, Bathurst, with all the settled country beyond the Blue Mountains, all the penal settlements unprovided with Roman catholic chaplains.

" According to the census of the colony taken in 1833, the catholic population amounted to 17,200; since that period 3,600 have been added to the number by transportation, besides the increase by births and by immigration. Of the free female immigrants, about 550 are catholics.

" In the view of this statement, I beg most respectfully to express my confidence, that your Excellency will not fail to perceive the justice and expediency of augmenting, for the catholic population of this colony and penal settlement, the number of chaplains.

" Firstly.—Inasmuch as a clergy not permanently resident, but moving from place to place, cannot be adequately efficient; passing visits leave only passing impressions.

" Secondly —Without an increase in the number of our clergy a considerable portion of the colony must still remain almost entirely destitute.

" Thirdly.—The numerous prison population have no means of procuring religious assistance and instruction, except through the provision of the Government. The duty of making such provision for persons so circumstanced is evident; without it, one of the great ends proposed to be gained by the system of transportation, viz. the reformation of the criminal, must be left, to a great extent, without the means of accomplishing it.

" Fourthly.—An increase of the number of clergy is most desirable for the sake of the free persons who arrive in the colony for the purpose of settling in the interior, whose emigration to this country is encouraged by Government, in order, amongst other motives, to raise the morals of the people deprived of the rites and consolations of their religion themselves, and their children deprived of all pastoral care and guidance, a bereavement and disappointment more afflicting to them than any other that may be named; they are in imminent danger of falling into the vices which they find prevailing around them, and thus most lamentably frustrating the praiseworthy object proposed on their immigration.

" Fifthly.—A greater number of clergy is required for the sake of the rising generation; these, in the absence of nearer guardians, have a claim to the protection of Government; without the aid of their clergy they must in very many instances grow up neglected, ignorant of their moral duties, and formed to criminal ways, guided by the depraved example of their neglected parents.

G

"Sixthly.—I have great reason to confide that the labours of a resident clergy amongst the catholic population will be followed by a considerable diminution of public crime, and consequently by a proportionate diminution in the expense of convicting and punishing crime. Out of the number of public criminals of the catholic religion executed during the last four years, it has been remarked not one has seen a clergyman so as to receive the rites of his church in this country, until after he was apprehended and lodged in jail; the remark may be extended to the 450 catholics of Norfolk Island; scarcely any amongst them are to be found who had attended even once to their religious duties, from the period of their transportation to the period of their re-conviction, and all, with an uniformity which cannot be deemed the chance of coincidence, attributed their career of guilt principally to the absence of clerical care, guidance, and support.

"On these grounds it is most respectfully submitted to your Excellency that six additional catholic chaplains are required to render the catholic a permanently resident and efficient clergy, besides the one to be stationed at Norfolk Island. Of this number I propose one to be stationed in a central part of the county of Camden, one in the Illawarra, one in Argyle, one at Bathurst, one additional chaplain in the district of Windsor and of the Hawkesbury, and an additional one in the district of the Hunter, to be stationed at Newcastle or Patrick's Plains. Even after this arrangement the settlements of Port Macquarie and of Moreton Bay can only receive occasionally spiritual assistance from Sydney.

"Having, as I hope, shown most satisfactorily the urgency of the case, and that this further addition to the number of catholic chaplains is not greater than is demanded by the pressing wants of the colony, my confidence in the successful result of this application is the more firm, being supported by the late Right Honorable Secretary of State for the colonies, Lord Stanley, as to the dispositions of your Excellency, and of the Honorable the Legislative Council. Lord Stanley states it to be his opinion 'that an addition of four chaplains was not more than was required by the urgency of the case.' A letter, dated 22nd January, 1834, to Edward Blount, Esq., a copy of which was transmitted from Downing-street to the Right Rev. Bishop Bramston, by the direction of Lord Stanley, and now in my hands, contains a similar sentiment. Having stated the opinion above quoted, his Lordship continues—'and should the demand increase, I am satisfied that the Legislative Council of New South Wales will be happy to make such further provision as may be in their power, consistently with the other claims upon the revenue, which it may be necessary for them to take into consideration.'

With great respect,
I have the honor to be,
Sir,
Your most obedient humble Servant,
J. B. POLDING."

The following excellent letters of Bishop Polding arose out of a discussion about Lord Stanley's system of education, which Governor Bourke wished to establish in the colony. Bishop Polding was favorable to its introduction, on the principle that half a loaf is better than no bread; and to give it a trial. The protestant bishop (Broughton) was opposed to the general system of education, because he thought it would be too much in favor of the catholics and obstruct his favorite scheme, which was to compel, or bring about, that all the children, whether catholic or dissenting, be taught the doctrine and catechism of the Church of England :—

(To the Editor of the Australian.

SIR,—A speech delivered by the Protestant Bishop of Australia at a meeting held on the 3rd August, at the Pulteney Hotel, has at length fallen into my hands. Of its existence in print I had heard; some portions of it in the public papers I observed, but to obtain it had been hitherto almost as hopeless an endeavour as to catch the gleams of light with which the marshes of Botany Bay sometimes favor us.

Its object, I perceive, is to discountenance the system of education it has been proposed to introduce into the colony. Thus it may be considered as a continuance of the series of petitions, resolutions, and protests which have emanated from the Pulteney of late, tending to the same purpose. This address, therefore, may be possibly the finale of the exhibition. Rocket-like, it scorns the base things of earth and takes its flight into the regions of theological disquisitions, displaying in the grand burst plainly and legibly the object of its author, and then, as best beseems the nature of all earthly things, descending into the covert of darkness and of silence.

That Dr. Broughton has a right, particularly in the situation he holds, to canvass a system of education, no one will deny ; each one will deem that he is employed in his proper function in canvassing such system if he have doubt respecting its utility and propriety. But neither eminence of station nor zeal for the cause we conscientiously embrace will justify glaringly incorrect and palpable misstatements. The former, in the person of Pilate, condemned the innocent Jesus; the latter, in the person of Paul, persecuted the church of God. On the ignobly intended shield of ignorance must be received the charge, which also will strike moral integrity to the heart. I regret deeply to find in the address now before me statements on subjects the most important equally incorrect with those which had been so gravely numbered amongst the resolutions and solemn declarations of the Pulteney. Amongst the latter I read, for instance, that "to prize the Bible is to forfeit the favor of the government." How impressively the alteration helps on the phrase! And again, that the population includes 16,000 catholics and about 1600 children, in the face of the census of 1833, which even at that time gave a return of seventeen thousand two hundred catholics, taken as it was, so carelessly that not one catholic is reckoned in upwards of nine hundred colonial seamen. As regards the number of catholic children, upwards of sixteen hundred have been baptised within the last four years. But these extravagant assertions of the Pulteney have been so regularly manufactured for the nonce that the grave formality of discussion respecting their truth would chase away the smile which they are good-naturedly intended to elicit to dissipate the tedium of continued lamentation.

To the statements in the address I shall proceed presently. As regards the system of education and its fitness for this colony permit me to say a word *en passant*. I cannot condemn, on the strength of the evidence now in my possession, a system which has received the sanction of such eminent divines and scholars as those confessedly are who compose the Board of Education in Ireland. I have every reason to believe the empire contains no individuals more attached to their country, more solicitous to promote its welfare, more capable of devising means for that purpose, or of carrying those measures into effect. It is truly delightful to see such men leaving the areopagus of controversial recrimination, sitting down together in the temple of concord to receive from the lips of heaven born charity, lessons informing them how their fellow creatures may be taught to preserve their faith and yet dwell in mutual love. In this matter I would not surrender my private judgment, yet who would not pay a reverential deference to the names of Murray, Whately, and Carlisle! *As regards its fitness for the colony; no evidence of its unfitness has yet been adduced ; the trial is to be made.* And after the success the system has met with in Ireland, it deserves a trial. There it has smoothed down animosities, it has encouraged the spread of education, it has introduced a nobler range of feeling than heretofore degraded the national character under the influence of Charter House and Kildare-street Schools. What radical distinction exists between the inhabitants of Australia and their Antipodes to prevent those blessings being produced by the system here, though one-third be catholics, and two-thirds of the population be of all shades of religious belief, from the scarcely visible tinge of enthusiasm to the lamentably broad expanse of entire indifference, is an enquiry I could wish to hear satisfactorily answered by the author of the Pulteney address. I can readily conceive that the conversation on religious subjects, which will take place sometimes, even amongst boys, will clear away many of the prejudices which were heretofore deemed sacred, that it will not be easy to poison the friendships that have been formed at school by the insinuation of deadly enmity; each catholic will not be deemed an inquisitorial torturer at heart. He who has never been known even in the thoughtlessness of youth to swerve from his word will not readily be deemed a purjurer on principle; and he who has uniformly shewn himself possessed of common sense, will be permitted to believe in transubstantiation without being insulted by the odious epithet of idolater. I acknowledge the consequence will be awful to some parties, there will be bewailing amongst dealers in anti-popery tracts. The fifth of November will loose its flaming honors; and many a preacher, with the candid Mr. Grinfield, will deplore that each cottage no longer makes Fox's Book of Martyrs its chief treasure; and may conclude his argument on the utility of such noble publications with the pathetic avowal of that reverend gentleman; "my brethren let Sophists disclaim as they may, man is too little a creature to be stripped of his prejudices."

As a catholic I am vastly amused with the contrariety of opinion expressed with regard to this system. The Pulteney oracles declare the system will be the means of establishing the catholic religion. A writer in the "Australasian" is quite as positive it will destroy the catholic religion. The sagacious editor of the "Monitor" rejoices that at length the book of Revelation will give an interlinear translation to the book of Nature, and we shall thus be enabled infallibly to resolve the mysteries of faith into the dicta of reason. Creeds, commentaries, and councils—priests and parsons—all books, save the Bible, will be forced into a pyramid from the top of which, with the book of

Nature in one hand and the of book Revelation in the other, the "Monitor" will instruct the world. But to be serious, religion, which springs from man, essentially partakes of man's infirmity, like him it is destined to decay—it is the creature of circumstances—it is "of earth earthly." The religion which has God for its author cannot be destroyed by human devices. It demands not to be exclusively bolstered up by external power, it refuses not support when proffered, it quails not before the terrors of persecution, it attributes not its flourishing to the smiles of an earthly potentate. True religion enshrouds not herself in prejudices, these she regards as habiliments degrading to her beauty. As a catholic, whether the system be permanently adopted or not, I have no fear of the result. Prohibit education—even use physical means to prevent it—we will still exert our efforts to educate our children, for, "it is better to obey God than man." Open schools to us, unhampered and unfettered on the fair principles of equality. We ask no more—and the form of religion that perishes under the test ought to perish, for it has within it the germ of mortality.

In my next letter I shall proceed to the proofs of my assertions, in the fact of misrepresentation of the doctrine of the catholic church, as defined by the council of Trent, respecting the reading of the scriptures; secondly, in the fact of misrepresentation respecting the Bull "Unigenitus" (no wonder the Venerable Marsden was deceived); thirdly, in the fact of misrepresentation respecting the introduction of the Bible as a school book.

I have the honor to be,
Sir,
Your most obedient servant,

CATHOLICUS IPSE.

Tuesday, August 23, 1836.

———

Remarks of the Editor of the *Australian.*—The tenor of his writing (Catholicus Ipse) must and will obtain, for his contributions, a prominent attention in this interesting discussion. The letter avows the ardent attachment of the writer to his own form of religion, but at the same time evinces how compatible that attachment is with an enlarged and enlightened spirit of christianity.

DR. BROUGHTON'S SPEECH

(To the Editor of the Australian).

Sir,—It has been for many years a subject of regret to me, that they who have stated, or take occasion to state, matters of catholic faith or doctrine as distinguished from their own protestant opinions, do not bring to the task that caution and discrimination demanded by the imp rtance of religious inquiry. This observation extends to practical o subjects of most serious import. By individuals' moving in the first circles of society, the catholic religion is, in a solemn appeal to the Deity, declared to profess articles superstitious and idolatrous. This is declared by persons who have never examined whether these things be so or not, and who, in the ordinary course of life, maintain that a conviction of the truth of the thing sworn to is necessary to relieve the conscience of him who swears from the horrible guilt of perjury.— " Væ tibi flumen moris humani! Quis resistit tibi ? Quamdiu non siccaberis ? Quousque volves Evæ filios in mare magnum, et formidolosum ? " The language of the penitent Augustine thus expresses how custom lends its deluding influence to self-deception; and oh ! how fatally. Our books are now to be met with, and even if they were not, we are ready to give an account of the faith that is in us, and application might be made to ascertain whether the tenets imputed to us, but generally disclaimed, do, or do not belong to catholic faith. How many prejudices would be cleared away, how narrow would become the isthmus of separation between the catholic church and numberless well-meaning people who are now floating about in search of truth, and weary for want of a standing place to their feet ! Were no doctrines ascribed and believed to belong to the catholic church, except such as she herself has declared to be articles of her faith, only that imperishable barrier would remain which the hand of the Almighty hath established to preserve pure and undefiled, from the turbulent ocean of human fallacies, the waters of salvation which have been, are, and will be to the end of time, poured over the earth from the fountain seated in Himself, and reflecting upon the surface, and in their depths, the beauty and purity of His own unchangeable existence. These thoughts have been brought to my mind by the perusal of a passage in Bishop Broughton's address, which I shall presently quote ; first observing how in gentleness is administered a castigation to certain individuals, who had, through the medium of the press, used words of scoffing and reviling ·towards the catholic church. We are so accustomed to language of this sort, that we had not noticed it as deserving of particular reproof ; nor indeed am I now sensible that it was merited. The game is started, the animals in pursuit give notice that they are in full chase—and they are chided for the natural development of their instinctive propensities. This is not as it ought to be. It grieves us to see them thus inopportunely surprised by a check. If the reality of catholic doctrine be such as Dr. Broughton exhibits, in their language and in that exhibition I can assuredly trace the connection between cause and effect.

I proceed to prove the first assertion contained in my last letter. The fact of misrepresentation of the doctrine of the catholic church as established by the Council of Trent respecting the use of the Scriptures. Preparatory, I will place before you the words of Dr. Broughton relating to the subject. " The rule of the Roman catholic church as to the use of the Scriptures we know is diametrically opposed to ours. It is this :—Forasmuch as it is manifest from experience, that if the Holy Bible, translated into the vulgar tongue, be indiscriminately allowed to everyone, the temerity of men will cause more evil than good to arise from it ; it is on this point referred to the judgment of the bishops or inquisitors, who may, by the advice of the priest or confessor, permit the reading of the Bible translated into the vulgar tongue by catholic authors to those persons whose faith and piety they apprehend will be augmented and not injured by it ; and this permission they must have in writing. But if any-one will have the presumption to read or judge the Scriptures without such written permission, he shall not receive absolution (fourth rule of the index of prohibited books; by order of the council of Trent). It is needless to perplex ourselves with a dis-cussion, whether this rule be a matter of doctrine or of discipline, which distinction is sometimes dwelt upon. It is the acknow-ledged rule of that church sanctioned by its declared authority."

Dr. Broughton asserts first, that the rule of the Roman catholic church, as to the use of the scriptures, is diametrically opposite to the protestant rule, and that we know it ; secondly, that this Roman catholic rule is contained in the fourth rule of the index, by order of the Council of Trent ; thirdly, that it is immaterial whether this rule be a matter of doctrine or of discipline ; fourthly, that it is the acknowledged rule sanctioned by its declared authority.

To try the correctness of the first proposition, we will place the protestant principle and the rule quoted as the catholic by Dr. Broughton in juxta position.

QUOTED BY DR. BROUGHTON AS THE CATHOLIC RULE.

For as much as it is manifest from experience, that if the Holy Bible translated into the vulgar tongue be indiscriminately allowed to everyone, the temerity of men will cause more evil than good to arise from it; it is on this point referred to the judgment of the bishops or inquisitors who may, by the advice of the priest or the confessor, permit the reading, &c., &c.

PROTESTANT.

Holy Scripture contains all things necessary to Salvation, and that the use of it should be put to every man who has a soul to be saved.

The parts, says Hooker, of every true (diametrical corresponds with that quality) opposition do always concern the same subjcet, and have reference to the same thing (with all due submission to Dr. Broughton's judgment, according to this definition the elements of opposition are wanting). Thus one proposition affirms and another denies. Applying this definition to the passages before us—what opposition exists between the proposition; the Scripture contains all things necessary to salvation, and the observation made in the quotation opposed that if the Holy Bible be indiscriminately allowed to every one, more evil than good will arise, does the one deny what the other affirms? Evidently not. But perhaps the diametrical opposition is to be found between the second principle and the unhappy fourth rule of the index. Let us try. The one asserts the free use of the Scriptures, the other requires a certain permission to be obtained to prevent abuse and injury to the unexperienced. But precaution is not prohibition. Am I debarred the free use of the Port of Sydney and its advantages, because to prevent destruction to the individual and loss to the public, a wise government requires me to take a pilot on board and to conform to regulations most easy to be complied with?

That the propositions are not adequate in terms, I readily grant; that they contradict each other, or are contrary to each other, I as readily deny it. To take up the metaphorical language of Dr. Broughton, though they do not exactly fall upon the same space or coincide, yet they are not diametrically opposite. Between two points on the circumference, diametrically opposite is an extent indefinitely devisable, what part of it and by consequence what position is occupied by the rule of the index.

relatively to the protestant rule, is a problem which might be
worked out, were the result when obtained worth the time and
trouble of obtaining it.

But it is unnecessary to dwell any longer on this subject, for
the regulation adduced by Dr. Broughton is neither an article of
catholic doctrine nor of catholic discipline, respecting the perusal of
the Scriptures nor published by order of the Council of Trent.

Indeed, whilst this quotation was under the pen, I suspect
some sort of uncertainty disturbed the writer's course of thought.
It is needless to enquire, observed Dr. Broughton, no, that is not the
word to perplex ourselves with the discussion, whether this rule
be a matter of doctrine or discipline. Quite as needless as to
perplex ourselves whether the number of catholics in this colony
be sixteen or six and twenty thousand; quite as needless as to
enquire whether or not the forfeiture of government favour has
been actually the consequence of prizing the Bible.

"*Sic volo sic jubeo stat pro ratione voluntas.*"

Why perplex ourselves? As regards the present subject, not
the least reason imaginable; to be perplexed, intimates to have
the presence of troublesome doubt, and troublesome doubt is very
inconvenient, but indeed there can be none. For what is matter
of catholic doctrine? "All that and that only is of catholic
doctrine which God has revealed and the church proposes to the
belief of all." In an article of faith or doctrine therefore there
are two things required,—revelation from God, for faith, says St.
Paul, comes by hearing, and hearing by the word of Christ; and
the second that it be taught by the church, either in a general
council by an express and definite decree, or practically
confirmed by the unanimous assent of the pastors of the church.

Till Dr. Broughton shall bring proof that the fourth rule of
the index has been in either way declared to be an article of
Faith, take, Sir, the assertion of Catholicus Ipse, that it is no
matter of catholic doctrine, propounding the rule of the Roman
catholic church as to the use of the Scriptures.

Secondly, neither is it a matter of catholic discipline in the
general sense of the word, for that law of discipline is not
obligatory, which neither proceeds from a general council, nor has
been promulgated to the church at large, and received by its
pastors. Now the regulations of the index, though received by
some countries, have never been enforced throughout the church,
nor received by its pastors at large as rules of general church
discipline, and wherever they have been adopted, it has been
because the local ecclesiastical authorities have deemed it
expedient as a matter of *prudence* and of temporary precaution

to do so. Thirdly, the rule in question is not by order of the Council of Trent. It is often objected against us, says Veron, for the sake of causing dissension and of rendering the catholic religion more odious, that the Council of Trent forbids the perusal of the Scriptures, in a vulgar tongue. This is a mere calumny. There is not a word which can possibly be construed in the decrees of the council, as even alluding to a prohibition of using the sacred Scriptures in a vulgar tongue. As to the fourth rule of the Roman index, which Dr. Moulin and others falsely ascribe to the Council of Trent, that council had nothing to do with it. The fact is—and Dr. Broughton ought to be aware of it, the council appointed certain individuals to consider what steps had better to be taken to prevent the dissemination of books dangerous to the faith and morals of the faithful. Amongst these were corrupted and perverted translations of the Scripture. The rules of the index were drawn up by these deputies, "but never received the sanction of the Council of Trent." In fact the council purposely abstained from giving its sanction to them. Hence Dr. Marsh, the Bishop of Peterborough, observes :—" The reading of the Scriptures, in an authorised version, is not prohibited to the laity (even of the Roman catholic church) by any decree or canon of the Council of Trent. And even the impediments which from other quarters had been thrown in the way of reading the Bible, such for instance as the requiring a license for that purpose, have been gradually diminished if not removed." *Comp. vide Chap. 6.* Who is the faithful witness, Dr. Broughton or Dr. Marsh ?

Dr. Broughton, the Protestant Bishop of Australia, asserts that it is needless to enquire whether the rule of the Roman catholic church respecting the use of the scriptures be a matter of doctrine or of discipline. I am astonished that this assertion should proceed from a theologian, who has before his mind a distinct knowledge of the difference between an article of doctrine and an article of discipline. Discipline considered in a general ecclesiastical sense regulates the internal policy of the church, connected indeed directly or indirectly with articles of faith or doctrine, but mutable, adapted to times and circumstances. Matters of doctrine are those truths which God has revealed, which all are bound to believe, immutable, received at all times and in all places. Do you not perceive, Sir, an immense difference which even Dr. Broughton might have condescended to notice ? He might, Sir. And instead of producing an unauthoritative regulation respecting the perusal of the scripture, he might at once have go to the fountain head and drawn from the council itself the catholic doctrine on this important subject. But as the writer of the address observes, "there is a meaning in these proceedings." Our doctrine is contained in the following decree of the fourth session of the council and in truth published by its order. The council—to curb the petulance of certain dispositions—defines, that on questions of faith and morals appertaining to the edification of christian doctrine, no one relying on his own discretion *pervert* the scriptures to his own meaning in opposition to that sense which our Holy Mother the church, to whom it belongs to judge of the true sense and interpretation of the scriptures, has held and doth hold, or presume to give an interpretation of the sacred text, contrary to the unanimous consent of the fathers. This is a decree of the catholic church : in this we avow our firm belief. To this we submit. Has she thereby prohibited the reading of the scriptures ? So far from prohibiting the perusal of the scriptures—the definition contained in this decree of the council is grounded on the fact of perusal—since abuse necessarily implies the power to use. It admonishes the faithful, lest in such perusal they may be led astray by their own fancies to destruction. No one is to presume to read them with a view of deriving from them articles of faith at variance with the doctrine "once delivered to the saints" and handed down by the church, the attested witness of their truth, to our times, either in the original languages or in copies authorised by her: she exhorts her children to read the scriptures in the spirit of humility and of piety, to apply to their own personal improvement its precepts of wisdom, its examples of charity, its counsels of perfection,—that thus they may become more conformable to our Divine Model Jesus Christ, our most blessed Lord. But she warns her children to repress the spirit of pride and presumption—not to be wiser than it behoveth to be, not to be deluded, by the wicked enemy whose advice is destruction, into conceited thoughts and vain imaginings, to set up individual judgment in opposition to the sense in which the books of God have been read by the fathers of the first ages of the church, which sense is embodied in the creed, liturgy, and prayers, which unite her children at all times and all places as one, in accomplishment of the prayer of Him who prayed that His people might be one, even as He and the Father. Thus is it now, thus it has always been, with those who are gone before, with those who are still in the mortal body, age preceding age, as wave precedes wave, till we come into the very source whence emanates the stream of eternal incorruptible truth. In this spirit the venerable pontiff, Pius the VI. in 1778, wrote to the Archbishop of Florence, to express his gratification

er of bad books were in circula-
ed by him to the reading of Holy
bled to read them more usefully
e sacred writings with judicious
the catholic bishops in England,
arnestly exhorts them to confirm
e in piety and virtue, and for that
pious books, but especially the
ns approved by ecclesiastical
prelates in their declarations of
e year 1829, state, "that the
den nor discouraged the reading
of the sacred scriptures in the
tions into modern languages, the
e shall be put into the hands of
acknowledged by ecclesiastical
onformable to the sense of the
e, that there never was a general
ibiting the reading of authorised
low correctly Dr. Broughton has
pecting the use of the scriptures
acular languages, is a conclusion
ratification than I may express.
ermit me to record the astonish-
l in page 22 of the address, that
of the Church of England, in the
her doctrine, on the ground that
a stand, "gave to them all the
nguage, yes, to you all." Again,
to the Church of England for
hat language." If this statement
plendide mendax. But possibly
ch of England has provided the
s to read the scriptures. In this
s own experience, and answer to

pe, a single civilized nation in
e national language had not been
ngland, as at present constituted,
England, there were many Anglo-
both of the   New Testa-
Sir Thoma   Lib.
es, " was b⸺
tongue

people with devotion and soberness well and reverently read." Mr. C. Butler, who has written his reply on this subject states, that he numbered in one bookseller's list alone, twenty-two different editions of the whole Bible or New Testament which had been published by the English catholics since the period of the Reformation. Sed Eheu! satis. For the sake of peace and of those well-meaning persons to whom I have before alluded, I rejoice that in her theory, at least, the doctrine of the Church of England respecting the free use of the scriptures, more closely approximates that of the catholic church as before detailed, than is stated by Dr. Broughton, and this I propose to discuss and demonstrate in my next letter.

I have the honor to be, Sir, &c., &c.,
CATHOLICUS IPSE.

_____

To the Editor of the Australian.

SIR,—Having shown in my last that Dr. Broughton had not given a correct statement of the doctrine of the Council of Trent, respecting the use of the scriptures, I shall now proceed to demonstrate that the doctrine of the Church of England on this subject approximates more closely to the doctrine of the Roman Catholic Church than might be supposed from the statement of the Protestant Bishop of Australia.

In the first struggles for change, civil or religious, the cry of liberty is raised loudly, and the abstract individual rights of man are asserted strongly. There is an object to be gained. Flatter the pride of man and he instantly becomes the instrument of his own subjugation. When that change has been brought about, and the transfer of power has been accomplished, a return to those principles of subordination and of restriction, the experience of ages has proved to be essential to the well being of society, is made invariably. Thus at the period of the boasted reformation, authority in matters of faith was denounced as intolerable despotism—the pages of the Bible were refused to those who could read and those who could not—the pride of the learned and the unlearned alike, welcomed the assurance that faith was to be the result of each one's interpretation of the word of God. The right of private judgment was the powerful lever used to wrest asunder the bond of catholic unity—and the alarming effects were soon visible. A monster, it was perceived, had been created that strode the land, east and west—anarchy rejoicing in its footsteps. They whom it had enthroned in the high places beheld the spread of ruin with dismay. They trembled for their own safety—parricide in itself became a virtue and protestants strove to annihilate the parent of protestantism. "The free use of the scriptures is each one's birth right." Thus exclaimed Luther, as he headed revolt against the church of God, and by the way of commentary he insisted upon his catechism being adopted, and denounced Zuinglius as an abettor of diabolical opinions, from presuming to use the scriptures in a sense different to his own exposition. Thus exclaimed Calvin too: but when he became supreme in Geneva, Servetus and others had to choose between the faggot and Calvin's interpretation of the scripture.

Thus also repeated our eighth Henry, having placed the tiara on his crown he sent forth his knightly pontifical degree, that his subjects should not presume to expound or take arguments from the scripture—*Burnet lib. 3.*—and indeed he had before given them to understand, that "whereas there were some teachers whose office it was to instruct the people, so the rest ought to be taught, and to those it was not necessary to read the scriptures, and that therefore he had restrained it from a great many, esteeming it sufficient for such to hear the doctrine of the scriptures taught by their preachers."

The same ambitious spirit which went forth at the commencement of the reformation has been abroad in this colony—accommodated however to circumstances. Now there is an object not to be gained, but to be retained within exclusive dominion. The church, heretofore dominant, has fallen from her lofty bearing; or rather a just and prudent hand, by placing all denominations of the christian religion on a level,—has filled up the iniquitous chasms which belted her as something sovereignly to be distinguished—into which she would have fallen. Let them stand or crumble away according to their deserving before God and man. No church founded in truth can perish under this fair state of things. No system of education which leaves the mind unbiassed and the communication between the pastors and pupil free and uncontrolled, can offer detriment for her well being. Yet the senseless cry of "the church is in danger," has been raised. I protest, I could not—could not remain a member of any church that required seclusion for the wholesome expansion of her tenets, or that could be endangered by any cause, save the physical destruction of its members. Can man destroy the work of God? The question approaches blasphemy; all, however are not of my opinion. Has   led to obtain favourable suffrages for the Churcl   " for that system of education which has thousands of public money, under the administration of the Church of England? and, alas! like the lean Kine of Pharoah, without becoming proportionately beautiful and well conditioned. Hence the supplications and petitions—hence the vulgar denunciations of the system, and the witless sarcasms, as if any thing good could come from Ireland; hence the prejudices excited on the score of religion, fostered and cherished—and furnished with a place to rest upon in the solemn warning of the bishop of Australia—that the fundamental principle of protestantism is about to be destroyed, and the fear of the foolish, and dreams of the ignorant have ample scope and verge enough in the appalling contrast between the free use of the Bible allowed the protestant—denied the catholic—a contrast founded, as we have seen, on grievous mis-representation. And why all this? There is a chance of detaining influence and at a venture it is grasped at; why this? Not that the fundamental principle of protestantism is in greater danger than it has been since the Church of England form of worship ruled dominant in the colony—as we shall presently see; but because, under the new system of education, truth and charity will occupy the ground hitherto cumbered by prejudice and sectarian exclusiveness. And this is becoming manifest to those who in their simplicity surrendered their judgment to the outcry. That outcry summoned all under the protestant name to the defence of their principles. "The free use of the Bible is endangered—it is to be taken away," exclaims Bishop Broughton, and the according response, so loud and general at first, has now died away to a lady's whisper.

But when I hear from the lips of Dr. Broughton, "that the free use of the scripture belongs to all who have souls to be saved," I do not forget he is chief dignitary of the Church of England form of worship in this colony, suffragan to the Archbishop of Canterbury, deriving ecclesiastical power from his ordination in that church, and a sworn observer of the thirty-nine articles of the Church of England. To whatever purpose, therefore, the Bishop of Australia uses the maxims above quoted, they receive their modification from that form of the protestant religion of which he is the colonial head. Now I think it will not be difficult to show, that the maxim which is so loudly proclaimed from the portals of the Church of England has been most carefully excluded from her precincts.

As regards the burden of authority in reference to the free use of the scriptures, which the great body of protestant dissenters regards with equal disdain, whether imposed by the hand of Canterbury or Rome; the right to impose it is claimed and exercised by the church of England with as much pertinacity and imperiousness of dominion, as may be found in the canons of the catholic church, which openly and honestly avows that right to have been deposited with her especially and inalienably. In proof, I shall not cite laws nor regulations, partial in extent and inoperative—disowned to be the canons of the church of England; we will appeal at once to the thirty-nine articles agreed upon by the archbishop and the whole clergy in convocation assembled; and solemnly confirmed by the king.—Art. 20. "The church has power to decree rites or ceremonies, and authority in controversies of faith; and yet it is not lawful for the church *to ordain* anything that is contrary to God's word written; neither may it expound one place of scripture that is repugnant to another. Wherefore though the church be a witness and keeper of Holy writ, yet as it ought not to decree anything against the same, so besides the same ought it not to enforce anything to be believed for necessity of salvation." * Here the church claims not only the power of regulating the ceremonial of religion—but also authority in determining controversies of faith, of expounding scripture and enforcing points of necessary belief, provided her decrees, her ordinances, and enforcements be agreeable to Holy writ as expounded by herself; but so expounded that no part be repugnant to another. Who is to judge of the discrepancy or the accordance? The appellant? To what purpose then the appeal? The scripture? This would be an appeal from the tribunal *de dernier ressort* constituted to determine; from the chancellor of the court to the equity he administers. The church declares herself the arbiter of controversies and the interpreter of scripture. Her judgment is set up and private judgment disallowed; for the church claims a right of enforcing her judgment, and if her judgment is to be enforced, what more is left for private judgment on doctrinal points? What becomes of the free use of scripture? If the individual understands the scriptural passages different from the church, and desires a different doctrine, he is called upon to suppress or renounce his own opinion and submit to authority. If he should refuse, then he is liable to be cast out of the society of faithful men, "as a heathen and publican;" so the visible church of God is defined by the nineteenth article, in the which it is declared the "pure word of God is preached and the sacraments duly administered."

---

* On what grounds of scripture does the Church of England prove the lawfulness or validity of infant baptism? the lawfulness of working on the Saturday, the Jewish sabbath; the abrogation of command to abstain from things strangled and from blood.—Acts 15, v. 29.

H

And the church of England has not only claimed, but exercised this authority in a manner the most ample. Read the thirty-nine articles: has she not declared her judgment upon, and interpreted the word of God on subjects of, mysteries, of sacraments, of truths, practical, and speculative? Has she not made a terrible inroad on private judgment, by proclaiming on her own authority the exact number of inspired books? Farewell, original sin, justification and predestination; all are determined by her in a manner intended to be most precise, whatever may be our opinion of their theological accuracy. In a word she gives a summary of christian belief, grounded on her own exposition of scripture. This is authoritatively required to be adopted, because it is either read in scriptures or may be proved by it. Who declares this? The Church of England. Thus the interpretation of the Bible by private judgment is completely interdicted on every vital point of religious belief.

Nor let it be supposed, sir, that these articles bind only the clergy and not the laity. Read the declaration prefixed to the thirty-nine articles; the preamble states that the object of the articles is to preserve the church in the *unity* of religion, not to suffer unnecessary *disputations, altercations, or questions to be raised.* The declaration itself has these decisive words: "We require all our loving subjects to continue the uniform profession thereof, and prohibit the least difference in the said articles."

And let it be further observed, that the entrammelling effects of the church of England's authority not only restricted the free use of the bible, but the free use of the limbs also. In 1551 it was enacted, "that all should resort where the book of common prayer was used under pain of church censure. If he be present under any other form of prayer he shall suffer imprisonment for life." .In 1558 it was enacted, "that any minister refusing to use the book of common prayer, or using any other rites or ceremonies, but what are set down in the said book, shall forfeit his benefice or be imprisoned for twelve months; on third conviction be imprisoned for life." I mention these enactments in no invidious sectarian spirit, nor to revive the remembrance of times and grievances I could wish to be obliterated from history, but to show that the authority, which as Supreme Governor of the church, ratified and confirmed the thirty-nine articles of the church of England, did in good earnest intend all liege subjects to abide by them. I think, Sir, it is sufficiently evident, that the church which Dr. Broughton acknowledges to be his mother, has appointed herself the judge of the true sense and interpretation of the scripture—that she has exercised that right and fenced about her prerogative with statutes cogent enough to obtain respect to its exercise, if not conviction to its consistency, with the boasted principle of the reformation. Now we will see what rule she has appointed, in order that her ministry may be directed to give the right interpretation of God's word to the people. I observe the rule was made and given to the clergy in the year 1571 by the convocation, the same year in which the thirty-nine articles, drawn up in the year 1562, were revised by convocation and confirmed by Act of Parliament.—*Canon de concion :* "Let them take care that they never teach anything which they would have the people to hold and believe, but what is agreeable to the old and new testament and which the catholic fathers and ancient bishops had collected from that very doctrine." It then declares such doctrine to be contained in the articles on Liturgy, and then concludes, "whoever shall be otherwise and disturb the people by contrary doctrines shall be excommunicated." "By this rule," says Dr. Brett on tradition, "I take it that all preachers are obliged to interpret the scriptures, not according to their own fancies, but according to the consentient tradition of the primitive and catholic fathers of the first ages of the christian church." Now sir, let me ask, where is the diametrical opposition Dr. Broughton good-naturedly informed us, was known to exist between the protestant and catholic rules in the free use of the scriptures ? Alas ! with the benefit of the information given, we are not much wiser on the subject. What becomes of the free use of the scriptures according to the protestantism of the church of England ? Verily, verily, Messieurs of dissent, I think it behoves you to be quite as wary in steering your barque of bible-use clear of the ecclesiastic institutions of comparatively modern date, as you doubtlessly are to keep clear of the ancient rock of Peter's orthodoxy. The former are most certainly quite as fatal to its existence as the latter.

In the commencement of this examination into the difference between the catholic and protestant rules respecting the use of the scriptures, I placed in juxtaposition the two rules stated by Dr. Broughton to be diametrically opposite. I am unable to discover the elements of opposition. I will conclude this letter by the juxtaposition of two rules respecting the free use of scripture, which I humbly conceive not to be substantially discordant—the one taken from the Council of Trent, the other from the articles and canons of the church of England.

Catholic Rule respecting the use and interpretation of the Bible.

Council of Trent, Sess. 4th.

The Council of Trent defines that on questions of faith and morals, appertaining to the edification of christian doctrine, no one relying on his own discretion, perverting the scripture to his own meaning, in opposition to that sense which our Holy Mother, the Church, to whom it belongs to judge of the true sense and interpretation of the scriptures, has held and doth hold, shall presume to give an interpretation of the sacred text contrary to the unanimous consent of the fathers.

Protestant Rule of the Church of England for the same.

The church hath power to decree rites, or ceremonies, and authority in controversies of faith. Art. 20, D. Concion. 1571, Canon 5. Let them take care that they (the clergy) never teach anything which they would have the people to hold and believe, but what is agreeable to the Old and New Testament, and which the catholic fathers and ancient bishops had collected from that very doctrine. Whoever shall do otherwise and disturb the people by contrary doctrine shall be excommunicated.

Surely the laity are not allowed a wider latitude in the exposition of the scripture than the clergy ?

Thus, it appears, the diametrical opposition between the doctrine of the two churches, on the most important subject, proves to be nearly a coincidence.

Would to God that all religious differences might thus terminate.

I have the honor to be, Sir,
Your most obedient servant,
CATHOLICUS IPSE.

CORRESPONDENCE.

(*To the Editor of the Australian.*)

Sir,—A letter appeared in the columns of the *Herald* animadverting on the lucubrations of " Catholicus Ipse." Its natural tendency to sink beneath the surface has been arrested by the friendly hand of the " Colonist." From this circumstance it may be supposed to contain a statement of some importance, how correctly the following observation will show :—

I pass by the preliminary surmises respecting " Catholicus Ipse," conceiving them to be of very little consequence, either to him or to the public.

The object of the writer is introduced by a certain query and wonderment it was not answered before. Why did not " Catholicus Ipse " cite the observation of Leo XII. on the Bible Societies ? For two obvious reasons : 1st.—The decree of the Council of Trent, to which allusion is made, has been cited as the foundation of the argument and the exposition of catholic belief : it was unnecessary therefore to repeat it. 2nd.—Because the observations of Leo XII. referred to the exceptions from the general rule respecting the use of the scriptures, which rule was the subject of discussion ; and therefore the observations were deemed irrelevant. But since " Colonist " has opened this subject of the Bible Society, and its translations into various languages,—and since the quotation from Leo XII. has doubtless caused numbers of pious ladies, of a certain age, to raise their eyes to heaven and ejaculate many devout sayings respecting the said very irreverent observations, I will cite for their further edification the judgment on this Society passed by other witnesses, perhaps more competent to give evidence respecting the mischievous effects produced by it than even Leo XII.:—"Surely it is enough to make the christian's blood run cold to think of the sacrilegious presumption of a society which has thus dared to trample and trifle with the revelation of the Almighty ; and dares to publish to the heathen, and attempts to foist upon its credulous supporters those schoolboy exercises of its agents as the sacred word of God. It is the circulation of such translations as these, that more than once at the meetings of the society have been blasphemously compared to the miraculous gifts of tongues. And such a system is supported and such comparisons applauded by many who on other occasions lay claims, and justly, to characters of piety and intelligence." Appendix to reasons why I am not a member of the Bible Society, by the Hon. and Rev. Phil. Arth. Percival, chaplain in ordinary to Her Majesty. Now for a sample of the doings of the Society. The Welsh translation was so incorrect that no use could be made of it. The Turkish, Dr. Henderson owns to be incapable of defence. The modern Greek was written in such a strange language that it could not be understood. In November, 1822, the Irish Society passed the following condemnatory resolution on the Irish translation of the British and Foreign Bible Society. "Resolved, that after a full enquiry, the members of this Society feel satisfied that material and very numerous errors exist in the version of the New Testament edited by the British and Foreign Bible Society." "With the exception," say the quarterly reviewers, "of three or four individuals, not one of those who have been employed, under the auspices of the British and Foreign Bible Society, either in translatingdor editing the scriptures, has received the benefit of a regular an learned education; whence their existing versions will be remembered hereafter only for the errors and blunders which disfigure them. It has even," they said, "been openly and repeatedly asserted, that amongst the foremost of the Society's continental supporters appear many individuals notorious for entertaining heretical or infidel opinions, whence the persons in question have succeeded in making serious innovations in the received versions." "With truth, Sir," Pope Leo observed, "there is just ground to fear, that in all the translations it will be discovered, as it has been found in those already examined, that, by bad translation, it has been found to be, instead of the Gospel of Christ, the gospel of men—or rather that which is worse, the gospel of devils." Now in this apprehension, and in this censure, the Sovereign Pontiff is in the company of the high church gentlemen of the Quarterly Review, and of other most staunch protestants. Of the eighty-nine new translations of the scripture there is not so much as one even tolerably accurate.—"Whence their existing versions (of the Bible Society) will be remembered hereafter only for the errors and blunders which disfigure them." And those are the writings, it is expected, the catholic church will acknowledge to be the inspired word of God, and recommend as such to the perusal of her children! Thus, Sir, in the language of Dr. Doyle, "the types sweat, the press teems,—vessels are freighted for this Society. It drives an immense trade, profitable no doubt to many, in Bibles and missionaries. Fortunes are made for the printers and booksellers, secretaries, and functionaries, and agents, and pawnbrokers: these be they to whom the Society is indeed of profit. In the meanwhile has the Society converted a single tribe or native to the faith? No, not one—and what is more, it is improbable they ever should." Excuse the parenthetical observation. Now Sir, we will take a view of the translations which had preceded the translations of the Bible Society. To begin with that of Luther—the foremost man of the reformation— he translated the scriptures. Let us have the testimony of his brother reformer, Zuinglius, respecting this translation. He stigmatizes him as a foul corrupter, and horrible falsifier of God's word—one who followed the Mareonites and Arians,—that he erased all such places of the Holy Scripture which were against him. In his New Testament alone not less than 1400 corruptions of the text were noted by Staphylus and Emserus. Not only did this man, who is said to have been deputed of God to reform the world, thus reform God's sacred word according to his own fancy, but he falsified the text also. Impartial justice to the entire exclusion of good works, is the fundamental principle of Luther's theology. Not only did he reject the epistle of St. James, which destroys this most dangerous tenet, profanely terming it a " chaffy production unworthy of an apostle," but to have a direct proof from scripture he inserted the word *alone* in the text of St. Paul in Romans iii, 28 :—We account a man to be justified by faith *alone*, without the works of the law. Accused of this presumptuous innovation on the inspired word, hear his defence :—*Sic volo, sic jubeo*—so I will, so I command. " Let my will be instead of reason, Luther will have it so. The word *alone* must remain in my testament. Although all the papists should run mad, they shall not take it thence. It grieves me, I did not also add those other two words, omnibus and omnium,— without all works of all laws." Zuinglius gave also his trans- lation of the New Testament. As Luther had introduced the word alone into the Epistle of St. Paul—to justify his doctrine of impartial justice, so Zuinglius inserted a word to meet his new idea of the figurative presence in the Holy Sacrament. The words St. Matt. xxiv, 26,—this is my body, hoc est corpus meum,—he translated "this signifies my body." Whereupon Luther returned the civilities of Zuinglius by rejecting his translation, calling him and his divines fools, asses, anti-christs, and deceivers. Calvin of course had his translation ; of its merits the learned Molinus speaks thus,—"Calvin in his harmony makes the text of the gospel to leap up and down. He uses violence to the letter of the gospel and besides this adds to the text—in *sua translat*. New Testament, Art. 12. And the translations of such men, for- sooth, we are invited to receive as the inspired word of God !— So far for the foreign translations. We will now turn our atten- tion to the translations into the English language.

I shall pass by that of Tyndal in the time of Henry VIII.—in the new testament alone two thousand corruptions were noted by Bishop Tunstal. Then we have Cranmer's Bible in 1546—the Geneva Bible of 1557 and 1560, and the Bible emphatically called the Bishop's Bible in 1572, and in many other editions. Now this translation was approved and authorized by the same powers, spiritual and secular, that gave authority to the present authorized version of the Church of England, which authority, it is insinuated, catholics ought to respect. In this translation the word church is supplemented by the word congregation—for idols, images are substituted—for traditions, ordinances. I need not observe there was a meaning in these proceedings. Lest, however, it may be supposed that the catholic eye is prejudiced, we will receive the testimonies of protestant authorities on the corrupt state of these translations. In an abridgement presented by the ministers of the diocese of Lincoln to King James, they denominate the English translation "a translation which taketh away from the text, that addeth to the text, a translation which is absurd and senseless, perverting in many places the meaning of the Holy Ghost." Mr. Broughton in his letter to the Lords of the Council stigmatizes the English translation as "full of errors." And in his advertisement of corruptions he plainly tells the bishops, "that their public translation of the scriptures into English is such that it perverts the text of the old testament in *eight hundred and forty-eight places*, and that it causes millions and millions to reject the new testament and to run into eternal flames." This Mr. Broughton, it is remarked, was one of the more zealous sort of protestants. King James, the royal divine, complained that he never saw a Bible well translated into English—as for the Geneva Bible, he pronounced that the worst of all. The character of these English protestant translations is thus described by a modern writer of eminence, D'Israeli. "Our English Bibles were suffered to be so corrupted that no books ever swarmed with such innumerable *errata*. These errata were in great part voluntary omissions, interpolated passages, reformed and forged for certain purposes."—Or as Dr. Broughton would say:—"There was a meaning in these proceedings." I think, sir, painful though it may be, "Colonist" will acknowledge that Leo XII. had just cause for the censure and caution expressed in the adduced extract. Respecting the present authorized version of the Church of England, I shall only observe that the authority which has sanctioned it, sanctioned the translations on which the severe censures I have quoted were passed—I will not draw the obvious conclusion. When the translation of the scriptures by the rev. missionaries to our aborigines is completed, we may perhaps be called upon to receive it also as the inspired word of God, together with the versions for the use of the Boothians and other Esquimaux. In the meantime "Colonist" may derive comfort from the sentiments expressed by Dr. Norris in his letter to Lord Liverpool.—" We conscientiously believe the Bible Society to be fraught with danger not only to our own church, but to the best interests of christian truth and unity throughout the world." "The current of public opinion," says Rev. Mr Callaghan, "has already set in against the established church; and the Bible Society, whether the prelates will see it or not, is unquestionably converted into an engine for its destruction." Bishop Marsh expresses a similar opinion—see inquiry p. 61. "The Socinians," observes the British critic, "are so convinced that the tendency of the Bible Society is hostile to the church, that they are unwilling, even though it circulates the authorized version of the scripture, to give their support."

Thus, sir, by protestant authorities are proved and confirmed the observations of Pope Leo XII., respecting the tendency of the Bible Society and its false and corrupt and school-boy translations. His past and emphatic denunciations of scriptures perverted to deceive and destroy, are founded on good sense and experience. The Bible delivered to her children by the church of God, and accredited by her authority to be the inspired volume of the divine revelation, ought to be received with veneration, read with reverence and humility not to be expressed; and deposited, when not in use, in an ark of cedar lined with gold. That which men or any set of men, not having authority from God, or not authorized by those having authority from Him, have sent, can only be received as the word of man. That translation which has knowingly perverted the sense of the original, and is sent forth to the world as the word of God, whereas it is man's own word corrupted to their own purposes, merits contempt as a vile imposture and is treated with too much honor when conveyed with a pair of tongs into a hole made for its reception, after the manner of the poor peasant mentioned by J. K. L., on whose devoted head the pious and gentle of the Bible Society have poured out so frequently their indignation.

I have the honor to be,
Sir,
Your most obedient servant,
CATHOLICUS IPSE.

PART II.

CHAPTER I.

*A great Protestant Meeting, held in the Pulteney Hotel, Sydney,
in the year 1836, in favour of the Denominational System of
Education.—An Account of the Foundation of Melbourne,
by Governor Bourke, in the year 1837.—The resignation of
Sir Richard Bourke, and the cause why he resigned.—The
Departure of the Governor.—The Address of Bishop Polding
and the Catholic Clergy to His Excellency before his departure,
and the Governor's Reply.*

By the passing of Sir Richard Bourke's Church Act, the
different principal religious denominations were placed upon an
equality before the Government, and aid was granted in proportion
to their numbers. At the same time Sir Richard Bourke was
most anxious to introduce, as the law of the land, a system of
Education which would not interfere with the religious views of
the different churches, and by which efficient help would be given
to all; and he was of opinion that Lord Stanley's system of
General Education, which had been lately established in Ireland,
would be admirably adapted for this purpose in the colony. The
measure of His Excellency, so justly and liberally conceived, by
no means met with the approval of some of the heads of the
religious bodies in the colony. The protestant bishop of the day,
Dr. Broughton, cried out loudly against it, and remonstrated by
sending a strong petition to His Excellency, to prevent Lord
Stanley's school system from becoming the law of the colony.
Besides, the non-conformists also sided with Bishop Broughton
against the system. A meeting was held in Sydney, on the 24th
of June, 1836, in the Pulteney Hotel. And this meeting was
presided over by Bishop Broughton, and there were represented
the Presbyterians, the Independents, the Baptists, and the
Wesleyans. They unamiously came to the four following resolutions. First, that this meeting having learned by official documents
recently published, that it is the intention of the Government to

propose the establishment in this colony, by an enactment of the local legislature, of a system of general education ; and that the schools introduced into Ireland a few years ago under the sanction of the British Government are thought to afford an appropriate model for that system, do unanimously express their decided opinion that any system of general education which shall be founded on the principle of interdicting, either wholly or in part, the use of the Holy Scriptures, according to the authorised version, and of prayer, in which the doctrine of the Blessed Trinity may be unequivocably acknowledged or implied, could not receive their countenance and support, *without a compromise of the essentials of their faith.* Second, that this meeting do now form itself into a committee of protestants, to be hereafter enlarged in numbers for the purposes of concerting measures to obtain the general co-operation of the protestant body throughout the colony of New South Wales, in petitioning His Excellency, the Governor, and the Honorable, the Legislative Council, on the subject of the plan of general education, setting forth their objections to the basis on which the same is founded, as being according to their conscientious conviction, *subversive to the fundamental principles of protestantism*, and, they are pursuaded, opposed also to the wishes of a very large majority of the people of this community. Third, that the petition now produced be adopted by this meeting, and signed by the members present. Fourth, that for the more effectual fulfilment of this purpose, a general committee be formed, to consist, in addition to the individuals here present, of all the protestant ministers having charge of congregations in Sydney, and of twenty-four protestant laymen resident in Sydney, or the vicinity thereof, of whom twelve shall be episcopalians, and twelve members of other protestant denominations ; and of this general committee any seven duly convened shall form a quorum. That they shall have power to fill up vacancies on the principle of the aforesaid proposition, and that the following ministers and laymen be requested to constitute such committee :—(*Signed*) The Right Reverend, The Bishop of Australia ; George Allen, Esq. ; Charles Campbell, Esq. ; Reverend William Cowper ; Prosper De Mestre, Esq. ; Reverend J. D. Lang, in all thirty-six.

Dr. Broughton, the protestant bishop, in his speech delivered at the Pulteney Hotel, on the 3rd of August, 1836, made some very extravagant assertions and misstatements ; for which Bishop Polding brought him to account in a series of letters, with the signature of " Catholicus Ipse." Which letters are inserted at the end of the first part. Dr. Broughton in those letters is taken to task, in a very able manner, for having asserted that the catholics of the colony only numbered 16,000, whereas by the census of 1833, their numbers were 17,200, and that instead of the catholic children only numbering 1600, within the four previous years more than 1600 catholic children had been baptized. He showed also how Dr. Broughton had misrepresented the doctrine of the catholic church, as defined by the Council of Trent, in respect to the reading of the scriptures ; and he explained his own views on the vexed question of the fitness of the system of general education proposed to be introduced into the colony by the Governor, Sir Richard Bourke. These letters show how vigorous was the mind of the gifted prelate at that time, and how capable he was of defending the dogmas of the catholic faith, and protecting the interests of that portion of the church which had been committed to his care.

It will not be irrelevant to my subject, having arrived at this time in my history, to give a brief acccount of the foundation of Melbourne, which rose so rapidly into importance and became the rival of Sydney ; and, on account of the sudden increase of the catholic population, required that it should be recommended by Bishop Polding to the Holy See, to be erected into a Bishopric.

The origin of Port Philip as a settlement, with its capital Melbourne, began in this way : The port and surrounding district were discovered by Captain Cook, when he surveyed the coast in his good ship the "Endeavour," so far back as the year 1770. From the accounts of those who visited the district from Sydney and Van Dieman's Land, it soon attracted notice on account of the capacious port, the richness of the soil, the picturesqueness of the scenery, and above all its admirable adaptability for cattle stations. The spirit of enterprise was very strong in those days, and many ambitioned to heap up wealth, by being shepherd kings, *alias* squatters. Several attempts in the beginning were made by private individuals to form settlements in Australia Felix, but failed. Messrs. Hume and Hovel travelled across the country from Sydney to the shores of Port Philip in the year 1824 ; but the first permanent settlement is said to have been made by Mr. Edward Henty, who landed at Portland Bay, to the south of Port Philip, and formed there a whaling station in the year 1834. A Mr. John Batman, although it seems more for his own private interests than the public good, bargained with the natives for land, and his first sheep station was where St. James' Cathedral now stands, in which place he had a shepherd's hut. He subsequently brought his wife and family from Van Diemen's Land, built a house on the western side of the part which is now Collins-street, and opened a general store. The New South Wales Government would not recognize the bargain which Mr. Batman and others had made with the natives. Sir Richard Bourke, Governor of New South Wales, issued a proclamation notifying that every treaty, bargain, and contract with the aboriginal natives for the possession, title, or claim to any crown lands within New South Wales is void, as against the rights of the crown; and that all persons found in possession of any such lands without license or authority from His Majesty's Government first had and obtained for such purpose, would be considered as trespassers.

Sir Richard Bourke in his dispatch to Lord Glenelg, stated that in consideration of the capital expended by Mr. Batman and his associates, he was inclined to recommend an early occupation of Port Philip. Mr. Batman had been negotiating with Governor Arthur of Van Dieman's Land for the acquisition of no less a quantity of land than 600,000 acres, and that in the vicinity of Port Philip; but Lord Glenelg in reply to a dispatch of Governor Arthur, July 4, 1835, checked the ambitious career of Mr. Batman and his associates, and said:—"That all schemes for making settlements by private individuals or companies in the unlocated districts of Australia, have of late years been discouraged by His Majesty's Government, as leading to fresh establishments involving the mother country in an indefinite expense, and exposing both the natives and new settlers to many dangers and calamities. And there is so much of prudence and of justice, and I think I may add of humanity in this policy, that I do not feel disposed to depart from it in the present instance."

There can be no question but that His Excellency Sir Richard Bourke, with the concurrence of Lord Glenelg, was the real founder of the Colony of Victoria, and but for his exertions and promptness, Melbourne would be now very small in all probability and surrounded in its immediate vicinity with cattle stations and sheep walks.

It was on the 4th March, 1837, that Governor Sir Richard Bourke landed on the banks of the Yarra Yarra, from H.M. ship "Rattlesnake" with Captain Hobson, R.N., for the purpose of founding the colony. He was accompanied by Captain Hunter, the military secretary; George Kenyon Holden, Esq., his private secretary; Captain P. P. King, as his travelling companion; and Mr. Robert Hoddle, surveyor in charge. His Excellency fixed the site for a township and called it Melbourne, after the then Prime Minister. The town of Melbourne was laid out by Mr. Hoddle. The principal streets were measured 99 feet.

wide. Collins-street was named after Lieutenant Governor Collins; Flinders-street after Captain Flinders; Bourke-street after Governor Bourke; Lonsdale-street after Captain Lonsdale; Swanston-street after Captain Swanston; and Russel-street after Lord John Russel. Governor Bourke then visited Mount Macedon and Geelong; he named Geelong after the native name of the hill on which Geelong is built. Hobson's Bay was named by the Governor after Captain Hobson, commander of H.M. ship the "Rattlesnake," which brought His Excellency to Port Philip. An address was presented to the Governor by the inhabitants before he left for Sydney, to which he made a suitable reply. The population then amounted to 600. During his stay three counties were marked out, viz.: Williams, Melbourne, and Geelong. During that short stay, not much more than a month, he accomplished a great deal and returned to Sydney, 7th April, 1837.

I have given this account of the foundation of Melbourne because I will often have to refer to it, when writing about affairs in connection with the church and its wonderful development in that part. Now, for the information of our friends in the northern hemisphere, who are so very apt to make mistakes as to our geographical positions in Australia, I will state that Melbourne is distant from Sydney about 500 miles to the south, lat. 37° 29′ 25″; east, longitude 144° 59′.

Before Governor Bourke went to Port Philip, he had tendered his resignation if Mr. Riddell, the colonial treasurer, were re-instated as a member of the executive council. He had removed him from his seat in the council, because he allowed himself to be nominated and elected chairman of the quarter sessions, at the instance of a hostile clique of magistrates, who had put him forward in opposition to Mr. Therry. This was an act of official impropriety on the part of Mr. Riddell and for which he deserved to be removed from his seat in the executive council which he held by virtue of his official position, which the Governor could not condone. A dispatch came from Lord Glenelg, which restored Mr. Riddle to his seat in the executive council, on the grounds that suspension for one year was sufficient punishment for his indiscretion. Another dispatch arrived shortly after urging the Governor not to carry out his resolution; but Sir Richard Bourke declined to sit with Mr. Riddell and consequently made preparations to leave the colony.

A public meeting was convened in Sydney, to devise measures to present the Governor with a suitable valedictory address; Mr. C. Wentworth was the principal speaker on this occasion; an address was agreed to by the meeting, and in due time presented. In this address the colonists and citizens of Sydney acknowledged the reforms, useful regulations, and works of the greatest public utility begun and completed by His Excellency : but the people in general were not content with this customary tribute of respect to a departing Governor, whom they held in the highest estimation, they would further testify their appreciation of the great good he had done to the colony, by determining to erect a statue to his memory. At the same meeting £680 were collected for this purpose ; and, not long after the departure of Sir Richard Bourke, his statue of bronze was erected in the Inner Domain of the Government House. The statue is raised on a pedestal of granite, on the base of which is inscribed an account of those services performed by him, which entitle him to the everlasting remembrance of the colonists.

I here transcribe this tribute to his worth :—" This statue of Lieutenant-General Sir Richard Bourke, K.C.B., is erected by the people of New South Wales, to record his able, honest, and benevolent administration from 1831 to 1837. Selected for the Government at a period of singular difficulty, his judgment, urbanity, and firmness, justified the choice. Comprehending at once the vast resources peculiar to this colony, he applied them for the first time systematically to its benefit. He voluntarily divested himself of the prodigious influence arising from the assignment of penal labour, and enacted great and salutary laws for the amelioration of penal discipline. He was the first Governor who published satisfactory accounts of the public receipts and expenditure. Without oppression or detriment to any interest, he raised the revenue to a vast amount, and from its surplus realised extensive plans of emigration. He established religious equality on a just and firm basis, and sought to provide for all, without distinction of sect, a sound and adequate system of national education. He constructed various public works of permanent utility. He founded the flourishing settlement of Port Philip, and threw open the wilds of Australia to pastoral enterprise. He established Savings Banks, and was the patron of the first Mechanics Institute. He created an equitable tribunal for determining upon claims to grants of land. He was the warm friend of the liberty of the press. He extended trial by jury after its almost total suspension for many years. By these and numerous other measures, for the moral, religious, and general improvement of all classes, he raised the colony to an unexampled prosperity, and retired amid the fervent and affectionate regret of the people, having won their confidence by his integrity, their gratitude by his services, their admiration by his public talents, and their esteem by his private worth."

The following address was presented by the Right Reverend Dr. Polding and his clergy to Sir Richard Bourke, shortly before his departure from the colony.

The Roman Catholic Bishop and Clergy to His Excellency Lieutenant Sir Richard Bourke, K.C.B., commanding Her Majesty's Forces in, and Governor of, New South Wales, &c., &c., &c.

We, the Roman Catholic Bishop and Clergy of New Holland, feel it our duty to express to your Excellency on the eve of your retiring from the administration of colonial government our sense of the moral and political benefits conferred by you on this portion of the British Empire.

While we give expression to the admiration and gratitude with which we contemplate the advantages derived by this country from your wise and impartial administration, it becomes our sacred profession, and the position we hold amongst our fellow colonists, more particularly to allude to those acts which have fallen under our episcopal observation. The solicitude you have evinced to establish on its proper basis general good, and in particular exigencies, the assistance which the state is to give to religious forms of belief, deserves to be mentioned with the highest respect; in a society so peculiarly constructed, assistance on the part of the state appears just and reasonable and not less so that it should be administered in proportion to the number of its component parts, you have adopted that happy medium which is the best and fittest for the wants of the colony. Total support would nurture internal weakness and helplessness, the total abstraction of aid would bring the zeal and efforts of individuals to abortive decay.

Consistent with those principles of even-handed justice you have so distinctly laid down and acted upon in your numerous legislative enactments and minutes, Your Excellency has shown respect for the rights of conscience, even in the infant. Perhaps no measure according to its extent has been productive of more gratification than the institution for the support of our destitute children. You have allayed the heart-burning with which a numerous class beheld the orphan deprived of its sole inheritance, the faith of its fathers. The mother is no longer borne down under the weight of her toil, by the afflicting reflection that her offspring is even then purchasing food and raiment at a price compared to which life is by her deemed valueless, that alienated from her in affection, and abhorrent of her creed, the meeting of child and parent is unnaturally shunned.

We have to express our thanks for the urbanity of manner, courteous attention, and prompt decision with which our official communications have been received and conducted, and in general for the cordial co-operation we have received from your government in our efforts to promote the moral good of the inhabitants of the colony. We would refer, however, in a particular manner to that class which in proportion to its wants will be made the object of his first care by the christian legislator. We allude to the convict population, a class doomed to punishment, but not to despair; degraded, yet not to be cast away; emblem of man in his fallen state, to be reclaimed, amended, reformed, not in the sternness of unmitigated justice, which is of the heathen, but in mercy, the essence of the christian institute. We are not accustomed, sir, to speak the language of adulation, but rather to declare the truth in plainness of speech, and we do not hesitate to state on extensive experience that your humane regulations have produced in the convict population, under our pastoral care, results the most gratifying; their numbers have been annually increased to a considerable amount, yet crime has diminished; a healthy contentedness of mind, under the influence of religion, has generated a disposition to improve the adverse circumstances of their condition; a high moral purpose has succeeded a misanthropic sourness and gloomy despondency which heretofore rendered the convict careless and reckless. We mention this fact, for it proves the course you adopted and pursued, unawed by intimidation and undisturbed by clamour, has been instrumental in effecting a great practical good.

In retiring, sir, from this government you will bear with you not only the conviction that your measures, the emanations of a mind singularly comprehensive and benevolent, were intended and directed to promote the best interests of the colony, but proof of their success. The testimony of your own conscience, that in the administration of your high office you have never, either from favor or aversion, passed the bounds of equity, receives a faithful and applauding response wherever judgment has not been misled by party or warped by prejudice.

Yes sir! this colony owes you an immense debt of gratitude, accumulating as the progress of time and the spread of population shall more fully develop, and more severely test the excellence of your policy and the depth of your foresight, and that debt future generations will gladly own in the reverence and love with which your name will be enshrined in their breasts. Religious intolerance you have crushed — all the arts of peace you have encouraged—you have opened sources of blessing to the miserable, the healing waters of which are and will be for ages doing the work of God. No honors, no demonstration of grateful feeling can be equal to the satisfaction derived from a consciousness of having lived for a purpose so noble, so becoming the man, the christian, the legislator. May you live long to enjoy it, and to witness the prosperity of this colony, which will ever number your Excellency among its chief benefactors! With our best wishes, in deep regret and respect, we bid you farewell !

(Signed.)

> JOHN BEDE, Bishop
> JOHN JOSEPH THERRY,
> C. V. DOWLING,
> T. C. SUMNER,
> H. G. GREGORY,
> J. B. SPENCER.

[REPLY.]

I have much satisfaction in receiving this token of respect and attachment from the clergy of a communion which reckons within its pale a large proportion of the inhabitants of New South Wales. I have observed with great pleasure the exertions which, though few in number, you have made for the reforming and improving the character and conduct of the unhappy persons of your persuasion, who quit their country under the penal sentence of the law. To these exertions is to be attributed the peaceable and orderly behaviour which has latterly been observed to prevail among the Roman Catholic convicts.

Continue, gentlemen, to instil into their minds the love of God and of their neighbour, and be assured that in thus consulting their temporal and eternal interests, and in conferring an important service to the State, you best manifest the g ati u which I am convinced you entertain for the religous freedom which in common with other denominations of christians you have lately obtained.

(Signed) BOURKE, K.C.B.

Governor Bourke left the colony on 5th December, 1837. A large concourse accompanied him to the place of embarkation, including the clergy of the various denominations, the officials, and persons of every grade and class.

CHAPTER II.

The first Ordinations which took place in the Colony.—The departure of the Vicar-General Dr. Ullathorne, for Europe, to procure more priests.—Public meeting of the Catholics held in St. Mary's Cathedral to raise funds for the completion of the building.—The first Oratorio given in the Colony.—The commencement of St. Mary's Seminary.—The labours of Bishop Polding..—The accidental death of the Revd. J. V. Corcoran.—Laying of the Foundation Stone of St Mathew's Church, Windsor, 20th December, 1836.—The Ordination of Revd. H .G. Gregory, to the order of Priesthood, 17th March, 1837.—The Arrival of the Revd. Charles Lovat, who takes charge of St. Mary's Seminary.

NOW I will continue to recount the events and affairs more intimately connected with the church and the administration of the Right Revd. Dr. Polding. I have stated that Messrs. Sumner, Gregory, and Spencer were professed monks of the Order of St. Benedict when they came to the colony, in the year 1835, with Bishop Polding. They were prosecuting their theological studies, which they had commenced in the College of Downside, at Bath, during the voyage, and continued so after their arrival in the colony. On Sunday, 8th May, 1836, Messrs. Spencer and Gregory were promoted to the order of Deacon in St. Mary's Cathedral; and on the following Monday the Revd. C. Sumner was ordained priest. He was the first priest ordained in the colony. It was considered advisable for the Vicar-General, the Very Revd. Wm. Ullathorne, to proceed to Europe to procure more priests. He and Dr. Polding, the Bishop, sailed together for Hobart Town, on Tuesday, 10th May, the day after the ordination. They arrived safely at Hobart Town and Dr. Ullathorne took shipping there for England. Bishop Polding remained at Hobart Town to look after the interests of the church, and settle some matters about church land, but returned to Sydney by 4th June.

The Bishop was most anxious to see St. Mary's Cathedral completed; he published a pastoral on the subject, and called a public meeting of the Catholics, which was held in the Cathedral, on 10th July, 1836. The pastoral was read at the meeting, which strongly urged the Catholics to exert themselves by subscribing towards the completion of the Cathedral.

The Church Act, introduced by Sir R. Bourke, was passed on 29th July, 1836. The Revd. T. Watkins was appointed Vicar-General of Hobart Town, and sailed from Sydney for that place on 13th August, 1836. There had arisen a misunderstanding between the Bishop and Revd. P. Connolly; Father Connolly was superseded by the Vicar-General, Father Watkins.

The first oratorio given in Australia took place in St. Mary's Cathedral, the 21st September, 1836. The orchestra was under the direction of Mr V. Wallace, and ably did he sustain his reputation on the occasion as the first musician of the colony; he led the music with the violin, of which instrument he was a master. This is the same Wallace who afterwards composed several operas in Europe, for which he is famous. The Cathedral contained on that occasion the most numerous assembly up to that time ever convened in the colony, 700 found suitable and pleasing accommodation. The orchestra was raised over the sanctuary. There were about 1,000 listeners in the church. The Bishop and clergy were present, as well as the public officials and distinguished individuals of the colony. The principal selections were from Handel's " Messiah " and Haydn's " Creation," and other beautiful pieces of sacred music were given. Mrs. Rust, a distinguished vocalist of the colony in those days, sustained her reputation. She sang " Comfort ye m people " and other pieces with great power and sweetness. Mrs. Chester, another favourite singer, gave "With verdure clad the fields appear." Miss Wallace, the sister of the distinguished conductor, sang "I know that my Redeemer liveth, &c." This young lady, it was remarked, possessed a fine flexible and powerful voice, which marked her out for eminence in the musical world. The proceeds of the Oratorio went to the building of St. Mary's Cathedral. The service of the church was not neglected in those early times. An advertisement appears in the "Australian" newspaper of 23rd December, 1836, that on Christmas day, at St. Mary's Cathedral, the first mass would be at six a.m.; the second at half-past seven a.m.; the third at half-past eight a.m. And that high mass would be celebrated by the Right Revd. Bishop at 11 o'clock. Mass to be celebrated at Liverpool at 7 o'clock by Revd. Mr. Sumner.

The nucleus of St. Mary's seminary was formed in the year 1836, when there were four students intended for the church pursuing their preparatory studies in the Bishop's house at Woolloomooloo, viz.—Messrs. Harding, Kenny, Reynolds, and Gorman. In the beginning of the year 1837, Mr. Reynolds and a Mr. Ferguson went to Europe to prosecute their studies for the church there. Mr. Reynolds studied at St. Sulpice in Paris, and Mr. Ferguson in the Propaganda at Rome. After three or four years family matters caused Mr. Reynolds to return to the colony, but he did not resume his ecclesiastical studies, but afterwards became a solicitor in Sydney. Mr. Ferguson was ordained in England, and he did not return to the colony. He the years 1836-37 the time of the good Bishop was very much occupied in corresponding with the government and visiting, from time to time, all the districts about Sydney with the view of preparing them for the placing of resident clergymen. When he obtained some leisure from the discharge of his onerous duties he did not forget his young charge, the hopes of the ministry; he would call them into his study in the quiet of the evening and hear them repeat those passages of scripture which he had given them to learn, and then he learnedly explained them, and never failed to put before them the sanctity, the glory, the responsibility, and the perils of the ecclesiastical state. Those homely and fatherly instructions of the saintly bishop always made a deep impression, and were never forgotten. The Mission, towards the end of 1837, sustained a great loss in the death of the Rev. J. V. Corcoran. But for the will of God, he could badly be spared. He was stationed at Windsor, 40 miles from Sydney. While seated in a gig, journeying towards Sydney, the wheel slipped into a rut near the old toll-bar—he was thrown out, and the vehicle passed over his head and neck. He was taken into the toll-house, but only survived about a quarter of an hour. All the Catholics were deeply affected at his sudden death, for he was greatly beloved by every one who knew him, and by none more so than the affectionate Bishop and those with whom Father Corcoran came to the colony. His remains lie in the old Catholic Cemetery in Devonshire-street. *Requiescat in pace.*

The following account of the inquest appeared in the papers of the day :—

New South Wales, Sydney, to wit. An Inquisition taken at the Toll Gate, Sydney-road, Sydney aforesaid, in the colony aforesaid, on the fourth day of August in the year of our Lord one thousand eight hundred and thirty-seven, before me John Ryan Brenan, gentleman, one of the coroners of our Lord the King for the colony aforesaid, upon view of the body of James Vincent Corcoran, then and there lying dead. Upon the oaths of Henry McDermott, George Langley, Henry Merritt, James Cosgrove, William Welch, Christopher Flinn, Edward Ryan, John Fisher, Patrick Maher, Edmund Fitzgibbons, James Roche, and Patrick Grace, good and lawful men of Sydney aforesaid, who being sworn and charged to inquire on the part of our said Lord the King, when, where, how, and after what manner the said James Vincent Corcoran came to his death, do say upon their oaths that the said James Vincent Corcoran on the fourth day of August in the year aforesaid, on the Parramatta-road leading to Sydney, in the district aforesaid, came to his death by being accidentally thrown from his gig on the said road, and then and there receiving an injury on the head, which then and there produced death and not otherwise. Witness as well the said coroner as the jurors aforesaid have to this inquisition, put their hands and seals on the day and year and at the place first above written :—John Ryan Brenan, coroner ; H. McDermott, foreman; Edward Ryan, Jas. Cosgrove Henry Bennett, William Walsh, Christopher Flynn, George Langley, Edmund Fitzgibbon, James Roche, John Fisher, P. Maher, Patrick Grace.

In the territory of New South Wales, Sydney, to wit. Informations of witnesses severally taken and acknowledged on behalf of our Sovereign Lord the King, touching the death of the Reverend James Vincent Corcoran at the Toll Gate, Sydney-road, on the fourth day of August in the year of our Lord one thousand eight hundred thirty-seven, before John Ryan Brenan, Esquire, one of the coroners for the said territory. Edward Ryan of Galong, county of King, being sworn, said :—I was in company with the deceased this afternoon in a gig, he was driving from Windsor to Sydney, after passing the Toll Bar on the entrance into Sydney about twenty or thirty rods, the wheel got into a rut or hole and threw him out of the gig, he went out head foremost, the gig was not upset, it was produced by a sudden jerk, I was thrown out of the gig, the wheel of the gig went over the deceased's head, the horse was trotting moderately at the time, I laid hold of the reins and stopped the horse, I got out of the gig and came up to the deceased, Mr. McDermott and the Reverend Mr. Summer came up to the body before me, the deceased was removed into the Toll Gate House. I was taking off his coat and I asked the deceased if his arm was broken and the deceased answered " No," he did not speak after this. Dr. Hosking and Dr. Smith were sent for and arrived before life was extinct. The deceased was not bled, the surgeons said if he was bled he would die immediately. The deceased departed about ten minutes after the arrival of Dr. Hosking and almost immediately after the arrival of Dr. Smith. I have no doubt on my mind but that it was purely accidental hy being thrown from the gig, and also that the injuries which the deceased received, as I have already described, were the cause of his death. Neither of the doctors then called in are in attendance. This circumstance occurred between five and six o'clock this evening to the best of my recollection. The mark which is observable on the right side of the cheek of the deceased, has been produced either by the fall or by the wheel passing over the head of the deceased. The body viewed by the jury on this inquest is the body of the Reverend James Vincent Corcoran. I was an intimate friend of the deceased. (Signed) Edw. Ryan.

It was noticed in the *Australian Newspaper* that the foundation stone of a church, dedicated to St. Matthew the Apostle, was to be laid and blessed by the Right Rev. Bishop Polding, at Windsor, on Wednesday, 28th December, 1836. It was during the incumbency of Father Corcoran in Windsor the foundation stone of St. Matthew's Church was laid by the bishop, Dr. Polding, on 28th December, 1836. He preached on the occasion, and all the Catholics of the district were assembled to witness the interesting ceremony of the commencement of the first Catholic Church in the Windsor district. I may note here, as it occurred at this time, that the Rev. Father Gregory was ordained a priest by the Right Rev. Dr. Polding, in St. Joseph's Chapel, on 17th March, 1837, and he was the second priest ordained in the colony, Father Sumner being the first.

Towards the end of the year 1837 arrived in the colony the Rev. Charles Lovat, he came to conduct the Seminary ; he was the first, perhaps, who brought to the colony a set of apparatus to assist in illustrating lectures on natural philosophy. He was a man of no ordinary abilities and attainments, and was well grounded in physical science and mathematics ; a distinguished classical scholar and a sound theologian. He came from Stonyhurst College, in England, and had been for some years the professor of physics and moral theology. He went through his theological course at the Propaganda, in Rome. Not long after the arrival of the Rev. Charles Lovat, there arrived in the colony two young theological students from the College of Waterford, in Ireland, their names were Messrs. Walsh and McGrath. They were received by the bishop, and immediately resumed the study of theology, and at the same time assisted by teaching in the Seminary. The first lay boarders of St. Mary's Seminary were Augustus Carter, William Carter, John McQuade, William McQuade, later on — Flanagan, William Gorman, Thomas Fennell, Gerard Philips, George Plunket, William Plunket, George Therry, and Joseph Leary, &c.

The first advertisement, relating to *St. Mary's Seminary*, appeared in the *Australian Newspaper*, of January, 1838,— " Seminary of St. Mary's, adjoining St. Mary's Cathedral. This institution will be opened *pro forma* on the 26th of this month. Studies will be commenced on the 1st February. It will be conducted under the direction of the Right Rev. Bishop. For terms and tickets of admission apply to the Rev. John McEncroe, Administrator, or the Rev. Charles Lovat, President. Only a limited number of boarders will be received."

The president, Rev. C. Lovat, formed the seminary (before it was removed to the building near St. Mary's) in the bishop's house at Woolloomooloo—a large commodious residence with an extensive garden, and from twenty to thirty acres of lawn in front facing the bay. But the property was only rented and belonged to the Reilly estate. The old house and garden have disappeared and the entire ground is now, in 1885, covered with houses and streets. The play ground is no longer discernible.

Next to the president in charge of the seminary in the beginning, was Mr. John Kenny, one of the ecclesiastical students who came to the colony with Bishop Polding, and Mr. Boyle, a good classical scholar, was the lay teacher. The president was well acquainted with college discipline, and he soon made excellent regulations for both studies and play.

CHAPTER III.

Strenuous efforts made for the completion of St. Mary's cathedral.—The arrival of two priests, Revs. Brady and Gould and two ecclesiastical students, 24th February, 1838—Grants of land given by catholics and others as sites for churches—The treatment of Father Brady when he applied to a protestant gentleman for a subscription to help in building his church—The efforts of Dr. Ullathorne to obtain priests in Ireland—The arrival of eight Roman catholic clergymen, 15th July, 1838—Some extracts and remarks on Dr. Ullathorne's pamphlet entitled "The Catholic Mission in Australasia."

DURING this year, 1838, strenuous efforts were being made, both by the clergy and the catholic community for the completion of St. Mary's cathedral. There appeared in the "Australian" newspaper of March, 1838, the following advertisement: "A subscription list has been opened for the purpose of completing the plastering of St. Mary's church; the roof is now nearly finished and on completion of the plastering, this spacious and handsome edifice will afford ample and convenient room to the large congregation of christians who resort to this church."

The following sums have been already subscribed:—

	£	s.	d.		£	s.	d.
Right Rev. the Bishop	25			Captain Carter	2	0	0
Roger Therry, Esq. ..	5			Mr. T. Maher	1	0	0
John Ryan Brenan, Esq...	3			Mr. Smith	5	0	0
Mrs C. H. Chambers ..	5			Mr. Kenny	1	0	0
William Davis, Esq. ..	5	0	0	Mr. Farrell, sen. ..	1	0	0
Adam Wilson, Esq. ..	2	0	0	Messrs. Coveny ..	2	0	0

I noticed a few pages back that Dr. Ullathorne went to England and Ireland to try and obtain more missionaries, for they were very much needed and the catholics were increasing rapidly in the colony. The first happy result of his endeavours was the arrival of two priests and two ecclesiastical students ; they came in the "Upton Castle," 24th February, 1838, which ship brought the new Governor, Sir George Gipps : they were the Rev. John Brady, an experienced and prudent priest, who had been for nineteen years a missionary in the Island of the Mauritius : the other was a young priest, Rev. James Gould, of the order of St. Augustine, lately ordained, who came direct from his monastery in Italy, where he had prosecuted his studies. Dr. Ullathorne first met him on the steps of St. Augustine's Church in the Piazza del Popolo at Rome, and induced him to labour on the Australian mission. He is now, in the year 1885, the Archbishop of Melbourne. Messrs. Farrelly and McPhilip who accompanied them were not in Holy Orders, but had finished their classical studies, they were prepared to commence philosophy, and whilst studying logic, metaphysics, and theology under the learned president, they assisted by teaching in the seminary. The senior priest, Rev. John Brady, was appointed after a short time to Windsor, which had been widowed of its pastor, through the untimely death of the Rev. James Vincent Corcoran. The Rev. James Gould remained for a considerable time in Sydney assisting the Rev. John McEncroe (whose duties were very arduous amongst the prison population). When the vicar-general Dr. Ullathorne returned to the colony, he was appointed to Campbelltown.

At this time very few catholics enjoyed the wealth of this world, houses or land; but some had acquired moderate riches, and from time to time gave donations to the church; but generally what they did accumulate was by the sweat of their brow. A Mr. Thomas Humphries, who followed with his sons the calling of fishermen at the Heads and Brisbane Water, had realised considerable property. Mr. Humphries gave a grant of three acres at Brisbane Water, as a site for a church and burial ground. By the direction of the Right Reverend Bishop Polding a meeting was held at Brisbane Water on 4th July, 1838, when a resolution was passed returning thanks to Mr. Humphries for his liberal donation. It will be seen by the resolutions, that some persons in that locality were very much disposed to find fault with the liberal provision of Sir Richard Bourke's Church Act, when they tried to induce the catholics to sign a petition, by which they promised to attend the protestant place of worship, and the police magistrate showed an earnest wish to return to the old system of oppression, when he enjoined that the catholics of that place should attend the protestant church. But the days of persecution were gone!

I adjoin the resolutions passed at the meeting:—

At a meeting of the Roman catholic inhabitants of the district of Brisbane Water, convened after the celebration of Divine service, on the 4th July, by direction of the Right Reverend Bishop—the Rev. John McEncroe in the chair—the following resolutions were passed:—

First—That this meeting records its approval of the sentiments expressed by his Excellency Sir George Gipps on various occasions, relative to the moral improvement of the colony, and hereby pledges itself to promote the same by example, and other laudable and honourable means.

Second—Resolved, that for this purpose a subscription be opened to obtain the funds requisite for the erection of a church, and we respectfully call upon the inhabitants of the district to assist us in the undertaking.

Third—That the thanks of this meeting are due, and are hereby given, to Mr. Thomas Humphries, for his donation of three acres of land as a site for the church and burial ground, in a situation central and convenient, and that the Right Reverend Bishop be most respectfully requested to accept the same.

Fourth—That a committee of three be appointed to take the names of Roman catholics willing to attend Divine service in the intended church; and this meeting, in making this appointment, expresses its regret that members of the Roman catholic faith have been cajoled to subscribe a declaration that they would attend a place of worship not of their own faith, under a pretence that it was a mere matter of form to obtain a clergyman's stipend; a pretence dishonourable and disgraceful to all parties connected with or concerned in it.

Fifth—That this meeting cannot separate without noticing an order of the Police Magistrate of the district, dated January 1st, requiring all assigned servants—catholics as well as protestants—to meet each Sunday at the usual places of protestant worship; and, whilst we appreciate at its proper value the privilege appended thereto, viz.:—that of allowing the catholics to remain outside till service is over—we detect in the granting of that privilege an assumption of authority destructive of religious freedom, and not sanctioned by any existing regulation or law.

Sixth—That the reverend chairman do present these resolutions to the Right Reverend Bishop for his Lordship's approval, and, if approved, they may be published.

The following committee was then appointed—consisting of Denis Dwyer, James Mullins, and Thomas Humphries; and subscriptions to the amount of £65 10s. were procured in a few minutes.

Signed on behalf of the meeting,

J. McEncroe,
Chairman.

† Approved, John Bede, Bishop and Vicar Apostolic of New Holland and V. D. Land.

5th July, 1838.

Not long after the arrival of the Rev. John Brady, by the directions of the bishop, he held a meeting of the Catholics of Penrith for the purpose of carrying out the provisions of Sir Richard Bourke's Church Act, in regard to the erection of churches, as the catholics of the district of Penrith were very much in want of a place of worship. Sir John Jamison, who was a member of the Executive Council and favourably disposed to catholics, lived on his estate in the vicinity of the township; he offered a piece of ground for the erection of a catholic church; another protestant gentleman, John Tindale, Esq., also offered ground for the same purpose.

I subjoin the resolutions which were passed at the meeting, and approved of by Bishop Polding.

[ADVERTISEMENT.]

At a meeting of the Roman catholic inhabitants of the district of Penrith, convened by the direction of the Right Reverend Bishop, in the Court House, after the celebration of Divine service, on Thursday, 26th April, 1838—the Reverend John Brady in the chair—Resolutions to the following purport were unanimously passed :—

First,—That this meeting has derived cordial satisfaction from the sentiments expressed by His Excellency, the Governor, on various occasions, relative to the moral improvement of the colony, and particularly of the prisoners of the Crown, sentiments in which the true spirit of christian philanthropy and justice is distinctly recognisable.

Second.—That a considerable portion of the population of the district of Penrith, free and bond, professing the Roman catholic faith, are in want of a place of worship which ought to be immediately supplied, in order to carry the benevolent intentions of His Majesty's Government, as expressed by His Excellency, into effect.

Third.—That for this purpose a subscription be commenced forthwith, and a committee be appointed to promote its progress.

Fourth.—That application be respectfully made to the magistrates and gentlemen of the district soliciting their aid, and this meeting assures itself of their liberal co-operation in the erection of the church contemplated, an object so essentially connected with the moral improvement of the Roman catholic assigned servants and others placed under their responsible care and control.

Fifth.—That the thanks of this meeting are due to Sir John Jamison for his kind offer of a site for the intended church, and the Reverend Chairman is requested to present the same.

Sixth.—That the thanks of this meeting are due to John Tindale, Esq., for his kind offer of a site for the church. That our Reverend Pastor be deputed most respectfully to request the Right Reverend Bishop to accept the same, it being a situation generally convenient to the inhabitants of the township.

Seventh.—That the Reverend Chairman be requested to submit these regulations to the approbation of the Right Reverend Bishop, and if approved of by His Lordship, that they be published.

JOHN PURCELL,
Secretary.

† Approved, JOHN BEDE, Bishop, Vicar Apostolic of New Holland and Van Dieman's Land

Sydney, April 28.

———

Not long after this meeting there was a singular display of bigotry shown by a protestant gentleman living not far from Penrith, and a landed proprietor. Father Brady in compliance with the fourth resolution passed at the meeting, called upon this gentleman soliciting a subscription from him for the intended church ; when the poor father, without being invited to sit down, was met with a tirade of abuse, charging the catholic church with superstition and error; and random texts of scripture were hurled at his head ; such was the conduct of this individual, full of rancour and animosity towards the humble priest, who begged for help to enable him to build a church in part for the benefit of the gentleman's assigned servants, who were tilling his broad acres and enriching him by the sweat of their brow, and at but a small expense to him. But this is not all—to add injury to insult, the same person, when Father John Brady wrote a letter, expostulating with him on the impropriety of his treatment, had this letter inserted in the *Gazette*, holding up the priest to ridicule. Father Brady had been speaking the French language for nineteen years, and had lost his former command over the English language ; he made a few orthographical mistakes in the letter, and for this reason it was published. *"Tantœne animis cœlestibus iræ ?"*

(To the Editor of the Australian.)

Sir,—You will much oblige by inserting the following article in refutation of one which appeared in the *Sydney Gazette* of Tuesday last, in your paper of to-morrow.

I remain, Sir, Yours &c.,

ERIGENA.

THE REV. MR. BRADY.

It requires considerable discrimination to decide on the relative claims of the Editor of the *Gazette*, and of the individual who furnished him with Mr. Brady's letter, to the rank of honorable men. Rev. Mr. Brady applies in a respectful manner to Mr. Cox for a subscription towards the erection of a place of worship for the use of the Roman Catholic servants and dependents of that gentleman—without being asked even to sit down, he is assailed by Mr. Cox with a volley of controversial texts, and stunned with the charge of superstitious and unscriptural doctrines. The Rev. gentlemen very properly declines entering the lists with this sturdy disputant in his own house. Mrs. Cox, on perceiving this uncourteous reception, endeavors by her kind attentions to remove the unfavorable impressions that her husband's theological wrath was calculated to make on the mind of a stranger, whom she at once recognizes to have been accustomed to better manners. On the next day the Rev. Mr. Brady writes a letter in French, which language he had almost exclusively used for the last nineteen years, and translates it into English, obviously retaining the French idiom and pronunciation, and thus commits two or three orthographical errors. The editor of the *Gazette* adds a few more of his own inventions with false punctuations, not to be found in the original.

Is it the act of a gentleman to send such a letter, under such circumstances to such a man as the yclept editor of the *Gazette!* Had the learned editor spent eighteen or nineteen years of his precious life in a foreign land, he might have lost some of that purely English and Johnsonian style, which he so perfectly formed during his long and extended literary pursuits in the Dublin University ! ! !

Mr. Cox has been handing about the letter to the great edification and delight of the elect "and elite." No candid mind will condemn the tenor of the letter—and Mr. Cox may rest assured that he would make but a poor exhibition in a critical or controversial Biblical discussion with the Rev. Mr. Brady. The profound editor himself with all his classical lore, may be put to his utmost to stand a few tilts over a Hebrew root, or a Greek particle with this "hedge" priest as he so elegantly designates this unoffending clergyman.

ERIGENA.

P.S. —The following note from Judge Filhole of the Isle of Bourbon, containing an extract from the "Feuille Hebdomadaire" of the 19th October, 1836, will show in what estimation the Rev. Mr. Brady was held by his parishioners in that island. The Gazette man and his correspondent no doubt are able to read French.

"Mon cher Abbé, voici l'article dont je vous ai parlé. 'L'Allier' porte en France Monsieur Brady, curé de la paroisse de Sainte Marie. Nous ne saurions trop faire l'éloge de cet ecclesiastique. C'est le vrai prêtre catholique d'un desintéressement parfait—Il consacrait toutes ses ressources au soulagement des pauvres, et a l'éducation des enfants de la paroisse. Homme d'ésprit et d'instruction, il a su se faire aimer et estimer dans la commune de Sainte Marie que de toutes les îles c'est celle dont les appréciations ressortent toujours les plus exemptes de prévention et d'enthusiasme.—Votre devoué Serviteur,

FILHOLE,
——— Juge d'Instruction."

The very Rev. Dr. Ullathorne was very much assisted in obtaining the young missionaries in Ireland by the Rev. Francis Murphy, who had been educated at Maynooth and was highly respected by the president and professors of the college. He had been on the English mission for a few years, and was, when Dr. Ullathorne met him, the senior priest of St. Patrick's church in Manchester; he then resigned his charge and consented to join the Australian mission. Father Francis Murphy was, without doubt, a great acquisition—he was both learned and pious, possessed of a very clear head and sound judgment; eminent as a preacher and an able controversialist; he also had great aptitude for business connected with the temporalities of the church. He became afterwards Bishop of Adelaide.

He took charge of the young missionaries who left Maynooth and accompanied them to the colony. When the old catholics read the names of these new arrivals, they will recall many reminiscences, it will remind them of former days and those who brought them back to the paths of virtue and happiness, encouraged them in their struggles through life, and took the deepest interest in both their spiritual and temporal welfare. Some of those good priests have gone to their everlasting rest, and some still labour with the same assiduity as they have ever done, expecting the promised reward. Arrived in Sydney Harbour on 15th July, 1838, the barque "Cecilia," Walker, master, which left Gravesend 23rd March, 1838. Passengers:— The Reverend Messrs. Murphy, M. O'Reilly, John Fitzpatrick, Edward Mahoney. John Lynch, John Rigney, Michael Brenan, and Thomas Slattery, Roman Catholic Clergymen. Mr. and Mrs. Davies, Mr. and Mrs. Hawksly, and two children, Mr. Brady Miss Fisher and Mr. McGrane. I have given the notice just as it appeared in the *Australian* of July 17.

The bishop lost no time in appointing and sending the new labourers to work in the vineyard of the Lord. They were sent immediately to the different districts where they were most wanted and for which in his judgment he thought they were best qualified. The senior of the party, the Rev. Francis Murphy, was retained in Sydney; the Reverend John Rigney was sent to Wollongong; the Reverend John Fizpatrick to Goulbourn; the Rev. Michal Brenan to Yass; the Rev. John Lynch to Patrick's Plain; the Rev. Edmund Mahoney to Maitland; the Rev. Michael O'Reilly and the Rev. Thomas Slattery to North and South Bathurst.

These gentlemen when going on their missions were provided with salaries according to the provisions of Sir Richard Bourke's Church Act.

I think it will not be out of place to make some remarks here and give some extracts from a pamphlet, published in England by Dr. Ullathorne in 1837, entitled "the Catholic Mission in Australasia." It was the reading of this production of the vicar-general, which partly was the cause of those excellent young priests volunteering to devote themselves to the Australian mission. Dr. Ullathorne lays bare in that pamphlet the defects of the system of transportation ; and considers the principal defect is not making the ministrations of religion the basis upon which the convict is to be reformed : he states that the number of criminals annually transported at about 6,000; the number in actual bondage in New South Wales, nearly 30,000 ; in Van Dieman's Land, 20,000 ; in the penal settlements of Norfolk Island, Moreton Bay, and Port Arthur, 3,000.

He writes :—The prisoners, amounting to two or three hundred, are sent in a ship to the colony ; they are mixed indiscriminately on board, young and old ; those immersed in vice, deep in every guilt, old in depravity, with those who have taken but the first steps in wickedness. True, some Bibles and Common Prayer Books are thrown in amongst them, but no prayer books or books of instruction for the catholic convict, in which he might find hope and motives for contrition. That when arrived ashore and lodged in the barracks allotted for them at Hyde Park and other places, there was the same neglect and want of precaution,—in fact the work of contamination continued ; when they were consigned to the settlers these did not look to the moral improvement of their assigned servants (thirty, perhaps, huddled together in a few huts), but to the quantity of work which would bring to them the most gain. No reward was held out to encourage the prisoner in industry and good conduct, but constantly kept in dread of being returned to Government, and continually under the apprehension of the lash. He cites a passage from a writing of Mr. Commissioner Therry, in the year 1832, describing the lot of the catholic convict :—" The moment he reaches the shores of Australia he is sent into the interior of the country, there to be assigned to a settler, at a distance of perhaps fifty, one hundred, or even two hundred miles from Sydney. There he is estimated according to the quantity of labour which he is capable of performing—there, amidst associates, reckless in their habits, and infamous in their vices, his days are passed without care and without solicitude,—there also, (and it is of this I complain), the voice of religion, with its salutary counsels and its blessed consolations, never comes. For him religion has lost all sanction, morality all attraction. Can it be wondered at, that when temptation presents itself anew, the miserable man continues his career of crime, until at length he expiates his offences on the gallows ; or by an equally terrible fate, is cast into a penal settlement, whose inhabitants consist of a populus virorum, the misery and the horror of which it is shocking to contemplate."

The Vicar-General finishes his heart-rending account of the misery and spiritual destitution of the unfortunate convict by this solemn appeal. "Oh remember the human lot and have pity! The presence of Christ is amongst them. His wounds and His agonies bleed anew: He calls on you to help; will you refuse Him? No; for you also are the child of His sorrows. The wild heathen walks through them deprived of light. The little children point with their finger, and ask you whether they shall become like these. From the shadow of death which covers them, ' bound in poverty and iron,' they stretch forth their arms with mine to supplicate you."

This pamphlet, at the time, caused the greatest consternation in the colony of N.S.W., especially amongst those who wished transportation to be continued, considering it the main stay and support of the agriculturalists and the owners of sheep and cattle, for they had the labour of the convict for nothing, comparatively speaking, and thus amassed wealth by over-strained muscles and sorrows unceasing, unpaid-for toil of degraded humanity, without attempting to lay before them the sanctions of religion to reform the unhappy men; whilst they made it appear by their representations that the lot of the prisoners was far from being an unhappy one, and that they had every comfort and consolation that could be allowed them. But the testimony of this pamphlet, as well as the evidence of Dr. Ullathorne before the Transportation Committee in London and the writing and evidence of others, dispelled for ever from the public mind this delusion. It is fair to state that some employers of convict labour in those days (but they were the exception) were kind and compassionate, and tried to reform those who were under their charge.

When Sir R. Bourke's Church Act came into full operation, and a good supply of priests were provided, then a decided change for the better was inaugurated. A clergyman was appointed for the spiritual wants of the prisoners on the voyage; the jails, iron-gangs, barracks, and factories were attended to by the priest; the stations in the interior were visited, and every assistance and co-operation with the clergy was afforded by the squatters for the moral improvement of their assigned servants.

K

CHAPTER IV.

*The arrival of the Right Rev. Dr. Pompalier in Sydney, the first
Bishop and Vicar-Apostolic of New Zealand, 8th Decr., 1837.
—The treatment which he met with at the hands of the
protestant missionaries when he arrived in New Zealand
—The letter of Mr. Thomas Poynton of Hokianga, N.Z.—
Public Meeting in St. Mary's Cathedral to repel the charge
made by Judge Willis, that "the worship of the Catholic
Church was idolatrous."— The opinion of the Protestant
Bishop in regard to the denominational system of Educa-
tion.—The opinion of Sir John Jamison. — Political
movements commenced in the Colony.*

THE Right Rev. Dr. Pompalier, the first Bishop and Vicar-
Apostolic of New Zealand, with one priest, Pere Servant, and a
lay brother Frere Michael, arrived in Sydney harbour on the 8th
December, 1837. He came by the schooner "Beatea," which left
Otaheite 6th October, and the island of Rotamah on the 20th
November. He was cordially received by the Right Reverend Dr.
Polding, and was his guest in Sydney for about six weeks, when
he left for the scene of his future labours in New Zealand and
the adjacent islands of the Pacific Ocean. I insert here a letter
from Mr. Thomas Poynton, a resident of Hokianga, which was
sent to the "Australian" newspaper of Sydney, giving an account
of the reception and treatment of the bishop when he arrived in
New Zealand. This letter exhibits a protestant minister in a no
very enviable light Our Saviour said to his disciples, " I send
you as sheep amongst wolves," but the Rev. Mr. Turner mentioned
in this account, termed a preacher on the river, acted rather the
part of the wolf, and stirred up the natives by saying the
catholic church was idolatrous, and Frenehmen were murderers, to
prevent the bishop from landing. Is this the "peace and good-
will" so strongly inculcated by the founder of Christianity ? and
what a demoralising effect such conduct must have on the minds
of the poor savage natives in regard to Christianity.

CORRESPONDENCE.

CATHOLIC MISSION IN NEW ZEALAND.

(To the Editor of the Australian.)

SIR.—As a correct account of the reception and treatment of
the Right Rev. Dr. Pompalier at New Zealand, may be

interesting to some of your readers, I send you the following straightforward statement from Mr. Thomas Poynton, a resident of Hokianga.—Yours, &c.,

A "SUBSCRIBER."

On the arrival of the Right Rev. Dr. Pompalier in Hokianga, that Right Rev. Prelate met with great opposition from a Mr. Turner, a preacher, stationed on the river. Mr. Turner was not contented with preaching against the catholic religion and its ministers on Sundays, and laying it down as black and idolatrous as his eloquence could paint—but he must carry his malice further. He represented to the natives that the bishop and his priest could be no good as they were Frenchmen; that all from their country were murderers, and if they were allowed to stop in New Zealand, in course of time Dr. Pompalier would burn them, tie the natives to a stake if they did not adhere to the catholic religion. On the 17th day of January Mr. Turner sent about fifty natives to my house, to force the catholic bishop from this river; they demanded to see the bishop—the bishop came out accordingly; they spoke to me, as the bishop did not understand them; they ordered him from New Zealand, and demanded his wooden gods that they might throw them into the tide.

It was time for me then to speak, when I saw they were determined to do something which was not just; but I soon convinced them that the best thing they could do was not to meddle with me or the catholic ministers; they thought so themselves and were soon satisfied, but told me that it was Mr. Turner who sent them or they should not have come to trouble the bishop or his priest—but that I knew what Mr. Turner's intentions were towards the catholic missionaries, and advised me to take such means as lay in my power to prevent Mr. Turner from sending them by native force from Hokianga.

I went down to Mr. Turner on that same day, to know by what right or by what authority he should send a party of natives to my place, to interrupt any person that might be there; he, Mr. Turner, denied having sent the natives, but told me he would oppose the catholic religion and its clergy as far as talk would go—but would not advise insult or persecution.

I represented to Mr. Turner what he might expect from the just indignation of forty or fifty British catholics if he persisted in persecuting the minister of their c   catholics, were allowed the free exercise of ou   tain and Ireland, and should be so in a free and independent country. I reminded him of the ill-advised plans to the natives, which caused them to slaughter one another. Not many months back I was an eye witness, as were ten Englishmen, to the complete slaughter of sixteen or eighteen natives, by what they style christian · natives. I told Turner, that if he commenced such work it would not be easy to put a stop to it : that I had the Europeans on my side, who were a match for what natives he could muster, not to mention the natives that would take our pa , and that would be the greatest number. I moreover told him I would make an appeal to the protestants on the river and at the Bay of Islands to judge his conduct in persecuting two men who never wronged him, and were strangers alike to his language and the language of the natives, that they were alike incapable of defending themselves in the English or New Zealand language.

I advised peace and good will, as it would be the only way to benefit the natives. This was the purpose for which the catholic missionaries seemed to have been sent from home, and not to raise dissensions and quarrels that might terminate in their destruction, and cause a good deal of bloodshed on both sides.

Mr. Turner told me that all the blame should be to me, for he was informed that I was the cause of the catholic clergy coming to New Zealand. That he and his family were safe—that catholicism was the worst of all religions, and particularly in New Zealand, as it had great attractions for the natives; that he was well aware the poor natives would be allured over to that religion by the splendour of their church and vestments—that it suited them. " But, Poynton," he said, addressing me, " you know we call all those who adhere to the Roman catholic religion, idolaters." " Well," I said, "there is no cause of quarrel on that point, for you know we are not idolaters, but you are heretics "—so we separated with a good understanding. Of course he was determined to drive the bishop and his priest out of New Zealand, and I was determined to keep them or perish in the attempt. I made an appeal to all the respectable protestants on the Hokianga River, and to most of them at the Bay of Islands, to know if they would sanction or allow Turner to carry on his persecution against the Catholic Bishop, and to their credit they said, to a man, that they would be the first to oppose Turner, and protect the bishop with their lives, and observed it was a good thing that the catholic missionaries came ; that it might cause the others to mind that for which they left home, for most of them forgot what they were before they came to New

Zealand, or for what purpose they arrived there. The bible was now only used as a mask for traffic; and our poor, meek, and humble English missionary is soon transformed into a complete New Zealand merchant, with the addition of the ignorant pride of a county magistrate. Their conduct but ill suits the purpose for which they have been sent out—and they call themselves Apostles of the Gospel. Oh how different from the first Apostles of Christ's church! Here they have their wives and children, their cows, and horses, their houses and land, and live in the greatest plenty. This was a general remark.

But to resume—there was not a chief in Hokianga of any consequence with whom Turner did not use his influence to see if they would drive the Catholic Bishop from New Zealand, but all to no purpose. Some would have nothing to do with it; and they that would, were afraid or over-ruled by those possessed of more power than themselves. There remained one more chance to be tried by Turner. This was a very influential chief who was from home, and Turner made no doubt when this man came back that he would execute his purpose. This man came back; Turner spoke to him to put the catholic bishop from New Zealand, but to his utmost surprise he made him this answer:—" No, I will not, do it yourself, if you think you can, and if you think the white men will allow you; as for me I will have nothing to do quarrelling with the white men, I never did nor will I now ;" so ended this much loved persecution. Turner is at great pains to disown having spoken to the natives, to put away the bishop; but the natives prove it to his face, that he sent them to my house to drive the bishop and priest from New Zealand and to break their service for the altar. The catholics during this dispute behaved with good conduct and prudence; they came every Sunday with their families to mass. Those catholics who lived with native women have all got married and had their wives and children baptized; the natives are quite surprised to see so many white men going to mass, when none go to Turner's preaching—men to whom the missionaries gave the name of devils; when the natives would ask, what was the reason they never came to hear him preach, he would say that they had no religion, that they were devils; but now the natives see that those devils, as they were called, have a religion and attend to the same.

The natives seeing so many white men go to mass on Sunday, and none, with the exception of two or three at most, go to the preaching of Turner, conclude that the catholic religion is the right one; and, many of the chiefs said to me t] only for being baptized in the Wesleyan church, they would be catholics; that they are ashamed to turn from it now, but that they can see that Turner wanted to drive the bishop from New Zealand for fear that they would all turn to him.

The bishop went to Weddenacey, situated about fourteen miles from my place on the River Hokianga (the natives on this river never would listen to Turner's teaching) I spoke to some catholics to go with the bishop, which they did in three boats; this was another insight to the natives; when we arrived at the settlement and the bishop went on shore, their first exclamation was, "Oh! that is the right missionary and he looks like the right one, we will have him and listen to him." I was on the spot when these words were spoken; we stopped all night, and the next morning when the bishop put on his vestments to read mass, I never before witnessed such surprise: they all consented to be of his flock. On an other river called Ollani, they also wish to belong to the catholic faith; twelve or fourteen of the principal men of that river were at mass at my house several times.

This week the bishop was sent for by two of the most powerful chiefs of the Hokianga, they and their people are about to embrace the catholic faith. There is another tribe called Isutiyes, the best part of the men attend every Sunday. I trust in God before many months expire, that we will have more catholic natives on this river than what the Wesleyans will have, as all those natives that have not turned to the Wesleyan preachers are determined to embrace our religion.

His Lordship has got on well in learning the English language since his arrival in this country; so much so that be can hear confessions; he labours hard in learning the English and New Zealand languages; the latter comes easy to him to articulate and he will not be long in learning it; sometimes he is up the most part of the night and very often all night; he has a great deal to do; but he is fit to accomplish it, he is just the man for it. Oh! what a blessing for all to have such a man, so meek, so humble, and devout, he is a saintly man—may the great God grant him health and long life to accomplish his great undertaking.

(Signed)   THOMAS POYNTON.

Hokianga, March 12th, 1838."

The following is an account of a public meeting of the members of the Roman catholic church in Sydney. It appeared in the *Australian* of July 31st, 1838.

At the close of the service at St. Mary's Cathedral on Sunday last, a public meeting took place, to take into consideration the best means of dispelling an error induced by a portion of the speech of His Honor Mr. Justice Willis, delivered at a meeting of the Diocesan Committee at the Old Court House, Castlereagh-street, on Thursday, 19th inst., in which that gentleman attributed to the Roman catholic community "idolatrous worship, and that they had departed from the pure Apostolic Faith."

His Lordship the Bishop took the chair and was supported by the Roman Catholic Clergy, who took their seats on either side on the platform. The chapel was crowded by the laity, and on the business of the meeting being opened, the bishop delivered the following address, premising that it might be remarked that several leading members of the lay community did not take an active part in the proceedings of this meeting. The reasons were so obvious and need not be specified, the meeting might be assured that they felt equally pained and aggrieved by reason of the slander thrown upon their religion with any individuals present.

——————

The Pastoral Address of John Bede, by Divine Providence, Bishop and Vicar-Apostolic of New South Wales and Van Dieman's Land, to his beloved in Jesus Christ—the Rev. Clergy and Laity of Sydney and its vicinity.

St. Paul has forewarned us that men will arise, speaking vain things, and the Royal Prophet in prophetic vision contemplating the spiritual kingdom of Jesus Christ and its assailants exclaims "How have the nations raged and people meditated vain things against the Lord, and against his anointed?"—Psalm 2. In every age, in every place, the church has experienced these predicted trials; and we could not expect that our Holy Faith would be planted unassailed and unmaligned within the limits of our jurisdiction in exception to the general law. Accordingly we have had proof that ridicule and misinterpretation are the portion of the people of God. For party purposes the tenets of our religion have been made the topic of unjust comment unceasingly. It was vainly imagined we should become like unto those who thus slandered us. They have done these things and we are silent. We sought after peace and followed her paths, for we knew they were filled with pleasantness.

But, my beloved brethren in Jesus Christ, circumstances have recently occurred which compel us to depart from the silent unobtrusive course which we deemed most fitting our sacred ministry. Our blessed Redeemer endured all in silence till His Eternal Father's name was used by one high in station for party purposes. And St. Paul, who prescribes patience and long-suffering, rebuked severely Elymas, who tried to pervert the right ways of the Lord in the court of Sergius the Proconsul. In like manner we cannot permit calumnious expressions, which, proceeding from the pen or lips of ordinary men, might pass by, to escape unnoticed and uncensured, when they come forth to the world impressed with a weight of authority, in itself entitled to the deepest respect. Our worship has been represented to the public as idolatrous by Mr. Justice Willis. A grave charge this! If true, it sweeps away from the fold of christianity a large proportion of the inhabitants of this colony, and with them four-fifths of the christian world. Such an accusation is in itself so far beyond credibility that we might leave it, as we before observed, unnoticed, had it not been stated that it proceeded from a high source. We ourselves could not credit the report. Our sincere respect for the individual implicated, and regard for our beloved flock unjustly maligned, induced us to write to Mr. Justice Willis, requesting to be informed whether the expressions imputed to him were correctly reported or not; to this request we received a reply by no means satisfactory.

One from whose breast the reverential love of truth ought to scare away every unseemly prejudice; from whose lips no words unseasoned by discretion ought to proceed, has volunteered the conviction that our worship is " idolatrous." Have we not reason to feel aggrieved ?

But since this charge of idolatrous worship has been brought against our holy religion, we deem ourselves called upon succinctly to expound those doctrines of the church which ignorance or malice has usually selected to justify this most dreadful imputation. We premise first, that we enter our solemn protest against those who, differing from us in religious belief, arrogate to themselves a claim to interpret our doctrines. " Every church," says a well-known protestant author, " is the properest judge of its own doctrines and government." Secondly, we declare that God alone is the end of all religious worship. The catholic church holds, as the foundation of all religion, that our first duty is to believe that God is the Creator and Lord of all things, and to love Him with all the feelings and faculties of our souls; to prostrate before Him all our mental and corporal powers; attaching ourselves to Him by a continued service of faith, of confidence and of love; for He is the source of all good.

Opposed to this duty is idolatrous worship, which consists in giving to any creature whatsoever that supreme adoration, honor, or worship which is due only to Almighty God.

Idolatrous worship consequently, as being opposed to the first duty of man, the catholic church teaches to be one of the greatest crimes which can be committed against the majesty of the one eternal God; and every sincere christian must feel grievously injured by an imputation alike destructive of his faith and of his hope.

For the catholic church moreover teaches that the fruition of God and the remission of sin are not attainable otherwise than in and by the merits of Jesus Christ, who, being God, became man, suffered and died in his human nature for the salvation of all mankind; that through his merits, gratuitously purchased for us, all may be saved; and that there is no other name under heaven given to men, in which salvation may be obtained. All spiritual graces in this life, all happiness hereafter, must come to us through the merits of Jesus Christ.

To God alone, therefore, do we offer the tribute of our supreme homage; in Jesus Christ alone, His blessed Son, do we rest the hope of our salvation.

In contradiction to these our doctrines it is said, we adore the elements of bread and wine in the mass—that we adore the Virgin Mary—that we worship the saints and images of Christ and of the saints. In the mass we believe that after the consecration, the substance of bread and wine is no longer present, but only the appearances. In the mass we do offer supreme adoration to Jesus Christ, the son of God, whom we believe to be truly, really, and substantially present, under the appearances only of bread and wine. Not indeed present according to that *sensible* manner and visible form of existence which He once assumed for our salvation, but after a spiritualized manner and in a sacramental form, not exposed to the senses nor to corporeal contingencies. Even as we believe the divine nature to have been truly present in Jesus Christ whilst He was visible on earth, though concealed, so in this, His sacramental form of existence, we believe Him to be truly present. The divine and human nature being alike concealed, and their presence being known to us by His own unerring word, which is the direct testimony of God. We adore, therefore, the Saviour in the mass, as we would have adored Him in the stable of Bethlehem under the form of an infant, or on Calvary under the appearance of a criminal dying upon a cross; relying on the testimony of God manifested to us by prophecy and miracles. In the mass we adore Jesus Christ, whom we believe to be present—whom we acknowledge to be truly God, the legitimate object of supreme adoration and love. The reality of the presence of Jesus Christ in the holy Eucharist may form a subject of theological discussion. The adoration of Jesus Christ in the holy Eucharist is a necessary consequence of a belief in the reality of that presence. And we hold we have an equal right to draw our own conclusions from the words of sacred scripture, in favour of the real presence, with those who deny it. They maintain a right of judging for themselves; this right we also maintain.

Before we proceed to answer the other objections, it will be proper to remark to you, that the words—worship, honour, adoration, with several others, are terms in themselves relative and ambiguous, varying in their sense according to the nature of the object to which the act, by the term expressed, is directed, and according to the intention of him by whom they are used (Compare Prov. v., 9, and Exod. xx., 12, Deu. xxviii., 47 and 48). In scripture we are commanded to honour God and to honour the king; children are commanded to honour their parents. Is it to be supposed that the honour due to the king or to parents is the same we owe to God? To God we owe supreme and sovereign honour, in which no created being can have any part. To the king we owe the highest civil honour. To parents children owe the honour of filial respect and obedience. Thus the words adoration, and worship are used in the ancient liturgies to signify supreme homage, and also affection and respect. How frequently is the former word to be met with in this sense in the language of poetry, or of excited feeling. The latter, with perfect innocence, may be used in the same sentence in reference to God and to man. Thus, in the first book of Chronicles, chap. 29, v. 20. And all the congregation blessed the Lord God of their fathers, and bowed down their heads and "worshipped the Lord and the king." Here evidently the word worship is used to signify supreme homage to God and inferior worship to the king.

Seeing, therefore, that these terms are in themselves ambiguous, and that their sense is determined by the intention of the person by whom they are employed, surely, no arguments can be more unfair than those derived from the use of terms merely relative, and construed in a sense disavowed by those against whom such arguments are brought.

We therefore declare the faith, which we have been taught from our infancy, when we state that we do not adore, nor worship, nor honour with the supreme adoration—worship and honour due only to God—no other than the one, living, true, and eternal God; the Creator of all things. Whatever may be the terms employed, we do not intend to express more than an *honour and respect infinitely inferior in kind,* and *infinitely inferior in degree* to this supreme homage. The honour we have in reference to the Blessed Virgin and the saints is precisely the same in *kind* with the respect and honour we would pay *to our fellow creatures on earth,* whom we deemed worthy of respect and honour.

How unjust, therefore, to say that we offer idolatrous worship to the Blessed Virgin and the saints! In like manner we renounce all divine worship and adoration of images and pictures, since we worship and adore God alone. Pictures, nevertheless, and especially the image of our crucified Redeemer, may be placed in our churches, to recall our wandering thoughts and to inflame our affections. What Christian can contemplate the image of his dying Saviour without veneration? It is a book to the unlearned; the Cross was the book of St. Paul, from which he derived his knowledge. We venerate the cross, as a son respects the image of his father —a parent the picture of his child—a friend that of a friend. To condemn the feeling which prompts this would be to condemn the finest feelings of our nature. It is manifestly unjust to stigmatize this veneration as idolatrous worship. Neither do we adore the saints. We believe in the communion of saints; that the church triumphant in heaven is one in Christ with the church militant on earth; that although faith and hope are absorbed in the vision and fruition of God, charity never faileth. Hence we believe that the blessed, who have died in the Lord, pray for us, their fellow-members on earth, and that they rejoice in the conversion of the sinner. We believe that the departed parents, when happy with God, may pray for their children, even as the parents did pray whilst on earth. We believe that God may be favourably inclined to hear the petitions made by them in our behalf; therefore we believe that it is good and profitable (not necessary) to desire their prayers. Can this manner of communication and invocation be more injurious to the merits and triumph of Christ, our only Mediator of Redemption, than it is for one Christian to beg the prayers of another? Above all, can this be deemed idolatrous worship?

Should anyone demand a more explicit declaration against this most anti-Christian accusation? We most solemnly pronounce anathema against him who commits idolatry, who prays to images, or worships them as gods. Anathema to him who believes the Blessed Virgin to be more than a creature ; who puts his trust in her more than in God. Anathema to the man who gives divine honour to any created thing, whether in heaven above or in the earth beneath, or who adores as God any but the *one true and living God*, to whom be honour and glory for ever and ever. Amen.

At the close of the address his lordship said that having now touched upon the leading points of their faith, as connected with Mr. Willis's allusion, he would proceed to the business of the meeting, and he had to express his deep regret that he was called upon thus publicly to acknowledge how much they felt aggrieved at the unfounded and illiberal charge made against the Roman catholic community generally by Mr. Justice Willis.

The Rev. Mr. Lovat then said, that to bring into effect the real purposes of the meeting, he had been induced to move the first resolution, and then proceeded to state :—That valuing peace as the greatest of all temporal blessings, and believing its preservation to be a sacred duty, we have studiously avoided giving cause of offence to any upon the subject of religion, which was given to man to be a bond of union with his fellow-man. For the same reason, when our doctrines have been impugned and misrepresented, we have not answered railing for railing, and we fearlessly appeal, in proof of this assertion, not only to the authorities of the colony, but also to our brethren of every religious denomination. We deem it criminal to bear false testimony against our neighbour ; and we consider, to charge any body of Christians with doctrines disavowed by them, is a false testimony—it is a calumny increasing in guilt in proportion to the numbers maligned and to the odiousness of the doctrines imputed. We consider that the charge of idolatrous worship against any body of Christians is most odious, for it strikes at the very root of their faith and of their hope ; it ranks them amongst the heathen ; their acknowledgement of the sole dependence on one God, the creator of all things, is denied ; their trust in one mediator between God and man, our blessed Lord and Saviour Jesus Christ is declared to be a lie ; their fitness for civilised life, which, as the experience of past ages proves, can only rest on these primary doctrines, is questioned. Moreover, this charge of idolatrous worship, first brought against the catholic church for the purpose of misleading the ignorant, and since resorted to for the purpose of exciting party feeling and prejudice, has been distinctly and repeatedly shown to have no foundation whatsoever in our belief nor our practice.

The resolution was seconded by Mr. Adam Wilson.

The bishop re-read the resolution, and stated if any persons had objections to make, they were invited to stand forward and make them The resolution was then put to the meeting, and carried unanimously by the show of hands.

The Reverend Mr. McEncroe rose and said—It was with deep regret he felt called upon to allude in public to an estimable and highly respectable personage, but his duty imperatively impelled him to do so, and his public duty must supersede all feelings of delicacy which he might have on the subject. These must give way to the solemn charge laid upon him, and for which he should have to account when standing before that highest of tribunals, before which all would be called to account. He admitted the right of every person to pursue his own course of salvation, and to declare his belief or disbelief in particular doctrines ; but in declaring his opinions he was not allowed to bear false witness against his neighbour. Any one had a right to state what he believed to be true, but he should arm himself with reasons and with facts—he should acquaint himself with the belief and practice, before he presumed to attack the doctrine of his neighbour : and above all he should not carelessly asperse any doctrine upon hearsay : he should not misrepresent and insult a large portion of his christian brethren who happened to differ from him in faith, without being fully prepared to answer for his assertions. If he had wished to attack the tenets of the Roman catholic church, he should have done so *fairly and honestly*, and not by giving expression to what was not catholic doctrine. Before making such unwarrantable assertions, he should have consulted the formulæ of the doctrine of their faith ; the expressed and written explanations and decrees of her prelates. If he had done so, and had expressed his dissent from doctrines correctly understood, no person could have censured his disagreement with the Roman catholic doctrines, nor with the candid expression of his disbelief. But if, on the contrary, he asserted what the catholic faith expressly denied—that which had been frequently attributed to it, and had as frequently been denied with abhorrence—then it became the duty, the urgent duty, not only of the clergy, but of the laity of that community, to assert their detestations of such calumnies, and publicly to disavow a participation in such doctrines. It was with the most painful feelings that he was called on to denounce the assertion of so exalted and influential an individual ; but he was bound to his God and to his flock to state aloud that the Roman catholics abhorred idolatry, and he could not sufficiently express his horror of the accusation. It was culpable to rob, to commit various offences which were amenable to the law; but the charge now brought against the whole Roman catholic people was ten thousand times worse than highway robbery, or any charge which could be brought against man. They were charged with robbing the Almighty of the honour due to Him alone; and it was not to be wondered that they felt indignant at the accusation of giving glory to the creature, which was alone due to the Creator. The slightest tinge—the shadow "of idolatrous worship," essentially corrupts and destroys the purity and singleness of divine worship of the " One only true God ;" for " the Lord is a jealous God," &c., " He will not bear a rival,"—" He will not accept a divided heart," —" He will not give His heart to another,"—" no one can serve two masters,"—" there is no union between light and darkness," —" there can be no union between God and Belial." Hence, if the Roman catholic worship be in any way " idolatrous," catholics are cut off from the true worship of the Living God in this world, and they can have no hope of mercy or glory in the world to come—an awful conclusion! and one forced on us by the astounding words of Mr Justice Willis. It was really painful for him to be forced to express himself in uncourteous and strong language; but standing as he did as the senior chaplain of the Roman catholic persuasion now in the colony, and having extended and great experience as a priest, he could not help rebutting the calumny which had either wantonly or ignorantly been thrown on their community.

He had been acquainted with catholics from South and North America, from the East and West Indies, from France, Germany, Spain and Italy, and he had never met with the idolatry imputed to the Roman catholics by Mr. Justice Willis. He could not find any excuse for such a cruel charge, which had every appearance of being thrown out to excite a prejudice against a large body of Christians, who were in every respect as devout and as well-conducted as any other body of religionists. To be accused of idolatry was a charge which no unprejudiced mind could believe against them, and which was not only uncharitable but untrue. It was with pain he had stated so much, but it was his duty to maintain the tenets of his church, and to contradict that which had not the slightest foundation in fact or doctrine. He begged leave to propose the second resolution, which was—" That this meeting cannot express in terms sufficiently strong its sense of the conduct of Mr. Justice Willis, who at a public meeting has declared that Roman catholics, by reason of their idolatrous worship, have departed from, or greatly erred in, the pure apostolic faith; an assertion containing a wanton and unprovoked insult, imputing to a large proportion of his fellow-citizens and inhabitants of this colony a practical doctrine which they hold in the utmost abhorrence. And that this declaration on the part of Mr. Justice Willis is uncalled for by reason of the circumstances of the meeting, and calculated to enkindle the flames of religious discord in this colony, being direct evidence that in his estimation we possess neither a moral nor a Christian character. We, the Roman catholics of Sydney and the colony at large, do hereby declare we can have no longer esteem for nor confidence in him."

The resolution was seconded by Mr. R. Murphy, and was carried without dissent.

The Rev. Mr. McEncroe said that in moving the third resolution, on the part of the Rev. H. G. Gregory, who was absent from the meeting, he must observe that it had been declared that many protestant gentlemen had expressed themselves equally indignant at the unjust and uncharitable aspersions thrown out against the Roman catholics, and that many of them would have attended the meeting, but that it was called in the name of the catholics only. It was very gratifying to him to state that many protestant gentlemen, with the kindest feelings, had come forward and contributed to the erection of temples for the worship of the only true God; and he thought it was a duty they owed to those gentlemen to rebut the presumption that they had contributed to the support of "idolatrous worship," which, if allowed to pass unheeded and uncontradicted, would indirectly attribute to them a culpability they deserved not. In justice and in gratitude to those gentlemen, who must truly have appreciated the doctrines of the catholic church, differing as it did in some points from their own, he was happy to propose the following resolution on the part of his brother-clergyman, the Rev. Mr. Gregory:—"That among the motives for this expression of our abhorrence of the imputed idolatry, not the least is our desire to rescue from so gross a calumny our respected protestant brethren who have so liberally and so generously contributed to the erection of this and other temples to be dedicated, not to the service of idols, but to the worship, in spirit and in truth, of the living God."

The resolution was seconded by Dr. Burke and carried unanimously.

It was then moved by the Rev. Mr. Murphy, and seconded by Mr. A. Ennis—"That a copy of these resolutions be presented to His Excellency the Governor, with a request that they might be transmitted to the Right Honourable the Secretary of State." Carried unanimously.

Mr. Adam Wilson moved that the Bishop should leave, and that the Rev. Mr. Murphy should take the chair.

The Rev. Mr. Lovat moved—"That the thanks of this meeting be given to our reverend bishop for his zealous and dignified conduct, and for the honour he has done us in the chair while presiding over this meeting." The resolution was seconded by Captain Carter, and carried unanimously.

The bishop then addressed the meeting, and said, that the proceedings of one of the most painful days of his existence had nearly come to a conclusion. They had been obliged to lay aside for a short space the unobtrusive and humble course they had always followed, to bring to the test of truth, what, if true, would debase them below the heathen nations, and render them a reproach to the name of Christians. They had met, and he hoped by their unqualified denial of the odious charge made against them, they had removed from the mind of their brother Christians the odium which the indiscreet avowal of a gentleman high in office, attached to them. Having done so, it was now their duty to fall back into their wonted course of quietude and charity. It rested with them to show to their opponents the real beauty of religion by the purity of their lives, and he earnestly prayed his flock to preserve and cherish feelings of peace and good will towards their brethren, of whatever denomination, regardless of the calumnies which might be thrown upon them, either by unkind or ignorant persons. These would in the end meet their own refutation, and recoil upon their propagators. He entreated them to remember that whatever difference existed in the forms of religion, there was one great commandment given to all,—that they should love one another like brethren—and this they were bound to obey, however others neglected it. With these words, he would dismiss them in peace.

The meeting was conducted throughout with the most perfect order, not a word being uttered, except by the speakers, from the beginning to the end ; and the bishop having given his benediction, the meeting broke up as if nothing uncommon had occurred.

This meeting was by no means uncalled for, it was necessary in order to dispel from the minds of protestants the revolting prejudice, that catholics were guilty of idolatrous worship. Indeed, this branch of the church catholic would have been unworthy of the Faith had they not repelled with indignation such an odious charge made by one of the judges of the land; and it would seem that those who were present at the protestant meeting (Bishop Broughton was in the chair) shared in the sentiments of Judge Willis; for not one rose to contradict his calumnious assertion; and the most influential members of the Church of England were at the meeting. The editor of the *Government Gazette*, in commenting on the meeting, stated that nine-tenths of the Church of England colonists "cordially acquiesced in the opinions of Judge Willis."

At this time the leading members of the Church of England, with some honourable exceptions, seemed to be highly incensed against the wise and liberal measure of the Church Act, introduced by Sir Richard Bourke, by which the Church of England in the colonies lost its ascendancy, and the lion's share of allowances.

The progress which the catholic church had made in the colony in such a short time, by the devotion and zeal of the bishop and clergy, alarmed the illiberals. They were disposed to resort to every means in their power to repress catholicity and prevent its advancement; but "magna est veritas et prevalebit"— *St. Aug.* A sure index of the rabid party feeling towards the Roman catholics may be found in the remarks which appeared in a public print at that time. When the ship " Cecilia " arrived, in July, 1838, the following were the observations of the *Government Gazette*:—" The ' Cecilia,' from London, has brought us eight additional Irish Roman catholic priests, being the first fruits of Dr. Ullathorne's pamphlet, at a cost to the colony, which he has calumniated and injured, to the extent of only £1200! We expect shortly to see the colony swarming with these adventurous spirits, if, as in the present instance, our emigration fund is to be taxed with the payment of £150 to each priest for the purpose of defraying the expense of his passage and to give the gentleman an outfit—a system of robbery of which we shall say more on an early day." How contemptibly this scribe writes of the catholic clergy; to him the introduction of learned, pious, and zealous ecclesiastics—to instruct and improve the morals of the people— was no benefit, and the statement was made as if the catholics monopolised the provisions of Sir Richard Bourke's Church Act. In regard to Dr. Ullathorne's pamphlet, by which, this writer states, the colony was " calumniated and injured," I need only cite the words of a liberal and intelligent cotemporary journal, wherein the editor writes that there is " not the slightest indication of that *malus animus*—of that personal vindictiveness, of that acerbity of temper which characterize the works of our other colonial slanderers. It breathes throughout rather a spirit of compassion for the religiously neglected prison population of his own, the R.C. community, and a feeling of sympathy for human suffering."

The meeting at which Judge Willis made the false charges was inaugurated by a dinner; here all the members of the Diocesan Committee were present, including Bishop Broughton, and Alexander Macleay, Esq., the Colonial Secretary, was in the chair. The second toast proposed by the chairman was "The Church and State," which he prefaced by saying it was rather a delicate toast, but one which he was assured would be well received. He might well say " delicate," because by the Church Act the connection between the State and the Church, by law established in the colony, was slender indeed, if not completely severed.

It was in consequence of the persistent opposition of Bishop Broughton and his party that the system of general education proposed by Governor Bourke was not introduced into the colony. They thought such a system of education too liberal in its object and unfavourable to protestantism. No doubt Bishop Broughton reasoned justly in favour of the denominational system when he wrote, "He was persuaded that the artificial substitution of a day for inculcating religion, instead of its being made always the subject of devout observation, will not accomplish the object proposed any more than in nature occasional irrigation could compensate for the failure of the rain and dew of heaven." They would only consent to the protestant catechism being taught in the schools; the public school system seemed to this party to favour the efforts of the Church of Rome. The liberal-minded and enlightened protestants accorded no approbation to the bigotry, prejudice, and religious rancour of these zealots. Sir John Jamieson, who was a man of cultured mind, a liberal and enlightened politician, in writing to a friend on the other side of the equator, states :—"At present the population of this colony is disturbed by religious controversy. Our Governor, Sir Richard Bourke, an enlightened and liberal man, is anxious to establish such a national system of education as would be most desirable to allay the prejudices of religious sects and most important in regard to economy in this thinly-peopled country. Against this our bishop has exerted all his influence with his numerous Tory friends to oppose the Governor's effecting his wishes, and keep up a system of exclusion. Thus the seeds of religious discord have been sown amongst us and destroyed the unanimity which for years bound the bulk of the colonists together."

There appeared at the time in a liberal and well-conducted protestant journal the following remarks :—"Our anti-popery alarmists have done most serious injury. . . . . . . They have been the first to sow the seeds of religious discord in our churches and in our society. . . . . . . To them alone belongs the guilt; their bigotry alone has been the means of stopping the spread of universal education. The means which have been resorted to are worthy of the end for which they have been employed. Not content with imputing to Roman catholics doctrines they abjure and purposes they abhor, some of our protestant zealots have heaped calumny upon calumny on the heads of the most virtuous and distinguished members of their own faith, whose measures they laboured to contravene."

It will be instructive and interesting to take a glance at the political movements going on in the colony about this time. There were two questions agitating the minds of the people the solution of which in after years may be said to have changed the destiny of the colony. The first question was, whether it would not be expedient to get transportation abolished; and the second, the natural outcome of the other, " ought not the colony to have representative government." In regard to the question of transportation, there existed a great difference of opinion. The home Government was decidedly averse to a change, because the colony was a very convenient and distant place to absorb the prison population of Great Britain; and the would-be autocrats who possessed large tracks of land in the colony, including the squatter, supported the transportation scheme, it being favourable to their interests: To do away with the prison population would be, they said, the death-blow to agriculture, and the money market would be shaken to its centre. It would involve the country in a colonial national debt, as a loan would have to be contracted, and the colony would be responsible for both principal and interest. They said the prosperity of the colony was bound up with the transportation system. The opponents to this view maintained that so long as the colony was a penal settlement, it was impossible for it to be prosperous and glorious in comparison to the other nations; it was like a leprosy which excluded her from the society of the world.

The agitators for a representative government asserted that, according to the law of nations, " every community had a right to govern itself;" that the prison population were vastly in the minority; that free immigrants were pouring in on our shores in great numbers every year; and that the colony could no longer be considered a penal colony, but must be considered a commercial dependency of Great Britain. There were only 20,000 prisoners and why should the free inhabitants, amounting to 80,000, be subjected to the arbitrary rule of a penal settlement ? Having a representative Government they could, with the approval of the Crown, make their own laws, tax themselves, and appoint competent officers to the State. How the colonists obtained their object I will briefly give an account of in another page.

CHAPTER V

The return of the Vicar-General, Dr. Ullathorne, to the colony with three priests, three ecclesiastical students, and five sisters of charity, December 31, 1838.—Great meeting of the Catholics in St. Mary's Cathedral, presided over by Bishop Polding.—Dr. Ullathorne's speech, giving an account of his travels in Europe.—The Sisters of Charity, their work, and the origin of their coming to the colony.—The able and statesman-like letter of Sir Richard Bourke in reply to the Bishop of Exeter, Dr. Philpotts, of Exeter Hall notoriety.

Now to return to ecclesiastical affairs. Dr. Ullathorne, after an absence of about two years and a half, returned to the colony. He brought with him the first nuns, Sisters of Charity, who ever landed in the colonies. In the *Australian* newspaper of Tuesday, January 1, appeared the following announcement :—" December 31, 1838—Arrived, The " Francis Spaight "; Sayers, master, with merchandize. Left London August 23. Passengers : The Rev. Dr. Ullathorne, Roman Catholic Vicar-General ; the Rev. Messrs. P. B. Geogeghan, Richard Marum and Thomas Butler, Roman Catholic clergymen ; Mrs. Cahil, Mrs. O'Brian, Mrs. Callen, Mrs. De Lacy and Miss Williams, Sisters of Charity ; Messrs. J. Dunphy, P. Magennis and J. Grant, ecclesiastical students."

The press at the time made the following remarks :—" On New Year's Day High Mass was celebrated in St. Mary's Cathedral, when the newly-arrived priests and sisters of charity attended at the altar. The cathedral was crowded to see the installation of the priests, and, no doubt, partly from curiosity to see the veiled sisters who have ventured so far from their homes for the purpose of contributing to the religious instruction of their fellow creatures."

After Divine Service on Sunday, January 6, 1839, a meeting of the Roman Catholics of Sydney was convened in the cathedral, the Right Reverend Bishop in the chair. The principal object of the meeting, as the resolutions indicate, was to raise funds for the completion of the cathedral.

We know not when we were more agreeably gratified than we were on entering this splendid structure, and in being present during the service which preceded the meeting. The whole of the roof had been completed. The grandeur and general appearance were well supported by the delicate minuteness with which the detail of ornament, peculiar to the style adopted, had been carried out. And we beheld the Bishop standing before the altar, under the canopy of an arch, beautiful in the simplicity of its form, and enriched in a manner peculiarly striking and novel by the introduction of stained glass into the ornamental spandrils, surrounded by the ministers of religion in their various gradations. The recently arrived priests made their obedience to the Right Reverend Bishop, and were formally received into the number of the clergy. The music was of the first order. We never heard the celebrated Gloria of Mozart, No. 12, to greater advantage. A most instructive discourse was delivered by the Reverend Mr. Geoghegan, one of the clergy who lately arrived with Dr. Ullathorne. The sisters of charity, we observed, occupied the first bench in front of the altar.

The service being finished, the business of the meeting commenced. The Bishop, having taken the chair, read the following address :—

" John Bede, by the grace of God and the appointment of the Holy See, Bishop, Vicar-Apostolic of New Holland and Van Dieman's Land, to the faithful of Sydney and its vicinity, greeting :

" Dearly beloved in Jesus Christ,—

" Two years and a half have elapsed since we first invited your co-operation and assistance in the completion of the structure in which we are now assembled. Then the bareness and nakedness of the walls, its roof just sufficient to protect the altar and the congregated multitude around it from the elements, its generally desolate appearance by reason of its unfinished state, served as arguments most cogent and irresistible to influence you to take up the sacred cause with vigorous generosity. Blessed be God, that space of time has not elapsed unproductive of the effects we wished to see realized. The building, commenced by that good pastor whom Providence selected to watch over and protect his infant church in these counties, has now grown up by your efforts into a structure, without and within, goodly and pleasant to behold, well seeming to its noble purpose. Cast your eyes around, survey the work of your hands, the result of your zeal, and you will take part in the joy of Holy David, when, having adorned, according to the extent of his means, the resting place of the Tabernacle—the mere type or emblem of our church—he exclaimed, ' Lord, how have I loved the beauty of Thy House and the place of Thy habitation? I will adore in Thy holy temple, and I will praise Thy name.' Not one amongst you now repines for that his contribution has been large and frequent, not one has been visited by distress in his own family because he has given generously to the Lord.

" In referring to the means we used for the purpose of regulating the donations of the faithful, so that the contributions might flow in channels easy of access to all parties, it will be recollected we instituted a society of persons who engaged to pay a sixpence per week towards the completion of the cathedral, and also of those who zealously engaged themselves to collect the sums so contributed. Amidst the labours of our Ministry it was gratifying, it was consoling to observe how energetically you exerted yourselves to obtain the means of completing the material structure which best might represent that spiritual edifice of faith, and of hope. and of love to God and man, which, with our beloved clergy, we were engaged in raising among you. In the lapse of time, however, various circumstances, as might be expected, have broken in upon the harmonious working of that society, and have clogged proceedings ; so that, though the good-will remains, the results of that good-will do not substantially appear. The consequence is, the channels no longer bring in their wonted contributions, the treasury from which the current expenses were discharged has become entirely empty. We are in debt. We think it right to state the fact in its plain simplicity. Upwards of £2000 have been paid to the contractors, Brodie and Craig ; several hundreds—the exact amount cannot yet be ascertained—remain to be paid. We cannot proceed to complete the cathedral unless our treasury be again replenished by the contributions of the faithful.

" We require an immediate supply to meet the demands now due ; we must provide for the future, so that the work may proceed uninterruptedly to its completion, unencumbered by the great evil of accumulated debt.

" To effect the first of these purposes we propose that an immediate subscription be commenced. Several gentlemen have already signified their willingness, and have evinced their sincerity by the payment of their subscription, others most laudably have engaged to pay annually considerable sums until the completion of the work. Thus encouraged we unhesitatingly call upon all to contribute of their substance to this great work. The Lord loves the cheerful giver; and that which shall descend into the general fund for erecting a temple to His name, which shall in some sort be worthy of its object (like the waters which have passed to the ocean, return from the clouds to the earth with a fertilizing power) the divine blessing will again restore to you with an hundredfold increase.

" But this will not be sufficient. Who would not regret the cessation of the work before completion? Yet this must be the case; even the sanctuary, the place most solemnly consecrated to the divine service, must remain in an unfinished state, unless we have steady supplies on which we can safely calculate; and these we do not doubt we shall have. To secure these supplies we propose that a society shall be formed having for its object the procuring of funds for the completion of the Cathedral This society, like the former, to consist of those who will contribute monthly at least one half crown to the funds, or a sixpence for each member of the family; and of others who will engage to collect these sums from the faithful. We do not doubt, after the proofs we have received of the devotedness and zeal of very many of our flock, that this association for the completion of St. Mary's Cathedral will accomplish the glorious object for which it has been formed.

" We cannot dismiss the subject which has principally urged us to assemble you, before we have expressed our sincere heartfelt gratitude to the author of all good for the unbounded mercies he has been pleased to bestow upon us in the interval of time to which we have alluded.

" The mission of our beloved Vicar-General has been attended with the most beneficial results His zeal, activity, and piety have created an extensive sympathy in our favor. Zealous, active, and pious laborers in the Lord's vineyard have beheld our wants, and have hastened to come to our succour. Our people are no longer as sheep gone astray in the absence of pastors. The cry of our little ones for bread—the bread of eternal life—will not be in vain, there are those now who will brake it unto them. The spirit of God hath filled with courage, not belonging to their sex, excellent ladies, who, deeming all things of small account to gaining souls to Christ, have, fearlessly traversing the ocean, come amongst us to consummate their sacrifice of charity on these shores in the abodes of sorrow and guilt. What return, dearly beloved in Jesus Christ, shall we make to the Lord for all he has done to us? Shall we refuse to devote a portion of our worldly substance to his service? Impossible!

That part of the sacred edifice destined for the use of the people we behold completed; now we are called upon to adorn the sanctuary of our God, in which he loves to dwell with the children of men. The donations we now request are more directly consecrated to Him. Dearly beloved, on this auspicious day, when we commemorate the oblations which were offered by our forefathers in the faith—the wise men to the infant Saviour—let us offer our gold as a testimony of our grateful homage unto Him who has given us to enjoy in the light of the true faith all its concomitant blessings. On this day when you behold, encircling the naked unfinished sanctuary, those who, to administer within its sacred precincts, have left all things—who have given their very lives for you—let the munificence of your present subscription, the energy of your future exertions in the completion of the Cathedral of St. Mary prove that you gratefully appreciate the sacrifice made by those apostolic men for your sakes.

"The Grace of God our Saviour be with you all. Amen."

The Rev. Francis Murphy, in moving the first resolution, expressed his conviction that a sum sufficient for the completion of the cathedral, and for the liquidation of its present debt, might easily be raised, if the labouring classes and the mechanics would only unite with their wealthier brethren in contributing, each according to his circumstances. Having resided for the last ten years in Liverpool, England, he could bear testimony to the extraordinary good which had been effected by the united exertions of the labouring classes amongst the catholic body in that town as well as in the neighbouring town of Manchester. In Liverpool and its vicinity three splendid catholic churches were erected, at an expense of upwards of twenty thousand pounds, the greatest part of which was raised by the weekly penny subscriptions of the poor, which amounted on an average to the sum of twenty-five pounds. In Manchester, the weekly subscriptions for the erection of a new church in that town amounted, at the time of his departure from England, to the sum of fifty pounds. He, therefore, was persuaded that if the town of Sydney was divided into districts and collectors appointed on a plan similar to that adopted by the catholics of England, the result would prove what stupendous things may be achieved by the united exertions of a whole congregation, animated with the Spirit of God, in love with the beauty of His house, and the place where His glory dwells. Captain Carter seconded the resolution, to the following effect:—"That an association be this day formed, entitled, an association for the completion of the cathedral of St. Mary. That the members thereof engage to pay one half crown per month, or at the rate of sixpence for each member of the family, towards this object. That members of the association be invited to offer themselves to become collectors to this fund. That collectors shall meet on an appointed day for the purpose of arranging their several districts and of organising the association, and that the funds being at present exhausted a general subscription be opened, to which all are most earnestly invited to contribute,"

Mr. Therry, Commissioner of the Court of Requests, in moving. the next resolution said, it was one which required no great amount of eloquence, as the sentiment of congratulation and gratitude it contained would find a ready response in the boscm of every member of the meeting. It was natural and just that, on such an occasion as the present, they should offer their warmest acknowledgements, and the assurance of their grateful esteem to Dr. Ullathorne, for all the toils and travels, both by sea and land he had undertaken, solely for their interests, and in their service. In the supply of the numerous and efficient clergy he had induced to visit these shores—some preceding, some accompanying, and others yet to follow him—he had given proof of the zeal, ability and energy with which he fulfilled the mission entrusted to him. They had for many years experienced his zeal while he was present amongst them; but they had now manifestation of it whilst he was absent; and the only question they had to determine respecting him was, whether absent or present his anxiety for their welfare was the more assiduous,. persevering and serviceable? It must be gratifying to Dr. Ullathorne to see the edifice in which they were now assembled,. which he had left in a roofless and unfinished state, now rapidly advancing towards completion—and to see the catholic religion,. which was but as a speck on the horizon when he first touched upon these shores, gradually enlarging in size and strength. On such an occasion it was impossible to be unmindful of the services and of the name of the founder of that church in which they were then met, the Rev. Mr. Therry—a name that could not be blotted out from the page of the religious history in the colony nor erased from the tenderest and most grateful endearance of its catholic inhabitants. (Applause.) Besides the congratulations with which they had welcomed Dr. Ullathorne and his associates, they owed him a large debt of gratitude for the success of his exertions in the mission, which was not undertaken in the pursuit of any personal advantage nor to advance the wealth of the colony, already accumulating wealth beyond any British colony, nor to promote its commercial or agricultural interests. While in England, he would venture to say, his reverend friend had not once enquired how wool sold at Garraway's, nor into the state of the oil market. (Laughter.) There were a sufficient number already engaged in these pursuits. The object of his mission was quite a different one—to cause those to be remembered who were forgotten, to relieve the wants of the depressed and deserted, and to place a limitation to their distresses; to attend to the neglected—these were the high and meritorious objects of his mission, so that his voyage, like that of the illustrious Howard, may be said to have been " a circumnavigation of charity." The presence of the numerous clergy assembled on that day was the best argument in favour of the resolution, as it furnished proof of the zeal and services of Dr. Ullathorne, and the sympathy he created in their favour.

The second resolution was then passed from the chair:— " That whilst we acknowledge with unfeigned gratitude the goodness of Almighty God in the arrival of the reverend clergy who have recently come amongst us, our thanks are also due, and are hereby given, to the very reverend the vicar-general, for the zeal, activity and ability with which he has accomplished the arduous mission entrusted to him by the right reverend the bishop; and this meeting tenders to him and the reverend clergy who have lately arrived our congratulations and the expression of our grateful esteem."

Dr. Ullathorne next addressed the meeting :—" My lord, why should praise and honor be given to me? Praise and honor belong only to God, and to Him I give back that which you, dear friends, have given to me. In your heart, my lord, my heart lives. I have been but the organ of your spirit. For, as Samuel about Elias, so was I brought up about you, to serve the temple; as Paul before Gamaliel, so was I brought up at your feet. I am but as it were an excrescence upon the large heart which God has given to you for great purposes. I have long since lost my personal identity, which has been merged in yours, because I saw that yours was merged in a great cause, and that cause is not less than the planting of the church, and the planting in its primitive fervour in a new world. I have had no other will than yours, for in yours I have always been accustomed to see the will of God. You spoke, and I went forth; you breathed into me your spirit, and that spirit prevailed. Let me expand in gratitude to God, who sent His angel to accompany me and made all my designs to prosper. You, the beloved flock whom I served, judge of my joy at being again amongst you. If the brother rejoices at the return of an absent brother, if the mother's heart yearns over the children whom she sees again after a long absence, and if the guardian angel receives enlargement of happiness at the sight of those received into heaven over whom he has had long care, judge how full is my soul, who am at once your brother, your parent and your guardian, because your pastor. I left you not for any personal object, but that I might serve you the more. My friend Mr. Therry has well remarked that I never once whilst in Europe mentioned the price of wool or of oil, though I was doubtless often asked the question.

"'Well,' it would be asked of me by various persons, 'how is land selling in N.S.W.?' 'really,' I would reply, I have been so much occupied with the cultivation of sheep, that I have not paid much attention to mere land. 'Well then, how is wool selling?' 'Why, you will think it very strange; but though my flocks are very numerous, they don't bear wool; and if they did we would not fleece them.' (Laughter.) During my long absence you were ever in my heart; I lived but for you. On the trackless seas you were my care; amongst the icebergs of the Horn, in a most severe winter, my prayers were constant for you. I landed in England; and wherever my steps fell, in public or in private life, I spoke of you and of our wants. I passed over to Ireland and pleaded your cause; I entered into France, and it was sufficient to know you were Catholic, and in want of aid, to obtain the co-operation of the faithful in that country. I crossed the snowy Alps, descended upon the plains of Lombardy, passed through the innumerable states of Italy: and when I stood before that venerable man, on whose mitred brow a trinity of crowns is pressed—the load of the spiritual—I thought I saw Peter and all his successors. I saw the halo of 1800 years gathered on the august temples of Gregory the XVI; and in my person you all did homage to the prince of pastors, to the corner stone of Unity, to the successor of Peter, to the Vicar of Christ. Many and kindly affable were his enquiries about you, and deep the interest he showed in this remote portion of his universal charge.

"When I stood in the noblest temple the world ever saw, an emblem of our religion in its universality, I beheld from its centre how to every quarter of the world it expanded an arm, and how, above all, its vast dome seemed to enclose heaven as well as earth; and how it seemed to have gathered to itself all the richest materials of the earth, mystically arranged in order to express the profusion of spiritual treasures which it emblematically represents. This did not most interest me; but I went down beneath its marble pavements, and stood upon the porphyry floors of that elder church which Constantine, the first Christian Emperor, and Pope Sylvester had raised more than 1500 years ago. I entered the silver sanctuary, where side by side lie the bodies of Peter and Paul, the dearest remains which are left us—for the body of Christ arose and ascended to heaven; yet was that sacred body with me there in another manner, as it was on the altar to-day, and upon the altar of that tomb you were then in my heart, and I offered up the eternal sacrifice, that the Apostolic spirit in its first fervour might descend upon Australia.

"And when on the Feast of the Pasch I mingled with the 150,000 men of Rome, who blended with the 60,000 strangers gathered together from every spot of the earth within the arms of that vast portico, which seems to invite and embrace the world, and when that venerable figure of the sovereign pontiff arose with uplifted arms to bless the city and the world, you then knelt in me and prayed through me that, ' as the odors of a full field,' so might the blessings of God come down in their plenitude upon you.

"In short, whoever knew me said, that I seemed to live and breathe but for your cause. When I arose in the pulpits of England and Ireland, of you only could I utter a word, and of your wants and claims. In whatever I have said or written of you, at home or in foreign lands, I had but one object—to deter poor weak, ignorant men from crime, and to arouse the zeal of good men to hasten with their help to the fallen. For this I had but one resource : to spread before their eyes a picture of what my eyes had seen—of the miseries in which my heart had mingled. I know of no politics, for I am set apart to religion, I know of no parties or party views—except to lament the disunion and uncharities which grow out of them—for I am a minister of peace. I care not for the temporal interest or material happiness of any man or class of men, when these strike against interests antagonistic to the interests of a higher and more widely spread order. My motto in such matters is that of the illustrious Bishop Milner, ' I know of no politics but those of religion, and no party but the Church.' What man then in any place on this petty globe shall dare to rise so far above the respect he owes himself, as a member of our common humanity, as sharing the same flesh, blood, soul and spirit with myself, as having part in the common fall of our Nature—though he may have a trifle of the elevation —who shall presume to say, that I, who as a man cannot be insensible to the miseries of any of my fellow men, who as a christian should bring health to every wounded spirit, and a refreshing cordial to every troubled heart; what man dares so far to depart from himself as to say that I may not use the truth in order to arouse the zeal of men, and to deter from crime by painting the bitter miseries of its punishment?

"What changes have I witnessed in the Mission of this country? It is not six years since I landed a solitary stranger; I found but three priests, zealous ones indeed, but what were these amongst so many, and these so widely spread? This building, now so magnificent, was more like a ruin than a temple; the walls of two others, only commenced, were hastening to decay. I have seen strange invisible things as though they were visible. I have seen circumstances and events follow and combine with each other in such numerous and strange ways, independently of human will in our regard, that I can no more doubt the finger of a special Providence over our affairs, than if I saw it incarnate before me. I have done nothing, I was but the empty capacious vessel of reception for the gifts of God as they unexpectedly came from many quarters. Ireland, as of old, supplied her Saints, and England gave her money; the Continent even claims a share in the good work and France, Italy, Austria, Switzerland, Belgium, Holland and many other parts of Germany, contributed each their mite to enable me to complete the good work. The history of our Mission is known not only to our countrymen at home, but 75,000 copies in the languages of Europe have made it familiar to the faithful of the Continent, from the peasant to the prince, from Paris to Vienna, and from Constantinople to the Baltic. We have now twenty priests engaged in the Mission, besides the provision for Van Dieman's Land; eight divines under your own eyes, my lord, are preparing soon to enter the field of our labors; three others are equally making their preparations in the college of Douai. Schools are increasing; our missionaries are men on whose brows are stamped the character of holy experience, our young men all fresh in their fervor from the altar of their vows. The institutions of the Church are being completed; holy women have forgotten the delicacy of their nurture and the tenderness of their bringing up, they have closed their senses to the blandishments, the fascinations, and accomplishments of the world; they have made themselves deaf to the syren-cry of kindred and friends; they only know that here was much crime and misery. Why do the angels of God visit this earth? Because in Heaven there is no misery, and the God they love is merciful and compassionate; and they saw the Son of God come down to our poverty, to heal our sorrow by labour and sufferings. And these, his daughters, saw also in Australia the Cross was lifted up, and Christ upon it in bitter suffering; like the Maries, they thirsted to be near Him in his agonies. Wherever human miseries are greatest, there also will they be found; they will seek the bruised, they will bind up the broken heart, they will pour in oil and wine and balm—the oil of mercy, the wine of charity, the balm of heavenly consolation. I am ashamed of myself when I think of their heroism. One word let me address to the particular object of this meeting, and I have done. It was the glory of our forefathers in faithful ages, whilst they lived themselves in holy guise, to consecrate all the best gifts of God to the honour of His worship. They thought nothing too good for the God of goodness, who gave them all. Let us rejoice to be like them. Remember that you are not building for yourselves only, but leaving the best legacy, the noblest and most lasting monument of yourselves, to your descendents. It is here your minds are unburdened in their sorrows, here you receive pardon for repentance: from this altar the mingled streams of celestial fire and celestial blood will flow for your spiritual strength and animation. Here will your children be purified at the font, here will they receive the light of heaven, here will they be united in holy bands, here will be brought your greatest sorrows, that you may leave them, and hence you will carry your greatest joys. And when the grave closes over your bodies, when every other monument and remembrance of you have decayed and disappeared, the children of your children's children will be praying in this place, and enkindling the fervour of their religion by that spirit which, whilst it animates with life this temple, will recall the piety and self-sacrifice of those ancestors who, through many difficulties, raised it up for the service of the Living God.

"My Lord, may I express in conclusion my confident hope that at the end of your labours, (may they be very long) the crown of brethren with whom you are encircled—I have added fifteen to the number—may still be yours, enriched with the load of their labours; may you be able to say to Christ, ' of these whom thou gavest to me I have not lost one.' At the terrible account, (may it be far distant, and may I pass away first) may the thousands of your people be also with you, and the words which the Almighty put into the mouth of the prophet Ezekiel will be your own, and presenting them to the Son of God you will say, these came to me from the north, and these from the south, and these from the Austral land."

J. R. Brenan, Esq., J.P., moved the next resolution, and said —"I have a gratification beyond expression in proposing the resolution with which I have been honoured, to this most respectable meeting. It refers to men of other countries and other colonies. It reminds me of scenes of unparalleled intensity in interest, of which I was an humble spectator. I allude to the exertions which at length accomplished the liberation of our country from the bane of the law and the restrictions of religious jealousy—to the unwearied zeal of those men of God who lived only to console their people under their affliction and lift up their oppressed souls; how these same good and great men have seen our distress, and with a disinterested spirit have laboured to procure good of which they will not participate, save by the consciousness of having enabled others to comfort the captive, and to heal the wounded in affliction. Their reward must not come from us, but from Him who alone knows the amount of good they have accomplished. The expressions of our gratitude we may offer, and this is embodied in the resolution I have the honor to propose :—

"That our grateful acknowledgements are due, and hereby given, to the several Members of Parliament and to the other friends of the mission in England and Ireland, who have so earnestly and generously evinced their sympathy in our spiritual wants; and this meeting does especially appreciate that truly Catholic spirit which has influenced the Right Reverends the Bishops of Ireland to surrender their claims to the spiritual services of the apostolic men who have devoted themselves to the Australian Mission; and in the name and on the part of the Catholics of New Holland and Van Dieman's Land, we most respectfully and affectionately tender to their lordships the homage of our gratitude, esteem and veneration."

Dr. Ullathorne, on the motion moved by Mr. Brenan, seconded by Mr. Coveny, again addressed the meeting to the following effect :—"My lord, to the enlightened hierarchy of Ireland we are under very great obligations. Wherever I met those venerable men, whether assembled or individually, I found but one sentiment in our regard. I went before them a stranger, they received me as a friend; I went among them as an Englishman, they received me as though I had been an Irishman; I went amongst them unknown, they saw but my cause, and gave me their respect and unanimous co-operation. I had but one brief word to say, "My lord, our people were once your children, and the good Father never forgets his children, our mission is but an appendage to the Church of Ireland." To particularize where all were so willing and ready, is almost invidious, and yet I cannot avoid mentioning the names of two prelates whose sacrifice of their best subjects was most generous: The Most Reverend Dr. Murray, the Archbishop of Dublin, and the Right Reverend Dr. Kinsella, the Bishop of Ossory. To another ecclesiastic of eminent dignity in the Church we owe a peculiar tribute of remembrance. He it was who by letter urged my visit to the Holy See, and entertained much care for us. I arrived but in time to console him with the intelligence of our progress and prospects, for a few days afterwards, I stood on the outskirts of the assembled princes of the Church, as they knelt round his dying bed. The illustrious Cardinal Weld was our protector before the Holy See; as he was a saint on earth, so he, doubtless, is now a protector before the throne of God. Yet are we not left without a successor to his kindness. There are several, and one in particular—a distinguished member of the sacred college—who will look with a vivid interest for the particulars of our progress: the illustrious and princely Cardinal Castricane.

"To many of the members of the legislature we owe a debt of gratitude for their solicitude in our behalf. You are aware, my lord, and no one more so, how difficult it is for a stranger, amidst a crowd of applicants, to obtain ready access to Her Majesty's Ministers without the aid of influential members of the legislature. Here, again, I feel it almost invidious to particularize, but there are names which the burden of my gratitude urges me specially to mention. Of the members of the House of Lords we are most particularly indebted to the noble lords Clifford and Stourton, and to the noble Earl of Fingal. Of the members of the House of Commons we are specially indebted for their zeal in our behalf to Daniel O'Connell, Mr. Moore O'Farrell, Mr. Lynch, Mr. Shiel, the Honorable Mr. Langdale, and to that personification of indefatigable zeal and benevolence in the cause of religion, Mr. Philip Howard, who seemed to live but to serve us."

The Reverend Mr. Geoghegan moved the next resolution, which was to solicit additional aid from the Government. He

Mr. Therry, before the resolution passed, recommended that the Committee should use its best exertions to obtain numerous signatures for the petition. After the liberal aid offered by the Legislative Council in other instances, during the former and last sittings of the Council, it would be an unjust and unworthy suspicion to doubt the impartial distribution of the public funds, which experience forbade them to entertain; to doubt that the prayer of this petition would receive all the fair and favourable attention to which the wants of the community, on whose behalf it was presented, and the reasonableness of the request entitled it.

It was then moved by the Very Reverend Dr. Ullathorne:—"That the Right Reverend the Bishop do leave the chair, and that the Reverend Mr. Murphy take it."

Moved by the Very Reverend Dr. Ullathorne:—"That the thanks of this meeting are eminently due to the Right Reverend the Bishop, for his dignified and, what they valued much more, his amiable conduct in the chair."

The Bishop briefly expressed the pleasurable sensations with which this meeting was closed. Having congratulated the clergy and people on the union which existed amongst them, and on the supply of all the branches of spiritual administration, His Lordship exhorted them most earnestly and affectionately to evince their gratitude by a faithful correspondence with the Graces of Heaven, and whilst, with becoming zeal, they laboured to complete the material edifice, let them not forget the spiritual edifice to be built up unto Christ, by the exercise of Faith, of Hope, and of all the virtues of a good life. Having received the episcopal benediction, the meeting was dissolved. The collection amounted to about £130.

The new arrivals, whilst arrangements were being made, stayed at the Bishop's villa in Woolloomooloo. For a short time the Rev. P. B. Geogeghan was attached to the district of St. Benedict, and I may say he formed that mission. This is the same Father Geogeghan who was afterwards Bishop of Adelaide : he was a Franciscan Father, and had been one of the Community of Adam and Eve, in Dublin. He made his philosophy and theology in Spain, in a house belonging to his Order. He was distinguished in Dublin as a preacher. When he came to the colony his zeal, eloquence and learning attracted many, and he was very successful, by reason of his piety and learning, in advancing the glory of God, and gaining souls to his service. Not very long after commencing his labours in Sydney he was appointed to Port Philip, as the first Catholic missionary to that new settlement

M

The Rev. Richard Marum was stationed at Liverpool, near Sydney. He distinguished himself at Maynooth College, and had been studying for two or three years on the Dunboyne establishment; but his health failing, he did not long survive; had he lived he would have been a great acquisition to the mission, on account of his piety and learning. He was nephew to Bishop Marum, of Kilkenny. The Rev. T. Butler was very soon sent out by the Bishop to Launceston, in Van Dieman's Land. We will have the opportunity of noticing, in another page, the great good he did for religion.

The Sisters of Charity, whose names I have given, were the first Nuns who landed on these Australian shores; and they were selected in Ireland by Dr. Ullathorne. It required all but heroic resolution on the part of these religieuse to separate themselves at the time from their Holy Sisterhood, surrounded as they were by the grandeur, influence, and opportunities of religion, breathing an atmosphere of faith and virtue, to encounter a long, dreary, and dangerous voyage to the extremities of the earth, for the purpose of reforming the unfortunate of their sex, and generally to help in the advancement of Faith and morals. But since the day when the order was founded by St. Vincent de Paul, the Sisters of Charity were always ready to make generous sacrifices; whether on the field of battle by attending the wounded, amongst the crowded poor and disconsolate of the cities, or in the prisons amongst the criminals. The charity of God, with which their breasts are filled, knows no difference in its object. The zealous Bishop was overjoyed at the arrival of the Sisters, anticipating the good they would effect in communicating the graces of God to the most degraded, most despised and hardened of their sex. In the account of his mission, which he sent to the Propagation of the Faith, he gives particulars of the circumstances in which they were placed on their arrival, and where they were established. These are the words of Dr. Polding :—" The locality at Parramatta in which we intended to place them not being prepared when they arrived, they remained for some time in the residence of the Bishop. After the space of three weeks they were able to enter on the battle field of their labours : and immediately were their labours blessed by the most consoling results. There is an extensive factory in Parramatta in which those females are confined until they have been assigned to employers in the interior ; and some prefer to remain in the establishment that they may not be exposed to temptation. There are sometimes 1,200 of those unfortunate women in the factory at the same time, and usually about one half of these are Catholics. Your Eminence (addressing the

Cardinal Prefect of the Propaganda) will judge how necessary it was to introduce into such a place the sweet and consoling instructions of the Sisters of Charity. The Governor immediately granted the sisters permission to visit that asylum of crime and misery and to visit it whenever they thought fit. . . . . .
In the Lent succeeding the arrival of the Sisters of Charity a general preparation for the Sacraments was proposed to those who were confined in the factory. Nearly the whole of them availed themselves of the invitation. The Bishop, Vicar-General and two other priests attended to hear the confessions; and the result of this combined force was clearly discernible in the improved conduct of the inmates; the officials of the prison candidly acknowledged this to be a fact. Those who had not been confirmed received the sacrament of confirmation. In the meanwhile the edifying and assiduous exertions of the sisters caused a great many protestants to apply to them for instruction, and every week persons were led to the Faith and sanctity of life. Besides the duties of the sisters in the factory, which they fulfil at least twice a day; they visit the hospital of the town as well as the infirm. Further, they have charge of a large school and give instruction, when required. Our orphan school also is placed under their superintendence. The omnipotent God in his goodness has blessed them, and by inspiring the young with a vocation to a religious life, they have been enabled to undertake their duties with an increase of their number. Four have entered into the convent since the arrival of the sisters; one of them is a convert from Socinianism. They have obtained a house and garden which have been secured to the institute for ever. We are indebted for this in a great measure to the Association for the Propagation of the Faith, for which we cannot be sufficiently grateful."

I find that the origin of the Sisters of Charity coming to the colony was this: In the year 1837 Bishop Polding made application to Mother Mary Augustine Aaikenhead, foundress of the Sisters of Charity in Ireland, for a community to be devoted to the Australian mission. The sisters of Charity founded the Magdalene Asylum in 1848. For this charitable purpose a house was provided by Sir George Gipps, the governor, who gave the establishment, formerly known as Carter's Barracks. In the year 1856 this institution was consigned to the care of the Sisters of the Good Shepherd.

The Benedictine Sisters arrived in 1848, and were settled at Subiaco, on the Parramatta River. They are cloistered nuns, and devote themselves to the education of young ladies in the higher branches of learning.

Allow me to advert here to a grievous charge of injustice which was preferred by the famous Bishop of Exeter, Dr Philpotts, of Exeter Hall notoriety, against Sir Richard Bourke when he was governor of New South Wales, which implicated also the council of the colony at the time: He was charged with partiality and giving preference, inasmuch as he recommended, with the advice of his council, that Government support be allowed to the Roman Catholic Bishop, to the amount of £500 annually without an equal sum being raised by the Catholics of the colony. This charge was made by Bishop Philpotts in a pamphlet which contained the address to his clergy. was published in the year 1839, when Sir R. Bourke was living retired on his estate in the county of Limerick. I here present the able and statesman-like letter of the former Governor of New South Wales, in which he refutes and repels the monstrous injustice of that bigoted ecclesiastic.

SIR RICHARD BOURKE AND THE BISHOP OF EXETER

11 Upper Belgrave Street, Nov. 30, 1839.

My Lord,—I have seen within these few days, for the first time, your lordship's published Charge to the Clergy of the Diocese of Exeter, at their late visitation. The pamphlet, I find, contains observations on the ecclesiastical establishments in Australia, and, with reference to them, your lordship's statement of a proceeding of the Governor and Council of New South Wales at the time when I held the Government of that colony. The statement and your lordship's remarks upon it contain a heavy charge against the Governor and Council, and as I have reason to know that it is unfounded, your lordship will allow me to repel the charge as publicly as it has been made.

Your lordship accuses the Governor and Council of having recommended the appropriation of a sum of public money in favour of a Roman Catholic clergyman in direct contradiction a principle of the Government, acted upon in all cases affecting clergymen of the Church of England, thus combining partiality with malversation in the discharge of their official duty. The facts of the case are simply these: The Right Reverend Dr Polding came out to New South Wales towards the close of the year 1835 to exercise episcopal authority amongst those of the Roman Catholic communion in that colony. His stipend was fixed by Lord Aberdeen, under whose authority he came out,

£150 a year, which, under certain circumstances, was to be raised to £200. At the first session of the Colonial Legislative Council, subsequent to the arrival of Dr. Polding, a memorial was addressed to the Governor and Council in the name of the Roman Catholic inhabitants of New South Wales, praying for the augmentation of their bishop's stipend. The memorial having been taken into consideration in the usual form, and the important duties which Dr. Polding had to discharge, and the expense which he must necessarily incur in their execution being adverted to, as well as the station he occupied amongst those of his communion, and the fact that the Bishop of Australia received an annual stipend of £2000 from the Colonial Treasury, the Council resolved to recommend to the Secretary of State to raise that of Dr. Polding to £500.

Upon this transaction your lordship informs your clergy as follows:—" The Council recommend £500 per annum, which was proposed to the Government at home, and forthwith assented to, although it was in direct contradiction to the principle established five months before, and acted upon in all cases of the Church of England, that the amount of private contribution should be the condition and measure of public aid, (p. 15). In this case there was no private condition whatever."—(Charge, p. 11).

Now, when I inform your lordship that no such principle or rule as that which you have stated affecting the stipends of the clergy of any religious persuasion in New South Wales prevailed at the time when it was recommended to raise Dr. Polding's, nor, as I believe, at any time before, or at any time since (except in one contingency, not bearing at all upon the case, but which, to avoid any possible cavil, I will state hereafter), and that consequently no clergyman of the Church of England could possibly have been affected by it, the monstrous injustice which has been done to the Governor and Council by the sweeping declaration to your lordship's clergy, as above quoted, is but too clearly shown. Had your lordship been pleased to pay attention to the papers through which you state elsewhere you had travelled to discover the Church to which I gave a preference, you could hardly have failed to see that it was proposed and authorised by the Home Government that for the erection of churches, chapels, and ministers' dwellings a sum equal in amount to private contributions might be issued from the Colonial Treasury, but it is nowhere proposed or directed in these papers to require any contribution in aid of the stipends of the clergy, which are, on the contrary, to be paid by the colony under a totally different regulation. It is possible your lordship may have merely adverted to the expression in Lord Glenelg's dispatch of the 30th Nov., 1835, which you quote; but, in a matter involving a charge of official delinquency against the representative of the Crown, and the Council appointed by the Crown in one of its foreign possessions, it would have been no unusual exercise of prudence to have ascertained by comparing Lord Glenelg's dispatch with that to which it replied, how far the expression you relied on related to the matter under consideration, and whether it fairly and fully supported the charge proposed to be founded on it.

The exception to which I have referred is to be found in Sec. 5 of the New South Wales Act, 7 Wm. IV., No. 3, which authorises a certain allowance in aid of private contributions to clergymen employed to visit at settlers' houses in remote districts, where no churches or chapels have been built; it would be available, by reason of the scattered condition of the inhabitants. This Act was not passed until August, 1836, and does not bear on the question of Dr. Polding's stipend.

In the paragraph of the Charge at p. 10, from which I have quoted, your lordship evinces a very laudable anxiety for the maintenance of due subordination in the Colonial Department and you state with seeming displeasure and regret, that "Sir R. Bourke scrupled not, in despite of the despatch of Lord Aberdeen, to take advice of the Council upon the amount of stipend which they would be willing to assign to Dr. Polding, if His Majesty's Government consented to enlarge it." But your lordship has omitted to state that the question arose upon a memorial addressed to the Governor and Council by a number of respectable gentlemen in the name and on behalf of the Roman Catholics of New South, which document is to be found with the despatch from which your lordship quotes. To this petition your lordship doubtless would at once have replied in the words you placed in italics, that "Lord Aberdeen was not prepared to sanction the augmentation of Dr. Polding's stipend." But I have yet to learn that it is the duty of Governor's to slight the petitions of Her Majesty's subjects, or to debar her Ministers from performing in her name, an act of grace and sound policy, even though it should be necessary to revise a former instruction. Sure I am, that a nobleman, whose name has just been mentioned, would more honor the breach than the observance of any command of his which was found to be at variance with the reasonable desires of any loyal and dutiful subject of the Crown.

The same charge is repeated in italics in the next paragraph of the pamphlet as applying to the Roman Catholic Vicar-General of New South Wales, and must for the reasons already given be declared unfounded.

Your lordship also imputes blame to the Lieutenant-Governor and Council of Van Dieman's Land for having granted in 1835 to the Roman Catholics of Hobart Town pecuniary aid for erecting a chapel, on terms more favorable than those granted to members of the Church of England proposing to build a church in the same town. Though I cannot pretend to have as intimate acquaintance with the affairs of Van Dieman's Land as with those of New South Wales, yet I will venture, in the absence of Sir George Arthur in Canada, to offer an opinion though opposed to your lordship's, that the Lieutenant-Governor and Council had good reasons for what they did. I find in Sir George Arthur's Minute of 1835 to the Legislative Council a document, not given with the Parliamentary Papers, No 112, the following statement of each case :—" In Trinity parish a church is much wanting. Subscriptions were invited two years since from the inhabitants, but from some unexplained cause the scheme has languished until very lately. I confidently rely upon your support in providing such sums as may be required for the erection of a church in that quarter of the town, keeping in view the principle laid down by his Majesty's Government." And in the paragraph next but one it is stated :—" You are aware that the Roman Catholics of Hobart Town have not at present any suitable place of Public Worship whilst His Majesty's Government has recently acquiesced in an increase of the number of chaplains. It has appeared to me, therefore, though I have received no direct instructions from home on the subject, to be proper that aid should be given them in building a chapel sufficiently large to accommodate them, and I have accordingly proposed that £1500 should be voted for that purpose. It will be remembered that a considerable number of the members of this communion are not in circumstances to subscribe largely, and I think, therefore, that this is a case in which an equal contribution by the people should not be rigidly required."

I believe at that period (1835) there was no official regulation in Van Dieman's Land by which the aid granted to Roman Catholics or Dissenters was to be measured ; and up to that date, I apprehend, little aid had been granted to them ; whereas a rule by which the building of churches and schools for the Church of England was to be aided to the amount of private contributions had been long in existence. The regulation under which other communions became entitled to similar aid, and to that only, did not reach Van Dieman's Land until 1836.

I will now beg leave to remark, that if I had not thought it necessary to refute the charge brought against the Governor and

Council of New South Wales, it is probable I should not have noticed what your lordship is pleased to say of myself at page 5 of the pamphlet in a strain certainly not remarkable for courtesy or candour. Your lordship observes, that "Sir R. Bourke, in all his numerous and voluminous despatches, so far as I can discover, does not appear in a single instance to indicate the slightest preference of any church, or any creed whatever, the only feeling on this subject expressed by this representative of the Sovereign in New South Wales being that of hostility to an established church." I will briefly reply that it was no part of my duty to lay before the Secretary of State for the Colonies my confession of faith, or to trouble him with my opinion on the advantages or disadvantages of an established church, except as related to the affairs of the colony whose affairs I administered. It need not, therefore, have surprised your lordship that in perusing my despatches, you find no display of my religious opinions. If the service of the colony had required their publication, they would have been given. That service did however require that I should convey to the Minister of the Crown the best information I could obtain as to the opinions and feelings of the colonists, for whose religious instruction a provision was about to be made. Sir George Arthur also thought it necessary to report the prevailing opinion upon the subject of church establishment in Van Dieman's Land. At page 70 of the Parliamentary papers, to which your lordship has so often referred, he observes:—"I very fully appreciate the views entertained and expressed in the Executive Council by the Chief Justice, and other equally reflecting and excellent persons, who seem to dread any countenance being given to other sects as injurious to the interests of the established church. I go all lengths with them in the conviction that some establishment is necessary; but I do not think that the support of an exclusive system was at any period wise. It is not only impolitic by defeating the end aimed at, but, in the present day, I conceive it would be impracticable to support it without such an opposition as would shake the Church itself." The representations made to the Secretary of State, as to the course of public opinion in New South Wales, produced a measure which has, I trust, secured the lasting peace, while it has excited the religious spirit of the colonists. In 1836 a Church Act was passed by the Council, without a dissentient voice, facilitating the erection of places of worship, and the appointment of ministers of religion. Of these advantages by much the largest share has been obtained, as was anticipated, by the Church of England. Several new churches have been built, or are in progress, and the number of chaplains of this communion has been nearly, if not fully, doubled since the passing of the Church Act˙ in 1836.

> I have the honour to be, my lord,
> Your lordship's most obedient, humble servant,
>
> (Signed)   RICHARD BOURKE.

To the Lord Bishop of Exeter.

————

CHAPTER VI.

The arrival of Sir George Gipps, 24th February, 1838—Instructions of Lord Glenelg giving the order of precedence of the Civil and Ecclesiastical Authorities—Complaint of Bishop Broughton against Bishop Polding, for having been received at the Government House in the habiliments appropriate to a Bishop of Rome—Letter of Bishop Polding in reply to the allegation made by the Protestant Bishop—The case submitted to the Catholic Institute in London, and their Answer.

His Excellency Sir George Gipps arrived in the colony by the ship Upton Castle, in the month of February, 1838; and by the same ship came—Rev. John Brady, (afterwards Bishop of Perth); Rev. James A. Goold (now the Archbishop of Melbourne), and Messrs. P. Farrelly and—M'Philips, ecclesiastical students. I have previously given an account of the arrival of these priests and students.

On the day of the arrival of the Governor, Sir George Gipps, he issued a proclamation to the effect that he had assumed the Government of the colony, and that her Majesty had been pleased to appoint the Bishop of Australia, the Colonial Secretary, and the Colonial Treasurer, to be members of the Executive Council.

In the beginning of the year 1838 the instructions from Lord Glenelg, the Secretary of State, were published in the colony, giving the order of precedence of the Civil authorities and the Ecclesiastical authority.

The following is the order laid down:—1, The Governor; 2, Lieutenant-Governor; 3, the Bishop; 4, Chief Justice; 5, Members of the Executive Council; 6, President of the Legislative Council; 7. Members of the Legislative Council; 8, Speaker of the House of Assembly; 9, Puisne Judges.

An occurrence took place in the year 1839, in regard to a complaint of the Protestant Bishop, which caused no little surprise amongst the Catholics of these colonies. Dr. Broughton complained that the Right Reverend Dr. Polding was received by the Governor at the levee " in the habiliments which are appropriate to a Bishop of the Church of Rome." He had complained before, in the time of Governor Bourke, but the practise being continued in the time of Governor Gipps, he took upon him to reprove that governor also for his indiscretion in receiving and recognising Dr. Polding as a Catholic Bishop. Governor Gipps acquainted Dr. Polding with the complaint of Bishop Broughton, and it was then that Bishop Polding sent a letter to the Governor in reply to the allegation made by Dr. Broughton. The Protestant Bishop must have been very much chagrined when he did not obtain that redress which he expected. The complaint was by no means creditable to him, and showed plainly the spirit of ascendency and exclusiveness by which he was actuated. The case was laid by Bishop Polding, with all the correspondence, before the Catholic Institute of London, which had been established not long before and that influential body completely vindicated the conduct of the Right Rev. Dr. Polding. I here give the correspondence..

The Catholic Institute was duly made acquainted with the act of Bishop Polding, in attending the Governor's levee in a costume becoming a Catholic Bishop; the being received in such a costume giving great offence to the Protestant Bishop, Dr. Broughton. In the notice taken by the Institute it states :— Dr. Polding has been in the habit of attending the levees of his Excellency the Governor in the costume referred to in his Lordship's letter of the 2nd July, 1839, hereinafter stated, and be so appeared at a levee holden on 24th May, 1839. On the day following, Dr. Broughton, who is the Protestant Bishop in the colony, addressed and sent a letter to Sir George Gipps, who is now the Governor, of which the following is a copy :—

Sydney, May 25, 1839

Sir,—Having yesterday had the honour of attending your Excellency's levee at Government-house, for the purpose of paying my respect to your Excellency, on the occasion of her most gracious Majesty's birthday, I witnessed the public admission and reception of the Right Reverend Dr. J. B. Polding, wearing those habiliments which are appropriate to a Bishop of the Church of Rome. On a similar celebration in the year 1837 a corresponding occurrence took place; and I then addressed to Governor Sir

Richard Bourke a letter expressive of my sentiments, a copy whereof I have the honour now to enclose. This letter I at that time withdrew, upon receiving from Sir Richard Bourke an assurance that such appearance of Dr. Polding at the levee was unforseen by him, and that it would not be repeated, unless the practice in that respect at London or Dublin should be altered. It appears to me, however, that no discretion now remains to me; but that having witnessed the renewed endeavour now made to obtain from your Excellency a recognition of Dr. Polding as a bishop within the dominions of her Majesty, and thereby of the jurisdiction of the bishops of Rome within this realm, I should be guilty of a neglect of duty, approaching perhaps to a high crime and misdemeanour, if I forbore to notice and oppose it.

I have the honour, therefore, to request that the letter now enclosed, and which was originally addressed to Sir Richard Bourke, may be considered as expressing my present views. I have further to request that the same may be transmitted by your Excellency to her Majesty's principal Secretary of State for the Colonies with an application for a legal decision of the question, how far such a public reception of a Roman Catholic Bishop,. avowedly and visibly in that capacity, is recognised by the Statute Law of England, and with the oath of supremacy especially which civil and ecclesiastic functionaries in general within her Majesty's dominions are required to take.

In addition to the above statement, I will with submission intrude upon your Excellency with the expression of my hope, that in making such a representation and remonstrance I am acting wholly upon public grounds and not with a design—which, indeed, I expressly disclaim—of manifesting any personal disrespect towards Dr. Polding.

I have, &c.,
(Signed)   W. G. AUSTRALIA.

His Excellency Sir George Gipps, &c., &c.

The Institute states:—It is not considered necessary to refer to the complaint of Dr. Broughton, made in 1837, further than to state that it was to the same effect as the one made by his letter of the 25th May, 1839.

His Excellency the Governor having communicated to Dr. Polding the complaints of Dr. Broughton, Dr. Polding on the 2nd July, 1839, addressed to the Governor a long letter on the subject, from which the following are extracts:—

"In the case as stated by Dr. Broughton, my appearance at the levee and your Excellency's reception of me, could only be construed as a testimony of respect paid by a foreign prelate, an alien to the representative of her gracious Majesty in the manner deemed by him most fit to testify respect; and your reception of him was nothing more than the courtesy a stranger bearing his character would assuredly receive from your Excellency. It is not easy to discern how in this transaction the Statute Law, or the oath of supremacy, or the Act of Settlement has been infringed. I proceed to the facts of the case. I did attend on the occasion alluded to, as became the head of one of the recognised religious denominations in the colony, and was received by your Excellency; but I did not attend, and of course was not received by your Excellency in the appropriate vestments of a Bishop of Rome. I have never attended (I should deem the exhibition unseemly and indecent) any secular solemnity in the appropriate vestments of the episcopal order. If by pontifical ornaments be meant the cross which I wear on my breast, and my ring, these I received on the day of my consecration to remind me of my vocation and its obligation; these I have worn ever since in every place, at every time; in the dining and drawing room, as in the church and the condemned prisoner's cell; and never till now were they made a matter of offence—with what propriety by one bearing the character of a Christian prelate, I leave your Excellency to judge.

"As regards the levee of 1837, with feelings of extreme pain I proceed to notice the second allegation, because it rests on the personal testimony of the Right Reverend Dr. Broughton. The Right Reverend Prelate declares that he witnessed the public admission and reception of myself wearing the habiliments appropriate to a Bishop of the Church of Rome. Truth compels me to place my solemn denial of the assertion, resting on the personal testimony of his lordship, in contraposition to that assertion and that testimony. I deliberately deny the correctness of the statement offered to your Excellency. At the same time I am fully aware how easily an error in judgment may be formed on this subject. I do not ascribe to the Right Reverend Prelate an intentional misstatement of fact; but when the Right Reverend Dr. Broughton proceeds from erroneous judgment on fact to gratuitous imputation of intention, when he ventured to take the range of my mind and to assert that I thus appeared for the purpose of obtaining a recognition as a bishop from your Excellency, I feel that a liberty is assumed in my regard, which I can find no palliating circumstances to excuse. Such intention never entered my thoughts. It is not by appearance at a levee in a dress tolerated or not censured that I would accept recognition of my sacred character by the Government your Excellency represents. That there is a recognised Catholic Bishop in the colony the legislative enactments of the constituted authorities bear evidence, as well as the Church Act in its clauses, the Church Act in its regulations, the Legislative Council in its regulations and decisions. Does not the entire body of your Excellency's official correspondence in reference to the Roman Catholic Church in the colony, that of your Excellency's predecessor from the month of October, 1835, give testimony that I am the individual honoured in the recognition of that name? Permit me to mention that before I acquiesced in my nomination, foreseeing the difficulties that might arise, I required that the Government at home might be consulted. The Right Reverend Dr. Bramston, who usually transacted business with the Colonial office in reference to the Roman Catholic Church in the colonies, applied to the Secretary of State to ascertain the feeling of the Government. Not only was consent given, but the extreme propriety of appointing a bishop to govern the Catholic community in this colony was distinctly expressed. It was with the formal approbation of the Government at home that I departed from England. To support my episcopal character and dignity, the honorable Legislative Council made a provision immediately after my arrival. No, sir, I did not attend the levee in pontifical vestments, or habiliments, or ornaments to obtain from your Excellency a recognition of myself as a bishop of the Church of Rome. I repudiate the charge, and deem myself aggrieved that an act and intention unworthy of my station should be groundlessly imputed to me by the Right Reverend Dr. Broughton, for no one in the colony ought more accurately to appreciate the pure and exalted motives which should influence a bishop in all the transactions of life.

"Having thus noticed the case *de jure,* and the facts on which that case has been raised, I might close this letter. Certain observations of the right rev. prelate, however, will justify me in a further trespass on your Excellency's time and patience. His lordship states that he withheld his first letter to Sir Richard Bourke on the assurance given him by his Excellency that no such appearance of mine would be repeated. Sir Richard Bourke did certainly speak to me on the subject, and mentioned that some person had taken offence, not specifying the name or station of the individual. He did not inform me that the Right Reverend Dr. Broughton had interfered and remonstrated, considering that appearance of mine as an inroad on his jurisdiction. Had I been in possession of this information, I assure your Excellency that

before your arrival in the colony, with the permission of yo
predecessor, the letter of the right rev. prelate, with my rep
would have been laid before the authorities at home.

"His Excellency Sir Richard Bourke is moreover inform
that the anxiety imposed on the mind of the right revere
prelate on the subject of his letter was widely diffused among t
Protestant portion of the community. Of the existence of t
widely diffused anxiety, till I received the communication fr
your Excellency, I was entirely ignorant. I am honored by a
unextensive acquaintance in that community, many particula
valued friends, holding influential rank, are in it. A we
expressive of offence taken by themselves or by others was ne
conveyed to me, and I rely so firmly on their interest in
welfare as to be certain that if they had heard that anxi
expressed they would not have permitted me to remain
ignorance of it. The public papers, some of which were incess
in their attacks on the Roman Catholic community, and habitua
using every plausible pretext for censuring the acts of the I
Governor, passed over this cause of widely diffused anxi
without a remark.

"I cannot refrain from adding my conviction that, considen
the purport and contents of the two letters of the Right Reven
Dr. Broughton, the question at issue regards not vestments
habiliments, crosses and rings, but something of higher impe
ance, namely, whether each religious denomination is to en
freedom of conscience on the footing of perfect equality,
whether a hateful exclusiveness is to be introduced and establia
—whether one whom the Right Honorable Lord Glenelg
distinguished as the Bishop of the Church of England in Austr
is to be the only recognised head in the colony, or whether c
religious denomination recognised by the Government in its b
and its members, looking up to Her Gracious Majesty a
common protector and friend, free from all unseemly jealousy
contentious bickering for exclusive favor and domination, a
exist on the distinctly avowed basis of perfect equality,
cultivate peace and social love."

Dr. Polding, having done the Catholic Institute the ho
of transmitting to it a statement of the facts, in order, as
lordship expresses himself, that its influential members u
"interfere in the affair so far as may be necessary," a meet
of the Committee of Grievances was held on the 18th Janur
1840, at which it was resolved to submit the case to Messrs. Ad

Bagshawe and Cook, barristers-at-law, members of such Committee, for their opinion as to the legal bearing of it, and the following is a copy of the report of those gentlemen :—

"It having been referred to us the undersigned, by the Committee of Grievances of the Catholic Institute, to consider the legal question arising out of the correspondence, and other documents, relating to the affairs of the Right Rev. Dr. Polding, Catholic Bishop and Vicar-Apostolic of New Holland and Van Dieman's Land, we certify that we have taken the matter so referred to us into our consideration ; and we are of opinion that if ever the Right Rev. Dr. Polding had, as alleged in the letter of the Bishop of the Church of England in Australia, appeared at the levee of his Excellency the Governor of Sydney in the appropriate vestments and Pontifical ornaments of a bishop of the Catholic Church, (called in the letter of the Protestant bishop "the Church of Rome,") that his lordship would not have violated any law in force ; for we are of opinion that, in point of law, the prohibition against the public wearing of the Pontificals and priestly vestments, appertaining to the bishops and clergy of the Catholic church, which is embodied in the 26th sec., of the 10th Geo. IV, C. 7. (the Emancipation Act) does not extend to the colonies. We beg to drawpthe attention of the Committee to the fact of the constant appearance of the Catholic prelates of Ireland at the levees of the Lord Lieutenant in Dublin, wearing the precise ornaments stated in the letter of the Right Rev. Dr. Polding to the Governor of Sydney, dated 2nd July 1839, to have been worn by his lordship, with the addition of the purple Episcopal cassock. We also beg to draw the attention of the Committee to the fact that his late Majesty King George IV., has on the occasion of his visit to Ireland, received the Catholic bishops in a costume similar to that worn by Dr. Polding. We are also of opinion that if the case of Dr. Polding required to be strengthened, the public sanction of his lordships ecclesiastical rank and functions by the Government of Sydney, (especially by the printed circular issued from the Colonial Secretary's Office, dated 4th Sept., 1836, would not only justify the appearance of his lordship at the levee of the Governor in the dress and wearing the dress appearing to have been worn by him, but would render it a breach of state etiquette if his lordship had appeared on such an occasion in any dress that did not in some manner indicate his officially acknowledged rank and functions.

Dated this 22nd day of January, 1840.

(Signed)　　HENRY R. BAGSHAWE
　　　　　　JOHN ATHANASIUS COOKE
　　　　　　CHARLES ADDIS

It has been subsequently resolved. by the Committee to submit this case to such of the Vice. Presidents of the Catholic Institute who are peers and members of Parliament, in order that they may lay the facts (if they should think proper so to do) before the Colonial Secretary in England.*

JAMES SMITH, Secretary.

I will now give an account of the establishment, in Sydney, of a Branch of the Catholic Institute. Bishop Polding considered it would be a great support and assistance to the Catholics in the colony to be united with our brethren in England by this means. The Catholic Church at that time was constantly assailed by bigoted and malevolent Protestants, the pulpit, the press, and the platform resounded with calumnies and misrepresentations against the Catholic Church. The zealous efforts which were being made by the bishop and his priests were represented as quite alarming. A Wesleyan minister, the Rev. J. McKenny, writing from Sydney in regard to the exertions of the Catholics states :—" This is not a matter of mere pounds, shillings and pence, for it now assumes this form:—Shall Australia be a Protestant or a Popish colony ? The number of priests who are being sent out is quite frightful. Eight arrived lately in one vessel, and received from the Home Government £150 each for their passage and outfit."

[* By private communication from a friend in London, we are given to understand that Lord John Russell had been waited on by one of the most influential of the vice-presidents, and that his lordship declared he considered Dr. Broughton's remonstrance unfounded and untenable. The Catholic Institute deserves the lasting respect and gratitude of Catholics in the colonies.—ED.]

THE RIGHT REV. DR. MURPHY.

CHAPTER VII.

A great public meeting of the Catholics in Sydney, 10th Sept.,
1840, when a branch of the Catholic Institute of Great Britain
was established, and also a branch of the Society for the
Propagation of the Faith—The general objects of the Catholic
Institute of Great Britain, with the names of the patrons—
The labours of Bishop Polding—Laying the Foundation
Stone of St. Joseph's Church at the Lower Hawkesbury—
Foundation Stone laid by Bishop Polding at West Maitland
—Ordinations in St. Mary's Cathedral, Sydney, 18th Oct.,
1840—Foundation Stone of the Church of St. Francis Xavier
at Wollongong laid by Bishop Polding—The Foundation
Stone of the Schoolhouse at Campbelltown blessed by Bishop
Polding.

A PUBLIC meeting was held in the Old Courthouse, Castlereagh-street, on 10th September, 1840, for the purpose of forming auxiliary branches of the Catholic Institute of Great Britain, and of the Society for the Propagation of the Faith. The house was crowded to excess, the platform being occupied by the Bishop and Clergy, the gentlemen forming the committee of St. Patrick's Society, and the delegates from the country districts. His Lordship, in opening the meeting, said that the establishment of a branch of the Institute seemed to be imperatively required on account of the incessant attacks made upon their religious tenets and liberty; moreover, their object was to organize an union with that Association whose effects and transactions filled the world, &c., &c.

The Rev. Francis Murphy moved the first resolution, viz. :—
"That the numerous attacks made by means of misrepresentation and in other unjustifiable ways upon the Catholic community of New South Wales by organised societies, by officials of the Government, and others, render it expedient that we should establish a branch of the Catholic Institute of Great Britain and her Colonies for the purpose of self-defence." Amongst many appropriate remarks he said that their object in furthering the views for which that meeting had been assembled was to unite the Catholics in one compact body, not for the purpose of attack, although they had been called idolatrous imposters and clerical scoundrels, but merely for the purpose of self-defence. Both the clergy and the laity expected uncontrolled enjoyment of the religion of their fathers; and that no dominant Church would be

N

allowed to rear its unhallowed head, fostered and cherished by the hand of power, to the prejudice of other religious denominations in this the land of their adoption.

Mr. Duncan, editor of the Catholic Australasian Chronicle, moved the second resolution. After a few introductory remarks in praise of the Catholic Institute, he said it was true, as the Rev. Mr. Murphy had remarked, that the Catholic Church of New South Wales had been attacked on all sides. They had been assailed by Diocesan committees, reviled in productions of Tract Societies, insulted by the abominable and ridiculous fabrications of catch-penny Protesant magazines, and attacked by public and private individuals of all ranks in society. Indeed he was well convinced that it was only the existence of an act of the legislature which prevented their enemies from coming upon them with all the force of determined physical oppression. There was one remark that he would make, undeterred either by the absence of one gentleman who was concerned in it or by the presence of the other, namely : That the work of the Very Rev. Dr. Ullathorne was a complete answer to the aspersions cast upon the Catholic community in the pamphlet by Mr. Justice Burton. He then moved :—" That the thanks of the meeting are eminently due, and are hereby presented, to the Very Rev. the Vicar-General for his able, eloquent, and satisfactory reply to Mr. Burton, judge of the Supreme Court, in vindication of the Catholics of the Colony : a reply which has added another to the many titles he had previously acquired to our respect, confidence, and gratitude." Before the resolution was put to the meeting Mr. Gibbons remarked that although he must admit the work of Mr. Justice Burton had been offensive to the Catholic people, yet it had still been productive of great ultimate benefit to them, inasmuch that it had called forth a reply which was unanswerable and had also compelled them to meet that evening for the purpose of organization against similar attacks. (Cheers). The resolution was seconded by Mr. McGuigan and carried amid loud acclamations. The Lord Bishop presented the resolution to the Very. Rev. Dr. Ullathorne, remarking that he did so with feelings of extreme pleasure, knowing the inward gratification the receipt of such a resolution, accompanied with such a demonstration, would give the receiver, embodying as it did the enthusiastic approval of all those in whose cause he had so worthily exerted himself The Very Rev. Dr. Ullathorne, amidst loud and continued greeting, returned thanks and rose to say he had been taken by surprise, as he did not expect the passing of such a resolution. . He felt sincere pleasure at the receipt of such a resolution, embodying as

· it did the approbation of those in whose defence ho had taken up his pen so often ; but however often he had found it necessary to do this in defence of the Catholics of New South Wales, he called all present to witness that he had never done so for the purpose of attack. The task which he had imposed upon himself to reply to Judge Burton he had found a comparatively easy one, for the moment he took up that gentleman's book he perceived the erroneous principle on which it was founded, and he had only to peruse the necessary official documents in order to establish a full and complete refutation of every assertion the Judge had made to the prejudice of their holy religion.

The third resolution was moved by Rev. Mr. Goold :—"That besides an Auxiliary Catholic Institute it is expedient that we should form a branch of the Society for the Propagation of the Faith." This Institution was not less important than the Catholic Institute, for it was by its influence and the exertions of its members that the sacred truths of Christianity were spread far and wide over the surface of the globe. The only way to resist the incessant attacks against their holy faith would be to form themselves into organized bodies, and by a liberal contribution from their purses to further the dissemination of useful publications. Thus the clouds of calumny might be removed by which the shining rays of truth had so long and so oppressively been overcast. The resolution was seconded by Rev. Mr. Fitzpatrick and carried unanimously.

The Very Rev. Dr. Ullathorne then moved the fourth resolution and said it required considerable energy and power of the mind to do it justice, but he was enfeebled by bodily indisposition and would therefore only read the resolution, which shewed its own intention :—"That the Catholic Institute and the Society for the Propagation of the Faith be formed in union with the Parent Institute and Society respectively, upon the fundamental principles, &c., &c." He then continued to say the circumstances of the Colony justified them in establishing the Institute, so as to combat as successfully as might be the numerous and unjust attacks which were being made upon the Catholic body collectively and individually. They were assailed by the judge on the bench, by the justice of the peace, by clergymen from the pulpit. The Catholic community did not wish to quarrel with anyone, but was rather desirous of associating peaceably with their fellow-colonists ; still it was necessary, in justice to their civil and religious safety, to defend themselves against the unprovoked assaults. At the very last meeting of the Diocesan Committee what had been said from the pulpit was carefully collected and afterwards printed, charging the Catholics with usurpation, and asserting that its followers offered all their prayers and sacrifices through another mediator than our Blessed Redeemer. It was no longer ago than the Tuesday before last when a person, a non-commissioned officer of a regiment, asserted at a public meeting held for the purpose of disseminating the gospel of peace, that Popery, Infidelity, and Satan were in league. Dr. Ullathorne spoke of the Tract Society and its publications which were distributed everywhere, filled with misrepresentations, calumnies, and falsehoods, which only perverted ingenuity could devise. He further referred to another production—the *Sydney Protestant Magazine.* In the number for June, 1840, it professed to give "the prices charged for indulgences in various sins by the present Pope." It appears there, according to the author of the paragraph, that a Catholic may murder a layman for £1 1s. 5d. If a layman murdered a priest he must pay £1 19s. 2d. To murder a bishop would cost £15 13s. 7d. The author of this precious document was the Rev. Mr. McIntyre. Where did he get his information? He (Dr. D.) would tell him. It came from a book written by one Laurentz Bank, a Swedish Protestant. The present Pope was not more than 75 years old, and this book was published in the year 1651. So far from being copied from any Papal document, it was immediately condemned by the Holy See for its falsehoods and placed on the index of prohibited books, where it remains to this day. It appeared to him truly astonishing when he saw gentlemen whose general character they were bound to respect............were yet capable of meeting together in a society, and contributing by the aid of their presence and influence to the circulation of productions which seemed to have no other object in view than to insult and degrade the catholic name. It was always insinuated in these productions that catholics were prohibited to read the Scriptures; whereas the clergy of the catholic church were most anxious for the laity to read the Scripture. Before the year 1440 the art of printing was not known, and the copies of the Scripture then in existence, were the work of laborious penmanship. Prior to the publication of Luther's Bible, there were twenty nine editions of the Catholic Bible circulating in Germany; in France not less than eighteen versions before the year 1541; in Spain two; in Italy, the heart and fountain of Popery, fifteen editions were published before that of Martin Luther, and all in the vulgar tongue. Nay, there was on an average a new Catholic edition of the Scriptures in Italy for every eighteen months during the course of some seventy years after the discovery of printing; fifty editions in seventy succeeding years. It could be clearly shewn, even at the earliest period of British history, that the Catholic clergy were employed on that good work. In the year 706 there was a translation of the Psalms and New Testament into the vulgar tongue, made by the conjoint efforts of an Abbot and a Bishop for the use of the common people. In the year 736 that truly venerable man Bede, a catholic monk, expired praising God, who had prolonged his life until he had completed the last line of his translation of the Holy Scriptures into the language of the people. King Alfred, who died in 900, made a translation of the Psalms. In 995 Elfric, Catholic Archbishop of Canterbury, made a new translation of nearly all the Old Testament. In the year 1290 a translation of the Scriptures was done in English, of which three copies are still in existence. On account of the persecutions at the time of the Reformation there was no new translation of the Holy Scripture. The first edition of the Rheims Testament appeared in 1582, and the first edition of the entire Douay Bible in 1610. He was informed by one catholic bookseller in Dublin that he sold 50,000 copies of the Catholic Bible in the course of ten years. In 1836 it was stated in the House of Commons that in the course of six years three Irish catholic bishoprics had printed and published 309,000 copies of the Sacred Scriptures among their people. He had said enough to show that Popery was in league with no party, however infamous or respectable, to stop the Word of Life; and having, as he thought, established the necessity of consolidating the catholic community into one body for the purpose of defence—owing to the weak state of his health he was unable to enter upon other important considerations—he moved the resolution, which was seconded by Rev. Mr. Platt, and then carried unanimously.

The Rev. Mr. Brennan moved the fifth resolution, viz:—That the funds of the two institutions be preserved distinct, and that after all expenses have been paid, they be remitted to the parent Institute and Society respectively." The resolution was seconded by Mr. Coveny and carried unanimously.

The sixth resolution, "That the Right Rev. the Bishop be President of the Institute, and of the Society for the Propagation of the Faith," moved by Dr. Harnett, and seconded by Captain Carter, was also carried without dissent

The Lord Bishop thanked the meeting for the honour they had done him, and expressed a hope that the satisfaction which he should give in the performance of the duties attached to that office would be equal to the pleasure which he should feel in fulfilling them.

The seventh resolution, "That the Very Rev. the Vicar-General and the Reverend Deans be *ex officio* Vice Presidents" was then carried.

The Very Rev. Dr. Ullathorne took advantage of the opportunity to return thanks on behalf of himself and his reverend brethren the Deans. He wished to say that the Catholic Institute of Great Britain was established in the year 1838, chiefly by the influence of that distinguished individual Daniel O'Connell, Esq., M.P. Its president was the Right Honourable the Earl of Shrewsbury, and its vice-presidents the Right Hon. the Earl of Newburgh, Lords Clifford, Stafford, and Lovat, the Hon. Sir Edward Vavasour, Bart., Sir Henry Bedingfield, Bart., Sir James Gordon, Bart., Sir Charles Wolsely, Bart., the Hon. Charles Langdale, M.P., the Hon. Charles Thomas Clifford, Daniel O'Connell, Esq., M.P., Philip H. H. Howard, Esq., M.P., (a gentleman to whom the catholics of the colony were greatly indebted), and fifteen other gentlemen of the highest rank and influence; besides which it had also been placed under the patronage of all the right reverend the catholic prelates of England and Scotland. The Society for the Propagation of the Faith, the object of which was to spread the doctrines of the catholic church over every part of the globe, was first formed by a few individuals in the city of Lyons, on the 3rd May, 1822. Among other evidences of its usefulness it would be gratifying for them to learn that the mission of the Right Rev. Dr. Pompallier in New Zealand, had been undertaken at the instance of this society, and that the expenses of that mission were defrayed from its funds. During the six years after its formation the sum of £600,000 had been expended from its treasury for the furtherance of religion; and in the seventh year no less than £102,000 was applied in like manner. To this eminently beneficial society, as well as to the Catholic Institute, auxiliary branches had been established in almost every part of the world.

Mr. McQuigan proposed, "That the Rev. Henry G. Gregory be appointed treasurer for the Australian Catholic Institute."

The Rev. H. G. Gregory moved the eighth resolution, and spoke as follows:—The resolution I have the honour to propose has for its object the assemblage of the members of the Institute for the purpose of electing its officials, and for other business connected with the well-being and continuance of the society. The reasons which have urged us to the proceedings of this evening point out the necessity of adopting measures proper for giving them permanency. These, if I mistake not, will be found in the resolution I have the honour to propose. An annual

meeting will invigorate our society; a knowledge of the proceedings of the past year, prosperous or adverse, for we may
expect an admixture of both, will be diffused, interest will be
created, and we shall re-commence our career with courage and
enthusiasm. And, my Lord, though important be the object, great
and glorious the cause we have taken in hand, yet we know by
experience all human institutions will fail unless some invigor-
ating process be entered into for their preservation. Moreover
we shall, I anticipate, derive great gratification from the accounts
which shall then be laid before us—peaceable victories obtained
over prejudice, bigotry, and intolerance—and the rights of truth
vindicated : whilst the shield of legal protection, sheltering alike
the weak and the strong against the oppressor and calumniator,
shall earn for the Catholic Institute of Great Britain and the
Colonies our respect and gratitude. I move, "That a month's
notice of the annual general meeting of the Institute be given,
at which the secretary and lay members of the general committee
shall be elected, and an account of the funds and proceedings of
the Institute and Society, of their condition and prospects, shall
be laid before the members, and that the discussion at such
meeting be limited to the foregoing objects." Seconded by Mr.
Smith.

The twelfth resolution was moved by Rev. Mr. Brady :—
"That the several congregations be invited to form branches of
the Institute." He then remarked that ever since his arrival in
the Colony he had been very anxious to see these catholic
institutions established, convinced as he was of their salutary
effects, and of the great and many blessings conferred by
Almighty God upon the members of these most noble, pious, and
charitable institutions. He had had the honour of being elected
vice-president of the Society for the Propagation of the Catholic
Faith, established in Bourbon; he had also had the happiness of
forming several branches himself; and in the several missions
committed to his care of receiving many thousand members into
it; he was therefore an old as well as a working member. He
felt therefore much pleasure in moving the resolution. It was
seconded by the Rev. Mr. Gould, and carried.

Moved by the Rev. Mr. Murphy—"That his lordship leave
the chair and that it be taken by the Very Rev. the Vicar-
General."

Moved by Mr. Duncan, seconded by Mr. Coyle ;—"That the
thanks of this meeting be respectfully presented to the Lord
Bishop for his able and dignified conduct in the chair during the
evening." (Tremendous applause.)

His Lordship said : He thought he had discharged his duty by simply acknowledging the kind feeling evinced. They might anticipate from the proceedings of that evening a cessation of hostility in many quarters. Frequently attacks were made on the presumption that no resistance would be offered. The attitude of defence alone often prevented the manifestation of attack. They had assumed that attitude in the love of peace, and for the same reason they intended to continue it. (Cheers and "We will") Now that they had determined upon this course it became them to consider how far they would permit a line of conduct in others of which they had not taken public notice; he alluded to the practice of certain persons who, earnest in the work of charity from time to time appealed to the public, and invited the cordial cooperation of all classes and creeds......... Charity, exalting and noble, forbade not merely the action, but the word, and thought even, which might give pain or be disparaging to the feelings and good name of another. To illustrate, ...he had been requested to take part in the proceedings at the annual meeting of that noble institution the Benevolent Asylum. He had attended under the presidency of one for whom he had a sincere respect. He was not surprised at the conduct of some; but that a chairman, whom he had deemed deserving of respect and veneration, should tolerate those things, should give them the sanction of his name, did cause him pain. At that meeting the humble individual now addressing you was classed with the infidel and the socialist; was described as the enemy of truth, and as linked with Satan. Does any action of mine merit that I should be flung into such a degrading association? Infidelity, Socialism, Popery!.........He who maligns my religion maligns me; he who insults my religion insults me........ ......That some individuals should have used such language I am not surprised; but that such expressions should pass unrebuked by the chair is not what I expected..................I am clearly of opinion that a man of upright mind and good intentions may have a conscientious attachment for that form of belief which he thinks to be true; but this should be tempered by a delicate tenderness for the faith and religious practices of others, and even for the prejudices of those who deem his form of christianity to be erroneous............I am quite convinced that there are numbers who subscribe to these societies (Bible Tract Societies), who are not aware of their working, or to what amount of ill-judged zeal they give their names and their purses...............Thank God we have no dominant church here—no one church exclusively by law established, nor yet, I imagine, for some years to be established.

185

But we have three forms of faith distinctly recognised by the legislature, placed on an equal footing; therefore by all in official situations to be equally protected and guarded against wrong and insult; for we all have an equal right to look up to the government as our common protector and friend. His Lordship then concluded by exhorting the people to preserve the same quiet, forbearing, peaceable demeanor, showing forth the beauty of their faith in the practice of their lives; and whilst determined to repel every unjust attack, in all calmness to defend their tenets, resting their principal dependance on Him, without whose aid the best efforts of man are vain and fruitless. (Loud cheers.)

The immense crowd then retired in the most orderly manner, every countenance beaming with satisfaction and delight—an auspicious beginning to two noble institutions, from which might be predicted the best results to the colony.

The catholic church made great strides during the years 1839 and 1840. Sir R. Bourke's Church Act was now in full operation, and it was deemed advisable by the Bishop and his Vicar-General to take advantage of its provisions without delay. Through the strenuous efforts of the good bishop and his clergy churches and schools were erected in the most populous parts of the colony, as a means most requisite for the advancement of religion. The Right Rev. Dr. Polding was then in the vigour of life, and he did not spare himself in the labour of the Lord's vineyard. Whenever his clergy required him to lay the foundation stone of a church, or to promote any other good work, he was sure to be present at the time and place—in fact, it may be said he then worked almost night and day. There were no good roads in those days, nor trains, nor telegraphs, and in many places only bridle paths. He travelled with his clergy from place to place, through the thick forest, exposed to a broiling Australian sun, and shared with them the terrible thirst, which sometimes there was nothing to quench but muddy water. Everywhere he was received by the people with joy and acclamation, and they bowed implicitly to his injunctions. The bishop was an excellent horseman, who bore well the heat and brunt of the day, and often at the end of a very long ride was less fatigued than the young clergy who accompanied him.

We find the Bishop on 22nd December, 1839, at the McDonald River, where he blessed the foundation stone of St. Joseph's Church, near Mount St. Joseph in the Windsor district; the incumbent of the district at the time was the Rev. John

Brady, afterwards Bishop of Perth. In Windsor there was about six hundred Catholics and six stations in the district, visited monthly, at distances from 12 to 35 miles, and the number of Catholics attending these varied from 60 to 130. It was reckoned that Father Brady travelled, about 8000 miles a year on an average. The address delivered by the Right Rev. Dr. Polding to the inhabitants of the Lower Hawkesbury and McDonald River, on the occasion of laying the foundation stone of St. Joseph's Church, was as follows:—

"Three years have elapsed since from the height of yonder mountainous tract I first beheld the lovely valley which extends its sinuous course on either side of us; through the morning's mist I discerned the sparkling waters of the river which gives its name to your district, and the tracts which in the highest state of cultivation, fringe and border its course. As I descended the precipitous path by which you hold communion with the outer world, I said to myself : O that my God may grant me strength, when the decrepitude of age warns me that ere long I must pass to my dread account, to creep to these quiet scenes before me and whatever of worldly wealth I may possess shall be devoted to the erection of a church wherein I shall lift up my hands to offer sacrifice for my people; and the remains of a voice and of an energy almost extinct shall be consecrated to the instruction consolation, and support of the simple minded inhabitants. I thought that years, many and tedious, must elapse before a temple unto the living God would be raised amongst you. Nor could I have lost sight of the consoling assurance from the pen of the prophet, that 'Every hill shall be brought low, every valley filled, every crooked path made straight, in order that all flesh may see the salvation of God ?'—words not merely to be understood as pointing to the victorious influence of divine grace manifested in the destruction of the prejudices, machinations, and determinations of Paganism, but generally prophetic of the removal of every difficulty from the path of the gospel, its holiness and truth. Four months have not elapsed since I attended your invitation to commence an oratory which might also be used as a school, some few miles from here, and now we are assembled to erect a church, a temple to the living God. Does not this zeal confer honor on you? Your school has been supported entirely at your own expense, yet you hesitate not to embark in an undertaking which will require considerable contributions. It is thus that 'He in whose hands are the hearts of men models them to his own purposes;' it is thus as we expected that your souls having become, by a holy life, the spiritual

ıples of God, your zeal would not be satisfied until the
terial temple, which is the church, should be raised, wherein,
ər the wont of your forefathers you might worship in spirit
in truth.

" A noble instance of disinterestedness, a gratifying proof that
right use of riches is not altogether forgotten, the church we
about to found will record. The land on which we stand is
en by Mr. Watson, who also deposited £300 as his contribution.
e Almighty has blessed his labours and he deems it right thus
return a part to Him who gave all. Already does he see
ınd him the rising families of children he and his excellent
e have adopted for their own. Placed by him on farms
rchased by his own honest and well-deserved earnings, he
oys the highest and most exquisite feast it is for man in his
sent state to make unto himself, in their happiness and
sperity. For their use and for the public benefit he devotes
large a sum for the erection of this church. I may mention
ther circumstance which, in my mind, lessens not the value of
donation nor diminishes my estimation of the man. Thirty
ırs ago, in a moment of thoughtlessness, that was done which
been the cause of great regret. Is not this amply expiated
atoned for ? Is the stain of such a fault to be made more
luring than the justice of God ? Not so thought that Blessed
gislator from whose code, as illustrated in his own example, we
accustomed to draw our rules of life. When the publican
ccheus, nay, even the chief of the publicans, by the adventitious
umstances sought, and succeeded, to see Jesus, was he not
thwith recognised by the Saviour and desired to prepare to
eive Him into his house, for that He intended to abide with
ı? What were the dispositions of Zaccheus? Lord, says he,
ive one-half of my goods to the poor, and if I have wronged
one I restore to him fourfold. Nor when we see those who
ve followed Zaccheus in his aberrations, imitating him in their
urn, striving by honest industry to raise themselves that they
y see Jesus and merit to be recognised by Him who came to
'e the sheep that was lost, shall we hold in eternal remembrance
fault of one moment ? It is not thus we shall prove ourselves
ministers nor even the disciples of Jesus Christ; never, never
ll be seen in the conduct of the true disciple of Jesus any
ıptons of aversion and contempt for a large class of fellow-
izens in which, if there be found the objects of punishment
ll-deserved, there are and must be, from the nature of human
titutions, many victims of misfortune. I have not read to a
itless purpose the history of Ireland for the last two centuries.

I have not seen with my own eyes the misery of that c
unhappy country, but now disinthralled, I trust, from the tyr:
of besotted and heartless faction, the details and consequer
which always result when the arm of power is stretched fort!
uphold a party against a people, without coming to a conclu
which right reason suggests, which religion sanctions, whic!
exemplified and illustrated in the conduct of the incarn
wisdom of the Godhead. I cannot fasten my judgment to
ever-turning wheel of fashionable opinion. I am not prep
to deem Joseph a degraded character, though sold as such by
malevolent brethren; nor to pronounce the Blessed Jesus gu
though condemned by those leagued together for his destruct
nor to throw a stone at the bidding of every Pharisee. I re
not of what classes the settlers and cultivators of the soil
composed; but wherever I go, and I have largely traversed
country, I meet men of industrious domestic habits, solicitou
give their children an education superior to their own. I perc
a deferential respect where respect is due, an attachm
combined with that proper sense of independence, which in
mind evinces a sense of propriety totally incompatible v
vulgar or mean thought. Take for instance this beautiful va
with its inhabitants! See those plains! How zealously has
the plough pursued its claims to the very mountain foot! N,
weed is visible amongst these families of corn plants which b
their deep green flags to the breeze—emblem, dear childre
Jesus Christ, of your own state, who are the 'cultivation of
Lord.' How often have I not reposed when neither lock
latch nor fastening protected! You support your school,
give proofs of the proper sense of the value of wealth and
purpose for which it is given of which you may be justly
Such being your state and your disposition, why shoul[
minister of peace make enquiries odious and uncharitable.
willingly do I bear my testimony that in no part of England,
I have seen much of her rural population there, have I obser
a middle class possessed of qualities more valuable, or whe
their conduct were more deserving of estimation and of t
than it has been mine to meet here and in other parts of
Colony which in the discharge of my pastoral duties I
visited. But to return from this digression to the immer
purpose for which we are this day assembled. Let us not imn
that we have done a great thing even when we have besto
our whole substance on charitable doings; we can claim no
to meritorious giving when we have none to possess. We ca
suppose that the Lord requires a temple built by mortal h

r his worship. The temple in which we are now assembled, in
uich the earth furnishes the flooring and the arch of heaven
rms the dome, surrounded by creation, animate and inanimate,
 the most becoming. Yet for man's accommodation God
ndescends to accept worship in a temple built by mortal hands;
d he deems that which is given towards its erection as bestowed
on himself. We think it right to offer publicly a proof of our
probation to the individual whose munificent donation we have
fore mentioned. In your name, dearly beloved, we present to
n a treasure, the value of which money cannot reach, a copy of
e written Word of God—the Book of Life, the Holy Scriptures—
d we feel an especial gratification in thus publicly with our
'n hands presenting this most sacred Book to one of our beloved
ck, because we are not without hope that the false idea which
il-minded men have spread abroad relative to unjust
ohibitions and restrictions will be thus dissipated. The
tholic Church is said to be hostile to the distribution of the
ly Scripture. Would to God I could deposit a copy in the
ttage of everyone disposed to read it with proper dispositions!
t, the Catholic Church neither now nor at any other period
shibited her children from reading the Sacred Volume. Only
en those wicked men, whose object was plunder and sensual
ttification under the pretext of the reformation of religion,
nslated the Word of God in the Sacred Scripture and fashioned
to their own purposes to gratify their misdeeds and rebellion,
en they transformed the truth into a lie, the Church warned
 children against these poisoned fountains of error, and hence
 outcry raised against her, hence the calumnious charge
peated a thousand times. Keep this book with reverence; let
laws be thy guide, its counsels thy support and consolation.
hen thou hearest its words or readest it, remember God speaks
to thee, and be as the Jews near the Mount of Sinai or the
vout St. John near the Cross of thy dying Redeemer."

His Lordship then proceeded to the celebration of the
remonies usual on such an occasion. It was most gratifying to
serve the devotion of the Protestant part of the assemblage—
e union of heart which seemed to predominate. The meaning
the ceremonies used was then explained; and all present on
nded knees having received the blessing of the Bishop, the
emony concluded. The interesting occasion will long be
nembered with delight by the inhabitants of the Lower
wkesbury and the McDonald River.

But to continue our account of the labours and travels of
hop Polding. On the 3rd October his lordship was in East

Maitland, and on the following day (Sunday) he officiated in the church to a crowded congregation. There were a great many Protestants present, and the sermon he delivered gave general satisfaction. In the evening he proceeded to Raymond Terrace, where he performed divine service on the following morning. The chaplains of West and East Maitland and the surrounding districts were the Rev. Mr. Mahony and Rev. J. Lynch. The population according to the census of 1836 of the town of Maitland was 1163 persons of which 365 were Catholics. The chaplains had to travel on an average 5000 miles during the year. There being no church, mass was celebrated under a tent erected for the purpose, and it rained nearly all the time. The Rev. Mr. Mahony said that he felt much pleasure in introducing that portion of his flock to the especial notice of the Bishop for their truly exemplary piety and general good conduct, and the bishop expressed himself highly pleased at the account given of them by their zealous pastor. A subscription list was opened for the erection of a church and a handsome sum was subscribed. His Lordship then proceeded to Hinton, about seven miles distant, where a great many Catholics were in attendance to meet him, whom he addressed, and earnestly exhorted to persevere in the path of virtue and good works. The bishop then went on to Cooley Camp, accompanied by many persons, and addressed the multitude for a considerable time. From thence the bishop proceeded to Glenham, the seat of Mr. C. H. Chambers, where the party arrived about ten o'clock at night. On the following morning, 5th October, the bishop celebrated mass to about sixty people, and selected the site for a new church, the land having been given by the lady of Mr. C. H. Chambers, who had also subscribed liberally towards its erection. He then went to Dungog, a distance of about 25 miles, where he was kindly entertained at the hospitable mansion of W. F. Mackay, Esq. Mass was celebrated the next morning to about seventy catholics, some respectable protestants being present. The same day the bishop and party returned to Maitland where they arrived at 10 o'clock p.m. A great change has taken place in this district in a very short time, through the zealous exertions of the Rev. Mr. Mahony.

On the 29th September, his Lordship having travelled overland from Sydney, arrived in the Wollombi district, where he laid the foundation stone of a church dedicated to St. Michael the Archangel. A Mr. McDougall presented the land, and the stone bore the following inscription:—" This church is dedicated to the honour and glory of God under the patronage of St. Michael the Archangel, by the Right Rev. John Bede

Polding, Bishop, Vicar-Apostolic of New Holland and Van Dieman's Land, on the 30th September, in the year of Our Lord,
1840—Sacerdos Rev. J. Lynch."

On Thursday, 8th October following, the foundation stone
of the church of St. John the Baptist was laid on Campbell's Hill,
West Maitland, by the bishop. There was accommodation for
600 persons on the ground. The procession, with the children
clothed in white, moved from the temporary church in the town.
The Sacrament of Confirmation was administered to about seventy
persons, young and old : at the close of the Mass nearly the same
number received the Holy Communion. When about to lay the
foundation stone, the bishop said :—" On that stone, an emblem
of the new life which you this day commence, deposit all irregular
affections ; increase in virtue ; raise higher the fabric of sanctity,
as the walls of this material building come nearer to their termination : and may this edifice, by being ever the habitation of
virtuous and pious souls, be a figure of the church triumphant in
heaven, where nothing defiled can enter, and where the prayers
of the saints ascend as a sweet odour before the throne of the
Lamb."

The following was the inscription on a plate laid under the
stone :—

ECCLESIÆ SUB PATROCINIO
SANCTI JOANNIS BAPTISTÆ,
ERIGENDÆ,
AD MAJOREM DEI GLORIAM PROMOVENDAM
HUNC PRIMARIUM LAPIDEM
POSUIT
REVERENDISSIMUS D. D. JOANNES BEDA, EPISCOPUS,
HIEROCŒSARENSIS
ET, IN NOVA HOLANDIA ET INSULA VAN DIEMEN,
VICARIUS APOSTOLICUS,
DIE OCTAVA OCTOBRIS ANNO SALUTIS
MDCCCXL,
VIGEBAT, SUCCESSOR SANCTI PETRI IN ROMA.
SUMMUS PONTIFEX GREGORIUS XVI.
ET IN BRITANNIS VICTORIA PRIMA SCEPTRUM TENENS
BENEVOLENTIAM OMNIUM SUB UNA DITIONE
CONCILIABAT.

SACERDOS REV. J. LYNCH.

The Bishop celebrated Mass in the temporary chapel,
Friday, in West Maitland, and the same day returned to Syd
by Newcastle

On the same day, on the catholic church ground, Campbel
Hill, a branch of the Catholic Institute was established, the Ri
Rev Lord Bishop in the chair. The Rev. V. Dowling, E. Mah
and J. Lynch were appointed presidents and Dr. Mallon secreta
the following persons to act as a committee, viz :—Messrs. I
Dee, Murray, Turner, Grace, Healy, Tierney, jun., Calla
McDougall, Byrne, Tierney, sen., Shinkivin, Haydon, O'B
Brown, Cullen, Clarke, O'Neill, and *(ex officio)* the Rev. Me
Dowling, Mahony, and Lynch.

On Sunday, 18th October, in St. Mary's Cathed
Sydney, the Lord Bishop conferred the holy orders of s
deacon and deacon upon the following gentlemen, viz:—
Rev. John Kenny, the Rev. James Dunphy, the Rev. Pat
Magennis, and the Rev. John Grant. A Pontifical Mass w
celebrated by his lordship, and a most learned and inter
discourse, suitable to the occasion, was delivered by the Very Rev.
the Vicar-General, who, as their theological instructor, pre
the postulants to the bishop, and attested in the usual form the
fitness for the sacred office.

Bishop Polding was in Wollongong on 12th October, where
he laid the foundation stone of the church of St. Francis Xavier,
on the following day. The catholics of Wollongong were joined
on the morning of the 13th by those of Dapto, Jamberoo, and
Shoalhaven. At the first note of the *Adeste fidelis* the procession
moved from the presbytery, consisting of the children to the
number of about 200, the members of the committee with cedar
rods, and the whole body of the people, walking two and two.
When assembled in the temporary chapel, and before the sermon,
the bishop offered up prayers, and the children sang the hymn
"Jesus, the only thought of Thee." The Rev. Mr. Brennan
preached the sermon, after which the procession moved to the
foundation stone close by. The bishop then proceeded according
to the ritual : a plate with an appropriate inscription was placed
under the stone ; and the bishop made a very effective address
to the people. The collection amounted to £55.

In the district of Illawarra the Rev. John Rigney is the
chaplain, and he resides at Wollongong. The attendance in the
temporary chapel there is 200. He officiates weekly at Dapto,
8 miles, with an attendance of 120 ; at Jamberoo, 25 miles,
attendance 80 ; at Shoalhaven, 50 miles, he officiates every month,
the communicants numbering 100. On an average the Rev. J.
Rigney travels 3252 miles during the year.

The Catholic Church at Campbelltown is a substantial stone building capable of accommodating 500, and was erected before Bishop Polding arrived in the colony. The interior of the church was finished in a most tasteful manner by the then chaplain (the Rev. J. A. Goold), now Archbishop of Melbourne. It is beautifully situated on elevated ground, and commands a fine prospect of the surrounding country. The school, the foundation of which was laid and blessed on the 17th of March, was designed by the chaplain to answer the twofold purpose of a school and chapel. During the week days and some of the festivals mass was celebrated in it, because the church itself is rather distant from the centre of the town. The Catholic population of Campbelltown was, according to the census of 1836, no more than 287, and the population of what is called the Hundred of Campbelltown, contained in Appin, Menangle, Narellen and Cooke, was returned by the same census as amounting to 810 persons ; but at the time when the school was built, in the year 1840, there must have been a good many more Catholics. The chaplain attended five stations monthly, at distances varying from eight to forty miles ; during the year he travelled about 2000 miles in the discharge of his clerical duties. The average attendance at each place was from 100 to 250. The Communicants in Campbelltown were about 50 at each mass. The Rev. C. Sumner, O.S.B, was at this time the chaplain of Appin, but resided in Campbelltown, attending three stations distant 15 to 30 miles, travelling in the year about 1040 miles.

We extract the following from the *Australian Chronicle* of March 24 :—

"Mr. Editor,—As an inhabitant of Campbelltown I am proud that we anticipated the object of your remarks on the first celebration of the day dedicated to the glorious patron of Ireland, St. Patrick. Mass was celebrated at half-past ten o'clock by the Rev. Mr. Goold, and an instructive address delivered by the Right Rev. Bishop. The virtues of St. Patrick were proposed for the imitation of the hearers, and his extraordinary abstinence and life of prayer were held up as a standard. These were contrasted with the excess and dissipation too frequently to be lamented as desecrating a day so holy, so full of grateful recollections. The Bishop dwelt with much feeling on the sufferings of Ireland, and called the attention of his hearers to the fact that notwithstanding those sufferings Ireland had clung to her faith—for thereon alone could she repose—this was the anchor of her hope. Those sufferings had been to her as the press in the vineyard, and the streams of life had been diffused amongst

o

her children throughout the habitable world. The feast
Patrick filled the universe with joy. On this day Christ
came to the nation who had returned her virginal fidelity
heavenly spouse undefiled, and with gratitude it acknowl
the Apostle of Ireland to be the Apostle of the World.

At one o'clock his Lordship, accompanied by the
Messrs. Goold and Sumner and a very numerous assembl
Catholics and Protestants, proceeded to bless the foun
of the New School, named after St. Patrick. The Bishop ob
that this ceremony was not indeed in the Ritual, but sug
by a sense of propriety. "Unless the Lord buildeth the
they labour in vain who build it." After some remarks
value of education, its principal objects, and the end which
to be kept in view by those to whom the important t
developing the moral and intellectual powers of the ch
committed, the Bishop congratulated the people of Campbe
on the public spirit evinced by them, and the glory the
acquired in being the first to erect at their own exp
schoolhouse, at once, in a moral and material sense, most
able to them. His Lordship complimented them on the
unanimity which seemed to animate all classes, and alludi
the donor of the ground, who was then not expected to r
he reminded those by whose exertions the present buildin
to be erected of the gratification with which in their last
they would recollect their donations to an object so praisew
The Bishop offered a prayer for the children, and then, surro
by the latter, implored a blessing on their parents and benef
After this most affecting ceremony the Bishop gave his b
and the assemblage departed highly gratified.

A handsome collection, amounting to £265, was made
occasion.—Erigena.

CHAPTER VIII.

Wesleyan lamentations about the progress of Catholicity—The Opening of St. Matthew's Church, Windsor, 21st Oct. 1840—The Foundation stone of All Saint's Church, Liverpool, laid by Bishop Polding—Departure of Dr. Ullathorne for Adelaide—The establishment of a Catholic Circulating Library, under the patronage of his Lordship the Bishop—Meeting held in the Catholic School-room, Castlereagh-street, to devise means for the erection of a new church in Sydney, to be dedicated to St. Patrick

WE extract the following from a European Journal as an evidence of the progress made by the church.

"Jonathan Crowder, a Wesleyan missionary, writing from Madras, 16th March, 1839, says :—' Papists, with the reinforcement which came out in December of an extra bishop and ten students, are making a considerable impression at Madras.' W. S. Fox, a brother missionary, under date of 14th March, writes thus :—' Our fears have not been a little excited of late by the arrival and subsequent operations of a Roman catholic bishop, accompanied by several associates. That the papists are exerting themselves in this country is an alarming fact; and if we may judge from the peculiar power of adaptation which distinguishes popery, they are likely to form a numerous church.'"

J. McKenny, writing from Sydney, says, in allusion to missionary efforts :—"This is not a question of mere pounds shillings and pence, for it now assumes this form — Shall Australia be a protestant or a popish colony? The number of priests who are being sent out is quite frightful; lately eight arrived in one vessel, and received from the Home Government £150 for their passage and outfit."

In the *Australian* of the 19th May there is an account of the conversion of T. C. Anstey, Esq., son of a respectable member of the Legislative Council of Van Diemen's Land. He went to England to study with the view to become a clergyman of the church of England. He commenced to study the grounds of both churches, which ended in embracing catholicity in 1834. Since his conversion he has contributed to the *Dublin Review* and other catholic periodicals. He turned his attention to the legal profession and became a barrister-at-law in January 7, 1839. He married Harriet, the second daughter of J. E. Strickland, Esq., of Loughlin House, Roscommon, Ireland.

In reference to the opening of St. Matthew's Church in Windsor, on 21st October, 1840, a gentleman writing to a protestant friend in Sydney, states :—" Bishop Polding and his Vicar-General attended, with fourteen priests. I was highly gratified at witnessing the grand ceremony of the consecration of the Church. The Vicar-General preached on the subject of King Solomon's dedication of the temple ; his Scriptural allusions were applied with peculiar fitness to the service of the day. To say Dr. Ullathorne is a highly gifted individual, and endowed with shining talent is merely to repeat public opinion, but I may add he turns the powers of his mind to the best advantage in using them for the glory of God and the benefit of mankind. Dr. Ullathorne is a quick-sighted investigator of the truth, and whilst he grasps with firmness the evidences of Christianity, with peculiar earnestness he invites his hearers to lay hold on them. He is a sound logician and able champion of the Catholic Church. The music was very grand : Mr. Bushelle and the band of the 80th Regiment attended Divine Service, as well as the officers, with a number of respectable protestant families. I was present at Vespers. The scene was imposing ; the greater part of the service was performed by the Bishop, the Vicar-General, and priests, in full chorus. Their voices were accompanied by a fine mellow seraphim, presented as a gift from his Lordship to St. Matthew's Church. The Bishop closed the service with an appropriate discourse on the consecration of the Church, in which he enforced, with persuasion and eloquence the essential doctrine of the Gospel, without entering into metaphysics, and endeavoured to convince his hearers that true religion is not only calculated to promote the glory of God, but the real happiness of man. He dwelt with energy on the virtue of charity, and charged his flock, in their daily intercourse with their fellow men, to be friendly with Christians of whatever denomination. *O si sic omnes.* Within the walls of the Catholic Church Christ crucified is tised, and in all her services presented to the eye. Surely this saving doctrine should induce protestants to overcome prejudices, and extend hands of love and charity to all I shall communicate more fully upon this subject when we I remain, my dear sir, ... P.S.—I have had the hon an interview with Bishop Polding. His lordship's manners highly prepossessing, and, uniting the dignity which becomes Prelate with the humility of the true Christian, he is not revered but beloved by his flock.

I must not omit to make mention of the condition of in the County of Bathurst, at this time. The resident clergyman re Dean O'Reilly and Rev. T. Slattery. In the town of hurst a church was in the course of erection; the temporary pel was attended by from 90 to 100 persons. The Chaplain nds twenty-six stations, once in the quarter, viz., Weagdon, 40 from Bathurst; Cabee, 60; Mudgee, 90; Jungy, 140; Mac- ie River, 120; Summers Hill, 30; Wellington, 100; Murrum- ee, 120; Dubbo, 130; Weny Plains, 20; Grobeingbon, 42; hlan, 60; Billabulla, 60; Lachlan River, 80; Carryamy, 90; pan's Creek, 25; Todd Walls, 35; Vale of Clwydd, 42; Mount toria, 52; Rose Vale, 40: Cherry Tree Falls, 70; and Berigan, miles.

In a letter Dean O'Reilly states: "During my last journey I was led to proceed on from one sheep or stock station to nother, until I found myself 350 miles from home. There were no residences, but many stations, and numbers of catholics, who often came from great distances, when they heard of me. Above 70 attended to receive the Sacraments. The Rev. T. Slattery per- forms service at Bathurst, when the Dean is absent, and when he returns, Father Slattery proceeds to visit eleven stations. The sum subscribed towards the erection of the above church was £1,041 8s. 6d.

The foundation stone of All Saints' Church, Liverpool, was laid by Bishop Polding on Sunday, the 8th November. There was a large concourse of people, many of whom had come from Sydney. The Rev. Mr. Marum, pastor of the district, was present. The Bishop administered the Sacrament of Confirmation to a con siderable number of the children. A Pontifical Mass was then celebrated. His Lordship, before laying the stone, delivered a most eloquent address. The collection amounted to £40 or £50. His Lordship, in addressing the assemblage again, expressed his high gratification at their pious and zealous demeanour during the day, and at the account given by their excellent pastor of the vast improvement of their moral condition. He further said that it would be one of his pleasing duties, if God spared him, after his return from Europe, to consecrate the building of which the foundation had been laid that day, to the honour and glory of God and all his blessed saints. His Lordship concluded by giving them his benediction, when the people cried out simultaneously " God bless you my Lord, God grant you a safe voyage," and immediately dispersed. The Chaplain in Liverpool is the Rev. R. Marum. Service was performed in a room of the Government Hospital, the average attendance being 200, of which the monthly communicants number about twenty-four.

On the 28th May, the Vicar-General, Dr. Ullathorne, for Adelaide, and remained there for some weeks, making ar ments for the building of churches, the appointment of c men, &c., &c.

A Catholic circulating library was established in Sydney (the year 1840, under the patronage of his Lordship the B Mr. E. J. Hawksley, who came to the Colony with the R Murphy, and who was a very competent person, was appe librarian. The books were kept in the Catholic School Kent-street North.

The following advertisement appeared in the Austr Chronicle of May 26, 1840 :—" A meeting of the Cathol Sydney will be held at the Court House, Castlereagh-stree Monday the 1st prox., at seven o'clock in the evening, to ap a Committee, and to devise means for erecting a new Ca Church in Sydney. We understand that beautiful plans fc new building will be submitted to the meeting. An exc site has been presented by Mr. Davis, and we are confiden so praiseworthy an example will act as a stimulant to the i our brethren to come forward liberally on so urgent an oc We believe it is the intention of the Lord Bishop to dedicat new church to Ireland's glorious apostle, St. Patrick. W let St. Patrick's new Church form a monument to future ag the piety of Erin's sons, and of that zeal which, under variety of circumstances, they have evinced for that faith the great St. Patrick taught them.

The following is an account of the meeting. The Righ the Lord Bishop in the chair.

His Lordship, on opening the meeting said, as the obje which they were assembled had been made public, he : not detain them with any needless repetition, but should allowed them at once to proceed to business, were it no he felt himself justified in giving expression to the joy and fication which he felt on the occasion. He had long wish the erection of a church in that quarter of the town where proposed to build the edifice now in contemplation, a distr which, he was fully satisfied, the exertion of the harmo influence of religion was more required than in any othe anticipation of the other advantages hereafter to follow, h not without hope that the very commencement of such a in the quarter alluded to would tend, in a great degree, prove the moral condition of the people. He would, mot observe that they had some reason to accuse themselves defect in point of gratitude by having permitted so long ؛

lapse without the erection of some temple for God's worship, a proof of their sense of the Divine goodness. At a vast distance from their native soil, they had ample subject of thanksgiving and gratitude to the Divine power for the glorious privilege of enjoying the free worship of their Creator; a privilege which their forefathers long and ardently struggled for in vain. When therefore these bounties of the Almighty were taken into consideration, gratitude alone would manifestly demand the erection of some monument in testimony of their feelings of religion; and what monument could be more proper than a temple consecrated to divine worship. under the glorious patronage of that great benefactor of mankind, St. Patrick; in whose diadem it would form an additional jewel. The spire of this temple would be, as it proudly stood, a perpetual and unfailing monitor to each passer-by to lift up his mind to the God who created him. It was a fact which needed no illustration, that wherever the Irish people were spread, they invariably carried with them their religion—the religion of their forefathers, in all its beauty and purity. The ground on which the proposed new church would be erected was the gift of one who gloried in the name of St. Patrick, and he hoped so good an example would not be lost upon others; but that if the present year should not behold the laying of the foundation stone and the carrying up of the spire, or, in other words, the commencement and execution of the design, the terms of its completion might not exceed the ensuing year (1841). Besides the ordinary method of collecting subscriptions, it was their intention to form a society or fraternity under the denomination of the "Society of St. Patrick," in order to concentrate the efforts of the community at large towards the accomplishing the great object in view; an object which would be easily effected by these means Having said thus much, he would not detain them any longer, but would request the gentleman who had undertaken to move the first resolution to proceed to business.

Mr. Roger Therry, in moving the resolution, and in the course of his remarks, said, in regard to Mr. Davis, that "too much praise could not be bestowed on Mr. Davis, who had made so noble a commencement of the good work. He had devoted the early portion of his life to pursuits and habits of industry, and he was now in its decline applying the proceeds and fruits of that industry to the best possible use to which they could be put—the happiness and benefit of his fellow citizens and the service of religion." His allusion to St. Mary's Cathedral was very happy. His Lordship, he said, who was comparatively a new comer among

them, must be highly gratified by the rapid advances towards completion made under his auspices by St. Mary's Cathedral—an edifice which, shortly before his Lordship's arrival, they almost despaired of seeing finished in their time. This and similar results must be the best and most gratifying reward to that respected prelate and the reverend gentlemen comprising his ministry, for their zeal and devotion in the service of the people. Those results were the fruits of the precepts which they taught, and of that piety of which their lives afforded a practical exemplification.

Mr. Therry here took the chair, and a vote of thanks was accorded to his Lordship for his able and dignified conduct during the proceedings of the evening.

His Lordship said that he received this mark of their kindness with feelings of high gratification. He was proud to be enabled to tell them they had discharged their duty. The general proceedings and result of this meeting must have impressed every one with a high sense of the unanimity which prevailed among the professors of the catholic faith, and the generosity with which each member stepped forward for the purpose of subscribing his quota to further the cause of our holy religion. They had already commenced the good work with every demonstration of a spirited determination to bring it to a speedy and happy conclusion, which desirable end would be greatly furthered by the efforts and known zeal of the highly respected reverend gentleman whom they had just now chosen as their president; whose name was hallowed by both poor and rich wherever his ministry had led him, and in whose praise he would have said a great deal more were he not then present. By the united energies and zeal of the new fraternity, he felt certain that in a comparatively short time such a sum would be raised as would at once be a source of gratification and astonishment. He had not the honour himself to be a native of Ireland; but if he might be excused for making use of what might be technically termed a bull, he was an Irishman born in England. He perfectly recollected that which he considered the dearest compliment he had ever received, was from the lips of a poor Irish woman—"Ah! my lord, you have an Irish heart!"—and blessed be God! he had an Irish heart, under the influence of which he had ever lived among his fellow men, and under the influence of which he would remain until death. He would now dismiss them with his thanks and blessing, and an injunction, when they were asked ‡by others as to what they had done at the meeting, to answer them by a desire that they would go and do likewise.

It was then moved by Mr. Callaghan, barrister-at-law, and seconded by Mr. Roger Murphy, That a society be formed under the designation of "St. Patrick's Society," for the purpose of collecting funds for the erection of the said church. The Rev. Mr. Murphy was appointed by the Meeting president, and the Rev. G. H. Gregory, treasurer. In the course of a few minutes the collection amounted to £1,012.

CHAPTER IX.

Preparations of the Catholic Committee of St. Mary's for the Departure of Bishop Polding and Dr. Ullathorne for England —Presentation of addresses to Bishop Polding and Dr. Ullathorne, and Rev. H. G. Gregory—Departure of Bishop Polding and party for England—The great estimation and respect in which the two catholic gentlemen, John Hubert Plunkett, Attorney-General of New South Wales, and Roger Therry, Esq., Commissioner of the Court of Requests, were held by the inhabitants of the Colony—The state of the Colony, Religion, and Education, when Bishop Polding left, in the year 140—An Abridgement of the reply of Dr. Ullathorne to Judge Burton's Book.

FOR some time previous to the departure of Bishop Polding for Europe, the Catholic Committee were engaged in getting up a Memorial, as a token of the respect in which the Bishop and his Vicar-General were universally held. On the Sunday before the Bishop left, he administered the sacrament of Confirmation to a number of children and adults. A Pontifical High Mass was celebrated in the cathedral, at which the Rev. Dean Brady officiated as assistant priest, the Very Rev. the Vicar-General and Rev. F. Murphy as deacons, and the Rev. Joseph Platt as sub-deacon. The Rev. Messrs. Mahony, Lynch and Grant assisted in surplices and stoles. After the gospel his lordship delivered a most affecting farewell address to his clergy and people.

In the evening at the Old Court House, Castlereagh-street, the addresses were read to his lordship, the Right Rev. Dr. Polding, and his Vicar-General, Dr. Ullathorne. Never was there a more numerous and respectable meeting than that assembled on the occasion. The Attorney-General, J. H. Plunkett, Esq., was called to the chair. Mr. Commissioner Therry commenced by reading the address to the Very Rev. Dr. Ullathorne, as follows:—

Very Rev. Sir,—The moment of your departure for England will, we trust, be not deemed an unsuitable one for receiving the

assurance of our grateful acknowledgements for the many and important services you have rendered to the catholics of the Australian colonies. On your first coming amongst us you found but one roofless church before you: the religious wants of the people for many years had been supplied by only one excellent clergyman; and many thousands of the people had heretofore lived and died in the interior of this colony without any religious consolation whatever. If brighter prospects now present themselves; if we see a hierarchy established on our shores; if we see every populous district of the colony provided with good and pious clergymen; if we witness under the genial influence of their precept and example, a moral regeneration and improvement prevailing among their respective flocks; if we behold the institution of the Sisters of Charity, famed throughout Europe for the great religious benefits it has dispensed, extending its usefulness to this colony, so exigent of its pious services, believe us Very Rev. Sir, we are duly sensible that these great services and daily augmenting advantages, are mainly to be attributed to your active and devoted exertions on our behalf, both here and in Europe; to the reliance which your character procured on the truth of your representations, as to the great want of religious aid and instruction under which these colonies suffered, and to the persevering assiduity with which you left no source unexplored that could be available to our advantage.

With hearts full of gratitude for these great and important services; with an earnest hope of soon seeing you again amongst us in the prosecution of your pious labours; and with a confidence that, whether absent or present, we shall live, as past experience assures us we have lived, in your regard and affections—we bid you a respectful, a grateful, and an affectionate farewell!

We beg your permission to accompany this address with a small token of our sincere respect and esteem.

The tribute of respect consisted of a snuff-box, valued at £60, with the following inscription:—Presented to the Very Reverend William Ullathorne, Doctor in Divinity, and Vicar-General of New Holland, as a testimony of the affection of the Catholics in the Colony; and their gratitude for his high services rendered to their religion and religious liberty; of regret at his departure for Europe, and of their anxiety for his safe and speedy return. November, 1840

Dr. Ullathorne's reply:—My dear friends, I thank you most sincerely. This is one of those rare moments in this earthly existence which drowns at once the recollection of a great many of its trials. If the feelings of my own breast could enlarge themselves to the extent of all your kindnesses and your many indulgences in my

regard of which this token is only the latest expression, I would endeavour to thank you worthily. As it is, I return your kindness and good wishes, as the best response I am capable of. It is a consoling reflection that, whilst in all other things I leave this colony as poor a man as when I first came to it, I am amply rich in your good opinions and warm affections. For these, and all those good works which I have seen done amongst you by the graee of God, I can never be sufficiently grateful. That I should have been an instrument, however by nature unworthy and unfit, of any part of so great a work of good, as the one to which you refer, will always fill me with happy recollections. But when, my dear friends, you see and bear witness to any qualities in me, except a very simple and earnest intention of serving you, and·a wish and endeavour to cherish and protect your faith, and to enlarge and quicken the growth of your charity, I there recognize the fallacy of your kindness. Warm and earnest in your good affections, you believe those qualities to exist in your friend and pastor which you well know ought to exist, and imagine he does possess what you wish and desire he should possess ; and it is my duty to pray that henceforward I may possess them. If on the occasion of the departure of our beloved bishop, I condole with you on the temporary loss of the presence of one, it is only the loss of his presence—his spirit will continue with you—whom you so truly and justly venerate ; I would also console you with the reflection that his absence is needful for your own best interests, and that it will not be of a very long continuance ; and I would cheer you by directing forward your hopes towards the happy period of his return, which may you all live, and live worthily and happily, to see accomplished ; and may his coming again amongst you, as it will, be crowned with joy and benedictions. For myself, whilst I most heartily thank you, and trust that I shall live in your recollections, as you will continue to live in mine, I am desirous of laying myself under new obligations by most earnestly recommending myself to your prayers.

His lordship was addressed in the following words :—On the eve of your lordship's departure, we beg leave to express our warmest wishes for your safe and prosperous passage to England, and our earnest hope for your early return to us. Whilst we deeply deplore even your temporary absence, our regret is subdued and softened by the conviction that your visit to Europe is prompted by a sense of duty, and by that devoted and untiring zeal for our welfare, of which we have so many and unmistakable manifestations. After the five years you have exercised the pastoral charge in these colonies with mild and firm efficacy, it

must be gratifying to you as it is to us, to look back on the great benefits that have been conferred on this community, and of which, under Divine Providence, you have been the chief and chosen instrument. The many churches founded and consecrated by your lordship; your frequent visits into all parts of the colony; the dispersion and establishment of a zealous clergy throughout the principal districts of New South Wales; the impartial attention paid to all classes of your congregation, without any distinction, except that where assistance was most required and needed, there it was largely bestowed; and not least, the truly paternal solicitude you have shown towards the orphan, and the affection with which you have cherished the little children of your flock, are among the enduring monuments of those useful labours, by which, in your high station, you have been distinguished, and which have made an indelible impression upon hearts not formed to be ungrateful. As it is under the deep impression of sentiments such as these that we bid your lordship farewell now, you will not be surprised or displeased that, next to the reverence and affection we entertain towards you, the feeling uppermost is the desire that you may be re-united to your flock at the earliest moment your sense of duty and zeal for our service will permit. We beg leave to accompany this address with a small token of our gratitude and veneration.

This tribute consisted of a Treasury Bill for £400

His lordship replied as follows:—Wishes so warm and generous, on the part of a people whose affections cannot be commanded, but may be obtained, I do feel sincere gratification in accepting. I knew not until the period of separation approached, how strong had become the bonds which united us. Only indeed a sense of duty the most cogent, and a conviction that my services elsewhere will prove more generally useful to my extensive charge, could influence me to consent to be temporarily absent from you. May your prayers for my speedy return be accomplished. Your kindness has attributed much to me I do not deserve. Patient enduring was the glory and merit of a preceding generation. The season of mercy and grace has been mercifully ours. Suffering and spiritual privation had disposed you to receive with gratitude the enlarged means of religious consolation Providence granted to you through us, the humble instrument of the divine benignity; and the gracious dispensation has not fallen on an unworthy soil. In the churches now in the course of erection; in the improved habits of our people; in the various charitable and religious institutions which have sprung into existence, in a space of time almost instantaneous; there is,

for his worship. The temple in which we are now assembled, in which the earth furnishes the flooring and the arch of heaven forms the dome, surrounded by creation, animate and inanimate, is the most becoming. Yet for man's accommodation God condescends to accept worship in a temple built by mortal hands; and he deems that which is given towards its erection as bestowed upon himself. We think it right to offer publicly a proof of our approbation to the individual whose munificent donation we have before mentioned. In your name, dearly beloved, we present to him a treasure, the value of which money cannot reach, a copy of the written Word of God—the Book of Life, the Holy Scriptures—and we feel an especial gratification in thus publicly with our own hands presenting this most sacred Book to one of our beloved flock, because we are not without hope that the false idea which evil-minded men have spread abroad relative to unjust prohibitions and restrictions will be thus dissipated. The Catholic Church is said to be hostile to the distribution of the Holy Scripture. Would to God I could deposit a copy in the cottage of everyone disposed to read it with proper dispositions! No, the Catholic Church neither now nor at any other period prohibited her children from reading the Sacred Volume. Only when those wicked men, whose object was plunder and sensual gratification under the pretext of the reformation of religion, translated the Word of God in the Sacred Scripture and fashioned it to their own purposes to gratify their misdeeds and rebellion, when they transformed the truth into a lie, the Church warned her children against these poisoned fountains of error, and hence the outcry raised against her, hence the calumnious charge repeated a thousand times. Keep this book with reverence; let its laws be thy guide, its counsels thy support and consolation. When thou hearest its words or readest it, remember God speaks unto thee, and be as the Jews near the Mount of Sinai or the devout St. John near the Cross of thy dying Redeemer."

His Lordship then proceeded to the celebration of the ceremonies usual on such an occasion. It was most gratifying to observe the devotion of the Protestant part of the assemblage—the union of heart which seemed to predominate. The meaning of the ceremonies used was then explained; and all present on bended knees having received the blessing of the Bishop, the ceremony concluded. The interesting occasion will long be remembered with delight by the inhabitants of the Lower Hawkesbury and the McDonald River.

But to continue our account of the labours and travels of Bishop Polding. On the 3rd October his lordship was in East

The reply of the Rev. Mr. Gregory:—

"I receive the token of affection with sincere gratificati
It is an emblem of that union between pastor and people, whi
no circumstance can alter, no distance dissever. Accept
thanks, and add to the favor conferred by remembering me
your prayers."

The chair being vacated by the Attorney-General, the R
Francis Murphy was requested to take it, when a vote of than
was proposed by Mr. Commissioner Therry and seconded by Jo
Ryan Brennan, Esq., P.M.: "That the thanks of the meeting
due, and are hereby presented, to the Attorney-General for
dignified conduct in the chair." Mr. Plunkett briefly retur
thanks, and expressed his gratification at having had the ho
to preside over so respectable a meeting, assembled on
interesting an occasion.

At half-past eleven o'clock a.m. on the Monday followi
16th November, 1840, the Catholic Committee accompan
the Bishop from his residence to the Cathedral, where
read at the altar the beautiful prayers appointed to be read
implore the blessing of heaven on their voyage. A proces
was formed of the whole people, under the direction of
Committee. There were many thousands in it. The girls of
Catholic Schools were first, the whole of them dressed in whi
then came the boys, followed by the congregation walking
and two; the Bishop and his Clergy formed the rear.
procession marched along Hyde Park, Macquarie-street, B
street, and Macquarie Place. When they arrived at the jetty
the Circular Quay the people divided, and the Bishop, Clergy,
Committee went to the boats. His Lordship and the Rev.
Gregory proceeded in the Government boat. Dr. Ullathorne
the clergy occupied the boat of the Crusader, furnished by Capt
Inglis. The vessel in which the Bishop and the Very Rev.
Ullathorne, Rev. H. Gregory, and the Bishop's Chaplain embark
was a brig, by name "Orion," Captain Saunders, master, bo
for Valparaiso; in their company were three young gentle
Messrs. Chambers, Therry, and Carter, going to Europe f
collegiate education. The brig was towed to the Heads by
splendid steamship "Clonmel," and this steamer was filled
upwards of 400 persons desirous of testifying to the last the
respect they had for their beloved Bishop. It was remarked
the press at the time of the departure of Bishop Polding: "T
not only every Catholic, but every Christian ought to sympat

eople, increasing in the enjoyment of a high degree of physical
nd moral health. If ever a bishop was worthy to be called a
astor of his flock, it is the Right Reverend Dr. Polding."

I certainly would not be doing justice to my narrative were
to pass by unnoticed the worth of two most estimable Catholic
entlemen, officers of the Government, who flourished in our
mmunity at this time; I mean John Hubert Plunkett,
ttorney-General of New South Wales, and Roger Therry, Esq.,
omnuissioner of the Court of Requests. They were conscientious
atholics, and lived up to their religious principles. They never
mpromised their religion, and were ever ready to speak and act
defence of the faith of their forefathers, and of their country,
eland. They gave all the weight of their character and
osition for the benefit of religion and charity. Mr. Plunkett
as for many years Attorney-General, and he went home on
ave of absence in the beginning of the year 1841. But before
left the colony, in such great respect was he held by his legal
rethren, that they entertained him at a dinner. The Chief
ustice, Sir James Dowling presided, and there was present
udge Stephens. The Governor, Sir Geo. Gipps, also honored the
tive board by his presence. The Governor, in returning
anks when his health was proposed, said: "He felt extremely
ppy in meeting such a large and respectable company of the
lonists of New South Wales, of every grade and of every
rsuasion, who, laying aside all other motives, had met together
at evening to pay a tribute of respect to a public officer who
ad discharged his great, important, and arduous duties with the
ighest degree of impartiality and firmness; he felt extremely
ppy to make one amongst them in bearing testimony to the
orth, ability, and integrity of that officer." The Chief Justice,
ir James Dowling said: "It was a pleasing reflection to Mr.
lunkett, notwithstanding the very peculiar community in
hich he lived, all men bore ample testimony to the just, upright,
anly, and impartial manner in which he had discharged the
uties belonging to his station; after many years of trial Mr.
lunkett had passed through the crucible of public opinion
ithout a stain being cast upon him." All the gentlemen present
at the banquet bore similar testimony to the high character of
Mr. Plunkett.

Before the departure of Mr. Plunkett, on leave of absence, a
handsome testimonial was presented to him in the shape of
several pieces of silver plate, and on each piece was engraved his
family crest, which is a trotting horse, with the motto "*Festina
Lente*." The silver service was purchased by public subscription
cost about £400.

The Bishop celebrated Mass in the temporary chapel, on Friday. in West Maitland, and the same day returned to Sydney by Newcastle

On the same day. on the catholic church ground, Campbell's Hill. a branch of the Catholic Institute was established, the Right Rev Lord Bishop in the chair. The Rev. V. Dowling, E. Mahony, and J. Lynch were appointed presidents and Dr. Mallon secretary: the following persons to act as a committee, viz:—Messrs. Lett, Dee. Murray. Turner. Grace. Healy, Tierney, jun., Callaghan, McDougall, Byrne. Tierney. sen. Shinkivin, Haydon, O'Brian, Brown. Cullen. Clarke. O'Neill, and *(ex officio)* the Rev. Messrs. Dowling. Mahony. and Lynch.

On Sunday. 18th October. in St. Mary's Cathedral, Sydney. the Lord Bishop conferred the holy orders of sub-deacon and deacon upon the following gentlemen, viz:—The Rev. John Kenny. the Rev. James Dunphy, the Rev. Patrick Magennis. and the Rev. John Grant. A Pontifical Mass was celebrated by his lordship, and a most learned and interesting discourse, suitable to the occasion. was delivered by the Very Rev. the Vicar-General, who. as their theological instructor, presented the postulants to the bishop. and attested in the usual form their fitness for the sacred office.

Bishop Polding was in Wollongong on 12th October, where he laid the foundation stone of the church of St. Francis Xavier on the following day. The catholics of Wollongong were joined on the morning of the 13th by those of Dapto, Jamberoo, and Shoalhaven. At the first note of the *Adeste fidelis* the procession moved from the presbytery, consisting of the children to the number of about 200, the members of the committee with cedar rods, and the whole body of the people, walking two and two. When assembled in the temporary chapel, and before the sermon, the bishop offered up prayers, and the children sang the hymn "Jesus, the only thought of Thee." The Rev. Mr. Brennan preached the sermon, after which the procession moved to the foundation stone close by. The bishop then proceeded according to the ritual : a plate with an appropriate inscription was placed under the stone ; and the bishop made a very effective address to the people. The collection amounted to £55.

In the district of Illawarra the Rev. John Rigney is the chaplain, and he resides at Wollongong. The attendance in the temporary chapel there is 200. He officiates weekly at Dapto, 8 miles, with an attendance of 120 ; at Jamberoo, 25 miles, attendance 80 ; at Shoalhaven, 50 miles, he officiates every month, the communicants numbering 100. On an average the Rev. J. *Rigney travels 3252* miles during the year.

The Catholic Church at Campbelltown is a substantial stone building capable of accommodating 500, and was erected before Bishop Polding arrived in the colony. The interior of the church was finished in a most tasteful manner by the then chaplain (the Rev. J. A. Goold), now Archbishop of Melbourne. It is beautifully situated on elevated ground, and commands a fine prospect of the surrounding country. The school, the foundation of which was laid and blessed on the 17th of March, was designed by the chaplain to answer the twofold purpose of a school and chapel. During the week days and some of the festivals mass was celebrated in it, because the church itself is rather distant from the centre of the town. The Catholic population of Campbelltown was, according to the census of 1836, no more than 287, and the population of what is called the Hundred of Campbelltown, contained in Appin, Menangle, Narellen and Cooke, was returned by the same census as amounting to 810 persons; but at the time when the school was built, in the year 1840, there must have been a good many more Catholics. The chaplain attended five stations monthly, at distances varying from eight to forty miles; during the year he travelled about 2000 miles in the discharge of his clerical duties. The average attendance at each place was from 100 to 250. The Communicants in Campbelltown were about 50 at each mass. The Rev. C. Sumner, O.S.B, was at this time the chaplain of Appin, but resided in Campbelltown, attending three stations distant 15 to 30 miles, travelling in the year about 1040 miles.

We extract the following from the *Australian Chronicle* of March 24 :—

"Mr. Editor,—As an inhabitant of Campbelltown I am proud that we anticipated the object of your remarks on the first celebration of the day dedicated to the glorious patron of Ireland, St. Patrick. Mass was celebrated at half-past ten o'clock by the Rev. Mr. Goold, and an instructive address delivered by the Right Rev. Bishop. The virtues of St. Patrick were proposed for the imitation of the hearers, and his extraordinary abstinence and life of prayer were held up as a standard. These were contrasted with the excess and dissipation too frequently to be lamented as desecrating a day so holy, so full of grateful recollections. The Bishop dwelt with much feeling on the sufferings of Ireland, and called the attention of his hearers to the fact that notwithstanding those sufferings Ireland had clung to her faith—for thereon alone could she repose—this was the anchor of her hope. Those sufferings had been to her as the press in the vineyard, and the streams of life had been diffused amongst

o

her children throughout the habitable world. The feast of St. Patrick filled the universe with joy. On this day Christianity came to the nation who had returned her virginal fidelity to her heavenly spouse undefiled. and with gratitude it acknowledged the Apostle of Ireland to be the Apostle of the World.

At one o'clock his Lordship, accompanied by the Revs. Messrs. Goold and Sumner and a very numerous assemblage of Catholics and Protestants. proceeded to bless the foundation of the New School, named after St. Patrick. The Bishop observed that this ceremony was not indeed in the Ritual, but suggested by a sense of propriety. "Unless the Lord buildeth the house, they labour in vain who build it." After some remarks on the value of education, its principal objects, and the end which ought to be kept in view by those to whom the important task of developing the moral and intellectual powers of the child is committed. the Bishop congratulated the people of Campbelltown on the public spirit evinced by them, and the glory they had acquired in being the first to erect at their own expense a schoolhouse, at once, in a moral and material sense, most credit-able to them. His Lordship complimented them on the cordial unanimity which seemed to animate all classes, and alluding to the donor of the ground, who was then not expected to recover he reminded those by whose exertions the present building was to be erected of the gratification with which in their last hour, they would recollect their donations to an object so praiseworthy. The Bishop offered a prayer for the children, and then, surrounded by the latter, implored a blessing on their parents and benefactors. After this most affecting ceremony the Bishop gave his blessing and the assemblage departed highly gratified.

A handsome collection, amounting to £265, was made on the occasion.—Erigena.

lapse without the erection of some temple for God's worship, a proof of their sense of the Divine goodness. At a vast distance from their native soil, they had ample subject of thanksgiving and gratitude to the Divine power for the glorious privilege of enjoying the free worship of their Creator; a privilege which their forefathers long and ardently struggled for in vain. When therefore these bounties of the Almighty were taken into consideration, gratitude alone would manifestly demand the erection of some monument in testimony of their feelings of religion; and what monument could be more proper than a temple consecrated to divine worship. under the glorious patronage of that great benefactor of mankind, St. Patrick; in whose diadem it would form an additional jewel. The spire of the temple would be, as it proudly stood, a perpetual and unfailing monitor to each passer-by to lift up his mind to the God who created him. It was a fact which needed no illustration, that wherever the Irish people were spread, they invariably carried with them their religion—the religion of their forefathers, in all its beauty and purity. The ground on which the proposed new church would be erected was the gift of one who gloried in the name of St. Patrick, and he hoped so good an example would not be lost upon others; but that if the present year should not behold the laying of the foundation stone and the carrying up of the spire, or, in other words, the commencement and execution of the design, the terms of its completion might not exceed the ensuing year (1841). Besides the ordinary method of collecting subscriptions, it was their intention to form a society or fraternity under the denomination of the "Society of St. Patrick," in order to concentrate the efforts of the community at large towards the accomplishing the great object in view; an object which would be easily effected by these means Having said thus much, he would not detain them any longer, but would request the gentleman who had undertaken to move the first resolution to proceed to business.

Mr. Roger Therry, in moving the resolution, and in the course of his remarks, said, in regard to Mr. Davis, that "too much praise could not be bestowed on Mr. Davis, who had made so noble a commencement of the good work. He had devoted the early portion of his life to pursuits and habits of industry, and he was now in its decline applying the proceeds and fruits of that industry to the best possible use to which they could be put—the happiness and benefit of his fellow citizens and the service of religion." His allusion to St. Mary's Cathedral was very happy. His Lordship, he said, who was comparatively a new comer among

them, must be highly gratified by the rapid advances towards completion made under his auspices by St. Mary's Cathedral—an edifice which, shortly before his Lordship's arrival, they almost despaired of seeing finished in their time. This and similar results must be the best and most gratifying reward to that respected prelate and the reverend gentlemen comprising his ministry, for their zeal and devotion in the service of the people. Those results were the fruits of the precepts which they taught, and of that piety of which their lives afforded a practical exemplification.

Mr. Therry here took the chair, and a vote of thanks was accorded to his Lordship for his able and dignified conduct during the proceedings of the evening.

His Lordship said that he received this mark of their kindness with feelings of high gratification. He was proud to be enabled to tell them they had discharged their duty. The general proceedings and result of this meeting must have impressed every one with a high sense of the unanimity which prevailed among the professors of the catholic faith, and the generosity with which each member stepped forward for the purpose of subscribing his quota to further the cause of our holy religion. They had already commenced the good work with every demonstration of a spirited determination to bring it to a speedy and happy conclusion, which desirable end would be greatly furthered by the efforts and known zeal of the highly respected reverend gentleman whom they had just now chosen as their president; whose name was hallowed by both poor and rich wherever his ministry had led him, and in whose praise he would have said a great deal more were he not then present. By the united energies and zeal of the new fraternity, he felt certain that in a comparatively short time such a sum would be raised as would at once be a source of gratification and astonishment. He had not the honour himself to be a native of Ireland; but if he might be excused for making use of what might be technically termed a bull, he was an Irishman born in England. He perfectly recollected that which he considered the dearest compliment he had ever received, was from the lips of a poor Irish woman—"Ah! my lord, you have an Irish heart!"—and blessed be God! he had an Irish heart, under the influence of which he had ever lived among his fellow men, and under the influence of which he would remain until death. He would now dismiss them with his thanks and blessing, and an injunction, when they were asked by others as to what they had done at the meeting, to answer them by a desire that they would go and do likewise.

It was then moved by Mr. Callaghan, barrister-at-law, and seconded by Mr. Roger Murphy, That a society be formed under the designation of "St. Patrick's Society," for the purpose of raising funds for the erection of the said church. The Rev. Murphy was appointed by the Meeting president, and the G. H. Gregory, treasurer. In the course of a few minutes collection amounted to £1,012.

CHAPTER IX.

Preparations of the Catholic Committee of St. Mary's for the Departure of Bishop Polding and Dr. Ullathorne for England —Presentation of addresses to Bishop Polding and Dr. Ullathorne, and Rev. H. G. Gregory—Departure of Bishop Polding and party for England—The great estimation and respect in which the two catholic gentlemen, John Hubert Plunkett, Attorney-General of New South Wales, and Roger Therry, Esq., Commissioner of the Court of Requests, were held by the inhabitants of the Colony—The state of the Colony, Religion, and Education, when Bishop Polding left, in the year 140—An Abridgement of the reply of Dr. Ullathorne to Judge Burton's Book.

For some time previous to the departure of Bishop Polding for Europe, the Catholic Committee were engaged in getting up a memorial, as a token of the respect in which the Bishop and his Vicar-General were universally held. On the Sunday before the Bishop left, he administered the sacrament of Confirmation to a number of children and adults. A Pontifical High Mass was celebrated in the cathedral, at which the Rev. Dean Brady officiated as assistant priest, the Very Rev. the Vicar-General and Rev. F. Murphy as deacons, and the Rev. Joseph Platt as sub-deacon. The Rev. Messrs. Mahony, Lynch and Grant assisted in surplices and stoles. After the gospel his lordship delivered a most affecting farewell address to his clergy and people.

In the evening at the Old Court House, Castlereagh-street, the addresses were read to his lordship, the Right Rev. Dr. Polding, and his Vicar-General, Dr. Ullathorne. Never was there a more numerous and respectable meeting than that assembled on the occasion. The Attorney-General, J. H. Plunkett, Esq., was called to the chair. Mr. Commissioner Therry commenced by reading the address to the Very Rev. Dr. Ullathorne, as follows:—

Very Rev. Sir,—The moment of your departure for England will, we trust, be not deemed an unsuitable one for receiving the

must be gratifying to you as it is to us, to look back on the great benefits that have been conferred on this community, and of which, under Divine Providence, you have been the chief and chosen instrument. The many churches founded and consecrated by your lordship; your frequent visits into all parts of the colony; the dispersion and establishment of a zealous clergy throughout the principal districts of New South Wales; the impartial attention paid to all classes of your congregation, without any distinction, except that where assistance was most required and needed, there it was largely bestowed; and not least, the truly paternal solicitude you have shown towards the orphan, and the affection with which you have cherished the little children of your flock, are among the enduring monuments of those useful labours, by which, in your high station, you have been distinguished, and which have made an indelible impression upon hearts not formed to be ungrateful. As it is under the deep impression of sentiments such as these that we bid your lordship farewell now, you will not be surprised or displeased that, next to the reverence and affection we entertain towards you, the feeling uppermost is the desire that you may be re-united to your flock at the earliest moment your sense of duty and zeal for our service will permit. We beg leave to accompany this address with a small token of our gratitude and veneration.

This tribute consisted of a Treasury Bill for £400

His lordship replied as follows:—Wishes so warm and generous, on the part of a people whose affections cannot be commanded, but may be obtained, I do feel sincere gratification in accepting. I knew not until the period of separation approached, how strong had become the bonds which united us. Only indeed a sense of duty the most cogent, and a conviction that my services elsewhere will prove more generally useful to my extensive charge, could influence me to consent to be temporarily absent from you. May your prayers for my speedy return be accomplished. Your kindness has attributed much to me I do not deserve. Patient enduring was the glory and merit of a preceding generation. The season of mercy and grace has been mercifull ours. Suffering and spiritual privation had disposed you to receive with gratitude the enlarged means of religious consolation Providence granted to you through us, the humble instrument of the divine benignity; and the gracious dispensation has not fallen on an unworthy soil. In the churches now in the course of erection; in the improved habits of our people; in the various charitable and religious institutions which have sprung into existence, in a space of time almost instantaneous; there is, surely, a demonstration, that beneath a surface unfortunately made the ground of rash surmises and rude theories, there did list a bounteous source of moral worth, which only required to be opened to the clear day, to diffuse streams of virtuous impulses, noble and disinterested well-doing, throughout our beautiful land.

My labours and their effects you value too highly. The zealous co-operation of the Vicar-General and of the clergy must held in grateful remembrance. My devotedness to my beloved country, my determination to use every exertion that can tend to use and establish on a lofty and imperishable basis her religious, r social and moral character, words cannot express. Let the it be an earnest of the future; and whilst I am absent continue your peaceable determined course to co-operate with me. The calumny of the graceless may fall undeserving of note. No position, statement, or misrepresentation detrimental to your civil or religious rights, which might derive importance from the station of him who utters it, must pass unnoticed. Cultivate peace,—I use the words of an apostle—as much as in you is have peace with all men, until the harmonious union which gloriously distinguishes our body shall, in the extinction prejudice, of bigotry, or of unseemly strife, pervade the entire the social order of New South Wales. I accept with thank-ness this token of your affectionate regard; may the Almighty dispenser of all good bestow upon you every blessing.

The ladies of Sydney on this occasion presented the Rev. H. Gregory with a handsome and valuable ring, accompanied with an address. These are the words of the address:—

"Rev. and Dear Sir,—We, the Catholic ladies of Sydney, having observed that our husbands and fathers have their feelings likely absorbed with the lamented departure of our excellent bishop and his Vicar-General, cannot suffer you, reverend Sir, to leave our shores without in some feeble manner testifying our sense of your piety and zeal for the honor and glory of God and for our spiritual welfare during the time the Catholics of Sydney have had the happiness of enjoying your pastoral care. We bow to the will of God, which for great and good purposes removes us from our pastor for a time, trusting that that time will be short, and that after a speedy and safe voyage and a successful mission, you will soon be restored to a people who till we shall never cease to pray for that event and for your welfare.

We beg to accompany this address with a small tribute of respect and reverence.

Reverend and Dear Sir, farewell."

The Bishop celebrated Mass in the temporary chapel, on Friday, in West Maitland, and the same day returned to Sydney by Newcastle

On the same day, on the catholic church ground, Campbell's Hill, a branch of the Catholic Institute was established, the Right Rev Lord Bishop in the chair. The Rev. V. Dowling, E. Mahony, and J. Lynch were appointed presidents and Dr. Mallon secretary : the following persons to act as a committee, viz :—Messrs. Lett, Dee. Murray, Turner, Grace, Healy, Tierney, jun., Callaghan, McDougall, Byrne, Tierney, sen., Shinkivin, Haydon, O'Brian, Brown, Cullen, Clarke, O'Neill, and *(ex officio)* the Rev. Messrs. Dowling, Mahony, and Lynch.

On Sunday, 18th October, in St. Mary's Cathedral, Sydney, the Lord Bishop conferred the holy orders of sub-deacon and deacon upon the following gentlemen, viz:—The Rev. John Kenny, the Rev. James Dunphy, the Rev. Patrick Magennis, and the Rev. John Grant. A Pontifical Mass was celebrated by his lordship, and a most learned and interesting discourse, suitable to the occasion, was delivered by the Very Rev. the Vicar-General, who, as their theological instructor, presented the postulants to the bishop, and attested in the usual form their fitness for the sacred office.

Bishop Polding was in Wollongong on 12th October, where he laid the foundation stone of the church of St. Francis Xavier on the following day. The catholics of Wollongong were joined on the morning of the 13th by those of Dapto, Jamberoo, and Shoalhaven. At the first note of the *Adeste fidelis* the procession moved from the presbytery, consisting of the children to the number of about 200, the members of the committee with cedar rods, and the whole body of the people, walking two and two. When assembled in the temporary chapel, and before the sermon, the bishop offered up prayers, and the children sang the hymn "Jesus, the only thought of Thee." The Rev. Mr. Brennan preached the sermon, after which the procession moved to the foundation stone close by. The bishop then proceeded according to the ritual: a plate with an appropriate inscription was placed under the stone ; and the bishop made a very effective address to the people. The collection amounted to £55.

In the district of Illawarra the Rev. John Rigney is the chaplain, and he resides at Wollongong. The attendance in the temporary chapel there is 200. He officiates weekly at Dapto, 8 miles, with an attendance of 120 ; at Jamberoo, 25 miles, attendance 80 ; at Shoalhaven, 50 miles, he officiates every month, the communicants numbering 100. On an average the Rev. J. *Rigney travels* 3252 miles during the year.

people, increasing in the enjoyment of a high degree of physical and moral health. If ever a bishop was worthy to be called a pastor of his flock, it is the Right Reverend Dr. Polding."

I certainly would not be doing justice to my narrative were I to pass by unnoticed the worth of two most estimable Catholic gentlemen, officers of the Government, who flourished in our community at this time; I mean John Hubert Plunkett, Attorney-General of New South Wales, and Roger Therry, Esq., Commissioner of the Court of Requests. They were conscientious Catholics, and lived up to their religious principles. They never compromised their religion, and were ever ready to speak and act in defence of the faith of their forefathers, and of their country, Ireland. They gave all the weight of their character and position for the benefit of religion and charity. Mr. Plunkett was for many years Attorney-General, and he went home on leave of absence in the beginning of the year 1841. But before he left the colony, in such great respect was he held by his legal brethren, that they entertained him at a dinner. The Chief Justice, Sir James Dowling presided, and there was present Judge Stephens. The Governor, Sir Geo. Gipps, also honored the festive board by his presence. The Governor, in returning thanks when his health was proposed, said: "He felt extremely happy in meeting such a large and respectable company of the colonists of New South Wales, of every grade and of every persuasion, who, laying aside all other motives, had met together that evening to pay a tribute of respect to a public officer who had discharged his great, important, and arduous duties with the highest degree of impartiality and firmness; he felt extremely happy to make one amongst them in bearing testimony to the worth, ability, and integrity of that officer." The Chief Justice, Sir James Dowling said: "It was a pleasing reflection to Mr. Plunkett, notwithstanding the very peculiar community in which he lived, all men bore ample testimony to the just, upright, manly, and impartial manner in which he had discharged the duties belonging to his station; after many years of trial Mr. Plunkett had passed through the crucible of public opinion without a stain being cast upon him." All the gentlemen present at the banquet bore similar testimony to the high character of Mr. Plunkett.

Before the departure of Mr. Plunkett, on leave of absence, a handsome testimonial was presented to him in the shape of several pieces of silver plate, and on each piece was engraved his family crest, which is a trotting horse, with the motto "*Festina lente*." The silver service was purchased by public subscription and cost about £400.

Roger Therry, Esq., was appointed Attorney-General, du
the absence of Mr. Plunkett. Mr. Therry had been Commissi
of the Court of Requests for eleven years, and discharged
onerous duties of his office with great rectitude and ab
When he was promoted to be Attorney-General, the pu
expressed their satisfaction for his past services, by present
him with a massive silver service, which cost £500. The sal
had the following inscription engraved on it, with Mr. Ther
crest, a lion rampant, bearing a cross, with the motto, " E Cr
Leo." The words of the inscription were the following:—" 'I
salver with an urn, dinner, dessert and tea-service, and ot!
articles, forming a service of plate, were presented to Ro
Therry, Esquire, Her Majesty's Attorney General, by the peo
of New South Wales, as a mark of their esteem and respect
the occasion of his retiring from the office of Commissioner of
Court of Requests, the duties of which he discharged in t!
colony for a period of eleven years, to the entire satisfaction
the community."

Judge Burton, who published in London " an account of
state of religion and education in New South Wales," returned
the colony in the year 1841. His party prepared a banquet !
him and the Governor was invited to attend, but he declined. "
account of his independent position as a judge in regard to
Executive; and because the circumstances were different fr
those of the Attorney-General, Mr. Plunkett, who was leaving
colony, whilst Judge Burton was returning to office." It
very wise of Sir George Gipps to decline the invitation, if he I
attended, there would have been some reason to believe that
ruler of the colony gave countenance and support to the fa
statements, sophistical arguments, and derogatory remarks
Judge Burton's religious history.

The Judge must have been terribly taken by surprise wl
he returned to find that all his visions of a dominant church w
baseless fabrics; he found Sir Richard Bourke's Church Act, wh
placed the principal religious bodies on an equality, work
admirably, and giving to each denomination a share of the pul
revenue. The Catholics whom he desired to be the last in sta
before the law, had, since his absence vastly increased in numb
and there were two most efficient catholic officers of the Cro'

When Bishop Polding left the colony at the close of the y
1840, he left the church in a flourishing condition. The Cath
population then amounted to nearly 20,000 souls; Syd
contained 14,000 Catholics. The entire population of the col
from a return published by the Government in 1839 amounted
114,386 the population of Sydney was 40,000 and contai

CHAPTER VIII.

Wesleyan lamentations about the progress of Catholicity—The Opening of St. Matthew's Church, Windsor, 21st Oct. 1840— The Foundation stone of All Saint's Church, Liverpool, laid by Bishop Polding—Departure of Dr. Ullathorne for Adelaide—The establishment of a Catholic Circulating Library, under the patronage of his Lordship the Bishop— Meeting held in the Catholic School-room, Castlereagh-street, to devise means for the erection of a new church in Sydney, to be dedicated to St. Patrick

WE extract the following from a European Journal as an evidence of the progress made by the church.

"Jonathan Crowder, a Wesleyan missionary, writing from Madras, 16th March, 1839, says :—' Papists, with the reinforcement which came out in December of an extra bishop and ten students, are making a considerable impression at Madras.' W. S. Fox, a brother missionary, under date of 14th March, writes thus :— ' Our fears have not been a little excited of late by the arrival and subsequent operations of a Roman catholic bishop, accompanied by several associates. That the papists are exerting themselves in this country is an alarming fact; and if we may judge from the peculiar power of adaptation which distinguishes popery, they are likely to form a numerous church.' "

J. McKenny, writing from Sydney, says, in allusion to missionary efforts :—" This is not a question of mere pounds shillings and pence, for it now assumes this form — Shall Australia be a protestant or a popish colony ? The number of priests who are being sent out is quite frightful; lately eight arrived in one vessel, and received from the Home Government £150 for their passage and outfit."

In the *Australian* of the 19th May there is an account of the conversion of T. C. Anstey, Esq., son of a respectable member of the Legislative Council of Van Diemen's Land. He went to England to study with the view to become a clergyman of the church of England. He commenced to study the grounds of both churches, which ended in embracing catholicity in 1834. Since his conversion he has contributed to the *Dublin Review* and other catholic periodicals. He turned his attention to the legal profession and became a barrister-at-law in January 7, 1839. He married Harriet, the second daughter of J. E. Strickland, Esq., of Loughlin House, Roscommon, Ireland.

In the year 1841 there were six public schools, Catholic, and
some private schools, indeed in all the principal towns and
localities existed now good schools under Catholic direction.
In Sydney about three times in the year, the children made their
first communion in St. Mary's cathedral with great solemnity.
This imposing ceremony, made by the children with much piety
and fervour, had the best effect on the minds of the parents and
others, and usually a great many conversions of hardened sinners
took place. The gentle expostulations of the fervent children
drew their parents to the sacraments, which had been abandoned
by them for many years.

For the information of the readers I will relate how the
Catholic schools were supported at this time and previously by
the Government. To premise: there were 35 schools, primary,
established in various places of the colony by the Church and
School Corporation, and these were charged on the Estimates for
the year 1834, at £2,756. In these schools were children of all
denominations, Catholic, Wesleyan, and Presbyterian, and the
only catechism allowed to be taught was that of the Church of
England. Now observe the contrast, in regard to the support
given by the Government in those days to the Catholic schools.
The first Catholic school was established in the time of Sir
Thomas Brisbane, in 1822. In the year 1828 the Government
only expended on the Catholic schools £68 3s.; the Protestant
schools of the same character received Government support to the
amount of £2650 15s 2d. The Estimates for the year 1833 were
for Catholic schools £350, for Church of England schools of the
same class £2,232 1s 4d. The sum of £800 was voted for the
Roman Catholic schools in the year 1834. The Estimates for
public education in the year 1841, which were laid before the
Council were, for Protestant education £6,106 0s 7d, and the total
for Catholic education £1,346 14s 4d. There was voted by the
Legislative Council in the year 1834, the sum of £2,300 for the
site and buildings of King's School, Parramatta, and the annual
salary of £100 towards the support of the head-master; this was
exclusively a Protestant establishment.

The system of public education which was followed since
1836 was one which was introduced by Governor Bourke, and
similar to the system of education established in Ireland through
Lord Stanley. By this system, no religious instruction was given
(that being left to the ministers of the different denominations
and parents of the children) select portions of the Scriptures were
read This system of education was carried in the Council by a
majority of eight to four.

In the year 1840, Sir George Gipps, in a minute explanatory of his views on the all important subject of education, found fault with the present system. He said that, " Although apparently based upon the principle of equality, it was very unequal in practice. The rule is :—' That the assistance given to any school shall be measured by the sum which is raised for its support by private contributions '; but it is well known that exceptions from this rule are made in favour of certain schools, solely because they have been established longer than others— exceptions which I cannot consider to be founded on any principle of utility, expediency, or justice." In the same minute the Governor proposed a plan of public instruction which he intended to carry into effect. According to this plan a public school was to be built in Sydney, and two others in two principal towns of the interior. The system he intended to establish was on the principle of the British and Foreign School Society, and for this purpose £3000 were placed on the Estimates, and £1000 for the Catholic schools, because the Catholics could not conscientiously send their children to those schools. The Governor at the same time expressed himself favourable to the Irish National system. This system was afterwards established in the colony.

The population of the Colony when Bishop Polding left for Europe in 1840 had increased to 129,463, and in the year following, 1841, a census was taken by the Government of the entire population of New South Wales and Port Philip, and the result showed a total of 130,856. The population of Port Philip District at this time was 11,728. In the year 1836, the year after the arrival of the Bishop, the number of the population of New South Wales was only 77,096. At the time of the census in 1836 the Catholics numbered 21,898 souls; but when the census was taken in 1841 they had increased to 35,690. The members of the Church of England were reckoned at 73,725.

The rapid increase of the population in such a comparatively short time was chiefly owing to the streams of emigration which had poured into the Colony. A statistical account of the emigration for five years, ending with 1829, was shown by a Parliamentary paper published in the year 1832. It stated that immigrants had been introduced into the respective Colonies of Australia, viz., New South Wales, Van Dieman's Land, and Swan River, in the following numbers : In 1825, 485 ; in 1826, 903 ; in 1827, 715 ; in 1828, 1056 ; in 1829, 2016.

In the year 1840 it was reported to Lord John Russell by the Agent-General for Emigration that there had arrived in Sydney, from 1st January, 1838, to 30th June, 1839, in Government ships, emigrants to the number of 14,644.

In reference to the opening of St. Matthew's Church in Windsor, on 21st October, 1840, a gentleman writing to a protestant friend in Sydney, states :—" Bishop Polding and his Vicar-General attended, with fourteen priests. I was highly gratified at witnessing the grand ceremony of the consecration of the Church. The Vicar-General preached on the subject of King Solomon's dedication of the temple ; his Scriptural allusions were applied with peculiar fitness to the service of the day. To say Dr. Ullathorne is a highly gifted individual, and endowed with shining talent is merely to repeat public opinion, but I may add, he turns the powers of his mind to the best advantage in using them for the glory of God and the benefit of mankind. Dr. Ullathorne is a quick-sighted investigator of the truth, and whilst he grasps with firmness the evidences of Christianity, with peculiar earnestness he invites his hearers to lay hold on them. He is a sound logician and able champion of the Catholic Church. The music was very grand : Mr. Bushelle and the band of the 80th Regiment attended Divine Service, as well as the officers, with a number of respectable protestant families. I was present at Vespers. The scene was imposing ; the greater part of the service was performed by the Bishop, the Vicar-General, and priests, in full chorus. Their voices were accompanied by a fine mellow seraphim, presented as a gift from his Lordship to St. Matthew's Church. The Bishop closed the service with an appropriate discourse on the consecration of the Church, in which he enforced, with persuasion and eloquence the essential doctrine of the Gospel, without entering into metaphysics, and endeavoured to convince his hearers that true religion is not only calculated to promote the glory of God, but the real happiness of man. He dwelt with energy on the virtue of charity, and charged his flock, in their daily intercourse with their fellow men, to be friendly with Christians of whatever denomination. *O si sic omnes.* Within the walls of the Catholic Church Christ crucified is practised, and in all her services presented to the eye. Surely this saving doctrine should induce protestants to overcome their prejudices, and extend hands of love and charity to all catholics. I shall communicate more fully upon this subject when we meet. I remain, my dear sir, ... P.S.—I have had the honor of an interview with Bishop Polding. His lordship's manners are highly prepossessing, and, uniting the dignity which becomes the Prelate with the humility of the true Christian, he is not only revered but beloved by his flock.

I must not omit to make mention of the condition of catholics in the County of Bathurst, at this time. The resident clergymen were Dean O'Reilly and Rev. T. Slattery. In the town of Bathurst a church was in the course of erection; the temporary chapel was attended by from 90 to 100 persons. The Chaplain attends twenty-six stations, once in the quarter, viz., Weagdon, 40 miles from Bathurst; Cabee, 60; Mudgee, 90; Jungy, 140; Macquarie River, 120; Summers Hill, 30; Wellington, 100; Murrumbidgee, 120; Dubbo, 130; Weny Plains, 20; Grobeingbon, 42; Lachlan, 60; Billabulla, 60; Lachlan River, 80; Carryamy, 90; Orpan's Creek, 25; Todd Walls, 35; Vale of Clwydd, 42; Mount Victoria, 52; Rose Vale, 40: Cherry Tree Falls, 70; and Berigan, 50 miles.

In a letter Dean O'Reilly states: "During my last journey I was led to proceed on from one sheep or stock station to another, until I found myself 350 miles from home. There were no residences, but many stations, and numbers of catholics, who often came from great distances, when they heard of me. Above 70 attended to receive the Sacraments. The Rev. T. Slattery performs service at Bathurst, when the Dean is absent, and when he returns, Father Slattery proceeds to visit eleven stations. The sum subscribed towards the erection of the above church was £1,041 8s. 6d.

The foundation stone of All Saints' Church, Liverpool, was laid by Bishop Polding on Sunday, the 8th November. There was a large concourse of people, many of whom had come from Sydney. The Rev. Mr. Marum, pastor of the district, was present. The Bishop administered the Sacrament of Confirmation to a considerable number of the children. A Pontifical Mass was then celebrated. His Lordship, before laying the stone, delivered a most eloquent address. The collection amounted to £40 or £50. His Lordship, in addressing the assemblage again, expressed his high gratification at their pious and zealous demeanour during the day, and at the account given by their excellent pastor of the vast improvement of their moral condition. He further said that it would be one of his pleasing duties, if God spared him, after his return from Europe, to consecrate the building of which the foundation had been laid that day, to the honour and glory of God and all his blessed saints. His Lordship concluded by giving them his benediction, when the people cried out simultaneously "God bless you my Lord, God grant you a safe voyage," and immediately dispersed. The Chaplain in Liverpool is the Rev. R. Marum. Service was performed in a room of the Government Hospital, the average attendance being 200, of which the monthly communicants number about twenty-four.

assurance of our grateful acknowledgements for the many and important services you have rendered to the catholics of the Australian colonies. On your first coming amongst us you found but one roofless church before you: the religious wants of the people for many years had been supplied by only one excellent clergyman; and many thousands of the people had heretofore lived and died in the interior of this colony without any religious consolation whatever. If brighter prospects now present themselves; if we see a hierarchy established on our shores; if we see every populous district of the colony provided with good and pious clergymen; if we witness under the genial influence of their precept and example, a moral regeneration and improvement prevailing among their respective flocks; if we behold the institution of the Sisters of Charity, famed throughout Europe for the great religious benefits it has dispensed, extending its usefulness to this colony, so exigent of its pious services, believe us Very Rev. Sir, we are duly sensible that these great services and daily augmenting advantages, are mainly to be attributed to your active and devoted exertions on our behalf, both here and in Europe; to the reliance which your character procured on the truth of your representations, as to the great want of religious aid and instruction under which these colonies suffered, and to the persevering assiduity with which you left no source unexplored that could be available to our advantage.

With hearts full of gratitude for these great and important services; with an earnest hope of soon seeing you again amongst us in the prosecution of your pious labours; and with a confidence that, whether absent or present, we shall live, as past experience assures us we have lived, in your regard and affections—we bid you a respectful, a grateful, and an affectionate farewell!

We beg your permission to accompany this address with a small token of our sincere respect and esteem.

The tribute of respect consisted of a snuff-box, valued at £60, with the following inscription:—Presented to the Very Reverend William Ullathorne, Doctor in Divinity, and Vicar-General of New Holland, as a testimony of the affection of the Catholics in the Colony; and their gratitude for his high services rendered to their religion and religious liberty; of regret at his departure for Europe, and of their anxiety for his safe and speedy return. November, 1840

Dr. Ullathorne's reply:—My dear friends, I thank you most sincerely. This is one of those rare moments in this earthly existence which drowns at once the recollection of a great many of its trials. If the feelings of my own breast could enlarge themselves to the extent of all your kindnesses and your many indulgences in my

regard of which this token is only the latest expression, I would endeavour to thank you worthily. As it is, I return your kindness and good wishes, as the best response I am capable of. It is a consoling reflection that, whilst in all other things I leave this colony as poor a man as when I first came to it, I am amply rich in your good opinions and warm affections. For these, and all those good works which I have seen done amongst you by the grace of God, I can never be sufficiently grateful. That I should have been an instrument, however by nature unworthy and unfit, of any part of so great a work of good, as the one to which you refer, will always fill me with happy recollections. But when, my dear friends, you see and bear witness to any qualities in me, except a very simple and earnest intention of serving you, and a wish and endeavour to cherish and protect your faith, and to enlarge and quicken the growth of your charity, I there recognize the fallacy of your kindness. Warm and earnest in your good affections, you believe those qualities to exist in your friend and pastor which you well know ought to exist, and imagine he does possess what you wish and desire he should possess; and it is my duty to pray that henceforward I may possess them. If on the occasion of the departure of our beloved bishop, I condole with you on the temporary loss of the presence of one, it is only the loss of his presence—his spirit will continue with you—whom you so truly and justly venerate; I would also console you with the reflection that his absence is needful for your own best interests, and that it will not be of a very long continuance; and I would cheer you by directing forward your hopes towards the happy period of his return, which may you all live, and live worthily and happily, to see accomplished; and may his coming again amongst you, as it will, be crowned with joy and benedictions. For myself, whilst I most heartily thank you, and trust that I shall live in your recollections, as you will continue to live in mine, I am desirous of laying myself under new obligations by most earnestly recommending myself to your prayers.

His lordship was addressed in the following words:—On the eve of your lordship's departure, we beg leave to express our warmest wishes for your safe and prosperous passage to England, and our earnest hope for your early return to us. Whilst we deeply deplore even your temporary absence, our regret is subdued and softened by the conviction that your visit to Europe is prompted by a sense of duty, and by that devoted and untiring zeal for our welfare, of which we have so many and unmistakable manifestations. After the five years you have exercised the pastoral charge in these colonies with mild and firm efficacy, it

must be gratifying to you as it is to us, to look back on the great benefits that have been conferred on this community, and of which, under Divine Providence, you have been the chief and chosen instrument. The many churches founded and consecrated by your lordship; your frequent visits into all parts of the colony; the dispersion and establishment of a zealous clergy throughout the principal districts of New South Wales; the impartial attention paid to all classes of your congregation, without any distinction, except that where assistance was most required and needed, there it was largely bestowed; and not least, the truly paternal solicitude you have shown towards the orphan, and the affection with which you have cherished the little children of your flock, are among the enduring monuments of those useful labours, by which, in your high station, you have been distinguished, and which have made an indelible impression upon hearts not formed to be ungrateful. As it is under the deep impression of sentiments such as these that we bid your lordship farewell now, you will not be surprised or displeased that, next to the reverence and affection we entertain towards you, the feeling uppermost is the desire that you may be re-united to your flock at the earliest moment your sense of duty and zeal for our service will permit. We beg leave to accompany this address with a small token of our gratitude and veneration.

This tribute consisted of a Treasury Bill for £400.

His lordship replied as follows:—Wishes so warm and generous, on the part of a people whose affections cannot be commanded, but may be obtained, I do feel sincere gratification in accepting. I knew not until the period of separation approached, how strong had become the bonds which united us. Only indeed a sense of duty the most cogent, and a conviction that my services elsewhere will prove more generally useful to my extensive charge, could influence me to consent to be temporarily absent from you. May your prayers for my speedy return be accomplished. Your kindness has attributed much to me I do not deserve. Patient enduring was the glory and merit of a preceding generation. The season of mercy and grace has been mercifully ours. Suffering and spiritual privation had disposed you to receive with gratitude the enlarged means of religious consolation Providence granted to you through us, the humble instrument of the divine benignity; and the gracious dispensation has not fallen on an unworthy soil. In the churches now in the course of erection; in the improved habits of our people; in the various charitable and religious institutions which have sprung into existence, in a space of time almost instantaneous; there is,

temples of God, your zeal would not be satisfied until the material temple, which is the church, should be raised, wherein, after the wont of your forefathers you might worship in spirit and in truth.

" A noble instance of disinterestedness, a gratifying proof that the right use of riches is not altogether forgotten, the church we are about to found will record. The land on which we stand is given by Mr. Watson, who also deposited £300 as his contribution. The Almighty has blessed his labours and he deems it right thus to return a part to Him who gave all. Already does he see around him the rising families of children he and his excellent wife have adopted for their own. Placed by him on farms purchased by his own honest and well-deserved earnings, he enjoys the highest and most exquisite feast it is for man in his present state to make unto himself, in their happiness and prosperity. For their use and for the public benefit he devotes so large a sum for the erection of this church. I may mention another circumstance which, in my mind, lessens not the value of the donation nor diminishes my estimation of the man. Thirty years ago, in a moment of thoughtlessness, that was done which has been the cause of great regret. Is not this amply expiated and atoned for ? Is the stain of such a fault to be made more enduring than the justice of God ? Not so thought that Blessed Legislator from whose code, as illustrated in his own example, we are accustomed to draw our rules of life. When the publican Zaccheus, nay, even the chief of the publicans, by the adventitious circumstances sought, and succeeded, to see Jesus, was he not forthwith recognised by the Saviour and desired to prepare to receive Him into his house, for that He intended to abide with him ? What were the dispositions of Zaccheus ? Lord, says he, I give one-half of my goods to the poor, and if I have wronged anyone I restore to him fourfold. Nor when we see those who have followed Zaccheus in his aberrations, imitating him in their return, striving by honest industry to raise themselves that they may see Jesus and merit to be recognised by Him who came to save the sheep that was lost, shall we hold in eternal remembrance the fault of one moment ? It is not thus we shall prove ourselves the ministers nor even the disciples of Jesus Christ; never, never will be seen in the conduct of the true disciple of Jesus any symptons of aversion and contempt for a large class of fellow-citizens in which, if there be found the objects of punishment well-deserved, there are and must be, from the nature of human institutions, many victims of misfortune. I have not read to a fruitless purpose the history of Ireland for the last two centuries.

I have not seen with my own eyes the misery of that once
unhappy country, but now disinthralled, I trust, from the tyranny
of besotted and heartless faction, the details and consequences
which always result when the arm of power is stretched forth to
uphold a party against a people, without coming to a conclusion
which right reason suggests, which religion sanctions, which is
exemplified and illustrated in the conduct of the incarnate
wisdom of the Godhead. I cannot fasten my judgment to the
ever-turning wheel of fashionable opinion. I am not prepared
to deem Joseph a degraded character, though sold as such by his
malevolent brethren; nor to pronounce the Blessed Jesus guilty,
though condemned by those leagued together for his destruction;
nor to throw a stone at the bidding of every Pharisee. I regard
not of what classes the settlers and cultivators of the soil are
composed; but wherever I go, and I have largely traversed this
country, I meet men of industrious domestic habits, solicitous to
give their children an education superior to their own. I perceive
a deferential respect where respect is due, an attachment,
combined with that proper sense of independence, which in my
mind evinces a sense of propriety totally incompatible with
vulgar or mean thought. Take for instance this beautiful valley
with its inhabitants! See those plains! How zealously has not
the plough pursued its claims to the very mountain foot! Not a
weed is visible amongst these families of corn plants which bend
their deep green flags to the breeze—emblem, dear children in
Jesus Christ, of your own state, who are the 'cultivation of the
Lord.' How often have I not reposed when neither lock nor
latch nor fastening protected! You support your school, you
give proofs of the proper sense of the value of wealth and the
purpose for which it is given of which you may be justly proud.
Such being your state and your disposition, why should the
minister of peace make enquiries odious and uncharitable. Most
willingly do I bear my testimony that in no part of England, and
I have seen much of her rural population there, have I observed
a middle class possessed of qualities more valuable, or who by
their conduct were more deserving of estimation and of trust,
than it has been mine to meet here and in other parts of the
Colony which in the discharge of my pastoral duties I have
visited. But to return from this digression to the immediate
purpose for which we are this day assembled. Let us not imagine
that we have done a great thing even when we have bestowed
our whole substance on charitable doings; we can claim no right
to meritorious giving when we have none to possess. We cannot
suppose that the Lord requires a temple built by mortal hands

people, increasing in the enjoyment of a high degree of physical and moral health. If ever a bishop was worthy to be called a pastor of his flock, it is the Right Reverend Dr. Polding."

I certainly would not be doing justice to my narrative were I to pass by unnoticed the worth of two most estimable Catholic gentlemen, officers of the Government, who flourished in our community at this time; I mean John Hubert Plunkett, Attorney-General of New South Wales, and Roger Therry, Esq., Commissioner of the Court of Requests. They were conscientious Catholics, and lived up to their religious principles. They never compromised their religion, and were ever ready to speak and act in defence of the faith of their forefathers, and of their country, Ireland. They gave all the weight of their character and position for the benefit of religion and charity. Mr. Plunkett was for many years Attorney-General, and he went home on leave of absence in the beginning of the year 1841. But before he left the colony, in such great respect was he held by his legal brethren, that they entertained him at a dinner. The Chief Justice, Sir James Dowling presided, and there was present Judge Stephens. The Governor, Sir Geo. Gipps, also honored the festive board by his presence. The Governor, in returning thanks when his health was proposed, said: "He felt extremely happy in meeting such a large and respectable company of the colonists of New South Wales, of every grade and of every persuasion, who, laying aside all other motives, had met together that evening to pay a tribute of respect to a public officer who had discharged his great, important, and arduous duties with the highest degree of impartiality and firmness; he felt extremely happy to make one amongst them in bearing testimony to the worth, ability, and integrity of that officer." The Chief Justice, Sir James Dowling said: "It was a pleasing reflection to Mr. Plunkett, notwithstanding the very peculiar community in which he lived, all men bore ample testimony to the just, upright, manly, and impartial manner in which he had discharged the duties belonging to his station; after many years of trial Mr. Plunkett had passed through the crucible of public opinion without a stain being cast upon him." All the gentlemen present at the banquet bore similar testimony to the high character of Mr. Plunkett.

Before the departure of Mr. Plunkett, on leave of absence, a handsome testimonial was presented to him in the shape of several pieces of silver plate, and on each piece was engraved his family crest, which is a trotting horse, with the motto "*Festina Lente*." The silver service was purchased by public subscription and cost about £400.

Roger Therry, Esq., was appointed Attorney-General, during the absence of Mr. Plunkett. Mr. Therry had been Commissioner of the Court of Requests for eleven years, and discharged the onerous duties of his office with great rectitude and ability. When he was promoted to be Attorney-General, the public expressed their satisfaction for his past services, by presenting him with a massive silver service, which cost £500. The salver had the following inscription engraved on it, with Mr. Therry's crest, a lion rampant, bearing a cross, with the motto, "*E Cruce Leo.*" The words of the inscription were the following:—"This salver with an urn, dinner, dessert and tea-service, and other articles, forming a service of plate, were presented to Roger Therry, Esquire, Her Majesty's Attorney General, by the people of New South Wales, as a mark of their esteem and respect on the occasion of his retiring from the office of Commissioner of the Court of Requests, the duties of which he discharged in that colony for a period of eleven years, to the entire satisfaction of the community."

Judge Burton, who published in London "an account of the state of religion and education in New South Wales," returned to the colony in the year 1841. His party prepared a banquet for him and the Governor was invited to attend, but he declined, "on account of his independent position as a judge in regard to the Executive; and because the circumstances were different from those of the Attorney-General, Mr. Plunkett, who was leaving the colony, whilst Judge Burton was returning to office." It was very wise of Sir George Gipps to decline the invitation, if he had attended, there would have been some reason to believe that the ruler of the colony gave countenance and support to the false statements, sophistical arguments, and derogatory remarks of Judge Burton's religious history.

The Judge must have been terribly taken by surprise when he returned to find that all his visions of a dominant church were baseless fabrics; he found Sir Richard Bourke's Church Act, which placed the principal religious bodies on an equality, working admirably, and giving to each denomination a share of the public revenue. The Catholics whom he desired to be the last in status before the law, had, since his absence vastly increased in numbers and there were two most efficient catholic officers of the Crown.

When Bishop Polding left the colony at the close of the year 1840, he left the church in a flourishing condition. The Catholic population then amounted to nearly 20,000 souls; Sydney contained 14,000 Catholics. The entire population of the colony from a return published by the Government in 1839 amounted to 114,386 the population of Sydney was 40,000 and contained

Polding, Bishop, Vicar-Apostolic of New Holland and Van Dieman's Land, on the 30th September, in the year of Our Lord, 1840—Sacerdos Rev. J. Lynch."

On Thursday, 8th October following, the foundation stone of the church of St. John the Baptist was laid on Campbell's Hill, West Maitland, by the bishop. There was accommodation for 600 persons on the ground. The procession, with the children clothed in white, moved from the temporary church in the town. The Sacrament of Confirmation was administered to about seventy persons, young and old : at the close of the Mass nearly the same number received the Holy Communion. When about to lay the foundation stone, the bishop said :—" On that stone, an emblem of the new life which you this day commence, deposit all irregular affections; increase in virtue ; raise higher the fabric of sanctity, as the walls of this material building come nearer to their termination: and may this edifice, by being ever the habitation of virtuous and pious souls, be a figure of the church triumphant in heaven, where nothing defiled can enter, and where the prayers of the saints ascend as a sweet odour before the throne of the Lamb."

The following was the inscription on a plate laid under the stone :—

ECCLESIÆ SUB PATROCINIO
SANCTI JOANNIS BAPTISTÆ,
ERIGENDÆ,
AD MAJOREM DEI GLORIAM PROMOVENDAM
HUNC PRIMARIUM LAPIDEM
POSUIT
REVERENDISSIMUS D. D. JOANNES BEDA, EPISCOPUS,
HIEROCŒSARENSIS
ET, IN NOVA HOLANDIA ET INSULA VAN DIEMEN,
VICARIUS APOSTOLICUS,
DIE OCTAVA OCTOBRIS ANNO SALUTIS
MDCCCXL,
VIGEBAT, SUCCESSOR SANCTI PETRI IN ROMA.
SUMMUS PONTIFEX GREGORIUS XVI.
ET IN BRITANNIS VICTORIA PRIMA SCEPTRUM TENENS
BENEVOLENTIAM OMNIUM SUB UNA DITIONE
CONCILIABAT.

SACERDOS REV. J. LYNCH.

The Bishop celebrated Mass in the temporary chapel, on Friday, in West Maitland, and the same day returned to Sydney by Newcastle

On the same day, on the catholic church ground, Campbell's Hill, a branch of the Catholic Institute was established, the Right Rev Lord Bishop in the chair. The Rev. V. Dowling, E. Mahony, and J. Lynch were appointed presidents and Dr. Mallon secretary : the following persons to act as a committee, viz :—Messrs. Lett, Dee, Murray, Turner, Grace, Healy, Tierney, jun., Callaghan, McDougall, Byrne, Tierney, sen., Shinkivin, Haydon, O'Brian, Brown, Cullen, Clarke, O'Neill, and *(ex officio)* the Rev. Messrs. Dowling, Mahony, and Lynch.

On Sunday, 18th October, in St. Mary's Cathedral, Sydney, the Lord Bishop conferred the holy orders of sub-deacon and deacon upon the following gentlemen, viz:—The Rev. John Kenny, the Rev. James Dunphy, the Rev. Patrick Magennis, and the Rev. John Grant. A Pontifical Mass was celebrated by his lordship, and a most learned and interesting discourse, suitable to the occasion, was delivered by the Very Rev. the Vicar-General, who, as their theological instructor, presented the postulants to the bishop, and attested in the usual form their fitness for the sacred office.

Bishop Polding was in Wollongong on 12th October, where he laid the foundation stone of the church of St. Francis Xavier on the following day. The catholics of Wollongong were joined on the morning of the 13th by those of Dapto, Jamberoo, and Shoalhaven. At the first note of the *Adeste fidelis* the procession moved from the presbytery, consisting of the children to the number of about 200, the members of the committee with cedar rods, and the whole body of the people, walking two and two. When assembled in the temporary chapel, and before the sermon, the bishop offered up prayers, and the children sang the hymn "Jesus, the only thought of Thee." The Rev. Mr. Brennan preached the sermon, after which the procession moved to the foundation stone close by. The bishop then proceeded according to the ritual : a plate with an appropriate inscription was placed under the stone ; and the bishop made a very effective address to the people. The collection amounted to £55.

In the district of Illawarra the Rev. John Rigney is the chaplain, and he resides at Wollongong. The attendance in the temporary chapel there is 200. He officiates weekly at Dapto, 8 miles, with an attendance of 120 ; at Jamberoo, 25 miles, attendance 80 ; at Shoalhaven, 50 miles, he officiates every month, the communicants numbering 100. On an average the Rev. J. Rigney travels 3252 miles during the year.

The Catholic Church at Campbelltown is a substantial stone building capable of accommodating 500, and was erected before Bishop Polding arrived in the colony. The interior of the church was finished in a most tasteful manner by the then chaplain (the Rev. J. A. Goold), now Archbishop of Melbourne. It is beautifully situated on elevated ground, and commands a fine prospect of the surrounding country. The school, the foundation of which was laid and blessed on the 17th of March, was designed by the chaplain to answer the twofold purpose of a school and chapel. During the week days and some of the festivals mass was celebrated in it, because the church itself is rather distant from the centre of the town. The Catholic population of Campbelltown was, according to the census of 1836, no more than 287, and the population of what is called the Hundred of Campbelltown, contained in Appin, Menangle, Narellen and Cooke, was returned by the same census as amounting to 810 persons ; but at the time when the school was built, in the year 1840, there must have been a good many more Catholics. The chaplain attended five stations monthly, at distances varying from eight to forty miles ; during the year he travelled about 2000 miles in the discharge of his clerical duties. The average attendance at each place was from 100 to 250. The Communicants in Campbelltown were about 50 at each mass. The Rev. C. Sumner, O.S.B, was at this time the chaplain of Appin, but resided in Campbelltown, attending three stations distant 15 to 30 miles, travelling in the year about 1040 miles.

We extract the following from the *Australian Chronicle* of March 24 :—

"Mr. Editor,—As an inhabitant of Campbelltown I am proud that we anticipated the object of your remarks on the first celebration of the day dedicated to the glorious patron of Ireland, St. Patrick. Mass was celebrated at half-past ten o'clock by the Rev. Mr. Goold, and an instructive address delivered by the Right Rev. Bishop. The virtues of St. Patrick were proposed for the imitation of the hearers, and his extraordinary abstinence and life of prayer were held up as a standard. These were contrasted with the excess and dissipation too frequently to be lamented as desecrating a day so holy, so full of grateful recollections. The Bishop dwelt with much feeling on the sufferings of Ireland, and called the attention of his hearers to the fact that notwithstanding those sufferings Ireland had clung to her faith—for thereon alone could she repose—this was the anchor of her hope. Those sufferings had been to her as the press in the vineyard, and the streams of life had been diffused amongst

o

The Agent for the Patriotic Association of Sydney, Mr. Buller, in a speech made by him in the Imperial Parliament in the year 1840, on colonial affairs, stated that the number of free emigrants amounted annually to 10,000, for the last five or ten years. He remarked at the same time that it was no longer practicable to make New South Wales a penal colony, that the convict labour was inadequate to supply the wants of the colonies. The chief source of immigration was the Land Fund, *i. e.*, the proceeds of the sale of lands in the Colony, and the Government was pledged to devote that revenue for the purpose of bringing emigrants to the Colony. There were two systems of emigration, one called the bounty system, the other assisted emigration; but both depended for the means of being carried out on the land fund. By the bounty system Government orders were issued, on condition that those who took them up should send to the Colony eligible emigrants, according to the orders received, and these orders were made payable when the emigrants were landed. The candidates for such bounties were entrusted with the selection of the emigrants and with whatever related to the arrangements of the voyage. By the system called assisted emigration, which was the Government system, the Government took all the responsibility; by their agents the emigrants were selected, and the greatest care was taken that they were eligible as to character, health, and employment. The vessel was chartered by the Government and provided with all the necessaries. All was effected through the supervision of the Agent-General for Emigration. The Government system gave satisfaction, but there was a popular outcry against the bounty system, which had been, it was alleged, woefully abused. Those who took up the bounty orders sold them at a premium, and it was said this premium was deducted by lessening the provisions and comforts of the emigrants. The emigrants of some ships were starved, and, horrible to relate, some females, it is said, bartered their virtue for food. The Government interfered, and rigid conditions were enforced for bringing out the emigrants by the Government system.

Some colonial authorities at this time objected to Irish immigration, because the Irish were contentious and quarrelsome, and in several respects an undesirable class to introduce into the Colony; nay, that some were sent out who had aided and abetted in murder. A Commission was appointed to enquire into the use which was made of the land fund and the working of the emigration system. The Commission in their report vindicated the Irish emigrants. It stated: "We cannot quit the subject of the alleged prejudice, to which we have had accidentally to advert, without expressing our regret at its existence, and we hope that no public officer will permit

CHAPTER VIII.

Wesleyan lamentations about the progress of Catholicity—The Opening of St. Matthew's Church, Windsor, 21st Oct. 1840— The Foundation stone of All Saint's Church, Liverpool, laid by Bishop Polding—Departure of Dr. Ullathorne for Adelaide—The establishment of a Catholic Circulating Library, under the patronage of his Lordship the Bishop— Meeting held in the Catholic School-room, Castlereagh-street, to devise means for the erection of a new church in Sydney, to be dedicated to St. Patrick

WE extract the following from a European Journal as an evidence of the progress made by the church.

"Jonathan Crowder, a Wesleyan missionary, writing from Madras, 16th March, 1839, says :—' Papists, with the reinforcement which came out in December of an extra bishop and ten students, are making a considerable impression at Madras.' W. S. Fox, a brother missionary, under date of 14th March, writes thus :— ' Our fears have not been a little excited of late by the arrival and subsequent operations of a Roman catholic bishop, accompanied by several associates. That the papists are exerting themselves in this country is an alarming fact; and if we may judge from the peculiar power of adaptation which distinguishes popery, they are likely to form a numerous church.' "

J. McKenny, writing from Sydney, says, in allusion to missionary efforts :—" This is not a question of mere pounds shillings and pence, for it now assumes this form — Shall Australia be a protestant or a popish colony? The number of priests who are being sent out is quite frightful; lately eight arrived in one vessel, and received from the Home Government £150 for their passage and outfit."

In the *Australian* of the 19th May there is an account of the conversion of T. C. Anstey, Esq., son of a respectable member of the Legislative Council of Van Diemen's Land. He went to England to study with the view to become a clergyman of the church of England. He commenced to study the grounds of both churches, which ended in embracing catholicity in 1834. Since his conversion he has contributed to the *Dublin Review* and other catholic periodicals. He turned his attention to the legal profession and became a barrister-at-law in January 7, 1839. He married Harriet, the second daughter of J. E. Strickland, Esq., of Loughlin House, Roscommon, Ireland.

prerogatives of the church of England, and how she had been unfairly dealt with by both governor and government; that the Roman catholics had been preferred in the distribution of that favours. He says the church of England "is a part of the State itself," that the fundamental laws of England became the laws of the colony when the settlement was made; and by one of those fundamental laws the church of England became the established church of the colony; "for nearly fifty years," the judge states, "no other denomination of christians was acknowledged by the government as an object of its support, beyond the limits of a charitable toleration;" and it was in this spirit of "charitable toleration" that the government assisted the catholics and dissenters. He extols to the skies the zeal and labours of the bishop and clergy of the church of England; but he has not much to record of the zeal and labours of the church of England for the poor prisoners during those fifty years. What has become of the Apostolic zeal of the church of England? He calls her the true Apostolic church, when, although "part of the State itself," she could not succeed in sending more than one clergyman to administer to the religious wants of the colony, and he in the end left the church and became a Moravian. When religion was left in such a condition by the Apostolic church, it was time for a separation between Church and State. Here is the description which the judge gives of the state of religion in the early years of the colony:—"Those indeed who should (had they been so disposed) have set about laying the foundation of their city in righteousness, were far otherwise engaged: deeply immersed in selfish pursuits, they were seeking their own future wealth in the means placed at their disposal of unpurchased lands and convict labour, of mercenery barter and petty dealings with their inferiors. That most pernicious article of traffic, which came soon afterwards to be the ordinary circulating medium of the colony (spirituous liquor), was early resorted in exchange for the necessaries of life; in the purchase of valuable property; in payment for labour, and as a reward offered by government for public services. Thus were the foundations of the new colony laid *in avarice and drunkenness.*" There must also be noted the indifference of those in authority to religious matters, so remarkable in the single fact, that one of the earlier governors had to be informed by the clergyman that *five* or *six persons only* attended divine service, and that it was then that he determined to go to church himself, and stated that "he expected that the example would be followed by the people." The church Apostolic—the church of England—could not complain but that ample provision

But we have three forms of faith distinctly recognised by the legislature, placed on an equal footing; therefore by all in official situations to be equally protected and guarded against wrong and insult; for we all have an equal right to look up to the government as our common protector and friend. His Lordship then concluded by exhorting the people to preserve the same quiet, forbearing, peaceable demeanor, showing forth the beauty of their faith in the practice of their lives; and whilst determined to repel every unjust attack, in all calmness to defend their tenets, resting their principal dependance on Him, without whose aid the best efforts of man are vain and fruitless. (Loud cheers.)

The immense crowd then retired in the most orderly manner, every countenance beaming with satisfaction and delight—an auspicious beginning to two noble institutions, from which might be predicted the best results to the colony.

The catholic church made great strides during the years 1839 and 1840. Sir R. Bourke's Church Act was now in full operation, and it was deemed advisable by the Bishop and his Vicar-General to take advantage of its provisions without delay. Through the strenuous efforts of the good bishop and his clergy churches and schools were erected in the most populous parts of the colony, as a means most requisite for the advancement of religion. The Right Rev. Dr. Polding was then in the vigour of life, and he did not spare himself in the labour of the Lord's vineyard. Whenever his clergy required him to lay the foundation stone of a church, or to promote any other good work, he was sure to be present at the time and place—in fact, it may be said he then worked almost night and day. There were no good roads in those days, nor trains, nor telegraphs, and in many places only bridle paths. He travelled with his clergy from place to place, through the thick forest, exposed to a broiling Australian sun, and shared with them the terrible thirst, which sometimes there was nothing to quench but muddy water. Everywhere he was received by the people with joy and acclamation, and they bowed implicitly to his injunctions. The bishop was an excellent horseman, who bore well the heat and brunt of the day, and often at the end of a very long ride was less fatigued than the young clergy who accompanied him.

We find the Bishop on 22nd December, 1839, at the McDonald River, where he blessed the foundation stone of St. Joseph's Church, near Mount St. Joseph in the Windsor district; the incumbent of the district at the time was the Rev. John would be the consequence if such an establishment continued to exist. He writes :—" How this vast scheme of church aggrandizement, unparalleled in the world's history, would have been ultimately found to operate ; how this monstrous monopoly of the soil, one seventh in extent and value, in one continuous and unbroken block, of each individual county—spreading like Briareus, from one body and one will, a hundred strong and mighty arms, over all the face of the country, how this would have affected the interests and the industry of the farmer, the grazier, and the merchant ; how the continually increasing weight and accumulating influence of such a corporation, which must soon have become an exclusive, a close-shut, and a secretly working ecclesiastical oligarchy, not merely claiming a tithe of produce in this place and that, but one seventh of the firm and solid earth—to which mere form the remainder must have continually alluviated, whilst all that lay along its endless boundaries would be at his mercy—what weight and influence, I say, such an ecclesiastical oligarchy must ultimately have exercised ; on one side, against the liberty and independence of the civil government, and, on the other side, against the freedom and rights of the people : above all, how uneven the pressure of such an all-pervading, illimitable, and irresistible domination ; and the more wealthy the more corrupt it must have become ; the more sacred in its own self-assumption, the more blind-sighted and terrible in its zeal : how, under such a church domination, the unfortunate catholic, and equally unfortunate dissenter, would be reduced to worse than Egyptian bondage. All this, with various other vistas of but gloomy promise that seem opening up to contemplation in these temporal regions of spiritual domination, belong rather to the pursuits of the politician, the economist and the philosopher, than to the consideration of the present writer. A clergyman may, however, be allowed to observe, that the power of this corporation church would not ultimately become a spiritualizing influence : it would be temporal and earthly, not heavenly. Separated from the people by independence, raised above them by affluence, enjoying the luxuries of life by right, and assimilated into an exclusive society ; whilst the good things of this world, combined with a natural desire to advance their families, would supply continual temptation to ambition and intrigue. Such an incorporate clergy would possess but little in common with the feelings, the wants, the cares and the thoughts of the great mass of the population. Their own connexions would be proud of their alliance, but between the clergy and the people the mutual relations would be at points of repulsion, and not of temples of God, your zeal would not be satisfied until the material temple, which is the church, should be raised, wherein, after the wont of your forefathers you might worship in spirit and in truth.

"A noble instance of disinterestedness, a gratifying proof that the right use of riches is not altogether forgotten, the church we are about to found will record. The land on which we stand is given by Mr. Watson, who also deposited £300 as his contribution. The Almighty has blessed his labours and he deems it right thus to return a part to Him who gave all. Already does he see around him the rising families of children he and his excellent wife have adopted for their own. Placed by him on farms purchased by his own honest and well-deserved earnings, he enjoys the highest and most exquisite feast it is for man in his present state to make unto himself, in their happiness and prosperity. For their use and for the public benefit he devotes so large a sum for the erection of this church. I may mention another circumstance which, in my mind, lessens not the value of the donation nor diminishes my estimation of the man. Thirty years ago, in a moment of thoughtlessness, that was done which has been the cause of great regret. Is not this amply expiated and atoned for? Is the stain of such a fault to be made more enduring than the justice of God? Not so thought that Blessed Legislator from whose code, as illustrated in his own example, we are accustomed to draw our rules of life. When the publican Zaccheus, nay, even the chief of the publicans, by the adventitious circumstances sought, and succeeded, to see Jesus, was he not forthwith recognised by the Saviour and desired to prepare to receive Him into his house, for that He intended to abide with him? What were the dispositions of Zaccheus? Lord, says he, I give one-half of my goods to the poor, and if I have wronged anyone I restore to him fourfold. Nor when we see those who have followed Zaccheus in his aberrations, imitating him in their return, striving by honest industry to raise themselves that they may see Jesus and merit to be recognised by Him who came to save the sheep that was lost, shall we hold in eternal remembrance the fault of one moment? It is not thus we shall prove ourselves the ministers nor even the disciples of Jesus Christ; never, never will be seen in the conduct of the true disciple of Jesus any symptons of aversion and contempt for a large class of fellow-citizens in which, if there be found the objects of punishment well-deserved, there are and must be, from the nature of human institutions, many victims of misfortune. I have not read to a fruitless purpose the history of Ireland for the last two centuries.

from time to time separated themselves into sects, dissenting in matters of religion from the general body of the State, yet, ever since the establishment of a Church in England, and the Union of the Kingdoms under one Sovereign head, the Church of England existed as the National Church; at first free and independent, then for a time overwhelmed by corruption of foreign growth, but again asserting and maintaining the independence of her foundation and the purity of her faith. And as such was by force of law, before the Statute 9th Geo. IV., c. 83, and by the express terms of the Statute, the established Church of the Colony." To this spurious assertion of the Judge the reply of Dr. Ullathorne is that the now established Church of England is founded on the Statute 13, Charles II. This Statute is entitled:— "An Act for the Uniformity of the Public Prayers and Administration of the Sacraments . . . . in the Church of England." And the Act of 5, Ann. 8, for securing the preservation of the Church of England by law established, which is cited by Mr. Burton, expressly quotes the "Act of Uniformity" as being the foundation of the establishment of that Church, and limits its settlement by law "within the kingdoms of England and Ireland, the dominion of Wales, and town of Berwick-upon-Tweed, and territories thereunto belonging." "Statue law, then," writes the Dr., "limits the Anglican establishment to England, Ireland, Wales, and Berwick. All these Acts contain and speak their own express local limitations. . . . . The Statute law, he states, is so far from giving the Anglican Clergy of the Colonies the *rights* and *privileges* of belonging to the establishment of the Church of England, that it expressly and by a special enactment excludes them from the rights and privileges of that establishment. The Act 59, George III, expressly states that the clergy destined for the cure of souls in His Majesty's foreign and colonial possessions are "not provided with the title required by the Can^{on} of the Church of England of such as are to be made ministers.

One word says the Dr. on Mr. Burton's argument from the Coronation Oath and the Catholic Official's Oath. The Judge's sophistry on this point is the same as that of his friend the Protestant bishop in his formal complaint to the British Government on the subject of the Catholic bishop's dress and appearance; it depends on a quibbling mistake of the meaning of the words, "realm" and "kingdom." There are three realms or kingdoms, and many vast dominions besides, which are beneath the sceptre of the British Crown, some of which never were either realms or kingdoms, and amongst these is the colony of New South Wales.

for his worship. The temple in which we are now assembled, in which the earth furnishes the flooring and the arch of heaven forms the dome, surrounded by creation, animate and inanimate, is the most becoming. Yet for man's accommodation God condescends to accept worship in a temple built by mortal hands; and he deems that which is given towards its erection as bestowed upon himself. We think it right to offer publicly a proof of our approbation to the individual whose munificent donation we have before mentioned. In your name, dearly beloved, we present to him a treasure, the value of which money cannot reach, a copy of the written Word of God—the Book of Life, the Holy Scriptures—and we feel an especial gratification in thus publicly with our own hands presenting this most sacred Book to one of our beloved flock, because we are not without hope that the false idea which evil-minded men have spread abroad relative to unjust prohibitions and restrictions will be thus dissipated. The Catholic Church is said to be hostile to the distribution of the Holy Scripture. Would to God I could deposit a copy in the cottage of everyone disposed to read it with proper dispositions! No, the Catholic Church neither now nor at any other period prohibited her children from reading the Sacred Volume. Only when those wicked men, whose object was plunder and sensual gratification under the pretext of the reformation of religion, translated the Word of God in the Sacred Scripture and fashioned it to their own purposes to gratify their misdeeds and rebellion, when they transformed the truth into a lie, the Church warned her children against these poisoned fountains of error, and hence the outcry raised against her, hence the calumnious charge repeated a thousand times. Keep this book with reverence; let its laws be thy guide, its counsels thy support and consolation. When thou hearest its words or readest it, remember God speaks unto thee, and be as the Jews near the Mount of Sinai or the devout St. John near the Cross of thy dying Redeemer."

His Lordship then proceeded to the celebration of the ceremonies usual on such an occasion. It was most gratifying to observe the devotion of the Protestant part of the assemblage—the union of heart which seemed to predominate. The meaning of the ceremonies used was then explained; and all present on bended knees having received the blessing of the Bishop, the ceremony concluded. The interesting occasion will long be remembered with delight by the inhabitants of the Lower Hawkesbury and the McDonald River.

But to continue our account of the labours and travels of Bishop Polding. On the 3rd October his lordship was in East

Maitland, and on the following day (Sunday) he officiated in the church to a crowded congregation. There were a great many Protestants present, and the sermon he delivered gave general satisfaction. In the evening he proceeded to Raymond Terrace. where he performed divine service on the following morning. The chaplains of West and East Maitland and the surrounding districts were the Rev. Mr. Mahony and Rev. J. Lynch. The population according to the census of 1836 of the town of Maitland was 1163 persons of which 365 were Catholics. The chaplains had to travel on an average 5000 miles during the year. There being no church, mass was celebrated under a tent erected for the purpose, and it rained nearly all the time. The Rev. Mr. Mahony said that he felt much pleasure in introducing that portion of his flock to the especial notice of the Bishop for their truly exemplary piety and general good conduct, and the bishop expressed himself highly pleased at the account given of them by their zealous pastor. A subscription list was opened for the erection of a church and a handsome sum was subscribed. His Lordship then proceeded to Hinton, about seven miles distant, where a great many Catholics were in attendance to meet him, whom he addressed, and earnestly exhorted to persevere in the path of virtue and good works. The bishop then went on to Cooley Camp, accompanied by many persons, and addressed the multitude for a considerable time. From thence the bishop proceeded to Glenham, the seat of Mr. C. H. Chambers, where the party arrived about ten o'clock at night. On the following morning, 5th October, the bishop celebrated mass to about sixty people, and selected the site for a new church, the land having been given by the lady of Mr. C. H. Chambers, who had also subscribed liberally towards its erection. He then went to Dungog, a distance of about 25 miles, where he was kindly entertained at the hospitable mansion of W. F. Mackay, Esq. Mass was celebrated the next morning to about seventy catholics, some respectable protestants being present. The same day the bishop and party returned to Maitland where they arrived at 10 o'clock p.m. A great change has taken place in this district in a very short time, through the zealous exertions of the Rev. Mr. Mahony.

On the 29th September, his Lordship having travelled overland from Sydney, arrived in the Wollombi district, where he laid the foundation stone of a church dedicated to St. Michael the Archangel. A Mr. McDougall presented the land, and the stone bore the following inscription :—" This church is dedicated to the honour and glory of God under the patronage of St. Michael the Archangel, by the Right Rev. John Bede influence and power, endorsed them with your name, and with the seal of your judicial character have stamped the falsehoods true."

"This is not the first occasion," the Doctor goes on to say, "you have given us to fear your especial presence on the bench. The catholics of the colony remember your commonly reported connection with that vile production of short-lived existence, the *Sydney Standard*, which was not inappropriately designated 'the high church and Burton paper, inasmuch as such of its columus as could be spared from insulting us were devoted to your particular opinions in politics."

In another paragraph Dr. Ullathorne writes:—"You have not only sought to sink us into a party of a degraded class, but that holy religion which is the basis of our morals; that religion which is the best motive of our social conduct; of those morals, of that conduct, whose acts and omissions you are called upon to decide in our utmost need; of that religion you have expressed your contempt; her teachings you have derided; at the boliest of her rites and sacraments you have mocked and scoffed............ Your prejudice against us and your efforts to degrade us are now matters of common fame.

In the concluding chapter the Doctor states:—"The object at which Judge Burton aims in his 'State of Religion and Education in New South Wales,' is evident; floating on the surface of the work, visible without search." • "A contest, he perceives, has already begun. He will not avoid," he says, "any part of his own proper duty on such an occasion. A member of the church of England in Australia, he turns for help to his brethren in England. The help he wants *is money*. Of this article his brethren in the colony, he tells us, are collecting considerable quantities, and are receiving yet greater sums from the government. It is likewise his wish to obtain for the clergy of his particular church, whose numbers he would increase to legion, a legal and everlasting possession of one-seventh part of the soil, that every one of them may be straightway constituted an independent gentleman; independent not only of his people, but, as time would quickly show, were it brought to the test, independent of the duties expected from him, and equally independent of any needful possession of the clerical qualifications for his office. This large and ample independence he prefers resting on the lands of the colony, as being 'the safest and securest.' To the other religious communions of the colony Mr. Burton and his friends make the gracious offer of 'toleration.' ....A member of the church of England in Australia," he says, "turns for help to his brethren in Great Britain. His object is undoubted. He is the recognized lay leader of a politico-religious party. Shortly previous to the arrival of this book, his health was drunk, *coram episcopo,* at the diocesan dinner, as the constitutional lawyer, who would never support any other doctrine than that the Established Church of England is the national church wherever the national 'Standard waves.'"—*Speech of Mr. Campbell. Sydney Herald, June 26, 1840.*

Such was the language of Mr. Campbell, when he proposed the health of Judge Burton, *coram episcopo,* in the year 1840. If Mr. Campbell survive, he must now be convinced, that outside of England, the established church is not the national church, wherever the flag of England waves.

LAUS DEO.

The Catholic Church at Campbelltown is a substantial stone building capable of accommodating 500, and was erected before Bishop Polding arrived in the colony. The interior of the church was finished in a most tasteful manner by the then chaplain (the Rev. J. A. Goold), now Archbishop of Melbourne. It is beautifully situated on elevated ground, and commands a fine prospect of the surrounding country. The school, the foundation of which was laid and blessed on the 17th of March, was designed by the chaplain to answer the twofold purpose of a school and chapel. During the week days and some of the festivals mass was celebrated in it, because the church itself is rather distant from the centre of the town. The Catholic population of Campbelltown was, according to the census of 1836, no more than 287, and the population of what is called the Hundred of Campbelltown, contained in Appin, Menangle, Narellen and Cooke, was returned by the same census as amounting to 810 persons; but at the time when the school was built, in the year 1840, there must have been a good many more Catholics. The chaplain attended five stations monthly, at distances varying from eight to forty miles; during the year he travelled about 2000 miles in the discharge of his clerical duties. The average attendance at each place was from 100 to 250. The Communicants in Campbelltown were about 50 at each mass. The Rev. C. Sumner, O.S.B, was at this time the chaplain of Appin, but resided in Campbelltown, attending three stations distant 15 to 30 miles, travelling in the year about 1040 miles.

We extract the following from the *Australian Chronicle* of March 24 :—

"Mr. Editor,—As an inhabitant of Campbelltown I am proud that we anticipated the object of your remarks on the first celebration of the day dedicated to the glorious patron of Ireland, St. Patrick. Mass was celebrated at half-past ten o'clock by the Rev. Mr. Goold, and an instructive address delivered by the Right Rev. Bishop. The virtues of St. Patrick were proposed for the imitation of the hearers, and his extraordinary abstinence and life of prayer were held up as a standard. These were contrasted with the excess and dissipation too frequently to be lamented as desecrating a day so holy, so full of grateful recollections. The Bishop dwelt with much feeling on the sufferings of Ireland, and called the attention of his hearers to the fact that notwithstanding those sufferings Ireland had clung to her faith—for thereon alone could she repose—this was the anchor of her hope. Those sufferings had been to her as the press in the vineyard, and the streams of life had been diffused amongst

o

years after the settlement, great numbers of skeletons and dead bodies of the natives were found in caves and under projecting rocks. Many of the survivors took to plunder and robbery as their only resource: and numbers of them were cruelly and mercilessly shot down: the remainder formed the boldest and most warlike portion of the race.

The Aboriginal population of New South Wales at the time of the settlement of the whites amounted to about one million; and it was reckoned there were fully three thousand natives of different tribes living between Botany Bay and Broken Bay.

The cooey of the blacks is no longer heard in the bush and valleys about Port Jackson. The corroberee or native war dance by moonlight, at which hundreds assembled, is no more to be seen: nor is the whizzing of the boomerang, thrown with such dexterity by the native, heard on the plains: nor the sound of the hatchet, when he notched the tree and climbed to secure the opossum, or the honey of the native bee: all is desolation to the Aborigine: the stranger has possession of his country!!

The Aborigines of Australia have been looked upon by many as a contemptible race; indeed, not far removed from the brute creation: but ethnographists have discovered, after investigation, that the native race of Australia is more ancient than all the races of the surrounding islands; that they date back to a time not far distant from the dispersion of the human race. We read in the eleventh chapter of the book of Genesis, that after the deluge all men assembled in the plain of Sennaar; they were of "one tongue and speech." After the attempt of man to build the Tower of Babel their tongue was confounded; "and so the Lord scattered them from that place into all lands," &c. We can imagine the primitive races after the dispersion wandering about from one land to another, and some tribes taking up their abode in caves and under projecting rocks, without fixed habitations; without implements of any kind except the stone hatchet; and without any covering, except the skins of beasts: their food would be the animals procured by the chase, ocean fish, wild fruit and indigenous roots. The natives of the Andaman Islands, in the Bay of Bengal are characterized by habits and customs such as these: so also the Negritos, or Indian negroes, and inhabitants of the Phillipine Islands, the originals of the Malayan Peninsula.

The stone hatchet period is that era when numerous tribes made use of that instrument: it was the most universal of all tools or weapons before the inventions in metal, that is, in the pre-metallic age of the world. The hatchet at first was formed by splinters being taken off a block of stone, until it was reduced to the shape of a hatchet; afterwards they made it a more serviceable instrument by rubbing or grinding down the stone to a proper shape. "The hatchet of this kind," says an author, "has been found in countless numbers, most of the specimens bearing a marvellous resemblance to each other, in every portion of the habitable globe, with the exception of China. In Europe, in Asia, in Africa, in both the American continents, from the great lakes to the Straits of Magellan, and throughout Polynesia and Australia."

When the primitive race of Australians arrived in Australia, is unknown; and from whence they immediately came: most ethnologists are of opinion that the Negritos, or Indian negroes, were probably the aborigines of the Malay Peninsula, and are still to be found there, as well as in almost all the islands from the Andamans in the Bay of Bengal, to the Phillipines in the Chinese sea. The people of the Andaman Islands appear to differ in no essential respect from the Australian Aborigines. They go quite naked; they build no permanent habitations; bone and stone weapons are the implements which they use; they live in families or very small communities, and, like the Australian natives, have no knowledge of metals or of textile fabrics or pottery; and their stature and general appearance are similar. But they bear still a closer resemblance to the now extinct Tasmanian Aborigines, who are regarded as belonging to the purest stock of all the Australian Aborigines. The writers on the Antiquity of Man connect by various and conclusive evidence the Andamans and Negritos with the Australians; and the Negritos, they say, are the types of the Bushmen of Africa, some of the hill tribes of India, the Vedahs of Ceylon, perbaps the Caribs of the Mexican Gulf, and probably the aborigines of Patagonia and Terra del Fuego. "All these people seem to belong to that ancient race known to ethnologists as Cave Dwellers. Their remains have been disentombed from caverns, or dug from beneath the alluvial deposits of thousands of years. In the chronology of man this race occupies the first place, and must be regarded not only as the most ancient, but also as the most widely spread of any section of the human family. Its vestiges are almost universal. From the snows of Scandinavia, from the torrid soil of the tropics, from the classic vales of Greece, from the shores of barbarous Patagonia, from the valleys of sacred Mount Sinai, from the caves of idolatrous India, from the plains of Australia, and from the Steppes of Central Asia, the stone implements of this most ancient, this once universal race, have been brought, in modern times, to enrich the cabinets of the curious few, and to excite the wonder of the ignorant many."

Q

Many of the learned in these subjects have maintained th
the Aborigines of Australia belonged to, and were descend
from the Papuans of New Guinea; but after recent researc'
they have come to the conclusion that the native Australian is i
connected with the Papuans. The very feasible reason on wh
they rested their opinion, was the proximity of the two countr
viz., Australia being only separated from New Guinea by To
Straits, which are not very wide, and there are many small isla
by which they could pass from New Guinea to Australia. U
investigation it was found that the inhabitants of these t
islands bear no relation whatever to each other. 7
Papuans of New Guinea may be taken as the mod
representatives of the lake dwellers of the old wo
The Australians are undoubtedly, it is said, the mod
representatives of the cave dwellers. Those are two disti
races. The Australians do not build permanent dwellings; tl
are content to live in caves, or under a few sheets of bark. 7
Papuans build substantial houses, on piles, on the margin
lakes, or inlets of the sea. The Australians do not, nor e
have cultivated the soil; the Haraforas, Arrufours, or Arafura
people inhabiting some parts of New Guinea, and a large clu
of islands to the west of that country, cultivate the soil w
considerable success. The Australian Aborigines know not,
ever have known the use of the plough; they do not till
ground in any way. The Papuans not only make use of woo
implements and bone, but they understand the use of metal,
they make textile fabrics and pottery: the Australian nat'
are ignorant of all these things; nor do they use the bow
arrow, a weapon so well known to savage nations. The Papu
live in rather large communities; but the communities of
Australians are very small. The Papuans of New Gu'
construct very serviceable canoes by hollowing out large tree
making which they show considerable mechanical skill: the c.
of the natives of Australia scarcely deserves the name, made f
sheets of bark, very frail and dangerous in a rough sea.

The physical appearance of the natives of New Guine
quite different from that of the Aborigines of Australia.
Papuans from their appearance give evidence of a mixed pec
There is found amongst them the face of the Indian negro, of
Malay, the Arab, and Polynesian; and they may be regarde
chiefly of Tauranean or Tartar origin. The language of
Australians is quite different from the language of the native
New Guinea: the language of the Australians denotes then
belong to the Aryan race. They have not the well-devel

were Dean O'Reilly and Rev. T. Slattery. In the town of Bathurst a church was in the course of erection; the temporary chapel was attended by from 90 to 100 persons. The Chaplain attends twenty-six stations, once in the quarter, viz., Weagdon, 40 miles from Bathurst; Cabee, 60; Mudgee, 90; Jungy, 140; Macquarie River, 120; Summers Hill, 30; Wellington, 100; Murrumbidgee, 120; Dubbo, 130; Weny Plains, 20; Grobeingbon, 42; Lachlan, 60; Billabulla, 60; Lachlan River, 80; Carryamy, 90; Orpan's Creek, 25; Todd Walls, 35; Vale of Clwydd, 42; Mount Victoria, 52; Rose Vale, 40: Cherry Tree Falls, 70; and Berigan, 50 miles.

In a letter Dean O'Reilly states: "During my last journey I was led to proceed on from one sheep or stock station to another, until I found myself 350 miles from home. There were no residences, but many stations, and numbers of catholics, who often came from great distances, when they heard of me. Above 70 attended to receive the Sacraments. The Rev. T. Slattery performs service at Bathurst, when the Dean is absent, and when he returns, Father Slattery proceeds to visit eleven stations. The sum subscribed towards the erection of the above church was £1,041 8s. 6d.

The foundation stone of All Saints' Church, Liverpool, was laid by Bishop Polding on Sunday, the 8th November. There was a large concourse of people, many of whom had come from Sydney. The Rev. Mr. Marum, pastor of the district, was present. The Bishop administered the Sacrament of Confirmation to a considerable number of the children. A Pontifical Mass was then celebrated. His Lordship, before laying the stone, delivered a most eloquent address. The collection amounted to £40 or £50. His Lordship, in addressing the assemblage again, expressed his high gratification at their pious and zealous demeanour during the day, and at the account given by their excellent pastor of the vast improvement of their moral condition. He further said that it would be one of his pleasing duties, if God spared him, after his return from Europe, to consecrate the building of which the foundation had been laid that day, to the honour and glory of God and all his blessed saints. His Lordship concluded by giving them his benediction, when the people cried out simultaneously "God bless you my Lord, God grant you a safe voyage," and immediately dispersed. The Chaplain in Liverpool is the Rev. R. Marum. Service was performed in a room of the Government Hospital, the average attendance being 200, of which the monthly communicants number about twenty-four.

inhabitants of the whole continent form, in fact, one people, all governed by the same laws and customs, the points of difference between the tribes being only such as might be expected from differences of circumstances and locality; and it is one of the most remarkable facts in the history of the human family that among different tribes, scattered over a region two thousand miles long by nearly fifteen hundred miles wide, possessing no written literature whatever, and traditions traceable for only a brief period, there should prevail a system of internal government almost identical and common to all; that this system must have prevailed through countless generations, and that every tribe has its own country, with as clearly defined a boundary as any estate in England—a boundary which is never crossed but at the risk of death, without diplomatic arrangements as elaborate and punctilious as those between two German principalities." Mr. Lang states that "The government is administered in each tribe by a council consisting of old and elderly men, no young man being admitted a member unless he has displayed unusual intelligence, courage and prowess. There is also a class privileged to go from tribe to tribe, to carry messages, to negotiate and arrange for meetings between the various councils, and to transact other business of a general character. These men are much honoured by all the tribes."

THEIR DEGRADING PRACTICES.—Circumcision is practised by some of the Northern tribes, and this may be accounted for from their proximity to the Malayan Peninsula, and their intercourse with the Arabs in former years, when the Arabs were navigators and merchants in those parts. "The practice of circumcision is almost general with the Malays and Arabs."

The tribes of Australia practise polygamy, and they have no law against it; but the law pronounces capital punishment against any one who marries one of the wrong sort. The practice of infanticide was common and enjoined by their laws under certain circumstances. The scarcity of food, it is supposed, prompted them to destroy their offspring. Among the more degraded and starving of the tribes cannibalism prevailed as the means of sustaining life or of gratifying a craving for animal food, although generally they hold the practice in abhorrence. We are not to be suprised at these degrading habits, as they are common to most savage nations.

Skulls of the Australian Aborigines have been exhibited in Europe, seemingly in support of the old theory that the natives of Australia are a very inferior race of the human family to those who have had good opportunities of judging.

means agree with this theory. The intelligence of a race constitutes its rank among human beings. Now I have shewn that their laws and customs by no means places them in an inferior condition to other uncivilized nations or races. The natives of Australia, although they do not build dwellings for themselves or live in large communities, or have the knowledge of any mechanical art, yet they have shewn great aptitude in acquiring the knowledge of many things. They are most skilful in using their own weapons—the spear, the boomerang, the stone hatchet, &c.; it is said their use of these instruments is perfection. "No one seeing " says Mr. Lang, whom I have before quoted, "the natives merely as idle wandering vagabonds among the white men, can judge as to what they are in their natural state. In their subtlety as diplomatists, and their skill and activity in war and in the chase, I consider them quite equal to the American Indians. The great weir for catching fish on the Upper Darling, and another described by Morrill, the shipwrecked mariner, who passed so many years amongst them, prove that they are capable of constructing works upon a large scale, and requiring combined action. Everything they have to do they do in the very best manner, and for every contingency that arises they devise a simple remedy."

When Sydney, some forty or fifty years ago, was a considerable depot for whaling and sealing vessels, the natives were employed on board, and made excellent hands in the business. Mr. Benjamin Boyd manned his fine yacht " The Wanderer," about thirty years since, with native blacks of the Twofold Bay tribe, and they made capital sailors.

A team of aboriginal cricketers was trained by a Mr. Wills, in Victoria ; they came to Sydney in 1867. A few days after they competed in a three days' match with the Albert Club; the natives lost the game, but played very skilfully. There were eleven aborigines, captained by Mr. Wills. A team of aboriginal cricketers went to England in the year 1868 for the purpose of contesting the game with the renowned English clubs. The team consisted of twelve blacks, captained by one Lawrence. The aboriginals scored their first victory over an English team at Ladywell, against eleven gentlemen of Lewisham. The spectators numbered upwards of 4000. A handsome silver cup was presented to Red Cap, an aboriginal player, by the captain of the Lewisham team, as the highest scorer on the Australian side.

If the native blacks of Australia shew such aptitude in acquiring a knowledge of these arts and contrivances of the white man, would they not, if pains were taken and sufficient means provided, become capable of participating in most of the advantages of civilized life? Nothing could shew more the adroitness and natural intelligence of the Aborigines than the treaty which they entered into with John Batman, said to be the founder of Victoria, for the purchase of land. Batman states: "After some time and full explanation I found eight chiefs amongst them, who possessed the whole of the territory near Port Philip. Three brothers, all of the same name, were the principal chiefs, and two of them men of six feet high, and very good looking; the other not so tall, but stouter. The other five chiefs were fine men. After a full explanation now of what my object was, I purchased two large tracts of land from them— about 600,000 acres, more or less, and delivered over to them blankets, knives, looking-glasses, tomahawks, beads, scissors, flour, &c., &c., as payment for the land; and also agreed to give them a tribute or rent yearly. The parchment the eight chiefs signed this afternoon, delivering to me some of the soil, each of them, as giving me full possession of the tracts of land."—*Men of the Times, Heaton, page 12.—Batman.* This account at once shews the ingenuity of the natives and the greed of Batman.

The purest stock of the aboriginal natives is said to have been that of Tasmania, which is now extinct. King Billy, or William Laune, last male Tasmanian aboriginal, died March 3rd, 1869. Queen Tawaunimai, or Lalla Rookh, the last of the Tasmanian aboriginals, died at Hobart Town, May 8, 1876; aged 73.

GOVERNOR ARTHUR OF TASMANIA.—When the blacks of Tasmania were troublesome to the settlers Governor Arthur made a cordon across the island to capture them, but only one was taken, and the cost of the expedition amounted to £30,000.

Three hundred, the last of the Tasmanian aboriginals, were transferred from the mainland to Flinders' Island, in Bass's Straits, through the instrumentality of Mr. George Augustus Robinson in 1837.

It is now nearly a hundred years since the white men invaded these lands, and took from the black man the country which he had inhabited for hundreds and hundreds of years— the land which "the Lord God gave unto him." Since 1788, when Governor Phillip, with his military settlers and prisoners, landed on the shores of Australia, what has been done by those on whom the responsibility rested, to ameliorate the condition of the unfortunate aborigines, to civilize and convert them? No strenuous efforts, either by the government or others who had it in their power, have been made to alter their deplorable condition. Commendable efforts have been made from time to time. Pro-

It was then moved by Mr. Callaghan, barrister-at-law, and seconded by Mr. Roger Murphy, That a society be formed under the designation of "St. Patrick's Society," for the purpose of collecting funds for the erection of the said church. The Rev. Mr. Murphy was appointed by the Meeting president, and the Rev. G. H. Gregory, treasurer. In the course of a few minutes the collection amounted to £1,012.

CHAPTER IX.

Preparations of the Catholic Committee of St. Mary's for the Departure of Bishop Polding and Dr. Ullathorne for England —Presentation of addresses to Bishop Polding and Dr. Ullathorne, and Rev. H. G. Gregory—Departure of Bishop Polding and party for England—The great estimation and respect in which the two catholic gentlemen, John Hubert Plunkett, Attorney-General of New South Wales, and Roger Therry, Esq., Commissioner of the Court of Requests, were held by the inhabitants of the Colony—The state of the Colony, Religion, and Education, when Bishop Polding left, in the year 140—An Abridgement of the reply of Dr. Ullathorne to Judge Burton's Book.

FOR some time previous to the departure of Bishop Polding for Europe, the Catholic Committee were engaged in getting up a Memorial, as a token of the respect in which the Bishop and his Vicar-General were universally held. On the Sunday before the Bishop left, he administered the sacrament of Confirmation to a number of children and adults. A Pontifical High Mass was celebrated in the cathedral, at which the Rev. Dean Brady officiated as assistant priest, the Very Rev. the Vicar-General and Rev. F. Murphy as deacons, and the Rev. Joseph Platt as sub-deacon. The Rev. Messrs. Mahony, Lynch and Grant assisted in surplices and stoles. After the gospel his lordship delivered a most affecting farewell address to his clergy and people.

In the evening at the Old Court House, Castlereagh-street, the addresses were read to his lordship, the Right Rev. Dr. Polding, and his Vicar-General, Dr. Ullathorne. Never was there a more numerous and respectable meeting than that assembled on the occasion. The Attorney-General, J. H. Plunkett, Esq., was called to the chair. Mr. Commissioner Therry commenced by reading the address to the Very Rev. Dr. Ullathorne, as follows :—

Very Rev. Sir,—The moment of your departure for England will, we trust, be not deemed an unsuitable one for receiving the

assurance of our grateful acknowledgements for the many and important services you have rendered to the catholics of the Australian colonies. On your first coming amongst us you found but one roofless church before you: the religious wants of the people for many years had been supplied by only one excellent clergyman: and many thousands of the people had heretofore lived and died in the interior of this colony without any religious consolation whatever. If brighter prospects now present themselves: if we see a hierarchy established on our shores; if we see every populous district of the colony provided with good and pious clergymen: if we witness under the genial influence of their precept and example, a moral regeneration and improvement prevailing among their respective flocks; if we behold the institution of the Sisters of Charity, famed throughout Europe for the great religious benefits it has dispensed, extending its usefulness to this colony, so exigent of its pious services, believe us Very Rev. Sir, we are duly sensible that these great services and daily augmenting advantages, are mainly to be attributed to your active and devoted exertions on our behalf, both here and in Europe: to the reliance which your character procured on the truth of your representations, as to the great want of religious aid and instruction under which these colonies suffered, and to the persevering assiduity with which you left no source unexplored that could be available to our advantage.

With hearts full of gratitude for these great and important services; with an earnest hope of soon seeing you again amongst us in the prosecution of your pious labours; and with a confidence that, whether absent or present, we shall live, as past experience assures us we have lived, in your regard and affections—we bid you a respectful, a grateful, and an affectionate farewell!

We beg your permission to accompany this address with a small token of our sincere respect and esteem.

The tribute of respect consisted of a snuff-box, valued at £60, with the following inscription:—Presented to the Very Reverend William Ullathorne, Doctor in Divinity, and Vicar-General of New Holland, as a testimony of the affection of the Catholics in the Colony; and their gratitude for his high services rendered to their religion and religious liberty; of regret at his departure for Europe, and of their anxiety for his safe and speedy return. November, 1840

Dr. Ullathorne's reply:—My dear friends, I thank you most sincerely. This is one of those rare moments in this earthly existence which drowns at once the recollection of a great many of its trials. If the feelings of my own breast could enlarge themselves to the extent of all your kindnesses and your many indulgences in my

of the heavens and the earth, whom they call Motogon; that
Motogon is believed by them to be a man of great strength, high,
wise, and of their own colour and country. They say that in the
creation of the kangaroo, the sun, and the trees, he used these
words :—'Terra Esci Fuori,' Let the earth exist, and breathed,
and the earth was created: 'Acqua Esci Fuori,' Let the water
exist, breathed, and the water was created; and so of other
things." *   Further on in his work Bishop Salvado writes, after
much conversation with the natives, that they admit two
principles; one, the author of good, and he is Motogon, the other
the author of evil, whom they call Cienga.

In regard to the Aborigines of eastern Australia, a Protestant
missionary, who carried on for many years, under the auspices of
the Church of England, a mission to the Wiradhuri speaking
tribes of Wellington Vale, confidently asserts, after diligent
enquiry and study amongst the blacks, that most assuredly they
cannot be called atheists. This also is the opinion of Count
Strezlewski, who wrote " A Physical description of New South
Wales and Van Dieman's Land." The Count travelled much in
Australia, and had many conversations with the *Indigènes*.

There is no question but that amongst all the tribes of both
north and south there is prevalent the idea of certain imaginary
beings, to whom they ascribe various attributes, and some of these
attributes are very contradictory. However, it shows they have
some glimmerings of the supernatural. All the tribes have an
idea, but not very definite, that their existence does not absolutely
end with the death of their bodies; from which it is concluded
that they have an indistinct notion of the immortality of the
soul. There is one thing which they testify to and believe; and
that is, the existence of an evil spirit, which they call Wondon.
Every thing adverse to them which happens, they attribute it to
the malignity of that spirit.. To the malignity of that spirit they
attribute the thunder, the lightning, the storms, floods, whirlwinds,
and hail.

They also believe in the transmigration of souls. "It is
singular the manner by which they represent that transmigration.
When they see a person who has much resemblance with one
already dead, they say he has returned to life. Also a belief
prevails amongst them that after death they will rise up white
men; and that the white people who inhabit other countries,
beyond the seas, are their ancestors, who ass away to live in
other bodies. Wonderful to say! I have found that belief to

prevail, identical, amongst the savages of the Liverpool Plains who inhabit the eastern coast of Australia, and amongst those of King George's Sound, who live on the western coast, distant more than two thousand miles, without communication with each other."* It is acknowledged by all who have had much intercourse with the natives, that they are very reticent in regard to their religious belief, and seem to have very confused notions of the supernatural.

Before the minds of the Aborigines became darkened by the abuse of those natural lights and graces which they had received, they knew their God, and adored Him as such. Romans, chap. I. ver. 2—"But when they knew God they did not praise and glorify Him, nor give Him thanks, but became vain in their thoughts, and their foolish hearts were hardened." St. Paul says: Rom., chap. 1, ver. 20—"For the invisible things of Him, from the creation of the world, are clearly seen, being understood by things which are made, His eternal power also and divinity; so that they are inexcusable."

It is evident that the savages of Australia are reasonable beings, made to the image and likeness of God, redeemed by Christ, destined to be saved like the rest of man. 1 Tim., chap. II, ver. 4—"God will have all men to be saved and to come to the knowledge of the truth."

They are included amongst those nations to whom our Lord commanded His Apostles to go and teach, and baptise in the name of the Father, and of the Son, and of the Holy Ghost. The words of our Lord when He commissioned His Apostles are these: "All power is given to me in heaven and in earth. Go ye therefore, and teach all nations, baptising them in the name of the Father, and of the Son, and of the Holy Ghost; teaching them to observe all things whatsoever I have commanded you; and behold I am with you all days, even to the consummation of the world."† This was a command given by Christ before His ascension and after His resurrection to His Church, in the persons of the Apostles, to teach the nations, and that His Spirit would be ever and always with them. Christ hath been true to His promise, He has been with His Church in all ages, converting and baptizing the nations, "enlightening those who sit in darkness and the shadow of death, and directing their feet in the ways of peace."‡ The Catholic Church at the present time has her missionaries in every part of the globe, dispelling the darkness of infidelity, making known the saving truths of

---

* Ottav. Barsanti Salvaggi Dell' Australia, p. 172.   † St. Matthew, xxviii. 18.

‡ Luke i, 79.

salvation, and in many parts laying down their lives for the sake of Christ; and the head of the Church, Pope Leo., appointed by Christ, directs all her energies.

God selects His own time for the baptizing and conversion of nations; the aboriginal of this land hath sat till now in darkness and the shadow of death. The Catholic missionary is now in the land, labouring to snatch these souls from the power of the devil, and bring them under the influence of the Gospel. Lately—in 1882—a mission has been begun in the Northern Territory, at the express wish of His Holiness, Leo. XIII. It is conducted by three members of the Society of Jesus; the Rev. A. Strele, S.J., is the superior. This first mission station is established on an aboriginal reserve near Palmerston, given for the purpose by the Colonial Government. Father Strele states in his prospectus that "The missionaries have the satisfaction to see their efforts and sacrifices producing good fruit among the aboriginals. Many of the latter have joined us in the work of cultivating the land and of erecting the most necessary buildings for a permanent station. They listen to the teaching, and about forty have received baptism." Father Strele goes on to state that "The satisfactory results obtained on the first station and an increase in the number of missionaries led to the resolution to form stations also among other aboriginal tribes For this purpose he had to confer with the Colonial Government, and was very successful in obtaining an area of one hundred square miles, a more inland position, on the Daly River, where the blacks are very numerous." He says, "For aboriginals live still in great numbers in this continent, and many thousands may yet be brought out from their wretched state of ignorance and barbarism. . . . . The undertaking, moreover, co-operates with the solicitude repeatedly expressed by Her Majesty's Government, that efforts should be made to ameliorate the condition of the aboriginal tribes. It also co-operates with the intentions of the Government of these colonies, which always second undertakings of this kind."

"The continual life," writes Father Strele, "which I lived with the blacks during two years, and the close observation which I had opportunity to make of them, force on me the persuasion that their race, especially in the northern parts of Australia, is well suited for instruction, for learning agriculture and the various mechanical arts, and I am confident that after not many years the stations will become self-supporting."

The Rev. D. McNab, now the Catholic Pastor of Perth, conducted a mission for the blacks a few years since in the country

The reply of the Rev. Mr. Gregory :—

"I receive the token of affection with sincere gratification. It is an emblem of that union between pastor and people, which no circumstance can alter, no distance dissever. Accept my thanks, and add to the favor conferred by remembering me in your prayers."

The chair being vacated by the Attorney-General, the Rev. Francis Murphy was requested to take it, when a vote of thanks was proposed by Mr. Commissioner Therry and seconded by John Ryan Brennan, Esq., P.M. : "That the thanks of the meeting are due, and are hereby presented, to the Attorney-General for his dignified conduct in the chair." Mr. Plunkett briefly returned thanks, and expressed his gratification at having had the honor to preside over so respectable a meeting, assembled on so interesting an occasion.

At half-past eleven o'clock a.m. on the Monday following, 16th November, 1840, the Catholic Committee accompanied the Bishop from his residence to the Cathedral, where he read at the altar the beautiful prayers appointed to be read to implore the blessing of heaven on their voyage. A procession was formed of the whole people, under the direction of the Committee. There were many thousands in it. The girls of the Catholic Schools were first, the whole of them dressed in white ; then came the boys, followed by the congregation walking two and two ; the Bishop and his Clergy formed the rear. The procession marched along Hyde Park, Macquarie-street, Bent-street, and Macquarie Place. When they arrived at the jetty on the Circular Quay the people divided, and the Bishop, Clergy, and Committee went to the boats. His Lordship and the Rev. Mr. Gregory proceeded in the Government boat. Dr. Ullathorne and the clergy occupied the boat of the Crusader, furnished by Captain Inglis. The vessel in which the Bishop and the Very Rev. Dr. Ullathorne, Rev. H. Gregory, and the Bishop's Chaplain embarked, was a brig, by name "Orion," Captain Saunders, master, bound for Valparaiso ; in their company were three young gentlemen, Messrs. Chambers, Therry, and Carter, going to Europe for a collegiate education. The brig was towed to the Heads by the splendid steamship "Clonmel," and this steamer was filled with upwards of 400 persons desirous of testifying to the last the deep respect they had for their beloved Bishop. It was remarked by the press at the time of the departure of Bishop Polding : "That not only every Catholic, but every Christian ought to sympathise in the sorrow at the absence of him who had given by his presence and labours a moral dignity to our adopted land, formerly represented as the abortion of nations, but now the abode of a fine

people, increasing in the enjoyment of a high degree of physical and moral health. If ever a bishop was worthy to be called a pastor of his flock, it is the Right Reverend Dr. Polding."

I certainly would not be doing justice to my narrative were I to pass by unnoticed the worth of two most estimable Catholic gentlemen, officers of the Government, who flourished in our community at this time ; I mean John Hubert Plunkett, Attorney-General of New South Wales, and Roger Therry, Esq., Commissioner of the Court of Requests. They were conscientious Catholics, and lived up to their religious principles. They never compromised their religion, and were ever ready to speak and act in defence of the faith of their forefathers, and of their country, Ireland. They gave all the weight of their character and position for the benefit of religion and charity. Mr. Plunkett was for many years Attorney-General, and he went home on leave of absence in the beginning of the year 1841. But before he left the colony, in such great respect was he held by his legal brethren, that they entertained him at a dinner. The Chief Justice, Sir James Dowling presided, and there was present Judge Stephens. The Governor, Sir Geo. Gipps, also honored the festive board by his presence. The Governor, in returning thanks when his health was proposed, said: "He felt extremely happy in meeting such a large and respectable company of the colonists of New South Wales, of every grade and of every persuasion, who, laying aside all other motives, had met together that evening to pay a tribute of respect to a public officer who had discharged his great, important, and arduous duties with the highest degree of impartiality and firmness ; he felt extremely happy to make one amongst them in bearing testimony to the worth, ability, and integrity of that officer." The Chief Justice, Sir James Dowling said : "It was a pleasing reflection to Mr. Plunkett, notwithstanding the very peculiar community in which he lived, all men bore ample testimony to the just, upright, manly, and impartial manner in which he had discharged the duties belonging to his station ; after many years of trial Mr. Plunkett had passed through the crucible of public opinion without a stain being cast upon him." All the gentlemen present at the banquet bore similar testimony to the high character of Mr. Plunkett.

Before the departure of Mr. Plunkett, on leave of absence, a handsome testimonial was presented to him in the shape of several pieces of silver plate, and on each piece was engraved his family crest, which is a trotting horse, with the motto "Festina Lente." The silver service was purchased by public subscription and cost about £400.

condition of the aborigines of Australia. He bitterly lament: that England has not made use of the means best adapted for christianizing the aborigines. "Anglicanism," he says." or Episcopalianism is nothing but a kind of popery, and popery has always been an obstacle to the civilization of people. The Americans never made any progress whilst they were under the government of a code which recognized an episcopal church. But after they became independent, then protestantism made wonderful progress." Nothing would satisfy Dr. Lang, in converting the savages, but that they should be taught pure presbyterianism. Dr. Lang states, " that he was enabled, by the assistance of Lord Glenelg, then Secretary of State for the Colonies, with all the means necessary to convey, for the establishment of the mission of the aborigines, two ordained presbyterian ministers, and twelve lay missionaries, eight of whom were married. That mission was placed under the presidency of the Rev. John Gossener, pastor in Berlin of the church of Bohemia, and already for many years a most zealous promoter of the gentile missions."* " The twelve lay missionaries and the two ordained ministers," says Dr. Lang, " established a mission at Moreton Bay, on the river Kidron, seven miles from Brisbane. But I am grieved to say, that although they who directed that mission were excellent persons and true christians, and exercised a great and salutary influence through all the other districts of that Bay, they entirely failed in their intention, and in the same way that all the other aboriginal missions of Australia failed in their design of imbuing a religious sentiment into the minds of the aborigines. The government aid was finally withdrawn, and the missions from that moment were dissolved." This happened during the administration of Sir George Gipps.

Let us enquire briefly, what has been the conduct of the English and Colonial governments towards the aboriginal population of Australia. Governor Phillip, in the beginning of the colony, manifested great sympathy for the blacks, and was very kind to them; but it was not in his power to protect them sufficiently from the violence and bad treatment of the prison-population; so that he neither established any system for their civilization, nor for their conversion to christianity : nor am I aware that the English government instructed him in the matter. But in the year 1841 Lord John Russell, when he was Secretary for the Colonies, vindicated the honour of England before the

---

* This Rev. J. Gossener, be it known, was an apostate, who, from being a Catholic priest, became a Lutheran minister.

ere Dean O'Reilly and Rev. T. Slattery. In the town of athurst a church was in the course of erection; the temporary hapel was attended by from 90 to 100 persons. The Chaplain ttends twenty-six stations, once in the quarter, viz., Weagdon, 40 iiles from Bathurst; Cabee, 60; Mudgee, 90; Jungy, 140; Macuarie River, 120; Summers Hill, 30; Wellington, 100; Murrumidgee, 120; Dubbo, 130; Weny Plains, 20; Grobeingbon, 42; achlan, 60; Billabulla, 60; Lachlan River, 80; Carryamy, 90; Irpan's Creek, 25; Todd Walls, 35; Vale of Clwydd, 42; Mount Victoria, 52; Rose Vale, 40 : Cherry Tree Falls, 70; and Berigan, 10 miles.

In a letter Dean O'Reilly states: "During my last journey I was led to proceed on from one sheep or stock station to mother, until I found myself 350 miles from home. There were no residences, but many stations, and numbers of catholics, who often came from great distances, when they heard of me. Above 70 attended to receive the Sacraments. The Rev. T. Slattery performs service at Bathurst, when the Dean is absent, and when he returns, Father Slattery proceeds to visit eleven stations. The sum subscribed towards the erection of the above church was £1,041 8s. 6d.

The foundation stone of All Saints' Church, Liverpool, was laid by Bishop Polding on Sunday, the 8th November. There was a large concourse of people, many of whom had come from Sydney. The Rev. Mr. Marum, pastor of the district, was present. The Bishop administered the Sacrament of Confirmation to a considerable number of the children. A Pontifical Mass was then celebrated. His Lordship, before laying the stone, delivered a most eloquent address. The collection amounted to £40 or £50. His Lordship, in addressing the assemblage again, expressed his gratification at their pious and zealous demeanour during the day, and at the account given by their excellent pastor of the improvement of their moral condition. He further said that it would be one of his pleasing duties, if God spared him, after his return from Europe, to consecrate the building of which the foundation had been laid that day, to the honour and glory of God and all his blessed saints. His Lordship concluded by giving them his benediction, when the people cried out simultaneously "God bless you my Lord, God grant you a safe voyage," and immediately dispersed. The Chaplain in Liverpool is the Rev. R. M. Service was performed in a room of the Government Gaol, the average attendance being 200, of which the monthly communicants number about twenty-four.

242

of the aborigines. In the report which they prepared they recommended the abolition of the Protectorate, as having failed in the object for which it was established; as being in fact, at this time, altogether useless; but they could not recommend a substitute. They advised the house that it was useless to form new reserves, as recommended by the Secretary of State: the education of adults they thought to be hopeless, and the young could be educated only by a compulsory separation from their relatives and tribes. They concluded by expressing an opinion that, without under-rating the philanthropic motives of her Majesty's government in attempting the improvement of the aborigines, much more real good would be effected by similar exertions to promote the interests of religion and education among the white population in the interior of the colony, the improvement of whose condition in these respects would doubtless tend to benefit the aborigines.*

An Italian writer comments upon this evasive reply of the committee of the Council in the following words:—" This report was sent officially to London, and produced its effect, because the parliament became persuaded that nothing could be done for the civilization of the Australians. Thus no more is said about them: they cease to exist in the minds of the government, either as a *race*, or as individuals, and with the colonists prevails the idea that *they are not men*, but *a kind of monkey*. Every plan was dismissed, every system, every institution for their amelioration; they were left to themselves, exposed to all the violence and cruelty of the colonists, and compelled to retire into the depths of their forests, to become more savage and degraded than they were before."†

" The colony is now nearly one hundred years old; the land which belonged to the black population has been taken possession of by the colonists who invaded their country; I ask again, what compensation has been made to the aborigines? Have many of them been baptised, and made christians, and civilised? Comparatively very few of the million which inhabited New South Wales. Are not the colonies responsible in a great measure for this being the case? They have the power and the means of ameliorating their condition. If they have obstructed the labours of the missionaries of Christ, who were commanded to baptize and instruct all men,‡ what a terrible account they will have to give to the Supreme Judge. They will be

---

* Flanagan, vol. 2, c. 4, s. 9.   † Barsanti Selvaggi dell'Australia, p. 197.
‡ Matt. xxviii, 19, 20.

to la se without the erection of some temple for God's worship, as approof of their sense of the Divine goodness. At a vast distance from their native soil, they had ample subject of thanksgiving and gratitude to the Divine power for the glorious privilege of enjoying the free worship of their Creator; a privilege which their forefathers long and ardently struggled for in vain. When therefore these bounties of the Almighty were taken into consideration, gratitude alone would manifestly demand the erection of some monument in testimony of their feelings of religion; and what monument could be more proper than a temple consecrated to divine worship. under the glorious patronage of that great benefactor of mankind, St. Patrick; in whose diadem it would form an additional jewel. The spire of this temple would be, as it proudly stood, a perpetual and unfailing monitor to each passer-by to lift up his mind to the God who created him. It was a fact which needed no illustration, that wherever the Irish people were spread, they invariably carried with them their religion—the religion of their forefathers, in all its beauty and purity. The ground on which the proposed new church would be erected was the gift of one who gloried in the name of St. Patrick, and he hoped so good an example would not be lost upon others; but that if the present year should not behold the laying of the foundation stone and the carrying up of the spire, or, in other words, the commencement and execution of the design, the terms of its completion might not exceed the ensuing year (1841). Besides the ordinary method of collecting subscriptions, it was their intention to form a society or fraternity under the denomination of the "Society of St. Patrick," in order to concentrate the efforts of the community at large towards the accomplishing the great object in view; an object which would be easily effected by these means Having said thus much, he would not detain them any longer, but would request the gentleman who had undertaken to move the first resolution to proceed to business.

Mr. Roger Therry, in moving the resolution, and in the course of his remarks, said, in regard to Mr. Davis, that "too much praise could not be bestowed on Mr. Davis, who had made so noble a commencement of the good work. He had devoted the early portion of his life to pursuits and habits of industry, and he was now in its decline applying the proceeds and fruits of that industry to the best possible use to which they could be put—the happiness and benefit of his fellow citizens and the service of religion." His allusion to St. Mary's Cathedral was very happy. His Lordship, he said, who was comparatively a new comer among

SYDNEY:

F. CUNNINGHAME & CO., PRINTERS,

146 Pitt Street.

—

1886.

assurance of our grateful acknowledgements for the many and important services you have rendered to the catholics of the Australian colonies. On your first coming amongst us you found but one roofless church before you: the religious wants of the people for many years had been supplied by only one excellent clergyman; and many thousands of the people had heretofore lived and died in the interior of this colony without any religious consolation whatever. If brighter prospects now present themselves; if we see a hierarchy established on our shores; if we see every populous district of the colony provided with good and pious clergymen; if we witness under the genial influence of their precept and example, a moral regeneration and improvement prevailing among their respective flocks; if we behold the institution of the Sisters of Charity, famed throughout Europe for the great religious benefits it has dispensed, extending its usefulness to this colony, so exigent of its pious services, believe us Very Rev. Sir, we are duly sensible that these great services and daily augmenting advantages, are mainly to be attributed to your active and devoted exertions on our behalf, both here and in Europe; to the reliance which your character procured on the truth of your representations, as to the great want of religious aid and instruction under which these colonies suffered, and to the persevering assiduity with which you left no source unexplored that could be available to our advantage.

With hearts full of gratitude for these great and important services; with an earnest hope of soon seeing you again amongst us in the prosecution of your pious labours; and with a confidence that, whether absent or present, we shall live, as past experience assures us we have lived, in your regard and affections—we bid you a respectful, a grateful, and an affectionate farewell!

We beg your permission to accompany this address with a small token of our sincere respect and esteem.

The tribute of respect consisted of a snuff-box, valued at £60, with the following inscription:—Presented to the Very Reverend William Ullathorne, Doctor in Divinity, and Vicar-General of New Holland, as a testimony of the affection of the Catholics in the Colony; and their gratitude for his high services rendered to their religion and religious liberty; of regret at his departure for Europe, and of their anxiety for his safe and speedy return. November, 1840

Dr. Ullathorne's reply:—My dear friends, I thank you most sincerely. This is one of those rare moments in this earthly existence which drowns at once the recollection of a great many of its trials. If the feelings of my own breast could enlarge themselves to the extent of all your kindnesses and your many indulgences in my

regard of which this token is only the latest expression, I would endeavour to thank you worthily. As it is, I return your kindness and good wishes, as the best response I am capable of. It is a consoling reflection that, whilst in all other things I leave this colony as poor a man as when I first came to it, I am amply rich in your good opinions and warm affections. For these, and all those good works which I have seen done amongst you by the grace of God, I can never be sufficiently grateful. That I should have been an instrument, however by nature unworthy and unfit, of any part of so great a work of good, as the one to which you refer, will always fill me with happy recollections. But when, my dear friends, you see and bear witness to any qualities in me, except a very simple and earnest intention of serving you, and a wish and endeavour to cherish and protect your faith, and to enlarge and quicken the growth of your charity, I there recognize the fallacy of your kindness. Warm and earnest in your good affections, you believe those qualities to exist in your friend and pastor which you well know ought to exist, and imagine he does possess what you wish and desire he should possess ; and it is my duty to pray that henceforward I may possess them. If on the occasion of the departure of our beloved bishop, I condole with you on the temporary loss of the presence of one, it is only the loss of his presence—his spirit will continue with you—whom you so truly and justly venerate ; I would also console you with the reflection that his absence is needful for your own best interests, and that it will not be of a very long continuance ; and I would cheer you by directing forward your hopes towards the happy period of his return, which may you all live, and live worthily and happily, to see accomplished ; and may his coming again amongst you, as it will, be crowned with joy and benedictions. For myself, whilst I most heartily thank you, and trust that I shall live in your recollections, as you will continue to live in mine, I am desirous of laying myself under new obligations by most earnestly recommending myself to your prayers.

His lordship was addressed in the following words :—On the eve of your lordship's departure, we beg leave to express our warmest wishes for your safe and prosperous passage to England, and our earnest hope for your early return to us. Whilst we deeply deplore even your temporary absence, our regret is subdued and softened by the conviction that your visit to Europe is prompted by a sense of duty, and by that devoted and untiring zeal for our welfare, of which we have so many and unmistakable manifestations. After the five years you have exercised the pastoral charge in these colonies with mild and firm efficacy, it

must be gratifying to you as it is to us, to look back on the great benefits that have been conferred on this community, and of which, under Divine Providence, you have been the chief and chosen instrument. The many churches founded and consecrated by your lordship; your frequent visits into all parts of the colony; the dispersion and establishment of a zealous clergy throughout the principal districts of New South Wales; the impartial attention paid to all classes of your congregation, without any distinction, except that where assistance was most required and needed, there it was largely bestowed; and not least, the truly paternal solicitude you have shown towards the orphan, and the affection with which you have cherished the little children of your flock, are among the enduring monuments of those useful labours, by which, in your high station, you have been distinguished, and which have made an indelible impression upon hearts not formed to be ungrateful. As it is under the deep impression of sentiments such as these that we bid your lordship farewell now, you will not be surprised or displeased that, next to the reverence and affection we entertain towards you, the feeling uppermost is the desire that you may be re-united to your flock at the earliest moment your sense of duty and zeal for our service will permit. We beg leave to accompany this address with a small token of our gratitude and veneration.

This tribute consisted of a Treasury Bill for £400

His lordship replied as follows:—Wishes so warm and generous, on the part of a people whose affections cannot be commanded, but may be obtained, I do feel sincere gratification in accepting. I knew not until the period of separation approached, how strong had become the bonds which united us. Only indeed a sense of duty the most cogent, and a conviction that my services elsewhere will prove more generally useful to my extensive charge, could influence me to consent to be temporarily absent from you. May your prayers for my speedy return be accomplished. Your kindness has attributed much to me I do not deserve. Patient enduring was the glory and merit of a preceding generation. The season of mercy and grace has been mercifully ours. Suffering and spiritual privation had disposed you to receive with gratitude the enlarged means of religious consolation Providence granted to you through us, the humble instrument of the divine benignity; and the gracious dispensation has not fallen on an unworthy soil. In the churches now in the course of erection; in the improved habits of our people; in the various charitable and religious institutions which have sprung into existence, in a space of time almost instantaneous; there is,

surely, a demonstration, that beneath a surface unfortunately made the ground of rash surmises and rude theories, there did exist a bounteous source of moral worth, which only required to be opened to the clear day, to diffuse streams of virtuous impulses, of noble and disinterested well-doing, throughout our beautiful land.

My labours and their effects you value too highly. The zealous co-operation of the Vicar-General and of the clergy must be held in grateful remembrance. My devotedness to my beloved country, my determination to use every exertion that can tend to raise and establish on a lofty and imperishable basis her religious, her social and moral character, words cannot express. Let the past be an earnest of the future; and whilst I am absent continue by your peaceable determined course to co-operate with me. The calumny of the graceless may fall undeserving of note. No opposition, statement, or misrepresentation detrimental to your social or religious rights, which might derive importance from the station of him who utters it, must pass unnoticed. Cultivate peace,—I use the words of an apostle—as much as in you lies have peace with all men, until the harmonious union which gloriously distinguishes our body shall, in the extinction of prejudice, of bigotry, or of unseemly strife, pervade the entire of the social order of New South Wales. I accept with thankfulness this token of your affectionate regard; may the Almighty dispenser of all good bestow upon you every blessing

The ladies of Sydney on this occasion presented the Rev. H. G. Gregory with a handsome and valuable ring, accompanied with an address. These are the words of the address :—

"Rev. and Dear Sir,—We, the Catholic ladies of Sydney, having observed that our husbands and fathers have their feelings entirely absorbed with the lamented departure of our excellent Bishop and his Vicar-General, cannot suffer you, reverend Sir, to leave our shores without in some feeble manner testifying our sense of your piety and zeal for the honor and glory of God and for our spiritual welfare during the time the Catholics of Sydney have had the happiness of enjoying your pastoral care. We bow to the will of God, which for great and good purposes separates us from our pastor for a time, trusting that that time will be short, and that after a speedy and safe voyage and a successful mission, you will soon be restored to a people who till then shall never cease to pray for that event and for your welfare.

We beg to accompany this address with a small tribute of our respect and reverence.

Reverend and Dear Sir, farewell."

The reply of the Rev. Mr. Gregory :—

"I receive the token of affection with sincere gratification. It is an emblem of that union between pastor and people, which no circumstance can alter, no distance dissever. Accept my thanks, and add to the favor conferred by remembering me in your prayers."

The chair being vacated by the Attorney-General, the Rev. Francis Murphy was requested to take it, when a vote of thanks was proposed by Mr. Commissioner Therry and seconded by John Ryan Brennan, Esq., P.M.: "That the thanks of the meeting are due, and are hereby presented, to the Attorney-General for his dignified conduct in the chair." Mr. Plunkett briefly returned thanks, and expressed his gratification at having had the honor to preside over so respectable a meeting, assembled on so interesting an occasion.

At half-past eleven o'clock a.m. on the Monday following, 16th November, 1840, the Catholic Committee accompanied the Bishop from his residence to the Cathedral, where he read at the altar the beautiful prayers appointed to be read to implore the blessing of heaven on their voyage. A procession was formed of the whole people, under the direction of the Committee. There were many thousands in it. The girls of the Catholic Schools were first, the whole of them dressed in white ; then came the boys, followed by the congregation walking two and two : the Bishop and his Clergy formed the rear. The procession marched along Hyde Park, Macquarie-street, Bent-street, and Macquarie Place. When they arrived at the jetty on the Circular Quay the people divided, and the Bishop, Clergy, and Committee went to the boats. His Lordship and the Rev. Mr. Gregory proceeded in the Government boat. Dr. Ullathorne and the clergy occupied the boat of the Crusader, furnished by Captain Inglis. The vessel in which the Bishop and the Very Rev. Dr. Ullathorne, Rev. H. Gregory, and the Bishop's Chaplain embarked, was a brig, by name "Orion," Captain Saunders, master, bound for Valparaiso; in their company were three young gentlemen, Messrs. Chambers, Therry, and Carter, going to Europe for a collegiate education. The brig was towed to the Heads by the splendid steamship "Clonmel," and this steamer was filled with upwards of 400 persons desirous of testifying to the last the deep respect they had for their beloved Bishop. It was remarked by the press at the time of the departure of Bishop Polding: "That not only every Catholic, but every Christian ought to sympathise in the sorrow at the absence of him who had given by his presence and labours a moral dignity to our adopted land, formerly represented as the abortion of nations, but now the abode of a fine

people, increasing in the enjoyment of a high degree of physical and moral health. If ever a bishop was worthy to be called a pastor of his flock, it is the Right Reverend Dr. Polding."

I certainly would not be doing justice to my narrative were I to pass by unnoticed the worth of two most estimable Catholic gentlemen,yofficers of the Government, who flourished in our community at this time; I mean John Hubert Plunkett, Attorney-General of New South Wales, and Roger Therry, Esq., Commissioner of the Court of Requests. They were conscientious Catholics, and lived up to their religious principles. They never compromised their religion, and were ever ready to speak and act in defence of the faith of their forefathers, and of their country, Ireland. They gave all the weight of their character and position for the benefit of religion and charity. Mr. Plunkett was for many years Attorney-General, and he went home on leave of absence in the beginning of the year 1841. But before he left the colony, in such great respect was he held by his legal brethren, that they entertained him at a dinner. The Chief Justice, Sir James Dowling presided, and there was present Judge Stephens. The Governor, Sir Geo. Gipps, also honored the festive board by his presence. The Governor, in returning thanks when his health was proposed, said: " He felt extremely happy in meeting such a large and respectable company of the colonists of New South Wales, of every grade and of every persuasion, who, laying aside all other motives, had met together that evening to pay a tribute of respect to a public officer who had discharged his great, important, and arduous duties with the highest degree of impartiality and firmness; he felt extremely happy to make one amongst them in bearing testimony to the worth, ability, and integrity of that officer." The Chief Justice, Sir James Dowling said: " It was a pleasing reflection to Mr. Plunkett, notwithstanding the very peculiar community in which he lived, all men bore ample testimony to the just, upright, manly, and impartial manner in which he had discharged the duties belonging to his station; after many years of trial Mr. Plunkett had passed through the crucible of public opinion without a stain being cast upon him." All the gentlemen present at the banquet bore similar testimony to the high character of Mr. Plunkett.

Before the departure of Mr. Plunkett, on leave of absence, a handsome testimonial was presented to him in the shape of several pieces of silver plate, and on each piece was engraved his family crest, which is a trotting horse, with the motto " *Festina Lente.*" The silver service was purchased by public subscription and cost about £400.

Roger Therry, Esq., was appointed Attorney-General, during the absence of Mr. Plunkett. Mr. Therry had been Commissioner of the Court of Requests for eleven years, and discharged the onerous duties of his office with great rectitude and ability. When he was promoted to be Attorney-General, the public expressed their satisfaction for his past services, by presenting him with a massive silver service, which cost £500. The salver had the following inscription engraved on it, with Mr. Therry's crest, a lion rampant, bearing a cross, with the motto, "E Cruce Leo." The words of the inscription were the following :—"This salver with an urn, dinner, dessert and tea-service, and other articles, forming a service of plate, were presented to Roger Therry, Esquire, Her Majesty's Attorney General, by the people of New South Wales, as a mark of their esteem and respect on the occasion of his retiring from the office of Commissioner of the Court of Requests, the duties of which he discharged in that colony for a period of eleven years, to the entire satisfaction of the community."

Judge Burton, who published in London "an account of the state of religion and education in New South Wales," returned to the colony in the year 1841. His party prepared a banquet for him and the Governor was invited to attend, but he declined, "on account of his independent position as a judge in regard to the Executive ; and because the circumstances were different from those of the Attorney-General, Mr. Plunkett, who was leaving the colony, whilst Judge Burton was returning to office." It was very wise of Sir George Gipps to decline the invitation, if he had attended, there would have been some reason to believe that the ruler of the colony gave countenance and support to the false statements, sophistical arguments, and derogatory remarks of Judge Burton's religious history.

The Judge must have been terribly taken by surprise when he returned to find that all his visions of a dominant church were baseless fabrics ; he found Sir Richard Bourke's Church Act, which placed the principal religious bodies on an equality, working admirably, and giving to each denomination a share of the public revenue. The Catholics whom he desired to be the last in status before the law, had, since his absence vastly increased in numbers and there were two most efficient catholic officers of the Crown.

When Bishop Polding left the colony at the close of the year 1840, he left the church in a flourishing condition. The Catholic population then amounted to nearly 20,000 souls ; Sydney contained 14,000 Catholics. The entire population of the colony from a return published by the Government in 1839 amounted to 114,386 the population of Sydney was 40,000 and contained nearly **14,000** Catholics. There were only in the year 1835 the Bishop, the Vicar-General, and eight priests. When he left they numbered nineteen priests and a convent of the Sisters of Charity. There were only three churches commenced at the time of his arrival in 1835; now nine churches were completed and six in course of erection. In various places small chapels were erected, and some not finished. The total number of churches and chapels amounted to twenty-five.

The distribution of the priests was as follows:—In New South Wales there were twenty-four; in Van Dieman's Land three; in South Australia three; in Norfolk Island two. The holy communions during the year 1840 were 23,130 and the confirmations 3,158. Two institutions had been established which were a great help to our holy religion, viz., the Catholic Institute of Great Britain and the Society for the Propagation of the Faith. I have given an account of these.

An object of the greatest solicitude to the Bishop was the seminary intended to supply the mission with priests, and to educate the children of the respectable classes in the higher studies. St. Mary's Seminary was established in the year 1838. In the seminary when the Bishop left there were, six ecclesiastical students, twenty boarders, and twenty day-scholars, and the bishop left detailed directions, both as to the scholastic and economical arrangements of the establishment. The course of classical studies comprised the study of Greek and Latin authors, regular instructions in reading and elocution, writing and arithmetic in all its branches, history sacred and profane, geography and the use of the globes. The elder students received lessons in Algebra, Geometry, Trigonometry, Land Surveying, Book-keeping, &c. The seminary was under the management of the Very Rev. Francis Murphy, and the Rev. P. Farrelly, President.

The Catholic orphans were more under the care of the church. Up to the year 1836, they were in Government orphan schools, and taught the Protestant catechism, but the Bishop in his own name and that of the Catholics petitioned the Government, remonstrating against the injustice. The petition was favourably received. In the following year the sum of £1000 was voted for the maintenance of the Catholic orphan children. A large house in the suburbs of Sydney, known as Waverley House, was rented, and there they were in the meantime located, under Catholic guidance. When the Bishop shortly before his departure for Europe saw the Governor, he told him that he had in contemplation to erect a large, commodious building in Parramatta for the lodgement of the Catholic orphans.

P

In the year 1841 there were six public schools, Catholic, and some private schools, indeed in all the principal towns and localities existed now good schools under Catholic direction. In Sydney about three times in the year, the children made their first communion in St. Mary's cathedral with great solemnity. This imposing ceremony, made by the children with much piety and fervour. had the best effect on the minds of the parents and others. and usually a great many conversions of hardened sinners took place. The gentle expostulations of the fervent children drew their parents to the sacraments, which had been abandoned by them for many years.

For the information of the readers I will relate how the Catholic schools were supported at this time and previously by the Government. To premise: there were 35 schools, primary, established in various places of the colony by the Church and School Corporation, and these were charged on the Estimates for the year 1834, at £2.756. In these schools were children of all denominations, Catholic, Wesleyan, and Presbyterian, and the only catechism allowed to be taught was that of the Church of England. Now observe the contrast, in regard to the support given by the Government in those days to the Catholic schools. The first Catholic school was established in the time of Sir Thomas Brisbane, in 1822. In the year 1828 the Government only expended on the Catholic schools £68 3s.; the Protestant schools of the same character received Government support to the amount of £2650 15s 2d. The Estimates for the year 1833 were for Catholic schools £350, for Church of England schools of the same class £2,232 1s 4d. The sum of £800 was voted for the Roman Catholic schools in the year 1834. The Estimates for public education in the year 1841, which were laid before the Council were, for Protestant education £6,106 0s 7d, and the total for Catholic education £1,346 14s 4d. There was voted by the Legislative Council in the year 1834, the sum of £2,300 for the site and buildings of King's School, Parramatta, and the annual salary of £100 towards the support of the head-master; this was exclusively a Protestant establishment.

The system of public education which was followed since 1836 was one which was introduced by Governor Bourke, and similar to the system of education established in Ireland through Lord Stanley. By this system, no religious instruction was given, (that being left to the ministers of the different denominations, and parents of the children) select portions of the Scriptures were read This system of education was carried in the Council by a majority of eight to four.

In the year 1840, Sir George Gipps, in a minute explanatory of his views on the all important subject of education, found fault with the present system. He said that, "Although apparently based upon the principle of equality, it was very unequal in practice. The rule is :—' That the assistance given to any school shall be measured by the sum which is raised for its support by private contributions'; but it is well known that exceptions from this rule are made in favour of certain schools, solely because they have been established longer than others— exceptions which I cannot consider to be founded on any principle of utility, expediency, or justice." In the same minute the Governor proposed a plan of public instruction which he intended to carry into effect. According to this plan a public school was to be built in Sydney, and two others in two principal towns of the interior. The system he intended to establish was on the principle of the British and Foreign School Society, and for this purpose £3000 were placed on the Estimates, and £1000 for the Catholic schools, because the Catholics could not conscientiously send their children to those schools. The Governor at the same time expressed himself favourable to the Irish National system. This system was afterwards established in the colony.

The population of the Colony when Bishop Polding left for Europe in 1840 had increased to 129,463, and in the year following, 1841, a census was taken by the Government of the entire population of New South Wales and Port Philip, and the result showed a total of 130,856. The population of Port Philip District at this time was 11,728. In the year 1836, the year after the arrival of the Bishop, the number of the population of New South Wales was only 77,096. At the time of the census in 1836 the Catholics numbered 21,898 souls; but when the census was taken in 1841 they had increased to 35,690. The members of the Church of England were reckoned at 73,725.

The rapid increase of the population in such a comparatively short time was chiefly owing to the streams of emigration which had poured into the Colony. A statistical account of the emigration for five years, ending with 1829, was shown by a Parliamentary paper published in the year 1832. It stated that immigrants had been introduced into the respective Colonies of Australia, viz., New South Wales, Van Dieman's Land, and Swan River, in the following numbers: In 1825, 485; in 1826, 903; in 1827, 715; in 1828, 1056; in 1829, 2016.

In the year 1840 it was reported to Lord John Russell by the Agent-General for Emigration that there had arrived in Sydney, from 1st January, 1838, to 30th June, 1839, in Government ships, emigrants to the number of 14,644.

The Agent for the Patriotic Association of Sydney, Mr. Buller, in a speech made by him in the Imperial Parliament in the year 1840, on colonial affairs, stated that the number of free emigrants amounted annually to 10,000, for the last five or ten years. He remarked at the same time that it was no longer practicable to make New South Wales a penal colony, that the convict labour was inadequate to supply the wants of the colonists. The chief source of immigration was the Land Fund, *i. e.*, the proceeds of the sale of lands in the Colony, and the Government was pledged to devote that revenue for the purpose of bringing emigrants to the Colony. There were two systems of emigration, one called the bounty system, the other assisted emigration; but both depended for the means of being carried out on the land fund. By the bounty system Government orders were issued, on condition that those who took them up should send to the Colony eligible emigrants, according to the orders received, and these orders were made payable when the emigrants were landed. The candidates for such bounties were entrusted with the selection of the emigrants and with whatever related to the arrangements of the voyage. By the system called assisted emigration, which was the Government system, the Government took all the responsibility; by their agents the emigrants were selected, and the greatest care was taken that they were eligible as to character, health, and employment. The vessel was chartered by the Government and provided with all the necessaries. All was effected through the supervision of the Agent-General for Emigration. The Government system gave satisfaction, but there was a popular outcry against the bounty system, which had been, it was alleged, woefully abused. Those who took up the bounty orders sold them at a premium, and it was said this premium was deducted by lessening the provisions and comforts of the emigrants. The emigrants of some ships were starved, and, horrible to relate, some females, it is said, bartered their virtue for food. The Government interfered, and rigid conditions were enforced for bringing out the emigrants by the Government system.

Some colonial authorities at this time objected to Irish immigration, because the Irish were contentious and quarrelsome, and in several respects an undesirable class to introduce into the Colony; nay, that some were sent out who had aided and abetted in murder. A Commission was appointed to enquire into the use which was made of the land fund and the working of the emigration system. The Commission in their report vindicated the Irish emigrants. It stated: "We cannot quit the subject of the alleged prejudice, to which we have had accidentally to advert, without expressing our regret at its existence, and we hope that no public officer will permit

himself or be suffered by the authorities over him to give it any
countenance. We can only say that as regards their conduct on
board ship, judging by the records of the Agent-General's Office,
no people seem to be more susceptible to the influence of kind
and judicious treatment than the Irish, or more capable of being
carried out in good health; and certainly none evinced better
feelings at the conclusion of the voyage towards those under
whose care they have been safely guided to their destination."
Mr. Pinnock, the immigration agent, in a report which he drew
up at the instance of the Home Government, was charged with
having given a high colouring to the case of certain immigrants
from Ireland. He had said that these people were concerned in
the murder of a magistrate, and that, notwithstanding, they had
been sent out as emigrants by the Irish Government. An inquiry
was made, and it was found that such were not the real facts.
For these false allegations Pinnock was removed from his office
of immigration agent. That is not all ; but the Immigration
Committee of the Legislative Council, in the year 1841, in their
report, wished to exclude Catholics from participating in the
general benefit of the land fund for immigration. The Right
Rev. Dr. Broughton, the Protestant Bishop, was chairman of the
Immigration Committee. In September of this year there was a
public meeting in Sydney, to take into consideration this report
of the Committee, Dr. Bland in the chair. A petition was laid
before the meeting, in which the designs of the Committee were
exposed in regard to Her Majesty's Catholic subjects; and the
petitioners asserted that "the spirit of sectarianism had been
created and encouraged by Bishop Broughton, who was chairman
of the Immigration Committee."

JUDGE BURTON'S BOOK, AND REPLY TO IT, BY DR.
ULLATHORNE. 1840.

There issued from the London Press in the year 1840 a book
entitled "The State of Religion and Education in New South
Wales, by Judge Burton, one of the Judges of the Supreme
Court," in that colony. The subjects of the book are very well
divided, and there is in it a great deal of useful information: the
letters, petitions, and statistical statements in the Appendix are
valuable, and must have taken considerable time to collect.
But he by no means gives an impartial account of the progress of
religion in regard to the different denominations—and in many
instances he suppresses the truth; he is constantly insisting on the

prerogatives of the church of England, and how she had been unfairly dealt with by both governor and government; that the Roman catholics had been preferred in the distribution of their favours. He says the church of England "is a part of the State itself," that the fundamental laws of England became the laws of the colony when the settlement was made; and by one of these fundamental laws the church of England became the established church of the colony; "for nearly fifty years," the judge states, "no other denomination of christians was acknowledged by the government as an object of its support, beyond the limits of a charitable toleration;" and it was in this spirit of "charitable toleration" that the government assisted the catholics and dissenters. He extols to the skies the zeal and labours of the bishop and clergy of the church of England; but he has not much to record of the zeal and labours of the church of England for the poor prisoners during those fifty years. What has become of the Apostolic zeal of the church of England? He calls her the true Apostolic church, when, although "part of the State itself," she could not succeed in sending more than one clergyman to administer to the religious wants of the colony, and he in the end left the church and became a Moravian. When religion was left in such a condition by the Apostolic church, it was time for a separation between Church and State. Here is the description which the judge gives of the state of religion in the early years of the colony:—"Those indeed who should (had they been so disposed) have set about laying the foundation of their city in righteousness, were far otherwise engaged: deeply immersed in selfish pursuits, they were seeking their own future wealth in the means placed at their disposal of unpurchased lands and convict labour, of mercenery barter and petty dealings with their inferiors. That most pernicious article of traffic, which came soon afterwards to be the ordinary circulating medium of the colony (spirituous liquor), was early resorted to in exchange for the necessaries of life; in the purchase of valuable property; in payment for labour, and as a reward offered by government for public services. Thus were the foundations of the new colony laid *in avarice and drunkenness.*" There must also be noted the indifference of those in authority to religious matters, so remarkable in the single fact, that one of the earlier governors had to be informed by the clergyman that *five* or *six persons* only attended divine service, and that it was then that he determined to go to church himself, and stated that "he expected that the example would be followed by the people." The church Apostolic—the church of England—could not complain but that ample provision at least in land, had been made at an early time; for His most gracious Majesty King George the Third gave instructions to the first governor, Governor Phillip, to allot in each township, which should be marked out, 400 acres for maintenance of the minister, and 200 was for the maintenance of a schoolmaster; and this was done by his Majesty only *two* years after the founding of the colony. When the Crown was so favourably disposed to religion and education, surely it would not have been a difficult matter for the heads of the State Church to obtain from the government of the day all the aid which they required for sending to the colony ministers of religion, catechists and schoolmasters. Since King George the Third and his advisers had such a paternal regard for the sacred object of religious education, I think from their want of sympathy and support in the case of the poor convict, in his spiritual wants, the church of England looses all claim to Apostolic zeal. The King of England, George IV., in his paternal solicitude for the endowment of a dominant church in the colony, was extravagant in his royal goodness. In the year 1825, under the royal sign manual, instructions were sent to his Excellency the Governor, "to make out and set apart to the body politic and corporate, in each and every county, hundred, &c., into which they may from time to time divide the said territory or tract of land, comprising one seventh in extent and value of all the lands in each and every such county, to be henceforward called and known by the name of *the clergy and school estate of such county.*"

The most extensive powers were given to the corporation, which was appointed by the home government, for the management of the church and school lands in the colony of New South Wales; and the laws and regulations were exceedingly exact and comprehensive. The intention seemed to be to establish the church of England on such a basis in the colony, which would make her independent, so far as regards temporalities, in all times to come. Notwithstanding, it was deemed wise in five years after, for His Majesty, George IV., to revoke the letters patent. The corporation was legally dissolved 28th August, 1833. During the time of the existence of the corporation the agent for the Church and School Lands, Henry Fisher, Esq., states in his return for Lands, that the amount of land granted to the late Church and School Corporation was 435,765 acres 2 roods 11 perches, and they sold 15,993 acres 34 perches; what remained unsold reverted to the crown.

Dr. Ullathorne in his reply to judge Burton makes some very judicious observations in regard to the magnificent endowments made to the church of England, and shows clearly what likely

them, must be highly gratified by the rapid advances towards completion made under his auspices by St. Mary's Cathedral—an edifice which, shortly before his Lordship's arrival, they almost despaired of seeing finished in their time. This and similar results must be the best and most gratifying reward to that respected prelate and the reverend gentlemen comprising his ministry, for their zeal and devotion in the service of the people. Those results were the fruits of the precepts which they taught, and of that piety of which their lives afforded a practical exemplification.

Mr. Therry here took the chair, and a vote of thanks was accorded to his Lordship for his able and dignified conduct during the proceedings of the evening.

His Lordship said that he received this mark of their kindness with feelings of high gratification. He was proud to be enabled to tell them they had discharged their duty. The general proceedings and result of this meeting must have impressed every one with a high sense of the unanimity which prevailed among the professors of the catholic faith, and the generosity with which each member stepped forward for the purpose of subscribing his quota to further the cause of our holy religion. They had already commenced the good work with every demonstration of a spirited determination to bring it to a speedy and happy conclusion, which desirable end would be greatly furthered by the efforts and known zeal of the highly respected reverend gentleman whom they had just now chosen as their president; whose name was hallowed by both poor and rich wherever his ministry had led him, and in whose praise he would have said a great deal more were he not then present. By the united energies and zeal of the new fraternity, he felt certain that in a comparatively short time such a sum would be raised as would at once be a source of gratification and astonishment. He had not the honour himself to be a native of Ireland; but if he might be excused for making use of what might be technically termed a bull, he was an Irishman born in England. He perfectly recollected that which he considered the dearest compliment he had ever received, was from the lips of a poor Irish woman—"Ah! my lord, you have an Irish heart!"—and blessed be God! he had an Irish heart, under the influence of which he had ever lived among his fellow men, and under the influence of which he would remain until death. He would now dismiss them with his thanks and blessing, and an injunction, when they were asked by others as to what they had done at the meeting, to answer them by a desire that they would go and do likewise.

It was then moved by Mr. Callaghan, barrister-at-law, and seconded by Mr. Roger Murphy, That a society be formed under the designation of "St. Patrick's Society," for the purpose of collecting funds for the erection of the said church. The Rev. Mr. Murphy was appointed by the Meeting president, and the Rev. G. H. Gregory, treasurer. In the course of a few minutes the collection amounted to £1,012.

CHAPTER IX.

Preparations of the Catholic Committee of St. Mary's for the Departure of Bishop Polding and Dr. Ullathorne for England —Presentation of addresses to Bishop Polding and Dr. Ullathorne, and Rev. H. G. Gregory—Departure of Bishop Polding and party for England—The great estimation and respect in which the two catholic gentlemen, John Hubert Plunkett, Attorney-General of New South Wales, and Roger Therry, Esq., Commissioner of the Court of Requests, were held by the inhabitants of the Colony—The state of the Colony, Religion, and Education, when Bishop Polding left, in the year 140—An Abridgement of the reply of Dr. Ullathorne to Judge Burton's Book.

FOR some time previous to the departure of Bishop Polding for Europe, the Catholic Committee were engaged in getting up a Memorial, as a token of the respect in which the Bishop and his Vicar-General were universally held. On the Sunday before the Bishop left, he administered the sacrament of Confirmation to a number of children and adults. A Pontifical High Mass was celebrated in the cathedral, at which the Rev. Dean Brady officiated as assistant priest, the Very Rev. the Vicar-General and Rev. F. Murphy as deacons, and the Rev. Joseph Platt as sub-deacon. The Rev. Messrs. Mahony, Lynch and Grant assisted in surplices and stoles. After the gospel his lordship delivered a most affecting farewell address to his clergy and people.

In the evening at the Old Court House, Castlereagh-street, the addresses were read to his lordship, the Right Rev. Dr. Polding, and his Vicar-General, Dr. Ullathorne. Never was there a more numerous and respectable meeting than that assembled on the occasion. The Attorney-General, J. H. Plunkett, Esq., was called to the chair. Mr. Commissioner Therry commenced by reading the address to the Very Rev. Dr. Ullathorne, as follows:—

Very Rev. Sir,—The moment of your departure for England will, we trust, be *not* deemed an unsuitable one for receiving the from time to time separated themselves into sects, dissenting in matters of religion from the general body of the State, yet, ever since the establishment of a Church in England, and the Union of the Kingdoms under one Sovereign head, the Church of England existed as the National Church; at first free and independent, then for a time overwhelmed by corruption of foreign growth, but again asserting and maintaining the independence of her foundation and the purity of her faith. And as such was by force of law, before the Statute 9th Geo. IV., c. 83, and by the express terms of the Statute, the established Church of the Colony." To this spurious assertion of the Judge the reply of Dr. Ullathorne is that the now established Church of England is founded on the Statute 13, Charles II. This Statute is entitled :— " An Act for the Uniformity of the Public Prayers and Administration of the Sacraments . . . . in the Church of England." And the Act of 5, Ann. 8, for securing the preservation of the Church of England by law established, which is cited by Mr. Burton, expressly quotes the " Act of Uniformity " as being the foundation of the establishment of that Church, and limits its settlement by law " within the kingdoms of England and Ireland, the dominion of Wales, and town of Berwick-upon-Tweed, and territories thereunto belonging." " Statue law, then," writes the Dr., " limits the Anglican establishment to England, Ireland, Wales, and Berwick. All these Acts contain and speak their own express local limitations. . . . . The Statute law, he states, is so far from giving the Anglican Clergy of the Colonies the *rights* and *privileges* of belonging to the establishment of the Church of England, that it expressly and by a special enactment excludes them from the rights and privileges of that establishment. The Act 59, George III, expressly states that the clergy destined for the cure of souls in His Majesty's foreign and colonial possessions are " not provided with the title required by the Canon of the Church of England of such as are to be made ministers.

One word says the Dr. on Mr. Burton's argument from the Coronation Oath and the Catholic Official's Oath. The Judge's sophistry on this point is the same as that of his friend the Protestant bishop in his formal complaint to the British Government on the subject of the Catholic bishop's dress and appearance ; it depends on a quibbling mistake of the meaning of the words, " realm " and " kingdom." There are three realms or kingdoms and many vast dominions besides, which are beneath the empire of the British Crown, some of which never were either realms or kingdoms, and amongst these is the colony of New South Wales.

regard of which this token is only the latest expression, I would endeavour to thank you worthily. As it is, I return your kindness and good wishes, as the best response I am capable of. It is a consoling reflection that, whilst in all other things I leave this colony as poor a man as when I first came to it, I am amply rich in your good opinions and warm affections. For these, and all those good works which I have seen done amongst you by the grace of God, I can never be sufficiently grateful. That I should have been an instrument, however by nature unworthy and unfit, of any part of so great a work of good, as the one to which you refer, will always fill me with happy recollections. But when, my dear friends, you see and bear witness to any qualities in me, except a very simple and earnest intention of serving you, and a wish and endeavour to cherish and protect your faith, and to enlarge and quicken the growth of your charity, I there recognize the fallacy of your kindness. Warm and earnest in your good affections, you believe those qualities to exist in your friend and pastor which you well know ought to exist, and imagine he does possess what you wish and desire he should possess ; and it is my duty to pray that henceforward I may possess them. If on the occasion of the departure of our beloved bishop, I condole with you on the temporary loss of the presence of one, it is only the loss of his presence—his spirit will continue with you—whom you so truly and justly venerate ; I would also console you with the reflection that his absence is needful for your own best interests, and that it will not be of a very long continuance ; and I would cheer you by directing forward your hopes towards the happy period of his return, which may you all live, and live worthily and happily, to see accomplished ; and may his coming again amongst you, as it will, be crowned with joy and benedictions. For myself, whilst I most heartily thank you, and trust that I shall live in your recollections, as you will continue to live in mine, I am desirous of laying myself under new obligations by most earnestly recommending myself to your prayers.

His lordship was addressed in the following words :—On the eve of your lordship's departure, we beg leave to express our warmest wishes for your safe and prosperous passage to England, and our earnest hope for your early return to us. Whilst we deeply deplore even your temporary absence, our regret is subdued and softened by the conviction that your visit to Europe is prompted by a sense of duty, and by that devoted and untiring zeal for our welfare, of which we have so many and unmistakable manifestations. After the five years you have exercised the pastoral charge in these colonies with mild and firm efficacy, it

must be gratifying to you as it is to us, to look back on the great benefits that have been conferred on this community, and of which, under Divine Providence, you have been the chief and chosen instrument. The many churches founded and consecrated by your lordship; your frequent visits into all parts of the colony; the dispersion and establishment of a zealous clergy throughout the principal districts of New South Wales; the impartial attention paid to all classes of your congregation, without any distinction, except that where assistance was most required and needed, there it was largely bestowed; and not least, the truly paternal solicitude you have shown towards the orphan, and the affection with which you have cherished the little children of your flock, are among the enduring monuments of those useful labours, by which, in your high station, you have been distinguished, and which have made an indelible impression upon hearts not formed to be ungrateful. As it is under the deep impression of sentiments such as these that we bid your lordship farewell now, you will not be surprised or displeased that, next to the reverence and affection we entertain towards you, the feeling uppermost is the desire that you may be re-united to your flock at the earliest moment your sense of duty and zeal for our service will permit. We beg leave to accompany this address with a small token of our gratitude and veneration.

This tribute consisted of a Treasury Bill for £400.

His lordship replied as follows:—Wishes so warm and generous, on the part of a people whose affections cannot be commanded, but may be obtained, I do feel sincere gratification in accepting. I knew not until the period of separation approached, how strong had become the bonds which united us. Only indeed a sense of duty the most cogent, and a conviction that my services elsewhere will prove more generally useful to my extensive charge, could influence me to consent to be temporarily absent from you. May your prayers for my speedy return be accomplished. Your kindness has attributed much to me I do not deserve. Patient enduring was the glory and merit of a preceding generation. The season of mercy and grace has been mercifully ours. Suffering and spiritual privation had disposed you to receive with gratitude the enlarged means of religious consolation Providence granted to you through us, the humble instrument of the divine benignity; and the gracious dispensation has not fallen on an unworthy soil. In the churches now in the course of erection; in the improved habits of our people; in the various charitable and religious institutions which have sprung into existence, in a space of time almost instantaneous; there is,

surely, a demonstration, that beneath a surface unfortunately made the ground of rash surmises and rude theories, there did exist a bounteous source of moral worth, which only required to be opened to the clear day, to diffuse streams of virtuous impulses, of noble and disinterested well-doing, throughout our beautiful land.

My labours and their effects you value too highly. The zealous co-operation of the Vicar-General and of the clergy must be held in grateful remembrance. My devotedness to my beloved country, my determination to use every exertion that can tend to raise and establish on a lofty and imperishable basis her religious, her social and moral character, words cannot express. Let the past be an earnest of the future; and whilst I am absent continue by your peaceable determined course to co-operate with me. The calumny of the graceless may fall undeserving of note. No opposition, statement, or misrepresentation detrimental to your social or religious rights, which might derive importance from the station of him who utters it, must pass unnoticed. Cultivate peace,—I use the words of an apostle—as much as in you lies have peace with all men, until the harmonious union which gloriously distinguishes our body shall, in the extinction of prejudice, of bigotry, or of unseemly strife, pervade the entire of the social order of New South Wales. I accept with thankfulness this token of your affectionate regard; may the Almighty dispenser of all good bestow upon you every blessing.

The ladies of Sydney on this occasion presented the Rev. H. G. Gregory with a handsome and valuable ring, accompanied with an address. These are the words of the address :—

"Rev. and Dear Sir,—We, the Catholic ladies of Sydney, having observed that our husbands and fathers have their feelings entirely absorbed with the lamented departure of our excellent Bishop and his Vicar-General, cannot suffer you, reverend Sir, to leave our shores without in some feeble manner testifying our sense of your piety and zeal for the honor and glory of God and for our spiritual welfare during the time the Catholics of Sydney have had the happiness of enjoying your pastoral care. We bow to the will of God, which for great and good purposes separates us from our pastor for a time, trusting that that time will be short, and that after a speedy and safe voyage and a successful mission, you will soon be restored to a people who till then shall never cease to pray for that event and for your welfare.

We beg to accompany this address with a small tribute of our respect and reverence.

Reverend and Dear Sir, farewell."

The reply of the Rev. Mr. Gregory :—

"I receive the token of affection with sincere gratification. It is an emblem of that union between pastor and people, which no circumstance can alter, no distance dissever. Accept my thanks, and add to the favor conferred by remembering me in your prayers."

The chair being vacated by the Attorney-General, the Rev. Francis Murphy was requested to take it, when a vote of thanks was proposed by Mr. Commissioner Therry and seconded by John Ryan Brennan, Esq., P.M.: "That the thanks of the meeting are due, and are hereby presented, to the Attorney-General for his dignified conduct in the chair." Mr. Plunkett briefly returned thanks, and expressed his gratification at having had the honor to preside over so respectable a meeting, assembled on so interesting an occasion.

At half-past eleven o'clock a.m. on the Monday following, 16th November, 1840, the Catholic Committee accompanied the Bishop from his residence to the Cathedral, where he read at the altar the beautiful prayers appointed to be read to implore the blessing of heaven on their voyage. A procession was formed of the whole people, under the direction of the Committee. There were many thousands in it. The girls of the Catholic Schools were first, the whole of them dressed in white ; then came the boys, followed by the congregation walking two and two; the Bishop and his Clergy formed the rear. The procession marched along Hyde Park, Macquarie-street, Bent-street, and Macquarie Place. When they arrived at the jetty on the Circular Quay the people divided, and the Bishop, Clergy, and Committee went to the boats. His Lordship and the Rev. Mr. Gregory proceeded in the Government boat. Dr. Ullathorne and the clergy occupied the boat of the Crusader, furnished by Captain Inglis. The vessel in which the Bishop and the Very Rev. Dr. Ullathorne, Rev. H. Gregory, and the Bishop's Chaplain embarked, was a brig, by name " Orion," Captain Saunders, master, bound for Valparaiso; in their company were three young gentlemen, Messrs. Chambers, Therry, and Carter, going to Europe for a collegiate education. The brig was towed to the Heads by the splendid steamship " Clonmel," and this steamer was filled with upwards of 400 persons desirous of testifying to the last the deep respect they had for their beloved Bishop. It was remarked by the press at the time of the departure of Bishop Polding: "That not only every Catholic, but every Christian ought to sympathise in the sorrow at the absence of him who had given by his presence and labours a moral dignity to our adopted land, formerly *represented* as the abortion of nations, but now the abode of a fine

people, increasing in the enjoyment of a high degree of physical
and moral health. If ever a bishop was worthy to be called a
pastor of his flock, it is the Right Reverend Dr. Polding."

I certainly would not be doing justice to my narrative were
I to pass by unnoticed the worth of two most estimable Catholic
gentlemen, officers of the Government, who flourished in our
community at this time ; I mean John Hubert Plunkett,
Attorney-General of New South Wales, and Roger Therry, Esq.,
Commissioner of the Court of Requests. They were conscientious
Catholics, and lived up to their religious principles. They never
compromised their religion, and were ever ready to speak and act
in defence of the faith of their forefathers, and of their country,
Ireland. They gave all the weight of their character and
position for the benefit of religion and charity. Mr. Plunkett
was for many years Attorney-General, and he went home on
leave of absence in the beginning of the year 1841. But before
he left the colony, in such great respect was he held by his legal
brethren, that they entertained him at a dinner. The Chief
Justice, Sir James Dowling presided, and there was present
Judge Stephens. The Governor, Sir Geo. Gipps, also honored the
festive board by his presence. The Governor, in returning
thanks when his health was proposed, said : " He felt extremely
happy in meeting such a large and respectable company of the
colonists of New South Wales, of every grade and of every
persuasion, who, laying aside all other motives, had met together
that evening to pay a tribute of respect to a public officer who
had discharged his great, important, and arduous duties with the
highest degree of impartiality and firmness ; he felt extremely
happy to make one amongst them in bearing testimony to the
worth, ability, and integrity of that officer." The Chief Justice,
Sir James Dowling said : " It was a pleasing reflection to Mr.
Plunkett, notwithstanding the very peculiar community in
which he lived, all men bore ample testimony to the just, upright,
manly, and impartial manner in which he had discharged the
duties belonging to his station ; after many years of trial Mr.
Plunkett had passed through the crucible of public opinion
without a stain being cast upon him." All the gentlemen present
at the banquet bore similar testimony to the high character of
Mr. Plunkett.

Before the departure of Mr. Plunkett, on leave of absence, a
handsome testimonial was presented to him in the shape of
several pieces of silver plate, and on each piece was engraved his
family crest, which is a trotting horse, with the motto " *Festina
Lente.*" The silver service was purchased by public subscription
and cost about £400.

years after the settlement, great numbers of skeletons and dead bodies of the natives were found in caves and under projecting rocks. Many of the survivors took to plunder and robbery as their only resource: and numbers of them were cruelly and mercilessly shot down: the remainder formed the boldest and most warlike portion of the race.

The Aboriginal population of New South Wales at the time of the settlement of the whites amounted to about one million; and it was reckoned there were fully three thousand natives of different tribes living between Botany Bay and Broken Bay.

The cooey of the blacks is no longer heard in the bush and valleys about Port Jackson. The corroberee or native war dance by moonlight, at which hundreds assembled, is no more to be seen: nor is the whizzing of the boomerang, thrown with such dexterity by the native, heard on the plains: nor the sound of the hatchet, when he notched the tree and climbed to secure the opossum, or the honey of the native bee: all is desolation to the Aborigine: the stranger has possession of his country!!

The Aborigines of Australia have been looked upon by many as a contemptible race; indeed, not far removed from the brute creation: but ethnographists have discovered, after investigation, that the native race of Australia is more ancient than all the races of the surrounding islands; that they date back to a time not far distant from the dispersion of the human race. We read in the eleventh chapter of the book of Genesis, that after the deluge all men assembled in the plain of Sennaar; they were of "one tongue and speech." After the attempt of man to build the Tower of Babel their tongue was confounded; "and so the Lord scattered them from that place into all lands," &c. We can imagine the primitive races after the dispersion wandering about from one land to another, and some tribes taking up their abode in caves, and under projecting rocks, without fixed habitations; without implements of any kind except the stone hatchet; and without any covering, except the skins of beasts: their food would be the animals procured by the chase, ocean fish, wild fruit and indigenous roots. The natives of the Andaman Islands, in the Bay of Bengal, are characterized by habits and customs such as these: so also the Negritos, or Indian negroes, and inhabitants of the Phillipine Islands, the originals of the Malayan Peninsula.

The stone hatchet period is that era when numerous tribes made use of that instrument: it was the most universal of all tools or weapons before the inventions in metal, that is, in the pre-metallic age of the world. The hatchet at first was formed by splinters being taken off a block of stone, until it was reduced nearly **14,000** Catholics. There were only in the year 1835 the **Bishop, the** Vicar-General, and eight priests. When he left they **numbered nineteen** priests and a convent of the Sisters of Charity. There **were only** three churches commenced at the time of his **arrival in 1835**; now nine churches were completed and six in course **of erection.** In various places small chapels were erected, and **some not** finished. The total number of churches and chapels **amounted to** twenty-five.

The distribution of the priests was as follows:—In New South **Wales** there were twenty-four; in Van Dieman's Land three; **in** South Australia three; in Norfolk Island two. The holy **communions** during the year 1840 were 23,130 and the confirmations 3,158. Two institutions had been established which **were** a great help to our holy religion, viz., the Catholic Institute **of** Great Britain and the Society for the Propagation of the **Faith.** I have given an account of these.

An object of the greatest solicitude to the Bishop was the seminary intended to supply the mission with priests, and to educate the children of the respectable classes in the higher studies. St. Mary's Seminary was established in the year 1838. In the seminary when the Bishop left there were, six ecclesiastical students, twenty boarders, and twenty day-scholars, and the bishop left detailed directions, both as to the scholastic and economical arrangements of the establishment. The course of classical studies comprised the study of Greek and Latin authors, regular instructions in reading and elocution, writing and arithmetic in all its branches, history sacred and profane, geography and the use of the globes. The elder students received lessons in Algebra, Geometry, Trigonometry, Land Surveying, Book-keeping, &c. The seminary was under the management of the Very Rev. Francis Murphy, and the Rev. P. Farrelly, President.

The Catholic orphans were more under the care of the church. Up to the year 1836, they were in Government orphan schools, and taught the Protestant catechism, but the Bishop in his own name and that of the Catholics petitioned the Government, remonstrating against the injustice. The petition was favourably received. In the following year the sum of £1000 was voted for the maintenance of the Catholic orphan children. A large house in the suburbs of Sydney, known as Waverley House, was rented, and there they were in the meantime located, under Catholic guidance. When the Bishop shortly before his departure for Europe saw the Governor, he told him that he had in contemplation to erect a large, commodious building in Parramatta for the lodgement of the Catholic orphans.

P

Many of the learned in these subjects have maintained that the Aborigines of Australia belonged to, and were descended from the Papuans of New Guinea; but after recent researches they have come to the conclusion that the native Australian is not connected with the Papuans. The very feasible reason on which they rested their opinion, was the proximity of the two countries, viz., Australia being only separated from New Guinea by Torres Straits, which are not very wide, and there are many small islands by which they could pass from New Guinea to Australia. Upon investigation it was found that the inhabitants of these two islands bear no relation whatever to each other. The Papuans of New Guinea may be taken as the modern representatives of the lake dwellers of the old world. The Australians are undoubtedly, it is said, the modern representatives of the cave dwellers. Those are two distinct races. The Australians do not build permanent dwellings; they are content to live in caves, or under a few sheets of bark. The Papuans build substantial houses, on piles, on the margin of lakes, or inlets of the sea. The Australians do not, nor ever have cultivated the soil; the Haraforas, Arrufours, or Arafuras, a people inhabiting some parts of New Guinea, and a large cluster of islands to the west of that country, cultivate the soil with considerable success. The Australian Aborigines know not, nor ever have known the use of the plough; they do not till the ground in any way. The Papuans not only make use of wooden implements and bone, but they understand the use of metal, and they make textile fabrics and pottery: the Australian natives are ignorant of all these things; nor do they use the bow and arrow, a weapon so well known to savage nations. The Papuans live in rather large communities; but the communities of the Australians are very small. The Papuans of New Guinea construct very serviceable canoes by hollowing out large trees, in making which they show considerable mechanical skill : the canoe of the natives of Australia scarcely deserves the name, made from sheets of bark, very frail and dangerous in a rough sea.

The physical appearance of the natives of New Guinea is quite different from that of the Aborigines of Australia. The Papuans from their appearance give evidence of a mixed people. There is found amongst them the face of the Indian negro, of the Malay, the Arab, and Polynesian; and they may be regarded as chiefly of Tauranean or Tartar origin. The language of the Australians is quite different from the language of the natives of New Guinea : the language of the Australians denotes them to belong to the Aryan race. They have not the well-developed

In the year 1840, Sir George Gipps, in a minute explanatory this views on the all important subject of education, found fault with the present system. He said that, "Although apparently based upon the principle of equality, it was very unequal in practice. The rule is :—' That the assistance given to any school shall be measured by the sum which is raised for its support by private contributions'; but it is well known that exceptions from this rule are made in favour of certain schools, solely because they have been established longer than others—exceptions which I cannot consider to be founded on any principle of utility, expediency, or justice." In the same minute the Governor proposed a plan of public instruction which he intended to carry into effect. According to this plan a public school was to be built in Sydney, and two others in two principal towns of the interior. The system he intended to establish was on the principle of the British and Foreign School Society, and for this purpose £3000 were placed on the Estimates, and £1000 for the Catholic schools, because the Catholics could not conscientiously send their children to those schools. The Governor at the same time expressed himself favourable to the Irish National system. This system was afterwards established in the colony.

The population of the Colony when Bishop Polding left for Europe in 1840 had increased to 129,463, and in the year following, 1841, a census was taken by the Government of the entire population of New South Wales and Port Philip, and the result showed a total of 130,856. The population of Port Philip District at this time was 11,728. In the year 1836, the year after the arrival of the Bishop, the number of the population of New South Wales was only 77,096. At the time of the census in 1836 the Catholics numbered 21,898 souls; but when the census was taken in 1841 they had increased to 35,690. The members of the Church of England were reckoned at 73,725.

The rapid increase of the population in such a comparatively short time was chiefly owing to the streams of emigration which had poured into the Colony. A statistical account of the emigration for five years, ending with 1829, was shown by a Parliamentary paper published in the year 1832. It stated that immigrants had been introduced into the respective Colonies of Australia, viz., New South Wales, Van Dieman's Land, and Swan River, in the following numbers : In 1825, 485; in 1826, 903; in 1827, 715; in 1828, 1056; in 1829, 2016.

In the year 1840 it was reported to Lord John Russell by the Agent-General for Emigration that there had arrived in Sydney, from 1st January, 1838, to 30th June, 1839, in Government ships, emigrants to the number of 14,644.

inhabitants of the whole continent form, in fact, one people, all governed by the same laws and customs, the points of difference between the tribes being only such as might be expected from differences of circumstances and locality ; and it is one of the most remarkable facts in the history of the human family that among different tribes, scattered over a region two thousand miles long by nearly fifteen hundred miles wide, possessing no written literature whatever, and traditions traceable for only a brief period, there should prevail a system of internal government almost identical and common to all ; that this system must have prevailed through countless generations, and that every tribe has its own country, with as clearly defined a boundary as any estate in England—a boundary which is never crossed but at the risk of death, without diplomatic arrangements as elaborate and punctilious as those between two German principalities." Mr. Lang states that "The government is administered in each tribe by a council consisting of old and elderly men, no young man being admitted a member unless he has displayed unusual intelligence, courage and prowess. There is also a class privileged to go from tribe to tribe, to carry messages, to negotiate and arrange for meetings between the various councils, and to transact other business of a general character. These men are much honoured by all the tribes."

THEIR DEGRADING PRACTICES.—Circumcision is practised by some of the Northern tribes, and this may be accounted for from their proximity to the Malayan Peninsula, and their intercourse with the Arabs in former years, when the Arabs were navigators and merchants in those parts. "The practice of circumcision is almost general with the Malays and Arabs."

The tribes of Australia practise polygamy, and they have no law against it ; but the law pronounces capital punishment against any one who marries one of the wrong sort. The practice of infanticide was common and enjoined by their laws under certain circumstances. The scarcity of food, it is supposed, prompted them to destroy their offspring. Among the more degraded and starving of the tribes cannibalism prevailed as the means of sustaining life or of gratifying a craving for animal food, although generally they hold the practice in abhorrence. We are not to be suprised at these degrading habits, as they are common to most savage nations.

Skulls of the Australian Aborigines have been exhibited in Europe, seemingly in support of the old theory that the natives of Australia are a very inferior race of the human family ; but *those who* have had good opportunities of judging, by no means agree with this theory. The intelligence of a race constitutes its rank among human beings. Now I have shewn that their laws and customs by no means places them in an inferior condition to other uncivilized nations or races. The natives of Australia, although they do not build dwellings for themselves or live in large communities, or have the knowledge of any mechanical art, yet they have shewn great aptitude in acquiring the knowledge of many things. They are most skilful in using their own weapons—the spear, the boomerang, the stone hatchet, &c.; it is said their use of these instruments is perfection. " No one seeing " says Mr. Lang, whom I have before quoted, " the natives merely as idle wandering vagabonds among the white men, can judge as to what they are in their natural state. In their subtlety as diplomatists, and their skill and activity in war and in the chase, I consider them quite equal to the American Indians. The great weir for catching fish on the Upper Darling, and another described by Morrill, the shipwrecked mariner, who passed so many years amongst them, prove that they are capable of constructing works upon a large scale, and requiring combined action. Everything they have to do they do in the very best manner, and for every contingency that arises they devise a simple remedy."

When Sydney, some forty or fifty years ago, was a considerable depot for whaling and sealing vessels, the natives were employed on board, and made excellent hands in the business. Mr. Benjamin Boyd manned his fine yacht " The Wanderer," about thirty years since, with native blacks of the Twofold Bay tribe, and they made capital sailors.

A team of aboriginal cricketers was trained by a Mr. Wills, in Victoria; they came to Sydney in 1867. A few days after they competed in a three days' match with the Albert Club; the natives lost the game, but played very skilfully. There were eleven aborigines, captained by Mr. Wills. A team of aboriginal cricketers went to England in the year 1868 for the purpose of contesting the game with the renowned English clubs. The team consisted of twelve blacks, captained by one Lawrence. The aboriginals scored their first victory over an English team at Ladywell, against eleven gentlemen of Lewisham. The spectators numbered upwards of 4000. A handsome silver cup was presented to Red Cap, an aboriginal player, by the captain of the Lewisham team, as the highest scorer on the Australian side.

If the native blacks of Australia shew such aptitude in acquiring a knowledge of these arts and contrivances of the white man, would they not, if pains were taken and sufficient means provided, become capable of participating in most of the advantages of civilized life ? Nothing could shew more the adroitness and natural intelligence of the Aborigines than the treaty which they entered into with John Batman, said to be the founder of Victoria, for the purchase of land. Batman states : " After some time and full explanation I found eight chiefs amongst them, who possessed the whole of the territory near Port Philip. Three brothers, all of the same name, were the principal chiefs, and two of them men of six feet high, and very good looking ; the other not so tall, but stouter. The other five chiefs were fine men. After a full explanation now of what my object was, I purchased two large tracts of land from them— about 600,000 acres, more or less, and delivered over to them blankets, knives, looking-glasses, tomahawks, beads, scissors, flour, &c., &c., as payment for the land ; and also agreed to give them a tribute or rent yearly. The parchment the eight chiefs signed this afternoon, delivering to me some of the soil, each of them, as giving me full possession of the tracts of land."—*Men of the Times, Heaton, page 12.*—*Batman.* This account at once shews the ingenuity of the natives and the greed of Batman.

The purest stock of the aboriginal natives is said to have been that of Tasmania, which is now extinct. King Billy, or William Laune, last male Tasmanian aboriginal, died March 3rd, 1869. Queen Tawaunimai, or Lalla Rookh, the last of the Tasmanian aboriginals, died at Hobart Town, May 8, 1876 ; aged 73.

GOVERNOR ARTHUR OF TASMANIA.—When the blacks of Tasmania were troublesome to the settlers Governor Arthur made a cordon across the island to capture them, but only one was taken, and the cost of the expedition amounted to £30,000.

Three hundred, the last of the Tasmanian aboriginals, were transferred from the mainland to Flinders' Island, in Bass's Straits, through the instrumentality of Mr. George Augustus Robinson in 1837.

It is now nearly a hundred years since the white man invaded these lands, and took from the black man the country which he had inhabited for hundreds and hundreds of years— the land which " the Lord God gave unto him." Since 1788, when Governor Phillip, with his military settlers and prisoners, landed on the shores of Australia, what has been done by those on whom the responsibility rested, to ameliorate the condition of the un- fortunate aborigines, to civilize and convert them ? No strenuous efforts, either by the government or others who had it in their power, have been made to alter their deplorable condition. Commendable efforts have been made from time to time. Protectorates, assisted by the government, and missions have been formed for their conversion to christianity; but all have turned out failures. Thousands and thousands are wandering as vagabonds, without any object in life. If protectorates had been established in every district, and abundance of land given to each to cultivate, and the natives supplied with all the implements of husbandry, and persons appointed to teach them the usages of civilized life, and the arts of reading, writing and arithmetic, I venture to say that thousands of them would be now enjoying the comforts of civilized life, and their children would be perfectly civilized. The invaders have taken possession of all their lands, from north to south of this great island; their tribal organisation has been broken up; cattle and sheep stations are everywhere; the kangaroo and other marsupials, upon which the natives lived by the chase, have been destroyed or driven into the scrubs or desert places; houses and fences surround them on all sides: they have received no compensation for the loss of country which they have sustained. Let it not be thought that they are indifferent to what has happened by the occupation of the stranger. Starvation has done its work; hope and vigour have forsaken them; they have become demoralised, and apathy or the recklessness of despair has overtaken them. They have a deep-rooted love for their country, and their feelings often rebel against the intruders. Not long ago a poor black gin was giving some annoyance at a station, and she was ordered by the squatter to go away, when she turned quickly round and told him that "he should go away, that this was her country."

When, driven by hunger and starvation they have speared the cattle and sheep of the white man, they were shot down without remorse. Great have been the outrages committed against the blacks in retaliation for depredations. It was no extenuation that the unfortunate blacks were savages, starving with hunger, and deprived of their hunting grounds. Oftentimes they have been slain without pity, without a shadow of excuse, except the desire to exterminate them. Who has not heard of the terrible outrage perpetrated at the Myall Creek in June, 1838? At that time 28 men, women and children were most barbarously murdered, no regard being paid to age or sex: they were actually cut to pieces and burned in a hidden part of the scrub. The massacre was said to be committed by stockmen and labourers of various stations. The outrage was done, they said, because the blacks speared the cattle; but there was reason for believing that those murdered were not given to violence and plunder. Seven of those who were charged with the murder of the aboriginals, were tried, convicted and executed in Sydney, December 18, 1838.

A foreign author writes, in regard to this tragedy, " Are these, the English, the heralds of civilization, the preservers of the human race, of which they boast? With what right can they proclaim themselves the benefactors of humanity, who, by virtue of their profession, undertake to bring to the savage, life, activity, religion, arts, science, glory, salvation and happiness!!!"

Dr. Lang, in his IV. Letter to the Earl of Durham, writes :— " We are accustomed to speak with noble indignation and abhorrence of the brutal atrocities of Cortez, Pizarro, and the bands of soldier-highwaymen who pursued their depredations in Mexico and Peru: but we forget that at this time, in the nineteenth century, we ourselves, although a nation civilized, and a colonizing people, have upon other lands followed the same tragedy of blood."

Besides this atrocity, innumerable are the outrages which, from time to time, were committed by the whites against the aborigines ; and now, in 1885, the fell work of extermination is going on. We read in "Heaton's Dictionary of Dates" that in the year 1857, a tribe of about sixty were slaughtered on the Dawson River. It is true that the blacks had murdered a Mr. Frazer, wife, children and governess, at the same place: but how is it shown that the tribe of sixty were all implicated in that massacre? In the Medway Ranges, Queensland, 170 blacks were slaughtered by police and others, in reprisal for the Wills' massacres, October and November, 1861. When the blacks, through hunger, have been guilty of petty thefts, the flour has been poisoned, and many of them died in consequence ; and by having contracted the vices of the whites they have died in great numbers from loathsome diseases and strong drink. The depredations of blacks on the whites are extenuated because the poor savage has only the light of reason to guide him ; but religion and civilization ought to teach the white man to act with christian compassion towards his uncultivated brother.

THEIR RELIGION.—It is very important to consider what is the religious belief of the aborigines of Australia. It is the opinion of many who have written on the subject, that they have no knowledge of the existence of God, the Creator and Ruler of the heavens and the earth ; others hold a contrary opinion—that the aborigines of Australia believe in an omnipotent Being who made the heavens and the earth, and they are far from being atheists. Bishop Salvado of Port Victoria, who resides at New Norcia (Abbey Nullins), (where there is a Catholic Settlement for the aboriginals of Western Australia, conducted under his superintendence), states, in a work written by him, on the savages of New Norcia, that, " they adore neither a true nor a false divinity ; *they have,* nevertheless, the idea of an omnipotent being, the **creator** of the heavens and the earth, whom they call Motogon; that Motogon is believed by them to be a man of great strength, high, wise, and of their own colour and country. They say that in the creation of the kangaroo, the sun, and the trees, he used these words :—'Terra Esci Fuori,' Let the earth exist, and breathed, and the earth was created: 'Acqua Esci Fuori,' Let the water exist, breathed, and the water was created; and so of other things." * Further on in his work Bishop Salvado writes, after much conversation with the natives, that they admit two principles; one, the author of good, and he is Motogon, the other the author of evil, whom they call Cienga.

In regard to the Aborigines of eastern Australia, a Protestant missionary, who carried on for many years, under the auspices of the Church of England, a mission to the Wiradhuri speaking tribes of Wellington Vale, confidently asserts, after diligent enquiry and study amongst the blacks, that most assuredly they cannot be called atheists. This also is the opinion of Count Strezlewski, who wrote " A Physical description of New South Wales and Van Dieman's Land." The Count travelled much in Australia, and had many conversations with the *Indigènes*.

There is no question but that amongst all the tribes of both north and south there is prevalent the idea of certain imaginary beings, to whom they ascribe various attributes, and some of these attributes are very contradictory. However, it shows they have some glimmerings of the supernatural. All the tribes have an idea, but not very definite, that their existence does not absolutely end with the death of their bodies; from which it is concluded that they have an indistinct notion of the immortality of the soul. There is one thing which they testify to and believe; and that is, the existence of an evil spirit, which they call Wondon. Every thing adverse to them which happens, they attribute it to the malignity of that spirit.. To the malignity of that spirit they attribute the thunder, the lightning, the storms, floods, whirlwinds, and hail.

They also believe in the transmigration of souls. "It is singular the manner by which they represent that transmigration. When they see a person who has much resemblance with one already dead, they say he has returned to life. Also a belief prevails amongst them that after death they will rise up white men; and that the white people who inhabit other countries, beyond the seas, are their ancestors, who pass away to live in other bodies. Wonderful to say! I have found that belief to

---

* Salvado, p. iii, chap. 3.

prevail, identical, amongst the savages of the Liverpool Plains who inhabit the eastern coast of Australia, and amongst those of King George's Sound, who live on the western coast, distant more than two thousand miles, without communication with each other."* It is acknowledged by all who have had much intercourse with the natives, that they are very reticent in regard to their religious belief, and seem to have very confused notions of the supernatural.

Before the minds of the Aborigines became darkened by the abuse of those natural lights and graces which they had received, they knew their God, and adored Him as such. Romans, chap. 1, ver. 2—"But when they knew God they did not praise and glorify Him, nor give Him thanks, but became vain in their thoughts, and their foolish hearts were hardened." St. Paul says : Rom., chap. 1, ver. 20—"For the invisible things of Him, from the creation of the world, are clearly seen, being understood by things which are made, His eternal power also and divinity ; so that they are inexcusable."

It is evident that the savages of Australia are reasonable beings, made to the image and likeness of God, redeemed by Christ, destined to be saved like the rest of man. 1 Tim., chap. 11, ver. 4—"God will have all men to be saved and to come to the knowledge of the truth."

They are included amongst those nations to whom our Lord commanded His Apostles to go and teach, and baptise in the name of the Father, and of the Son, and of the Holy Ghost. The words of our Lord when He commissioned His Apostles are these : "All power is given to me in heaven and in earth. Go ye therefore, and teach all nations, baptising them in the name of the Father, and of the Son, and of the Holy Ghost ; teaching them to observe all things whatsoever I have commanded you ; and behold I am with you all days, even to the consummation of the world."† This was a command given by Christ before His ascension and after His resurrection to His Church, in the persons of the Apostles, to teach the nations, and that His Spirit would be ever and always with them. Christ hath been true to His promise, He has been with His Church in all ages, converting and baptizing the nations, " enlightening those who sit in darkness and the shadow of death, and directing their feet in the ways of peace."‡ The Catholic Church at the present time has her missionaries in every part of the globe, dispelling the darkness of infidelity, making known the saving truths of

---

* Ottav. Barsanti Salvaggi Dell' Australia, p. 172.   † St. Matthew, xxviii, 18.
‡ Luke i, 79.

ation, and in many parts laying down their lives for the sake
hrist ; and the head of the Church, Pope Leo., appointed by
st, directs all her energies.

God selects His own time for the baptizing and conversion
ations ; the aboriginal of this land hath sat till now in
ness and the shadow of death. The Catholic missionary is
in the land, labouring to snatch these souls from the power
e devil, and bring them under the influence of the Gospel.
ly—in 1882—a mission has been begun in the Northern
itory, at the express wish of His Holiness, Leo. XIII. It is
ucted by three members of the Society of Jesus ; the Rev.
trele, S.J., is the superior. This first mission station is
lished on an aboriginal reserve near Palmerston, given for
urpose by the Colonial Government. Father Strele states
s prospectus that " The missionaries have the satisfaction to
heir efforts and sacrifices producing good fruit among the
iginals. Many of the latter have joined us in the work of
vating the land and of erecting the most necessary buildings
permanent station. They listen to the teaching, and about
r have received baptism." Father Strele goes on to state
" The satisfactory results obtained on the first station and an
ase in the number of missionaries led to the resolution to
stations also among other aboriginal tribes For this
ose he had to confer with the Colonial Government, and was
successful in obtaining an area of one hundred square miles,
re inland position, on the Daly River, where the blacks are
numerous." He says, " For aboriginals live still in great
bers in this continent, and many thousands may yet be
ight out from their wretched state of ignorance and barbarism.
. . . The undertaking, moreover, co-operates with the
itude repeatedly expressed by Her Majesty's Government,
efforts should be made to ameliorate the condition of the
riginal tribes. It also co-operates with the intentions of the
ernment of these colonies, which always second undertakings
his kind."

" The continual life," writes Father Strele, " which I lived
the blacks during two years, and the close observation which
d opportunity to make of them, force on me the persuasion
t their race, especially in the northern parts of Australia, is
l suited for instruction, for learning agriculture and the
ious mechanical arts, and I am confident that after not many
rs the stations will become self-supporting."

The Rev. D. McNab, now the Catholic Pastor of Perth, con-
ted a mission for the blacks a few years since in the country

surrounding Brisbane, and at Port Mackay, under the auspices of Bishop Quinn. He obtained from the Government for the purpose about four hundred acres of land, and gathered around him a considerable number of the aborigines, many of whom he instructed and baptized; but ill-health and want of assistance compelled him to leave them. He said it was very difficult to civilize and christianise those blacks, because they were so much contaminated by association with whites.

I have seen in a letter from the Rev. D. McNab, dated 3rd March, 1886, that he is establishing a native mission in Western Australia, on the south side of King's Sound. He has obtained from the governor a reserve for a native mission, consisting of 600 acres; and the blacks in those parts have consented to settle down and cultivate the land; to catch and cure fish; and send their children to school. The reserve is about eighty miles from Derby. At the penal settlement, where he was for four months, he instructed and baptized between twenty and thirty natives.

A Community of Benedictine monks was established in Western Australia, upwards of fifty miles from Perth, on the extensive Victoria Plains. It was founded by the Right Rev. Rosendo Salvado, O.S.B., about the year 1867. The monastry is called New Norcia, and the bishop resides there. The community consists of fifty-eight monks and lay brothers. In conjunction with the monastry there is a settlement for the aborigines. In the year 1866 Governor Irwin gave 30 acres of good land in perpetuity, and for the use of pastoral purposes 1000 acres of grazing land. The *indigénes* have been instructed by the monks with great success. There may be, from time to time, as many as 300 blacks living on the establishment. The boys and girls at New Norcia are in number about 50. They have two separate buildings, one for the boys and another for the girls, where they receive from the monks religious and secular education. They are taught reading, writing, arithmetic, and sacred history.

New Norcia is a little colony of Australian blacks, and they are provided with every necessary. 300 acres of land were prepared in 1859, and 200 were put under cultivation. The produce from the labour of the aborigines and the brothers amounted to 3000 bushels of wheat, 15 tons of grapes, a ton of tobacco and 200 gallons of wine.

They have an elegant church built in the Italian style; a monastry, schools, houses for the adults, workshops, granaries, and an hospital. The blacks are taught how to cultivate the soil. They learn the useful trades of shoemaking, tailoring, carpentry, &c., &c., and how to build in stone and brick. The females are taught to knit and to cook and to do laundry work. Miss Florence Nightengale, famed at the time of the Crimean war for her attention to the wounded, in a work published by her in London, after her voyage to Australia, says, "in no part of this world have they succeeded in educating and civilizing the savage races, except in the Benedictine monastry of New Norcia."

The Anglican bishop of Perth, understanding that the success of the monastic colonization was a cruel reproach to the indifference of his co-religionists in the question of the civilization of the Australians, endeavoured by public conferences to engage the English colonists to contribute to the foundation of a new Protestant mission for the savages of his diocese; but neither the inhabitants of Perth, nor the colonists would listen to it; and when he returned again to the charge, the journals answered him in the following manner:—"It is our profound conviction that the Anglican missions for the savages in Western Australia, as well as in other parts, have failed, because the principal object of the founders was to make of the Australians, elegant and well-informed men. We believe that if the missionaries of New Norcia have succeeded, it is only because, without neglecting the development of the intelligence of the savages, they have above all sought to correct their manners after the precepts of Christ, and to unite the moral to the physical education, so as to make the Australian a working man and useful to society."—*The Inquirer*, of New Perth, 15th November, 1865.

All the young girls, natives, at New Norcia, know how to sew, and some are as expert with the needle as any seamstress of Europe. Every week two of them do the cooking for the rest, and two of them bake the bread. The result is that when they are to be married they are perfectly acquainted with their household duties.

Bishop Salvado writes, 28th August, 1878, "On the 15th August, the Feast of the Assumption, I administered the Sacrament of Confirmation to forty savages and three Europeans, who a few days before had abjured protestantism and received baptism." In a letter written 13th April, 1878, Bishop Salvado writes these remarkable words:—"The Australians received and instructed in our monastic colony do not return to the savage life, as the protestant neophytes generally do, when, for one reason or another, they leave New Norcia. Last year some of my savages who were baptized, left the mission, but they have not dishonoured it. The first has gone to establish himself as a shoemaker at Perth, our capital. Another savage civilized by our monks, is gone to work with an English colonist, and he has his wife with him, who is also an *indigéne*. The colonist was so satisfied with him that he has built them a small house and given them a garden. The man acts as servant, groom and gardener; his wife as cook and laundress. A third Australian took service with another colonist; he soon discovered the fitness of this *indigéne*, and not content with giving him three pounds per month, with board and lodging, he made him his butler; the other domestics, who were English and Irish, obeyed him, and did it with cheerfulness. Another *indigéne* who was in the service of a horse-trainer, seeing one of the domestics, an Englishman and catholic, become seriously ill, took care of him and assisted him piously in his last hour. During his agony he recited all the prayers which he knew. When the domestic was dead he buried him with respect, dug his grave, and after having interred him, recited over his tomb the psalms and prayers for the repose of his soul." Such is the race, remarks the writer of these extracts, of men whom the English protestants declare so incapable of any civilization that they seek by every means to exterminate them; and whom professor Darwin, with his credulous dupes, points out to us as the direct descendants of the Chimpanzee and Orang-Outang, after the amusing theory which would make us all to come from a great baboon.

The Rev. George F. Dillon, a Roman Catholic missionary, founded a mission for the aboriginals at Burragorang, a place about 65 miles from Sydney. Many of the blacks have been baptized and instructed there; the mission still exists, and is bringing forth good fruit.

Notwithstanding the cruel treatment and slaughter of great numbers of the blacks by the whites, together with the neglect and contempt to which they have been subjected, they are still very numerous in the year 1886. In 1788, when Governor Phillip established the colony, he estimated the number of blacks in New South Wales at 1,000,000; 3,000 of these were supposed to be between Broken Bay and Botany Bay. The number of blacks in Australia in 1848 was estimated at 3,000,000. At the first colonization of Port Phillip the aboriginals numbered about 5,000. When Victoria became an independent colony, in 1857, the number was officially stated to be 2,693. In 1879, the secretary to the Central Board for the Protection of the Aboriginals estimated the total number of aboriginals in the colony of Victoria at 1553. Aboriginals numbering 557, or more than a third, are living on Aboriginal Stations, which are under the control and partial support of the government. The remainder wander about the colony at large. Every effort is made to induce them to follow profitable employments, and the education of the young receives attention. They are trained to labour; but they are also taught reading, writing and arithmetic, and they are, as a rule, apt scholars."—*J. H. Heaton's Dictionary of Dates. p. 5.*

EFFORTS MADE TO INSTRUCT AND CIVILIZE THE BLACKS BY NON-CATHOLICS.—The first great effort made to educate and civilize the aborigines was made by Governor Macquarie. He formed an establishment at Black Town, on the Richmond Road, and placed it under the superintendence of a missioner of the South Sea Islands. A branch of this institution was afterwards established at Castle Hill, near Parramatta, but soon after the departure of Governor Macquarie, both of the institutions failed.

Messrs. Tyerman and Bennett were deputed by the London Missionary Society to establish missions for the aborigines, and with the consent of the society they formed one at Lake Macquarie, which lies to the north of Broken Bay; but whether it was that the expenses were too great to support it, or that the place was not well adapted for the purpose, the fact is that the society gave orders that it should be broken up: the government assigned to a protestant missionary a salary of £150, but notwithstanding the mission failed.

Another mission was undertaken in the district of Wellington for the aborigines, under the auspices of Archdeacon Broughton, who was afterwards bishop of Sydney. The protestant propaganda of London showed a lively interest for the prosperity of this mission, because it represented the work of the Church of England in the first colony of Australia. After a few years of useless efforts the mission was abandoned.

The Wesleyan Church made another attempt. They saw, in the district of Port Phillip, now the colony of Victoria, that there were numerous tribes of native blacks: they thought it would be a fine field for their exertions: they established there a mission: the plans for its success could not be better devised, says my author, and they deserved a better fate. Notwithstanding, "periit memoria eorum cum sonitu."—Psal. xi, 7.

The famous mission of Dr. Lang cannot be passed over unnoticed. It was different from all the others in its formation. Were one to believe the doctor, from what he has written, his name should be ranked amongst the greatest philanthropists of the Southern hemisphere, and held as one of the noblest defenders of the cause of the savages before the tribunal of humanity and politics, so great is the love which he shows for them; so animated are the expressions he makes use of in addressing the government and the agents, to induce them to ameliorate the

condition of the aborigines of Australia. He bitterly lament
that England has not made use of the means best adapted fa
christianizing the aborigines. " Anglicanism," he says " or Episca
palianism is nothing but a kind of popery, and popery has alway-
been an obstacle to the civilization of people. The American
never made any progress whilst they were under the government
of a code which recognized an episcopal church. But after they
became independent, then protestantism made wonderful progress." Nothing would satisfy Dr. Lang, in converting the
savages, but that they should be taught pure presbyterianism.
Dr. Lang states, " that he was enabled, by the assistance of Lord
Glenelg, then Secretary of State for the Colonies, with all the
means necessary to convey, for the establishment of the mission
of the aborigines, two ordained presbyterian ministers, and twelve
lay missionaries, eight of whom were married. That mission was
placed under the presidency of the Rev. John Gossener, pastor in
Berlin of the church of Bohemia, and already for many years a
most zealous promoter of the gentile missions."* " The twelve
lay missionaries and the two ordained ministers," says Dr. Lang,
" established a mission at Moreton Bay, on the river Kidron, seven
miles from Brisbane. But I am grieved to say, that although they
who directed that mission were excellent persons and true
christians, and exercised a great and salutary influence through
all the other districts of that Bay, they entirely failed in their
intention, and in the same way that all the other aboriginal
missions of Australia failed in their design of imbuing a religious
sentiment into the minds of the aborigines. The government aid
was finally withdrawn, and the missions from that moment were
dissolved." This happened during the administration of Sir
George Gipps.

Let us enquire briefly, what has been the conduct of the
English and Colonial governments towards the aboriginal population of Australia. Governor Phillip, in the beginning of the
colony, manifested great sympathy for the blacks, and was very
kind to them; but it was not in his power to protect them
sufficiently from the violence and bad treatment of the prison-
population; so that he neither established any system for their
civilization, nor for their conversion to christianity: nor am I
aware that the English government instructed him in the matter.
But in the year 1841 Lord John Russell, when he was Secretary
for the Colonies, vindicated the honour of England before the

---

* This Rev. J. Gossener, be it known, was an apostate, who, from being a
Catholic priest, became a Lutheran minister.

...tions, to a certain extent, in regard to the aborigines. He wrote ...despatch to Governor Gipps, and recommended " that fifteen per ...nt. of the Land Fund should be applied exclusively to the ...vilization and protection of the aborigines, leaving to the colonial ...thorities the details of the expenditure, but requiring that a ...arly report should be laid before the governor of the colony, ...howing, by statistical and other data, the progress made in improving the condition of the black population."*

The reply from the colony to this despatch was, that many experiments had been made to ameliorate the condition of the blacks, but without fruit ; and if they were to judge of the future by the past, there was reason to believe that every hope of changing the habits and customs of these savages was vain.

In the year 1845, Sir George Gipps received another despatch from Lord Stanley, about the civilization of the *indigène*. " I cannot conclude this despatch," says Lord Stanley, " without expressing my sentiments upon the importance of the object ; that is, to receive from your Excellency a general plan, by the carrying out of which we can satisfy our obligation towards that unfortunate race of beings. I will not admit without extreme reluctance, that nothing can be done for them ; and that only in regard to them the doctrines of christianity are inefficacious, and the benefits of civilization incommunicable. I cannot be persuaded that they are incapable of improvement, and that their extinction cannot be prevented, in contact with the colonists. I recommend them to your favourable solicitude and protection, assuring you at the same time with all faithfulness, that I charge myself to co-operate with you in that which will be considered opportune to execute, in order to their civil advancement."

Lord Stanley could not speak with more justness and interest than he did by those words of the despatch. But what was the result of the despatch ? A society was formed in Sydney to give an answer to the Secretary for the Colonies. The members of this society were composed not only of seculars, but also of protestant missionaries, who pretended to know the habits and dispositions of the savages. Every one gave his opinion : finally the conclusion was, that no plans, no systems availed to ameliorate the condition of the Australians.

The account given by Flanagan in his history is the following, in regard to the despatch.—" A committee of the Council, having reference to a despatch of the Secretary of State, received during the preceding year, was appointed to inquire into the condition

---

* Flanagan, vol. 2, c. 1, s. 6.

R

of the aborigines. In the report which they prepared the recommended the abolition of the Protectorate, as having faile in the object for which it was established; as being in fact, : this time, altogether useless; but they could not recommend substitute. They advised the house that it was useless to for new reserves, as recommended by the Secretary of State: t education of adults they thought to be hopeless, and the youn could be educated only by a compulsory separation from the relatives and tribes. They concluded by expressing an opinic that, without under-rating the philanthropic motives of h Majesty's government in attempting the improvement of t aborigines, much more real good would be effected by simil exertions to promote the interests of religion and education amor the white population in the interior of the colony, the improv ment of whose condition in these respects would doubtless ter to benefit the aborigines.*

An Italian writer comments upon this evasive reply of th committee of the Council in the following words:—" This repor was sent officially to London, and produced its effect, because th parliament became persuaded that nothing could be done for th civilization of the Australians. Thus no more is said about them they cease to exist in the minds of the government, *either as race*, or as individuals, and with the colonists prevails the ide that *they are not men*, but *a kind of monkey*. Every plan wa dismissed, every system, every institution for their amelioratior they were left to themselves, exposed to all the violence ar cruelty of the colonists, and compelled to retire into the depths their forests, to become more savage and degraded than they we before."†

" The colony is now nearly one hundred years old; the lar which belonged to the black population has been taken possessic of by the colonists who invaded their country ; I ask again, wh compensation has been made to the aborigines? Have many them been baptised, and made christians, and civilised? Con paratively very few of the million which inhabited New Sou Wales. Are not the colonies responsible in a great measue f this being the case? They have the power and the means ameliorating their condition. If they have obstructed th labours of the missionaries of Christ, who were commanded baptize and instruct all men,‡ what a terrible accou they will have to give to the Supreme Judge. They will l

---

* Flanagan, vol. 2, c. 4, s. 9.   † Barsanti Selvaggi dell'Australia, p. 197.
‡ Matt. xxviii, 19, 20.

...ked amongst those to whom our Lord will say, after pronouncing the awful sentence,—' For I was hungry and you gave me not to eat; I was thirsty and you gave me not to drink; I was a stranger and you took me not in; naked, and you clothed me not; sick and in prison, and you did not visit me............... then, I say to you, as long as you did it not to one of *these least*, neither did you do it to me.' " *

I will now conclude my short essay by a quotation from a celebrated writer, Count Joseph De Maistre, in regard to whom belongs the work of missions. "To the Pope," he says, "and the missionaries sent from the Holy See, belong the work of missions. Consider that famous Bible Society, the weak, and perhaps dangerous rival of our missions. It informs us every year how many copies of the Bible it launches into the world; but it always omits to tell us how many new christians it has produced. But if the money which this society spends on the Bibles were given to the Pope, to be devoted to the expenses of missions, he would by this time have made more christians than there are pages in all the Bibles of the association............Although such men had nothing against them but their divisions, nothing more would be necessary to render them powerless,—Anglicans, Lutherans, Moravians, Methodists, Baptists, Puritans, Quakers, &c.,—such are the people with whom heathens have to deal. The Scripture says, ' How shall they hear if no one preach to them ?' It may be said with equal truth, ' How will they be believed, if they do not understand one another.' " †

" An English protestant," continues the Count, " has felt this curse of sterility, and has expressed himself in regard to it with candour, delicacy, and truly religious sincerity, which show that he was worthy of that mission which was wanting to him."

" The missionary," he says, " ought to be far above a narrow bigotry, and ought to possess a truly catholic spirit. It is not his duty to teach Calvinism, or Arminianism, but Christianity. It is not his object to propagate an Anglican hierarchy, nor the principles of the protestant dissenters, but to serve the universal church. I wish the missionary to be well persuaded that the success of his ministry by no means depends on the points of separation, but on those which enjoy the concurrent assent of all religious men." ‡

---

* Matt. xxv, 41.
† De Maistre, book 3, c. 1.
‡ Melville Horne, late Chaplain of Sierra Leone, in Africa.

Lightning Source UK Ltd.
Milton Keynes UK
UKHW021517090219
336936UK00007B/923/P

9 780365 299509